THE BIG PICTURE OF U.S. NATIONAL GOVERNMENT

RICK SWANSON, J.D., PH.D

ISBN 13 (paper): 978-1-935754-90-9

Distributed by:
University of Louisiana at Lafayette Press
P.O. Box 43558
Lafayette, LA 70504-0831
http://ulpress.org

Printed in the United States on acid-free paper.

Table of Contents

PREFACE

CONTENTS OF THIS BOOK

The Big Picture of U.S. National Government is a comprehensive introductory text for entry-level political science or civics courses in U.S. national government and politics in colleges and universities. It could also be adapted for high school use as well, such as in Advanced Placement (AP) courses. The text provides a basic yet thorough overview of the history, theory, and practice of U.S. government, politics, and public policy. The guiding philosophy in this book is to give the reader a "big picture" of U.S. politics and government. In any field of study, it's often easy to get bogged down and lost in endless trivial details. Yet without an understanding of how those details fit together, the pieces don't make sense. Imagine, for example, trying to put together a complex 10,000 piece puzzle without having an image of what the completed puzzle should look like. It could be done perhaps, but only with great difficulty. Knowing the "big picture" first would be extremely helpful in seeing how the seemingly endless and disconnected puzzle pieces fit together.

Politics is much more complicated than any picture puzzle. There are at least many *millions* of political facts one could possibly learn. Without understanding first how to make sense of those endless facts, one would not know which details were important compared to the ones that were relatively trivial. For every one important political fact such as a key guiding philosophical principle or basic truth about human psychology and behavior, there are thousands of trivial details such as names, dates, places, and numbers. This book thus tries to focus on the "big picture" of U.S. politics. The goal is to help you come away with a broad framework of understanding, focusing on the most important underlying concepts rather than endless minor facts. Seeing the larger context will allow you to make sense of details. The ability to "see how it all fits together" is critical in allowing you to understand the meaning of new pieces of political information you'll encounter throughout your life.

We can analogize this approach to the study of plant biology. We would first have to understand the ecosystem in which a plant lives to understand why that plant has evolved to look and function as it does. Then we could examine more closely particular parts of the plant. Finally, we could zoom in with a microscope to see small details of how the plant's cells function. If you didn't first know you were looking at a plant cell, you wouldn't have any idea what the blobs and lines meant that you were seeing in the microscope. Indeed, this plant metaphor applies to politics since political systems are themselves living things. Political systems are ever-changing, adapting, and evolving. Thus, first we must understand the larger "ecosystem" in which politics arises: human psychology and behavior. Then we can look at specific organizational components of the political system, such as particular political institutions. We also must understand the guiding philosophies used by those who designed these institutions. Finally, we can "zoom in" to see how individual voters and government officials behave within these system constraints. For example, do the parts of the system work as they were intended? Only by understanding this broader background framework will particular detailed facts make sense. We will "know what it is we're looking at."

For example, let's say that while reading about political history you encounter the sentence "There have been four U.S. presidents that were assassinated while in office: Abraham Lincoln, James A. Garfield, William McKinley, and John F. Kennedy." Without understanding the "big picture" of U.S. history and politics, merely encountering or memorizing this list of assassinated presidents has relatively little meaning, and relatively little worth as a piece of knowledge. If all you know is this isolated list, you might be able to answer a question in a trivia game. On the other hand, if you understood the larger context of history you would know that two of these assassinations (Lincoln and Kennedy) changed the course of U.S. history. The other two of those assassinations (Garfield and McKinley) have been largely forgotten because of how relatively little historical impact they had. For example, without knowing who Lincoln was, or what he accomplished and was in the process of further accomplishing, you wouldn't know how Lincoln's premature death radically changed the course of racial politics in the U.S. for the next two centuries.

The organization of this book is therefore arranged to go in order from the "biggest" picture to the smallest. Tiny details can not be understood without first considering the larger and broader theoretical, legal, and historical frameworks into which those details fit. This hierarchy of meaning can be diagrammed as follows:

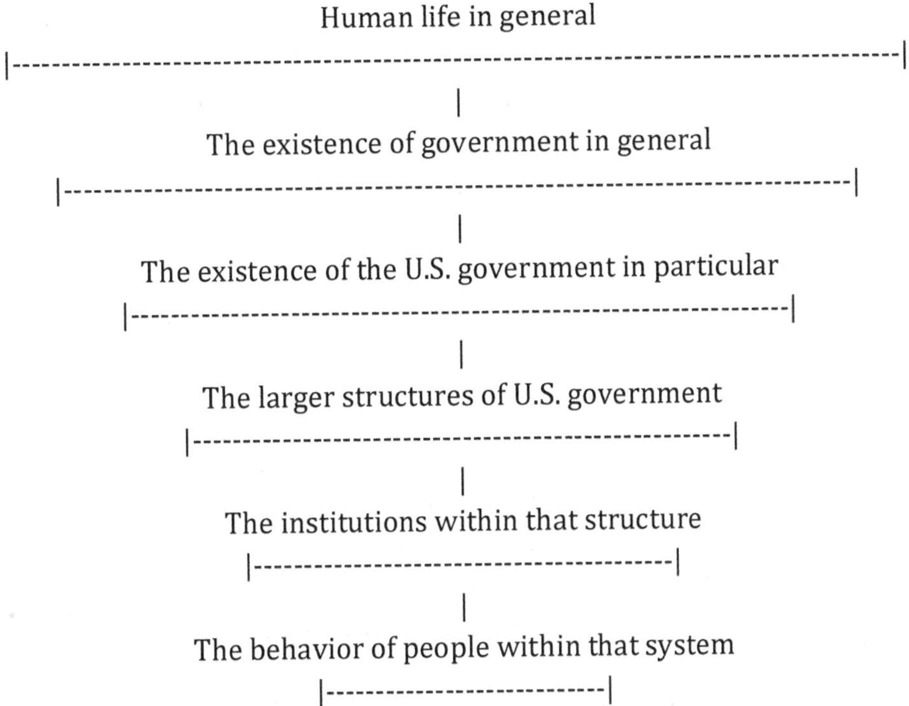

Consistent with this "bigger-to-smaller" philosophy, this book is divided into five different parts. Each part consists of multiple chapters. Part I, *Foundations of Government,* has two chapters that together cover the three highest levels of meaning shown above. Chapter One explains the role and importance of politics and government in human life. Chapter Two then describes the philosophical justification for the existence of government in general and for the founding of the nation known as the United States of America in particular.

Part II of this book is titled *Constitutional Framework.* It consists of Chapters Three through Six, which describe the overall structures of U.S. national government. This core framework of U.S. government includes, among other things, democracy, the separation of powers, checks and balances, mixed government, political pluralism, and federalism.

The substantive constraints on these larger political structures are then described in Part III, *Rights and Liberties.* Part III is comprised of chapters Seven through Ten. These chapters describe the history and current status of civil liberties and civil rights in the U.S. Such a detailed discussion of rights and liberties is needed given that almost every political issue today involves a claim of some sort of "right."

Next, Chapters Eleven through Thirteen comprise Part III, titled *Institutions.* The three branches of U.S. national government are described in those three chapters. In order, the chapters examine the legislative, executive, and then judicial branches.

Finally, Chapters Fourteen and Fifteen comprise the last part of this book: Part V, *Political Behavior*. This covers how individuals and groups, including public officials, behave within the political system described in the previous chapters. Chapter Fourteen discusses major sources of political information, and how that information then organizes itself into public opinion and political ideology. Chapter Fifteen then examines several common ways people participate in politics, such as through voting, political parties and interest groups. That same chapter concludes by reconsidering the "big picture" of the overall nature of political power in the United States.

Acknowledgements

I wish to thank many people for helping me to improve earlier drafts of this textbook. Feedback from many dozens of students in several sections of my introductory course on U.S. National Government course in the past couple years have greatly helped improve the organization and clarity of the material. Also, several fellow political science scholars with doctorate degrees provided in-depth review of the manuscript. These extremely helpful evaluations came from professional colleagues here at the University of Louisiana at Lafayette. McKinzie Hall reviewed the entire manuscript. Christie Maloyed reviewed chapters 1-10 and 14-15. Jason Maloy reviewed chapters 11-13. All of these political science scholars graciously gave of their time. Their comments provided immensely valuable improvements and resulted in numerous refinements to the manuscript. Also, my amazing wife Anne, who has a degree in public relations and marketing along with years of professional expertise in copyediting, helped proofread the entire manuscript for clarity, organization, and stylistic flow. Her input (as well as moral support) was also invaluable. I wish to greatly thank all of the above people who helped me. Of course, I take sole responsibility for any flaws or errors in the content of the resulting final version, since such ultimate editorial decisions were made by me alone.

I also wish to thank the Department of Political Science, the College of Liberal Arts, the Office of Distance Learning, and UL Press, all here at the University of Louisiana at Lafayette. These departments, offices, and organizations encouraged my efforts to provide free or low-cost textbooks to my students. High college costs and the resulting student loan debt that results from such costs have become an increasing financial obstacle to students who hope to obtain a college education. Expensive textbooks merely add to this difficulty. In my own life, I made it through all my years of higher education without my family being able to pay anything towards that education. As a result, I'm particularly sympathetic to the desire and need to keep college costs down for students who are struggling to pay for school. I've thus worked to keep the costs of this textbook as low as possible. This included doing most of the formatting of the book myself, and negotiating with UL Press to offer the book at the lowest price possible while still being financially worthwhile for UL Press to publish the book.

One such tactic for keeping costs down was to prevent potential copyright lawsuits or royalty issues by avoiding the use of images. This includes even images that appear to be in the public domain or claim to be available for free use through a "creative commons" license. Even though any legal claims against this book for using such images would have no merits, disputing frivolous copyright claims can be costly, time-consuming, and stressful. Including images would thus unfortunately raise the cost of this textbook so as to cover the potential cost of defending against such claims. As a result, a decision was made that the goal of minimizing the cost of this book outweighed any educational advantage that might result through the addition of images. Only a few simple author-created tables and diagrams have been provided in the text where such are especially helpful. Perhaps, and hopefully, a future edition of this textbook will use photographs or other images. For now, though, I trust that course instructors, or even students researching on their own, may easily supplement the text by finding relevant images online. I hope and believe I made the right decision through the chosen trade-off, but I leave it to the reader to make that judgment as well.

Part I: Foundations of Government

Chapter 1: Politics and Civics

The Big Picture

Politics is the competition for power in the making of rules governing human behavior. Since civilization does not exist without rules, politics is an essential part of human life. Indeed, the ideal goal of politics is to improve human life. One of the core purposes of education is to help students achieve knowledge about politics. That way, wise rules can be made that promote the flourishing of human society. The study of government and politics is also extremely helpful and necessary for success in several different careers.

Chapter Objectives

After reading this chapter, the reader should be able to:

1. Define politics and describe its central importance in human life.
2. Explain the role and importance of education in promoting political knowledge and wisdom.
3. Explain the relevance of political science to several possible careers.

Politics

Should college tuition be provided free to all students? If so, who would pay for it and how? And should only those students who have financial need be given tuition? Or only those students who have the best high school GPAs or college entrance test scores? Or only those students who agree to perform community service after college? Or some combination of the above? And should only U.S. citizens be eligible for free tuition? What about non-citizens who have legal permission to be in the United States? What about students whose parents brought them here as children in violation of U.S. immigration laws?

Along the same lines of addressing the high cost of living, should the prices of apartment rentals, medical insurance, automobile insurance, child day care, or college textbooks be regulated by law? Should there be a minimum hourly wage that businesses must pay college students? If so, what should that wage be? Should college students be guaranteed a job when they graduate? Should there be a minimum guaranteed wage for students who have a job that requires a college degree?

We could ask countless other questions as well that many college students are interested in these days. For example, should medical marijuana be legalized? What about recreational use of marijuana? If so, what should the legal age be? Should the drinking age be lowered to 18 years old? Should 18-year-old women be required to register for the military draft just as 18-year-old men currently must?

Should colleges provide separate men's and women's bathrooms, or should they provide only common bathrooms shared by people of all sexes?

Of course, college students are interested in every other political question as well, such as questions involving war and peace, the environment, crime, and many other issues. The particular questions listed above illustrate only a few of the endless issues that affect the lives of college students. What all these questions have in common, though, is that politics decides how to answer these questions. So what is "politics?"

There is no generally agreed-upon definition of the term "politics." A dozen different textbooks will give you a dozen different technical definitions. There is one definition, however, that is most often quoted. Harold Lasswell was a prominent political scientist who wrote in the 1920s. Lasswell finally gave up trying to create a clear, precise technical definition of "politics." He finally concluded that politics is simply "who gets what, when, and how." Put differently, politics is the struggle for the power to decide who gets what, when, and how. This means that politics is the struggle over how to allocate scarce resources.

Why does politics even exist? Why are there wars and political conflict? Why must we fight about things? Why is human life filled with such drama? Why can't we all just get along? If we had infinite resources, then we wouldn't need to ask the question "who gets what, when, and how." Everyone would get everything they want, whenever they want it. Even if resources were not scarce, we would never have disagreements if we all thought exactly alike. This is not the nature of reality, however. People don't all think the same, even with the same family, educational and cultural upbringing. And, it's human nature to want to take care of oneself and one's family and friends over people one doesn't know. So, since we live in a finite world, we have differences in opinions over values and priorities about how best to use limited resources. The question "who gets what, when, and how" must be asked in any situation where resources are finite. This results in conflict.

By "resources" we don't just mean natural resources like land, minerals, agricultural products, or clean air or water. "Resources" includes anything that can be divided among people. This includes money, jobs, health care, education, political positions, civil rights, and so on. For example, which is more important: logging jobs or wildlife preservation? Universal access to unlimited free college tuition and free health care, or financially sustainable government? Even rights themselves are a limited resource. Not everyone can have endless rights, because rights conflict with each other. For example, the right of the community to have a positive culture in which to raise children conflicts with the free speech rights of people who advocate bigotry and hate. Even a resource like a "right" in these cases is finite, because unlimited "rights" for one person means limited or no rights for someone else. The resulting battle to determine how government will decide these questions is called politics.

Even with scarce resources, there would be no politics if we all agreed how to allocate those resources. The reason we disagree on how to divide resources is because people disagree on *values*. There are many different political values all human societies agree with in varying degrees, such as order, freedom, morality, equality, and pragmatism. Yet these values inherently contradict each other.

As one example of conflicting values, perfect equality cannot occur with perfect freedom. There is an inherent tension between the two. If we maximize economic freedom, there will be less income equality because some people will end up earning much more than others. If instead we equalize income, then economic freedom must be greatly reduced. Since these values necessarily contradict each other, societies must decide which value to sacrifice. Should people be allowed to keep their own hard-earned money as reward for their successful efforts, or should we take some of their money from them through taxes so we can give poor persons a minimum quality of economic life?

As another simple example of the tension between values, perfect freedom cannot exist with perfect order. The more freedom we have, the less order. The more order, the less freedom. For example, let's say we wanted to maximize the prevention and punishment of crime and terrorism. This would require non-stop monitoring of the entire population, which could be done using current technology. We could have artificially intelligent computers read every e-mail, listen to every phone call, and remotely observe every internet website people visit on their computer. Some people believe and claim we already do this. But we could go much farther than this. We could put government cameras on every street and road, and in all private homes, yards, and businesses. Every room in every house could be monitored by a camera. In addition, we could require that people present identification at regular checkpoints along roads and in buildings every time they travel. We could make every car and person carry a tracking chip that records their every movement. No society, especially no democratic society, has chosen to do these things. By maintaining freedom of privacy, we allow many criminals and probably even terrorists to go uncaught and unpunished. Yet majorities of every society today have concluded so far that after reaching a moderate degree of order, they value privacy more. As technology improves and the tactics of criminals and terrorists change, societies will continue to struggle over where the proper balance lies in upholding the conflicting values of privacy versus security, freedom versus order.

Because people disagree which values should guide how scarce resources are used, politics will always exist. Indeed, unanimity of human opinion is impossible. Because not everyone thinks and believes identically on all topics, fierce disagreement will regularly occur. There will always be some people who dislike or even loathe the final decisions reached. This means there will always be a segment of the population, sometimes large, that will be angry about how resources are allocated. What seems "fair and common sense" to some people will seem "outrageously unjust" to others. Rightly or wrongly, for better or worse, this is the reality of human politics.

Because battles over resources happen in many contexts, the struggle of politics occurs everywhere, not just at the government level. Politics occurs in the family, in the workplace, in schools, and in private organizations. As one simple example, let's say you're living with a roommate in an apartment, dorm room, or house. What if you want to be asleep by 9:00 p.m. but your roommate wants to have a late-night party? What if you prefer a clean, tidy room but your roommate wants to leave dirty clothes and half-eaten food all around the room? What if you hate cigarette smoke but your roommate smokes? What if you don't want overnight guests in your room but your roommate does? The two of you will have to figure out a way to co-exist in the room together. How the two of you go about trying to find a solution to your differences will be a political interaction.

A similar situation occurs if you share your workspace with others. You and your fellow coworkers must decide what kind of pictures, posters, or symbols you will allow each other to display. What if you want to post a religious quote but your coworker is offended by it? What if your coworker wants to display a poster of a celebrity in a skimpy swimsuit and you are offended? Who gets to decide whether and what type of public displays will be allowed at your workplace? Whether the employees, the business, or the government settles these disputes, this question will be a political decision.

Government

Although politics is everywhere that human relationships occur, the greatest power in society is the government.

Just because there is a struggle for power over scarce resources doesn't necessarily mean there are any express rules that society has created for the allocation of those resources. Once there are such rules, though, there is now "law." The people who make and enforce those laws are "government." Just as there's no universally agreed upon definition of "politics," the same is true of "government" and "law." At its simplest, government is the institutions and rules that regulate the people living in a particular geographic area. Private organizations like social clubs can also have "governments," but these rule over their members only and not over a geographic territory. Thus, in using the term "government" here, we're referring to government that has the authority to create rules that apply to the general public within a defined territory and then to coerce obedience to those rules. The enforcement of rules can be done through fines or other punishment by using the police, courts, prisons, or even the military.

The right to use violent force if necessary in order to enforce geographical rules is the one feature common to all governments. All people have an "ability" to use force. You, I, and a robber all have the *ability* to use force, but not a legal a *right* to use force. Only the government has a legal right to use violent force if necessary to enforce obedience to the law. In other words, government has a monopoly on the "legitimate" use of force. This means that regardless what one thinks about the *moral* use of violence, only government can claim to *legally* use force to mandate obedience. For example, if a robber demands money from you, it's an illegal crime. You have a legal right to self-defense and so may resist the robber. If an individual or organization has no legal authority to use force to make you do as it says, then that entity is not "government." If the government demands money from you, however, that's taxation. You have no legal right to refuse to pay the taxes you owe. If you knowingly avoid paying your taxes, the government can fine you, imprison you if you're defrauding the government, and use violent force if necessary if you resist attempts at capture or imprisonment. You have no legal right of self-defense if the government is using force to make you obey the law.

So why do we have government? Why not just let all individuals and groups decide political disputes privately among themselves? There are a few people who argue there should be no government. These people are called *anarchists.* The word "anarchy" comes from the Greek "an" plus "archea," meaning "no rulers." Throughout history and across all cultures, however, the vast majority of societies have believed that having government is better than having no government. The main argument for having government is to maintain peace and order in society. If we leave private individuals to settle disputes themselves, there's no way to guarantee both sides will use peaceful means to settle those disputes. It could simply become a case of "might makes right." Whoever is bigger, stronger, or better armed would be able to have their way robbing, kidnapping, beating, raping, or murdering anyone for any reason. Indeed, if we look around the world at "failed states" that have little in the way of functioning governments, it usually is rule by various armed groups led by competing warlords.

Given the chaos that typically happens in the absence of government, government ideally exists to keep society in peaceful order. The law provides common rules of behavior. If there is any disagreement about our rights against each other under the law, we must take that dispute to the government. We may not rely on self-enforcement to resolve our disputes. In this way, the existence of government prevents violence between people due to fights over scarce resources. Instead, conflict is channeled into legal, peaceful means. If people refuse to use the lawfully provided peaceful means of resolving disputes, then government may use violence if needed to enforce those rules. As we'll see in a much later chapter, however, when we consider people disagree greatly on *how much* power government should have to make and enforce laws.

The laws and other rules of behavior made by government are called *policies*. The word "policy" comes from the ancient Greek root word "polis" meaning "city" or "state." All governments at the local, state, and national level make both substantive and procedural laws. These laws become the policies of those governments. For example, deciding that people cannot buy alcohol until they are 21 years old is a policy. Deciding to provide Social Security pensions to retired persons is a policy. The procedure one must go through to apply for Social Security benefits is also a policy. The standards that determine whether one is eligible for those benefits is also a policy. Most if not all organizations and businesses have policies as well. This can include how employees are hired, evaluated, compensated, promoted, disciplined, and fired. As another example, hospitals will have policies regarding how to admit patients, how to diagnose, treat, and monitor them, how to discharge them, how to bill them for their treatment, and how to collect those payments if the bill goes unpaid. Even your family has "policies," such as "you must take your shoes off before you come into the house if your shoes have mud on them."

In the context of government, though, policies are somewhat different. First, government-made policies apply to the entire public, not just members of a particular family or particular organization. And, as noted earlier, government may use force if needed to make people obey those policies. The term *public policy* is therefore used to distinguish policies made by government from policies made in other contexts. We can call a private business' hiring rules "policy," and a private hospital's patient treatment guidelines "policy." Neither, however, can be called "*public* policy." When one asks "What is public policy on health care?", one is asking "What are the laws the government has made that involve health care?"

The Importance of Politics and Government

Why does politics matter? Throughout history, philosophers, theologians, and other thinkers have wondered "what is the most important question a human being can ask?" They have agreed it comes down to a single, most important, all-encompassing question: "What is the meaning of life?" All the other great questions of human existence are either included in that question, or secondary to it. But what does it mean to ask about the meaning of life? The reason we ask this question is to know how to have the best human life possible. What this question is asking, then, is "How am I supposed to live?" or, "What is the best way to live?" We don't live alone on isolated, deserted islands, however. We live in families, communities, and societies. So the question "What's the best way to live?" is actually asking "What's the best way to live *together with other people?*"

The question of how we should ideally behave is usually answered by the fields of religious and ethical philosophy. Philosophers and theologians debate this question endlessly in the abstract. Yet society as a whole does not have the luxury of time. Life goes on and we need to live it. We must make immediate, practical decisions about how to live together. How do we obtain food, clothing, shelter, an education, a means of income, a family, and protection against those who would do harm to our family or property? Deciding how best to achieve these goals together necessarily means asking "What common rules should we live together by?" and coming up with at least temporary answers quickly.

Once we've agreed we need common rules, we have now agreed to create *government* and *laws*. That is, we now must answer all the questions about how our society should be structured and governed. What laws will we have? How will those laws be made? Will there be any limits as to what laws can be made? Who will make those laws? Who will have the power to enforce those laws? How will those laws be enforced? What limits will there be on enforcement of the laws? How will the meaning of the laws be clarified if people disagree as to the meaning of those laws? Who will make these interpretations? And so on.

Human nature is such that people will disagree about these answers. We will debate, argue, sometimes fight, and perhaps even go to war about the answers to these questions. *Politics* is this process of competition between competing individuals or groups to gain the power to decide the answers to these questions. *Public policy* is the answers our society collectively provides to these questions. This means that questions of government, law, politics, and public policy all involve the deepest and most important religious, moral, and ethical questions known to humanity. The field of *political science* is the study of how these questions are decided at the local, regional, national and international level. Each culture or nation answers these questions in a different way. This book will consider how the United States of America has answered these questions in the past and answers them today.

The study of how governments at all levels work to answer these questions is also called *civics*. This requires an understanding of the rights and responsibilities of citizenship. By "citizenship" we mean not just membership in the society a particular country, but also as members of a global culture. Since we are all human, we are all citizens of our planet. Thus, regardless of one's formal legal status or membership in any particular society or nation, we all share the common responsibilities of being members of the human race. For us to best improve our world, we must understand politics, government, and public policy at the local, regional, national, and international levels. Regardless where one lives, then, education in civics is essential.

What are those responsibilities of shared global citizenship? Education in civics and government is essential for freedom and democracy to exist and succeed. Without informed voters, democratic decisions will be based on ignorance or irrational emotions. *Demagogues* are leaders who manipulate public opinion through lies, illogic, and appeal to emotion rather than reason, all merely for the demagogue's own political gain. If the public is politically uninformed, demagogues can first manipulate the public to elect them. Then the demagogues can convince the public to go along with them in ways that are unhealthy, dangerous, immoral, or even barbaric.

Perhaps the most infamous example of this is pre-World War II Germany. Germany began as a democracy. Yet throughout the early 1930's, Nazi leader Adolf Hitler gradually threatened, outlawed, and murdered all political opposition. On August 19, 1934, Hitler had the German people endorse his total political power as "Fuhrer" (leader) of Germany in a public referendum. It was a sham election given that voting against Hitler could jeopardize one's life. The vote was therefore 90% in favor of giving Hitler absolute power. The day after the election, the New York Times reported:

> By every appeal known to skillful politicians and with every argument to the contrary suppressed, they [the Germans] were asked to make their approval [of Hitler] unanimous. Nevertheless 10 per cent of the voters have admittedly braved possible consequences by answering "No" . . . The endorsement gives Chancellor Hitler . . . dictatorial powers unequaled in any other country, and probably unequaled in history since the days of Genghis Khan. . . . The question that interests the outside world now is what Chancellor Hitler will do with such unprecedented authority.

Of course, as we now know from history, with such power Hitler went on to cause the deaths of *many tens of millions* of people in World War II. This included around 7 million of his own people, mostly his blindly obedient soldiers and his own Jewish citizens that he systematically murdered.

To prevent this kind of outcome, any democracy needs its citizens to be highly politically informed and involved. Unless this is the case, it is not democracy. An analogy is informed consent in medicine. Medical patients can only give genuine consent to treatment if they have been informed about all the alternative possible medical treatments and their risks. Similarly, people who are politically uneducated cannot make genuine political choices about who should govern or how. In such a case, the system is either a mere façade of democracy, or is extremely fragile. In either case, a demagogue might be able to manipulate public opinion to agree to eliminate freedom and democracy, as Hitler was able to do. Education in basic civics knowledge, such as this book hopes to provide, is therefore essential to maintaining the freedom and democracy that we cherish.

Even if one cares nothing about maintaining democracy or improving society, understanding politics is essential to protect oneself and one's family. Laws affect our lives from cradle to grave—and even before and after that! In today's world, government regulates what we may do, and what may be done to us, when we are fetuses, infants, children, adults, retired individuals, dying persons, and deceased corpses. Almost every aspect of our entire life is covered by legal requirements. Only by being aware of these laws can we obey them so that we can avoid the hassle of going through the criminal justice system. Only by understanding how these laws are made can we work to change them if we don't like them. Only by figuring out the bureaucracy can we get the government benefits that we and our families might qualify for. In short, we stand much to gain if we understand government, and much to lose if we don't. Our lives, and the lives of our loved ones, will be much better if we know how to navigate within the political system.

"HIGHER" EDUCATION

Our understanding of politics can be greatly aided by education. Since higher education is called "higher" to distinguish it from primary education (elementary school) and secondary education (high school). The term "higher" has several meanings here. The level of learning is higher in age and higher in information level. More importantly, though, this type of knowledge is more weighty, vital, and consequential. It is the "highest' or "most ultimate" learning one can partake in. It is therefore the most meaningful learning as well. In other words, it occurs at the very grandest level of thought. Higher education asks the question we considered at the start of this chapter: "*How can we best live together with each other?*" This question *is* the study of politics, government and law.

Not just universities, but even the first public elementary schools were based on this philosophy of the purpose of education. As merely one example, we can look to the role of Thomas Jefferson in promoting civics education. In 1779, Thomas Jefferson proposed a system of public schools for the state of Virginia. His "Bill for the More General Diffusion of Knowledge" was supported by a fellow Virginian, James Madison. The bill was not passed, but with continued support from Jefferson and Madison, the state legislature eventually created a system of public schools in the 1790's. In his bill, Jefferson explained the reason for having public education. It was to give the population the political wisdom to stop tyranny and preserve liberty and democracy:

> Whereas it appeareth that however certain forms of government are better calculated than others to protect individuals in the free exercise of

> their natural rights, and are at the same time themselves better guarded against degeneracy, yet experience hath shewn, that even under the best forms, those entrusted with power have, in time, and by slow operations, perverted it into tyranny;
>
> and it is believed that the most effectual means of preventing this would be, to illuminate, as far as practicable, the minds of the people at large, and more especially to give them knowledge of those facts, which history exhibiteth, that, possessed thereby of the experience of other ages and countries, they may be enabled to know ambition under all its shapes, and prompt to exert their natural powers to defeat its purposes;
>
> And whereas it is generally true that the people will be happiest whose laws are best, and are best administered, and that laws will be wisely formed, and honestly administered, in proportion as those who form and administer them are wise and honest;
>
> whence it becomes expedient for promoting the publick happiness that those persons, whom nature hath endowed with genius and virtue, should be rendered by liberal education worthy to receive, and able to guard the sacred deposit of the rights and liberties of their fellow citizens.

Jefferson became President of the U.S. in 1800. After he had finished his two terms as President, he led the charge for Virginia to create a state-run public university system in Virginia. Along with James Madison and over a dozen other Virginians, Jefferson was appointed to the Board of Commissioners of the new University of Virginia. The Commissioners met in 1818 to decide on the purpose of the University, and what subjects would be taught in fulfillment of this purpose. The Commissioners then issued their "Report of the Commissioners for the University of Virginia" in 1818. As head of the Commission, Jefferson wrote the goals of "the higher branches of education" should include:

> To form the statesmen, legislators and judges, on whom public prosperity and individual happiness are so much to depend;
>
> To expound the principles and structure of government, the laws which regulate the intercourse of nations, those formed municipally for our own government, and a sound spirit of legislation, which, banishing all arbitrary and unnecessary restraint on individual action, shall leave us free to do whatever does not violate the equal rights of another;
>
> To harmonize and promote the interests of agriculture, manufactures and commerce, and by well informed views of political economy to give a free scope to the public industry;

> To develop the reasoning faculties of our youth, enlarge their minds, cultivate their morals, and instill into them the precepts of virtue and order;
>
> To enlighten them with mathematical and physical sciences, which advance the arts, and administer to the health, the subsistence, and comforts of human life;
>
> And, generally, to form them to habits of reflection and correct action, rendering them examples of virtue to others, and of happiness within themselves.

Jefferson concluded in the report that along with language, math, and science, the "higher grade of education" should include "Government, Political Economy, Law of Nature and Nations, History, being interwoven with Politics and Law."

This understanding of the purpose of a university remains with us today. The purpose is not merely to teach students how to earn money for living through acquiring a trade such as business or medicine. More importantly, higher education is supposed to be truly "higher." Ideally it should help us enhance our knowledge and morals so that we can improve ourselves, and thereby become good and wise leaders for the betterment of our shared society. Without such education included in one's studies at a college or university, a student will only receive a *degree*, but not a higher *education*. Hopefully, then, this book is a step towards you, the reader, receiving a higher education.

Political Science

The primary study of power is the study of power in and through government. Within the context of higher education, *political science* is the specialized academic field that studies this broad arena of power. Other academic subfields study power in other contexts. For example, sociology studies power in relationships, in families, in the workplace, in organizations, and between social groups. However, as we just discussed, advanced knowledge of *governmental* politics is necessary for successful, flourishing societies. This is the most important historical reason why political science has long been a standard area of study at colleges and universities.

Indeed, political science has always been at the core of the study of the liberal arts. The word "liberal" comes from the Latin word *liber*, meaning liberty or freedom. The Latin *liberalis* meant "appropriate for a free person." A "liberal" education is thus the art of living well as a free person. An imprisoned person or enslaved person cannot flourish while imprisoned or enslaved. Only a free person is able to fully explore and achieve their potential. However, a person can flourish in this way only if they learn how to do so. A liberal education therefore teaches how to live the best life possible as a free person. Throughout Western history, obtaining the knowledge how to flourish has been the ultimate, guiding goal of human learning and education. The liberal arts include the study of philosophy, politics, religion, history, language and communication, math, the natural sciences, and the creative arts such as music and painting.

Apart from the benefits of improving oneself and humanity, the study of government and politics is helpful and often necessary for the fulfillment of many different careers. One of the most common careers that students of political science eventually enter is law. Knowledge of government and politics is essential to understanding how laws are made and enforced. To be most successful, lawyers must know how to work within the entire political system, not just the legal system. For example, even the best legal expert can lose cases if they refuse to play the local politics needed to stay on good terms with local judges. Political knowledge similarly helps prosecutors, defense attorneys, corporate lawyers and solo practitioners all maximize their chances of winning for their clients.

There are many other careers in government and politics besides law. This includes elected officials, their long-term support staff, and their campaign staff. There are over 11 million civil service jobs in the U.S. This includes at least eight million jobs at the state and local level, and at least three million jobs at the federal level. Despite regular calls by politicians to shrink the size of government, the number of government positions keeps expanding. The job outlook for government employment therefore remains as positive as ever.

Similar politically related positions exist throughout numerous professional organizations, interest groups, and not-for-profit entities. The fields of education, health care, the environment, criminal justice, civil rights, affordable neighborhood housing, domestic violence shelters, food banks, animal rescue efforts, employment training, youth sports leagues, and numerous other community activities, private charities, and social support services must all follow legal guidelines. These groups also have input in the making of laws governing their respective domains. This requires understanding how political support can be gained for enacting, modifying, or repealing laws. In this situation, knowledge is truly power.

Entrepreneurs, business owners and managers all must understand the ever-increasing patchwork of government regulations that applies to them. Only by knowing how to work within the political system can these affected parties hope to navigate a complicated legal maze to maximize success and avoid potential liabilities.

Moreover, political science knowledge is essential to teachers of government. Instructors at all levels of civics education must be trained in this knowledge so as to pass on thorough and accurate political information to learners. Elementary and high schools usually require civics education as a result of state education laws. Community colleges and universities also often require a basic government course of all students. Even if not, as mentioned earlier, political science is one of the most popular majors for students going to law school. As a result, there is a regular demand for college instructors who can teach background concepts in government and politics.

Journalists also must understand the political system. Probably the largest share of all news involves the action of some level of local, state, national, or international government and politics. Reporters for newspaper, radio, television, and internet news companies will excel at what they do only if they can actually understand the content they are covering.

SUMMARY

Politics is the struggle for power to decide how to allocate scarce resources in society. Government is the institutions that make those decisions, and the decisions themselves become public policy. Government, and not private individuals, make law so that disputes will be decided peacefully rather than violently. The philosophical purpose of a "higher' education is to teach students greater concepts than one learns about in elementary school or high school. This means higher education is intended to consist of something more than mere money-making knowledge or skills such as math or reading. Instead, students in higher education should be taught to think about "higher" questions of human existence. These especially include how to make oneself a better person, and how best to improve human society, such as by using the tools of government. This question is the same thing as asking "how can we best live together on this Earth?" This question in turn is akin to asking "what is the meaning of life?" This means that only by studying politics, government, and law (along with ethical, moral, and religious philosophy) can one actually receive a "higher" education. Even apart from this more noble purpose in learning about government, in the U.S. there are millions of jobs throughout many different careers that require political education as an important background for success. Finally, understanding the political system is essential if one is to protect oneself and one's family either from government, or with the help of government.

QUESTIONS FOR REVIEW AND SELF-ASSESSMENT

1. What is politics, government, and law?
2. What is the role and importance of government in human life?
3. What is the role and importance of higher education in promoting political knowledge and wisdom?
4. How is political science relevant to many different possible careers?

CRITICAL THINKING QUESTIONS FOR REFLECTION AND DISCUSSION

1. Is politics actually a necessary part human life?
2. Could a person live the best human life possible if they never knew anything about politics, government, or law?
3. How would you define the best possible life?

Suggested Reading Supplements

- Preamble to the Constitution of the United States

For Further Advanced Reading

- Thucydides, *The Peloponnesian War*
- Aristotle, *Politics*
- Frans de Waal, *Chimpanzee Politics: Power and Sex among Apes*

Chapter 2: Origins of Government

The Big Picture

Politics is the struggle between humans for power. The outcome of politics is official government policies. Historically, rulers typically claimed that government policies came from god. This theory was largely overthrown by the idea that government gets its authority from the people. This means that all legitimate governments must be created by the public. This concept is illustrated by the founding of the United States of America as an independent nation.

Relevant Timeline

- 1620 Mayflower Compact
- 1680 Robert Filmer publishes *Patriarcha*
- 1690 John Locke publishes *Two Treatises on Government*
- 1765 Stamp Act
- 1770 Boston Massacre
- 1773 Tea Act
- 1775 American Revolution begins
- 1776 U.S. Declaration of Independence

Chapter Objectives

After reading this chapter, the reader should be able to:

1. Explain the theory of divine right of kings.
2. Describe the basic elements of John Locke's social contract theory.
3. Explain the philosophical cause of the U.S. Revolutionary War.
4. Describe the philosophical meaning and importance of the U.S. Declaration of Independence.

Divine Right

As we saw in the first chapter, an understanding of politics and government comes through the study of political science. This knowledge is necessary so we can decide how to best live together as a human beings so that we can flourish as individuals and as a society. But where does government come from? Why do those in political power get to make the laws? What right do our leaders have to tell us what to do? To understand the answers to these questions today, one needs to understand how these questions were originally answered hundreds of years ago. For example, a person waking up with amnesia cannot remember their own past. In that case, they wouldn't understand who they were, or what they were doing or why. Likewise, throughout this course a knowledge of history is necessary to understand the United States today. Context is always critical.

One answer to the question "why do our leaders get to be the ones in charge?" would be to simply say "might makes right." This was, in fact, essentially the answer commonly given for thousands of years, but with a little more subtlety. For most of human history, across most cultures, the leaders justified their rule by claiming they were gods, or prophets of gods, or descendants of gods. At the very least, the ruler typically claimed that the gods had directly given them authority to rule. Indeed, throughout the middle ages in Europe, the theory of *divine right of kings* justified the rule of monarchs by using the Bible. The most famous and detailed written defense of the divine right of kings was by the English scholar Robert Filmer, in his work titled *Patriarcha* (roughly meaning "rule by fathers") published in 1680.

Filmer used many Biblical passages were used in support of this theory, including parts of the Christian New Testament such as Romans 13:1-2. This verse states "Everyone must submit himself to the governing authorities, for there is no authority except that which God has established. The authorities that exist have been established by God." (New International Version). Filmer defended the right of the kings and queens of Europe to claim "We have the right to tell you what to do because God says so." Under the theory of divine right, god did not grant only the *king* authority to rule, but the king's *family*. Political authority therefore passed on through the king's bloodline. When the king died, his children ruled, and then his children's children, and so on.

A detailed set of rules determined which particular descendant got to be king. The preference was first-born male heirs. This meant that when a king died, the king's firstborn son became king. If the firstborn son was dead, then the second-born son was made king, and so on. If there were no male heirs to the throne, then the firstborn daughter became queen, then the second-born daughter, and so on. If the king had no children, then either the King's eldest brother became king, and then the next eldest brother, and so on. If none of the King's brothers were alive, then the eldest sister became queen, and so on. The rules then passed on the throne to other relatives, such as uncles, aunts, and cousins, as long as they were related to the king by blood. Notice the King's *wife* did not become queen because she was part of the family only through marriage, and *not* by blood. (Sometimes, though, marriages were arranged to a queen that was blood- related to the king to make extra sure the throne stayed in the hands of the same family.)

An important implication of the divine right of kings was that no one could disagree with king's authority or any laws the king made. Since the king was put there by god, to disagree with the king was to disagree with *god*. An analogy is that there is no such thing as a "right" to disagree with the physical laws of the universe such as gravity. Similarly, there is no "right" to disagree with the moral laws of the universe put there by the same god who created the physical laws. This would be political and religious *heresy* (disagreement with accepted ideas), punishable by harsh sentences. These could include fines, imprisonment, torture, and perhaps even execution. In short, under the divine right of kings, the "freedom of speech" did not exist, nor much religious liberty, either.

Political writers began to question the theory of divine right. Perhaps the first thinker to do so was Thomas Hobbes. In 1651, Hobbes published a book titled *Leviathan*, named after the mythical sea monster. In the work, Hobbes said that government comes not from God. The people give an all-powerful government named "Leviathan" the power to make all laws and settle all disputes. In doing so, each person voluntarily surrenders the right to individual self-defense that would otherwise be used to settle disputes privately. According to Hobbes, the grant of this absolute political power is irrevocable. This means the government (typically an all-powerful king) may use any means necessary, including violent force against the people, to enforce order if need be. The people may never take back their grant of total rule to the government.

As you can imagine, the theory that governments are rightfully both totalitarian and unchangeable was not a popular idea. Such a government would be little different in practice from a government justified by divine right. Other political thinkers, though, began to offer more alternative, more attractive theories of government.

Locke's Social Contract

Just ten years after Filmer published *Patriarcha*, an English philosopher named John Locke published an important and influential work of political thought. Locke greatly disliked the theory of divine right of kings, because it offered a convenient excuse for any tyrant to have absolute rule without question. In 1690, Locke published *Two Treatises on Government.* A "treatise" is a detailed scholarly work. It's not necessarily the case that Locke was the first one to think of all the concepts he presented in his *Two Treatises*. Other thinkers had begun to formulate ideas about civil government based on concepts other than divine right. Locke did, though, develop the ideas more fully, modify and expand some of them, and present them in a clearer, more coherent way than anyone had done before. Thus, his work became an influential political writing that helped kill the theory of divine right. Locke did so by offering an alternative theory to justify the existence of government instead of divine right.

In Locke's *First Treatise on Government*, he systematically, point-by-point, attacked the theory of divine right of kings as defended by Filmer in his *Patriarcha*. Locke argued in detail that nothing in the Christian Bible could be used to justify absolute rule by any particular king, queen, or family bloodline. After destroying the theory of divine right, Locke realized that government still needed a justification for its existence. Locke's *Second Treatise on Government* did this by providing (among other things) an alternative theory of government. Although Locke didn't give his political theory a name, it has since come to be called *social contract theory.* Again, other thinkers before him developed some of these ideas, but Locke's is the most well-known version, and some historians consider it to be the most influential one.

Locke begins his argument by having the reader imagine going back in time before there was any human civilization. Humans were living just as animals do, without any laws or government. This was, as Locke called it, living in the *state of nature.* Yet he declared that even without any human-made laws, there are moral laws that exist in nature, just as there are physical laws of nature like gravity. Locked suggested these moral laws were created by a supreme deity. This moral law includes *natural rights.* These rights are comprised of a right to life, a right to liberty, and a right to "estate," meaning property.

Even though these natural rights are inherent in the universe as provided by a god, they are unprotected. That is, in the state of nature, any person can easily interfere with our rights at any time. Murderers, rapists, kidnappers, and thieves can injure or destroy us or our property. People don't like feeling so insecure. The solution is to join together in groups for our mutual protection. Within these groups, everyone agrees to live by common rules by which everyone's rights are respected. Once a group forms laws to follow for each other's benefit, that group is no longer living in a state of nature, but in a *civil society.* The mutual agreement to create, obey, and enforce common rules can be verbal or written. However, the rules are provided, this agreement is called a *social contract.* This concept is also sometimes referred to by the term *social compact.*

Under social contract theory, a government of laws is formed for everyone's mutual advantage and protection. According to Locke, the *only* reason government exists is to protect our natural rights. Indeed, government power is based on the fact that the people have agreed to give the government the power to enforce the social contract. The source of government authority is therefore not god, but the people themselves. This makes the consent of the governed necessary for any government to claim it has legitimate moral authority to rule. If the people do not give the government the right to rule over themselves, then the government has no right to rule.

Moreover, by definition a creator is greater than a creation. For example, a pottery-maker is supreme over a piece of pottery, parents are supreme over their young children, and any creator god is supreme over humans. Similarly, since the people have created the government (and not the other way around), the people are supreme over the government. This concept is called *popular sovereignty.*

"Sovereignty" simply means supreme political power. In social contract theory, the people have the highest political authority. Locke's concept of popular sovereignty is merely another way to state that the government has no right to rule without the consent of the people who will be governed. In essence, Locke argued that the only morally legitimate form of government is *democracy*—rule by the people. All other types of government would have no moral authority.

Locke took this idea to its logical conclusion. In a legal contract, each of the parties has rights and responsibilities. If one party to the contract violates the terms of the contract, the other party is free to break the contract as well. Similarly, in a social contract, people have rights protected by law but also corresponding duties to obey those laws. If one party to the social contract violates its side of the bargain, the other party is free to ignore its side of the agreement also. So, if the government begins to violate its obligations under the social contract to protect the people's natural rights, then the people are no longer bound by their promise to obey the government. This could happen, for example, if the government begins to abuse the people's rights by oppressing the people rather than protecting them. Since the people are supreme, they would then be free to withdraw their consent to be ruled by that government. That is, the people would have a right to abolish that government and replace it with it new one. Locke pointed out that the people might even have to use violence if necessary, in case the illegitimate rulers refuse to give up their power. That is, the people have a right to revolution if the government infringes on the natural rights of the people. Put simply, the democratic masses may rightly rebel against the government if the government becomes undemocratic.

The Mayflower Compact is a famous example that illustrates some of Locke's basic concepts even though it was written over a half-century before Locke published his *Two Treatises on Government.* Written in 1620, the Mayflower Compact is a simple example of a written social contract. It is comprised of merely a single paragraph authored by a group of Puritans. The Puritans were coming from Europe on route to what would become their new home in Plymouth, Massachusetts. They were still on their ship the *Mayflower,* traveling across the Atlantic Ocean, when they formed an express agreement to create a political community together in the new world. In their compact, the adult men on board the ship all signed their names promising that they will live together in a shared society for each other's mutual benefit and protection. Towards these ends, they agreed to form a common government and laws, and pledged obedience to them.

The Mayflower Compact

In the name of God, Amen. We, whose names are underwritten, the Loyal Subjects of our dread Sovereign Lord, King James, by the Grace of God, of England, France and Ireland, King, Defender of the Faith, etc.

Having undertaken for the Glory of God, and Advancement of the Christian Faith, and the Honour of our King and Country, a voyage to plant the first colony in the northern parts of Virginia; do by these presents, solemnly and mutually in the Presence of God and one of another, covenant and combine ourselves together into a civil Body Politick, for our better Ordering and Preservation, and Furtherance of the Ends aforesaid; And by Virtue hereof to enact, constitute, and frame, such just and equal Laws, Ordinances, Acts, Constitutions and Offices, from time to time, as shall be thought most meet and convenient for the General good of the Colony; unto which we promise all due submission and obedience.

In Witness whereof we have hereunto subscribed our names at Cape Cod the eleventh of November, in the Reign of our Sovereign Lord, King James of England, France and Ireland, the eighteenth, and of Scotland the fifty-fourth. Anno Domini, 1620."

[There followed the signatures of 41 of the 102 passengers.]

Again, even though it was written before Locke defined his ideas, the Mayflower Compact shows how simple a social contract can be. In theory, it would only take one short sentence to create a social contract. This could be a declaration that says something like this: "We the undersigned agree to form a government and laws together for our common good." Of course, most real-world social contracts are much more detailed. They typically set out the structure, functions, powers, and limitations of government. More detailed social contracts are typically called *constitutions*. The verb "to constitute" means to create, form, establish, make up, comprise, or compose. A constitution thus "constitutes" the social contract that forms the essence of that society. In short, a constitution is what makes up a political system.

The American Revolution

So far we've looked at the proposed origins of human government in general, but now let's look at the origins of the United States government. At the time Locke published his *Two Treatises on Government*, social contract theory was considered by many people to be a dangerously radical idea. First, Locke and other social contract thinkers were directly repudiating parts of the Christian Bible such as Romans 13:1-2, which we saw earlier states that all government comes from god. Second, since there were no democracies at the time, Locke was declaring all governments and rulers on the planet at that moment to be morally illegitimate. Although those with political power did not like his ideas, the educated classes widely read Locke and other political writers. These ideas began to gain popularity among political thinkers who wanted greater political rights. Some of these thinkers lived in what were called the "Thirteen Colonies" of the British Empire along the eastern coast of North America.

Great Britain was not just a major European power, but arguably the greatest world power at the time. Although it had an elected national legislature called the parliament, the King still had primary political authority. King George III was the monarch during this time. Also, under British law at the time, English citizens living in British colonies had all the same rights of other English citizens, except the right to vote. The Thirteen Colonies in America thus had no right to vote for members of the British Parliament. This meant that the Thirteen Colonies received no direct representation in the British Parliament, and British law could overrule any of their decisions.

Yet the Thirteen Colonies provided vast wealth for England. This was especially true in regard to natural resources and agriculture in particular. The Thirteen Colonies also made much money for themselves, both by trading among themselves and by trading with other nations. In the late 1760's and early 1770's, the English parliament imposed a series of taxes on the colonies. The British government was in debt, especially from fighting the French and Indian War. The British victory keep the territories of the British colonies out of the hands of France and Native American tribes, but had been costly to fight. Thus, Britain decided to raise money by taxing sugar, stamped paper, tea, and a few other goods in the Thirteen Colonies.

By today's standards, the number and the amount of the taxes the British government imposed on the Thirteen Colonies were relatively small. Yet the Americans were increasingly outraged. They were not angered so much by the number or amount of the taxes, but by the fact they had no democratic input into the making of the taxes. Soon the philosophical objection "no taxation without representation" became the rallying cry of the colonies. Both the King of England and the British Parliament refused to consider requests to allow English colonist the right to vote. England was not even open to the possibility of negotiation on the issue. This simply created more opposition within the Thirteen Colonies in America, which led to a downward spiral of escalating hostility between England and the colonies.

Probably the most hated tax was the tea tax. Tea was by far the most popular non-alcoholic drink in the colonies. This traditional habit had been inherited from their mother country, England. At first, the colonists began to refuse to pay the tea tax along with other taxes. This led Britain to enforce tax collection through tougher administration. This simply caused resistance to increase, which in turn caused Britain to impose harsher administration. As part of this, the King ordered more British troops to the colonies to enforce the tax laws and protect tax collectors. The colonists then began to boycott tea, since no sales taxes would be owed if there were no sales. In all the colonies, sellers of tea were coerced to quit and send their tea back to England.

It also occurred to some of the colonists that no taxes would be owed on merchandise that did not exist. Only in Boston had the sellers of tea not resigned their jobs. To deal with this, some of the colonists organized and decided to destroy a large shipment of tea due to arrive in Boston. This famous incident in 1773 became known as the "Boston Tea Party." Colonists disguised as Mohawk Indians destroyed the incoming shipment of tea by dumping it overboard three ships while they were anchored in the Boston harbor. These actions of the colonists led Britain to close the port of Boston and impose still harsher laws. In 1774, Britain passed what the colonists called "The Intolerable Acts." Among other things, this law prohibited Massachusetts from having any self-government, as punishment for the Boston Tea Party. Boston became an occupied city, and was essentially an armed encampment of British troops. (Fun Fact: the Thirteen Colonies' mass rejection of tea is why coffee became the favorite non-alcoholic drink in the United States rather than tea, which is still widely consumed in England today.)

Up to this point, violence between the colonists and British troops had occurred only sporadically. This included the "Boston Massacre" in 1770, in which several British troops were killed by an angry mob of protestors. Yet by 1775, the colonists were organizing and arming themselves for war. In April of that year, British troops set out from Boston to destroy stockpiles of such weapons in the nearby towns of Lexington and Concord. On April 19, 1775, the first shots of the American Revolutionary War were fired as colonists fought with British troops in the battles of Lexington and Concord. These battles immediately became known as the "shot heard 'round the world." This was because a colony of England was now in open, armed rebellion against its mother country, the most powerful empire on the planet.

At first, the war was not a war for independence, but a war for representation. In 1774, colonial leaders had formed a *Continental Congress* to aid the colonies in cooperating against England. Now that the colonies were in rebellion, the Continental Congress sent delegates to England to attempt to negotiate for voting rights. Most of the colonists still wished to remain loyal to England, and simply wanted the equal rights of other English citizens. King George and the majority of the English parliament, however, insisted on unconditional surrender and laying down of arms. In short, Britain showed no openness to discussing voting rights for the colonists.

Because of the refusal of England to negotiate, only a year after the war began the tide of public opinion in the colonies had turned against the mother country. Many colonists now spoke openly of independence. The most widely-read writing in this regard came from an American patriot and thinker named Thomas

Paine. He published a book in February 1776 called *Common Sense*, in which he argued for American independence. The book was enormously influential in the colonies. Based on the percent of the population that bought and read the book at the time, it is still the best-selling American publication in history. (Fun fact: Paine later wrote *The Age of Reason* in 1794, in which he ridiculed religion, especially Christianity. In 1796, he viciously criticized highly popular U.S. President George Washington. When he died in 1809, only six people came to his funeral).

Finally, in early June 1776, the Continental Congress assigned a five-person committee to write a draft of a statement declaring the Colonies' independence from Great Britain. Together the committee chose Thomas Jefferson to write the first, main draft of a "Declaration of Independence" for their new nation. The draft was then reviewed and revised by two other members of the committee, John Adams, and Benjamin Franklin. All three represented their colonies in the Continental Congress. Jefferson was a lawyer from Virginia who later became Vice-President and then President of the United States. Adams was a lawyer from Massachusetts, and also later became a Vice-President and then President of the United States. Franklin was a widely respected writer, inventor, and politician from Pennsylvania. After the three of them polished the draft, the Continental Congress made further revisions. After several days of debate, on July 2, 1776, the Continental Congress voted in favor of the declaration, in which Jefferson had named the new nation the "United States of America." This makes July 2 technically the birthday of the United States. The public announcement of the Declaration of Independence was not made until two days later, however. Because of this, by tradition the date of July 4, 1776 is recognized and celebrated in the United States as its Independence Day.

The Declaration of Independence

Publicly proclaiming the Declaration of Independence was a radical act and vast political experiment. It was the first time in modern world history that a major colony attempted to throw off the rule of its mother country. Doing so challenged the authority of every national government then existing on the planet. This was especially true regarding all the major European empires at the time, such as England, France, and Spain. It was important, then, that the colonists do more than merely declare independence. They also needed to philosophically explain and morally justify their independence to the entire world. This is what the U.S. Declaration of Independence did.

The Declaration of Independence describes and applies every major step in John Locke's social contract theory. Jefferson and the Continental Congress didn't quote or cite Locke as a source. However, Locke's ideas were so well-known at the time that every educated person who read the Declaration of Independence realized Locke's ideas were being used to justify American independence. The first paragraph of the Declaration of Independence first admits that such a momentous decision needs to be explained to the world. The second paragraph then describes Locke's social contract theory in these terms:

> "We hold these truths to be self-evident, that all men are created equal, that they are endowed by their Creator with certain unalienable Rights, that among these are Life, Liberty and the pursuit of Happiness.--That to secure these rights, Governments are instituted among Men, deriving their just powers from the consent of the governed, --That whenever any Form of Government becomes destructive of these ends, it is the Right of the People to alter or to abolish it, and to institute new Government . . ."

The bulk of the remainder of the Declaration of Independence then gives a detailed list of the ways in which the King of England (that is, the country of Great Britain) had broken the social contract with the colonies. The Declaration notes that these breaches of the political bargain between England and the colonies have continued despite repeated pleadings by the colonists to have their rights as English citizens respected. Since England has broken its side of the bargain and refuses to change its ways, the American colonies have been forced to consider their former mother country to be an enemy. The new United States of America therefore dissolves its political ties with England, and justifiably declares itself a free and independent nation.

The concepts contained in the U.S. Declaration of Independence make it much more than merely a historical document. It is also a philosophically important work because of its use of Locke's social contract theory. In justifying political independence, the Declaration goes far beyond a mere one-sentence statement such as "We, the United States of America, declare ourselves independent." This would be all it would technically take to issue a "declaration of independence." In this sense, the U.S. Declaration of Independence is either misnamed, or at least incompletely named. A more accurate and complete title would be "The Declaration of, and Philosophical Justification for, Independence." That's not quite as easy to remember or say as "The Declaration of Independence." The point, though, is that the Declaration of Independence is an important historical document not only because of its historical significance, but especially because of its *philosophical* significance. The Declaration of Independence is the philosophical justification for the existence of the United States of America as a separate, independent nation. The Declaration bases that existence on a moral, philosophical, and religious belief that every human being has equal rights to liberty. Put differently, according to the Declaration of Independence, god does not give only *one* individual the right to rule as divine right theory had argued. Instead, under Locke's social contract theory, everyone is "created equal" by god in a political sense. This means everyone has an equal right to rule. Under the moral law of the universe, then, democracy is the only morally defensible form of government.

The Declaration of Independence is the first social contract of the United States. All other founding documents like the Constitution and Bill of Rights merely build upon it. Indeed, *everything* that comes later merely builds upon it. The U.S. Constitution, for example, sets out the structural details of the U.S. government, but the Declaration of Independence is the foundation for that structure. Indeed, during the period leading up to and during the U.S. Civil War, President Lincoln rarely referred to the Constitution in his speeches, since the Constitution allowed slavery. Instead, Lincoln regularly quoted the Declaration of Independence. He argued that the United States should finally implement the principles expressed in it, especially the moral-religious statement that "all men are created equal." Just as a house can be wiped away by a storm yet rebuilt on the foundation, even if the Constitution or U.S. government were temporarily destroyed, the United States would still exist as a nation due to the Declaration of Independence. The Declaration of Independence is therefore every bit as politically important, if not more so, as the U.S. Constitution.

After the United States declared its political independence from the British Empire, the governments of the rest of the world were morally cheering for Britain to defeat the rebellion. A defeat of the United States would be a defeat of the ideas it represented. Otherwise, a successful revolution in America would challenge the political authority of all governments at the time. Indeed, the only government that sided with the U.S. was the French Monarchy. King Louis XVI of France did not care about American democracy but wanted to embarrass England, France's main political and military rival. By October of 1781, with help from France, the U.S. military under the leadership of General George Washington defeated the major English forces on American soil. England finally signed a peace treaty with the U.S. in 1783, thereby ending the American Revolution with the United States gaining full independence. The success of the ideas of the American Revolution inspired people in other lands to demand democracy in their own nations. Ironically, the very first nation in which this occurred was France. Beginning in 1789, the French monarchy that had helped the United States gain independence was itself brutally overthrown by the French masses.

Summary

The original theory of government was the theory of the divine right or kings. This theory argued that god gave the government the authority to rule. English philosopher John Locke, however, replaced the theory of divine right with his social contract theory. Locke's theory argues that the people decide when and how to create government over themselves. Locke's social contract theory was extremely influential on the political thought of England's Thirteen Colonies in North America. When England refused to give the colonists equal voting rights as English citizens, the colonists turned to Locke's theory. In 1776, colonial leader Thomas Jefferson and the Continental Congress used social contract theory to morally defend their right to political independence from their mother country. This written justification was called the Declaration of Independence, and the new nation was called the United States of America.

Questions for Review and Self-Assessment

1. What is the theory of divine right of kings?
2. What are the basic elements of John Locke's social contract theory?
3. What was the philosophical cause of the U.S. Revolutionary War?
4. What is the philosophical meaning and importance of the U.S. Declaration of Independence?

Critical Thinking Questions for Reflection and Discussion

1. Does government come from god, the people, or something else?
2. Are there natural rights? If so, what are those rights, and how can we know what they are?
3. Would we be better off without government?

Suggested Reading Supplements

- Thomas Paine, *Common Sense*
- U.S. Declaration of Independence
- Preamble to the U.S. Constitution

For Further Advanced Reading

- Robert Filmer, *Patriarcha, or the Natural Power of Kings*
- John Locke, *Second Treatise on Government*
- Robert Middlekauf, *The Glorious Cause: The American Revolution 1763-1789 (Oxford History of the United States)*

PART II: CONSTITUTIONAL FRAMEWORK

Chapter 3: New Government

The Big Picture

The founders of the United States at first created a new U.S. government where the states (the former colonies) would be supreme over the national government. After this design quickly failed, a new Constitution was written which still governs the U.S. today. Several major political bargains were reached in writing the U.S. Constitution. These included compromises on how states would be represented in the national government, on how political power would be divided between the state governments and the U.S. government, and how the new Constitution would address the issue of human slavery. Each of these decisions has had enormous, long-term influence on politics within the United States.

Relevant Timeline

- 1776 U.S. Declaration of Independence
- 1777 Articles of Confederation
- 1783 American Revolution ends (U.S. defeats Great Britain)
- 1787 Philadelphia Convention writes the Constitution
- 1789 U.S. Constitution ratified; George Washington 1st President

Chapter Objectives

After reading this chapter, the reader should be able to:

1. Define the three different types of government based on how many people are sharing political rule.
2. Define the three different types of government based on how power is divided between the central and regional governments within a nation.
3. Describe the U.S. Articles of Confederation and explain why it failed.
4. Explain the political compromises in the U.S. Constitution that created a federal system and a bicameral national legislature.
5. Explain the three separate compromises in the U.S. Constitution that involved slavery.

Autocracy, Oligarchy, and Democracy

The U.S. declared its political independence from Great Britain in 1776. Now that the United States was a new nation, it needed a government and a constitution defining that government. The Continental Congress had several major decisions to make in this regard. Indeed, a committee had already begun work on a proposal for the U.S. government while the Declaration of Independence was being drafted. Only eight days after declaring independence from England, the Continental Congress was given a proposal for a constitution titled the *Articles of Confederation*. The Continental Congress quickly adopted this proposal as the working form of government for the United States. However, the Congress did not formally vote for the plan until November 1777, and the states did not finish ratifying the proposal until 1781. Since it was the working plan of the U.S. government since its initial consideration by the Congress, 1777 is generally considered the birth year of the Articles of Confederation. It lasted until 1789, at which time a new constitution replaced the Articles of Confederation as the constitution of the United States. This new constitution was uncreatively called simply "The Constitution." As we shall see, the failures of the Articles of Confederation heavily influenced the thinking that went into the design of the U.S. Constitution.

One of the first things any new nation must decide is who is going to rule. Going as far back as the ancient Greek philosophers Plato and Aristotle, political thinkers have been classifying types of governments. There are different ways governments can be classified. Most political scholars today, however, agree there are roughly three different general types of government based on the number of people ruling. There are also many variations of each of those three basic types. Shown in the table below are only a few of the most common subtypes (there are dozens of different kinds of oligarchies, for example).

Table: Types of Government

Name of Government (with Greek word origin)	**Basic Definition**	**Examples** (subtypes) (with Greek word origins)
autocracy (*auto* = self + *kratos* = power)	Rule by one.	--**monarchy** (rule by a king or queen) (*mono* = one + *archia* = rule) --**dictatorship** (absolute rule by a tyrant)
oligarchy (*oligoi* = few + *archy* = rule)	Rule by an elite few (rule by a relatively small percent of the population).	--**plutocracy** (rule by the wealthy) (*ploutos* = wealth + *kratos* = power) --**aristocracy** (rule by those most fit to rule→wisest, smartest, morally best, etc.) (*aristo* = "best" + *kratos* = power) --**theocracy** (rule by religious leaders) (*theos* = god + *kratos* = power)
democracy (*demos* = people + *kratos* = power)	Rule by the majority (rule by most or all of the population).	--**direct democracy** (everyone votes directly on all laws; no representatives) --**representative democracy** (people elect representatives who vote on laws)

When it came to deciding the nature of the United States government, most of the American founders wanted a democracy (rule by the majority of people). A few leaders would have preferred a monarchy (rule by royalty), as that was the type of national government they were familiar with as English citizens living under the King of Britain. Some few others believed that because they were the revolutionary leaders, they were by definition the aristocracy (the most fit to rule) and so should make themselves the rulers. There was also an element of plutocracy (rule by the wealthy) to U.S. politics at the time since several of the states did not allow a person to vote unless they owned land. However, those voting restrictions were eliminated in a few short years, so any overtly plutocratic elements in the government were soon ended. Finally, several of the American colonies had originally been founded as theocracies (rule by religious leaders). However, by the time of the American Revolution none of the colonies had theocratic rule. Only very few people—and none of them prominent leaders in the revolution—wanted a theocracy. Instead, the large majority of the leaders of the American Revolution believed concentrated political power is inherently dangerous. After all, the United States was fighting a rebellion against a strong central government, as the King of England had nearly absolute authority. Any form of monarchy, as well as any form of aristocracy, plutocracy, theocracy or other oligarchy, would put too much political power in the hands of too few people (or one person).

The founders of the United States therefore concluded that democracy would be the least dangerous form of government. This is because democracy spreads out political power among the greatest number of people. Dispersing power rather than concentrating it makes tyranny less likely. The word *tyranny* comes from the ancient Greek *turannos*, which roughly means "one who has absolute rule." The word "tyranny" originally meant any kind of rule (good or bad) by one person. However, the term has come to mean any form of government that is cruel and oppressive. Tyranny is thus not a form of government, but an abusive *manner* in which *any* type of government might operate depending on the circumstances. The founders of the U.S. decided that to minimize the danger of tyranny, the legislative bodies of the national government and all the state governments would be elected by "the people." As we shall see, though, originally only white males were considered as "the people" because only they could legally vote.

Unitary, Federal, and Confederal Systems

Another major decision any new nation must decide regarding their government is how to divide power between the nation's capitol and regional capitols. This might not at first sound like an important issue. Yet, how this question is answered can often make or break the survival of a government, and hence of a nation itself. The central government is called the national government. Regional governments are also called subnational governments.

We can look at an example from outside the United States to show how critical this issue can be. In the Middle-Eastern nation of Iraq, there are three major groups: The Shias, the Sunnis, and the Kurds. The Kurds are a different ethnic group apart from the Shias and Sunnis. Also, the Shias and Sunnis are defined by their religious differences between each other. These three groups mostly live in different regions of Iraq. The also each want political control over their own separate regions. If each group is given too much authority to govern their own regions, the country of Iraq might break up. This could perhaps even happen through civil war. Yet each group is always afraid to give the central Iraqi government too much power. The Kurds, Shias, and Sunnis each fear that if one of the other groups controls the central government, it will use that power to oppress the other groups. The Iraqis are thus always trying to walk a political tightrope. They are trying to balance between preventing two opposite dangers: an oppressive central government on the one hand, versus disintegration of their nation on the other.

The founders of the United States had a similar choice to make. There are three basic ways any nation can choose to divide power between the central and regional governments. The simplest way is to not create any separate regional governments that have their own lawmaking authority. Instead, there would be only one central capitol that makes a uniform set of laws that applies equally throughout the nation. This type of arrangement is called a *unitary* system of government. "Unitary" comes from the root word "*uni*," meaning "one." In other words, in a unitary system, there is only a single government throughout the nation. The large majority of nations throughout history have been unitary systems. This is still true today, including for most democracies.

A second way to allocate power in a nation is to create two levels of government. There would be a central national capitol, along with separate regional governments. Both the central and regional governments each have independent lawmaking powers. The *central* government, however, is politically supreme over the *regional* governments. If there is any dispute or contradictory laws between the capitol and regional governments, the central government overrides the regional governments. This type of two-level government is called a *federal* system of government. A federal system of government can also be referred to as a *federation*. Only about two dozen nations on the planet today have federal systems. Among these are Australia, Brazil, Germany, Canada, Germany, India, Iraq, Mexico, Russia, and the United States. (Fun Fact: for Star Wars fans, a long time ago in a galaxy far, far away there is the fictional interstellar "Trade Federation." For Star Trek fans, in the future there is the fictional interplanetary "Federation," of which Earth is a founding member. It's not poli-sci, it's poli-sci-fi!)

A third alternative method of power sharing in a nation is the opposite of the federal system. As with federalism, there would be two levels of government: a central national capitol, along with separate regional governments. Both levels also still would maintain independent lawmaking powers. The difference, though, is that the *regional* governments are politically supreme over the *central* government. That is, if there is any dispute or contradictory laws between the capitol and regional governments, the regional governments override the central government. This is called a *confederal* system of government. It can also be referred to as a *confederation* or a *confederacy*, or sometimes as a *league*. Confederal systems of government are relatively uncommon. A famous example is the Confederate States of America, the government of the Southern slave-owning states during the U.S. civil war, although in practice they differed little from a federal system. Also, the European Union is a hybrid system of government that contains elements of both federalism and confederalism, depending on the policy area involved.

The founders of the United States faced the question regarding which of these three systems their United States should have: unitary, federal, or confederal. Prior to independence, the Thirteen Colonies each had their own separate government, laws, and currencies. People were raised to identify themselves with their colony of birth. After U.S. independence, the people likewise identified with their individual states. They did not think of themselves as "Americans." Instead, they called themselves "Virginians" and "New Yorkers" and so on, and were fiercely loyal to their states. They were citizens of essentially 13 different mini nation-states with relatively little political unity. Their main political commonality was that they were fighting for independence against their shared enemy, the British Empire. Because of their state's separate identities, when it came time to form a nation together, the members of the Continental Congress favored a form of government that gave primary power to their state governments. The national government of the U.S. would be mostly just a coordinating body. That is, it would merely help provide economic and military organization and cooperation. However, the states would have authority to disregard the national government. To emphasize that the new nation would be a confederation, the founders of the U.S. named their first-ever national constitution the *Articles of Confederation*.

The Articles of Confederation

Recall from the first chapter that a document that comprises or "constitutes" the structure and powers of a government is called a "constitution." The U.S. Declaration of Independence created the United States, but it did not set out any details of the government of the United States. This is what the Articles of Confederation did instead, and so the Articles of Confederation made up the first constitution of the United States. Because the founders of the U.S. wanted power within the U.S. to remain with the state governments, the Articles of Confederation created an extremely weak central government. This led let to several serious problems in attempting to hold the new nation together.

First, the U.S. government had no power to impose mandatory taxes. The U.S. government could only ask the state governments to voluntarily donate money to it. The states rarely agreed to provide such funding. As a result, the U.S. government remained essentially bankrupt. This meant it could not pay its debts left over from fighting the Revolutionary War. These debts included huge loans from foreign nations, especially its primary ally France. This caused a great deal of diplomatic tension between the United States and foreign governments. Even apart from paying war debts, there was little budget to accomplish anything else.

According to the Articles of Confederation, the U.S. government also could not regulate trade and commerce between the states, or between the states and foreign nations. As a result, the state governments each entered into their own separate commercial treaties with foreign nations. The state even imposed trade tariffs (taxes and fees) on goods coming into their states from other states. This was done to protect producers and sellers within their own states from outside competition. Moreover, although the U.S. government printed its own money, the state governments were free to do so as well. Most states did so, and so the states had their own separate banking systems. State courts also commonly refused to order their own states' citizens to pay debts to citizens of other states. And, the states had conflicting business regulations so that it was hard for businesses to operate in more than one state. In short, there were thirteen separate isolated economies rather than a single unified national economy.

In addition, under the Articles of Confederation, the U.S. government was allowed to have a military. However, it could not draft U.S. citizens into the military, and it had almost no budget for military operations given its inability to tax. This resulted in the United States having almost no functioning national army or navy. This left the American coasts almost completely unprotected against the hostile British or Spanish navies. Even pirate ships had nearly free reign in attacking and seizing American merchant vessels without fear of the U.S. government reacting.

The Articles of Confederation also created a minimal national government. The legislature was a continuation of the Continental Congress, and it became known as the Confederal Congress. Yet it was the only branch of national government. There was no President or any executive branch of government. Nor was there any national U.S. court system. This meant that the state governors and state judicial systems were the top executives and top courts in the United States.

To make matters worse, the Articles of Confederation made it difficult for the U.S. government to use what little power it had. Any decisions by the Confederal Congress needed more than just a majority vote. Instead, decisions had to be agreed to by nine out of the thirteen states, which equates to a 70% supermajority. To top it all off, the Articles of Confederation was extremely hard to modify. Even if the Continental Congress or the state governments thought that changes needed to be made--which they clearly were—amendments needed the unanimous agreement of all 13 states. This meant that even a single objecting state could block any attempts at revising or reforming the Articles of Confederation. In short, problems went unaddressed.

It was not until late 1781 that the Revolutionary War (also called the War for Independence) was won by the U.S., and the war was not officially declared over by Congress until 1783. During all this time, under the Articles of Confederation, the United States was "united" in name only. In practice, it was really the "Disunited States." The states were quickly becoming 13 separate mini nation-states. Increasingly, those who wanted to maintain a common nation realized something had to be done soon if the United States were to continue to exist as one nation.

The last straw that showed how badly the Articles of Confederation needed to be fixed was Shay's Rebellion. This was a rebellion by Massachusetts farmers in the winter and spring of 1786-87. During the Revolutionary War, the state of Massachusetts had borrowed lots of money from wealthy urbanites mostly in Boston. After the war, the Massachusetts government lacked funds to repay the debts. To get this money, the state legislature decided to heavily tax rural farmers living mostly in Western Massachusetts. Many of the farmers went into bankruptcy when their farms were seized to pay the taxes. About 1500 farmers finally rebelled against the taxes. They were led by a fellow farmer named Daniel Shay. The farmers first attacked a weapons arsenal to gain more rifles. Then they attacked a courthouse and shut it down to stop foreclosures on their farms. The U.S. government requested money from the states to create a national army to put down the armed rebellion. Only one state, though, gave any money. Eventually, after several months, the Massachusetts state militia was able to quash the revolt by the farmers. The total inability of the U.S. government to prevent or stop Shay's Rebellion revealed to everyone how powerless the U.S. government was. The U.S. government did nothing but make unenforceable requests of the states, making it the laughingstock of the world.

The Constitution

After the end of Shay's Rebellion, in May of 1787 the Confederate Congress decided a convention was needed to fix the Articles of Confederation. Delegates from the states were sent to Philadelphia. Their assignment was to fix the problems with the Articles of Confederation. As soon as the convention delegates began to consider possible changes, they realized the Articles of Confederation were hopelessly beyond repair. The United States needed an entirely new constitution with a new national government. A few delegates disagreed, left the convention, and made public statements and writings in protest. Most of the delegates, however, agreed a new constitution was needed. At the end of the summer of 1787, the Philadelphia Convention had finished writing a proposal for a constitution that would replace the Articles of Confederation. They called this proposed new constitution simply "The Constitution."

The Constitution was ratified (adopted) by the states in 1789. The Articles of Confederation had lasted only a dozen years: 1777-1789. So why was it so important to discuss the Articles of Confederation in detail? As we've said before, we can only understand who we are if we know where we came from. Almost everything that was put into the Constitution was directly because of the failures of the Articles of Confederation. Learning about the Articles of Confederation thus tells us a great deal about the intentions behind the Constitution. And, as we shall see in upcoming chapters, disagreement over the intended meaning of the Constitution is still a huge issue in U.S. politics today. Modern debates surrounding the powers of the President, Congress, Supreme Court, and state governments regularly refer to the intentions of the framers and ratifiers of the Constitution. At every step of our discussion of the Constitution, then, it's critical to examine the original understanding of those designs.

Table: Key Differences between Articles of Confederation and Constitution

The Articles of Confederation	The Constitution
Congress had no power to tax, regulate commerce, have an army or navy, or do just about anything	Congress is given power to tax, regulate commerce, have an army and navy, along with two dozen other specific powers
The United States had a confederal system of government	The United States is given a federal system of government
The U.S. government had no executive or judicial branches, just a legislative branch only	The U.S. government is given executive and judicial branches in addition to the legislative branch
Amendments to the Articles of Confederation require unanimous (100%) agreement by the states	Amendments to the Constitution require agreement by 2/3 of Congress and ¾ of the states

So what were the main differences between the Constitution and the Articles of Confederation? In other words, what were the biggest changes made to the Constitution as a results of the lessons learned from the failure of the Articles of Confederation? As can be seen by the table above, the single most critical difference between the Articles of Confederation and the Constitution is that the U.S.

government was given more power in the Constitution than it had under the Articles of Confederation. Congress was given specific powers to make certain types of laws, especially the powers it lacked under the Articles of Confederation. Most significant among these powers was the power to tax, regulate commerce, and have a military. Most importantly, any laws Congress makes will be supreme over the states due to the new federal system. Consistent with this increase in power, the U.S. government was expanded from one branch to three branches. Also, in case problems arose with the Constitution, it would not be quite as difficult to make changes to the Constitution as it had been to make changes to the Articles of Confederation.

From the records of the Constitutional Convention, we know that the delegates pushed their own individual agendas. Several of the delegates took notes during the debates, especially James Madison. His ideas contributed heavily to the making of the Constitution, and he was referred to as the "Father of the Constitution" even in his own lifetime. Madison's detailed notes are the primary source of the early drafts of the Constitution and the debates surrounding the writing of it during the Philadelphia Convention. Almost everything in the Constitution, and certainly every major detail, was a political compromise. Sometimes deals were reached only after fierce political debates which sometimes included threats to leave the convention. In short, just like politics today, there was a lot of down-and-dirty political haggling in the mud while writing the Constitution. Decisions were made by majority vote of the states, and the delegates did not always agree on the final product. In short, no "magic formula" was used to create the Constitution. Indeed, the writing of the Constitution was somewhat like a hot dog: the end result may taste good, but you don't want to know how it's made.

The delegates did agree on one thing, though. If the Constitution were to replace the Articles of Confederation, it would become the new detailed social contract of the United States. Recall that Locke's social contract theory said the people have supreme political power. Also recall this concept is known as *popular sovereignty.* To emphasize this point, the writers of the Constitution placed this fact at the very start of the Constitution. The "Preamble" to the Constitution establishes that supreme political power is in the hands of the people. The Preamble contains no substantive rights, but firmly declares that the people have created and "ordained" the Constitution. This indicates that the people, as creators of the Constitution, are by definition supreme over their creation, the Constitution. In full, the Preamble states:

> "We the People, in order to form a more perfect Union, establish justice and ensure domestic tranquility, provide for the common defense, promote the general welfare, and secure the blessings of liberty to ourselves and our

posterity, do ordain and establish this Constitution for the United States of America."

Since almost every line in the Constitution was a compromise, entire books have been devoted simply to examining the writing process of the Constitution. For purposes of this book, we'll look at only certain key issues that were debated during the writing of the Constitution. Initially, we'll examine the three fiercest political debates that occurred during the Philadelphia Convention. Each of the three political compromises we'll discuss were the toughest agreements to reach. That is, the biggest political fights occurred over these three issues: the division of power between the states and the national government, the representation of big states versus small states in the national government, and slavery. The last two of these issues almost caused the convention to break up, especially the issue of slavery.

There also was another major compromise that occurred after the initial Constitution was written. The "Massachusetts Compromise" involved an agreement to add a list of basic political rights to the constitution after its ratification (formal adoption). The Massachusetts Compromise, however, will be discussed in Chapter 7: Civil Liberties when the U.S. Bill of Rights is discussed.

Federalism and Enumerated Powers

Given the failure of the Articles of Confederation, all the delegates at the 1787 Philadelphia Convention agreed that the national government needed *some* additional power over the states. The question was *how much more*? The delegates were deeply divided about how much new power the U.S. government should have. There were many different options debated. Explaining the options and why they rejected some of them will help us understand the final choice. Although there were many variations, there were basically five different options the writers of the Constitution considered. Each option would give a different additional amount of power to the national government. In order of greatest additional power to smallest additional amount of power, the five alternatives were as follows (the delegates didn't number these options or necessarily discuss them in this order; these are simply arranged this way for convenience of our discussion here):

1. Create a unitary system. The Constitution could create a U.S. government only and abolishes the state governments. One of the delegates from New York, Alexander Hamilton, was in favor of this proposal. As was discussed earlier, though, most people at the time were fiercely loyal to their state government. The delegates thus rejected this option as giving too much additional power to the U.S. government.

2. *Create a federal system which gives the U.S. government the "police power."* In this plan, the states would still exist, but the national government would have all-encompassing power. The term "police power" comes from the verb "to police," meaning "to oversee" or "to regulate." For example, parents police their children, and teachers police their classrooms. In the political arena, the police power is a broad, blanket grant of authority. In legal language, it is the power to regulate and promote the public "health, safety, welfare, and morals." In other words, this power is so broad, it includes the power to do basically anything and everything. In U.S. law, the state governments have always had and still do have the police power. Alexander Hamilton favored giving the U.S. government this broad police power as well, since his first choice of creating a unitary system was rejected. The exact language Hamilton proposed was that "Congress shall have power to pass all laws whatsoever." Again, though, the fierce loyalty of most of the delegates to their state governments caused them to reject this option as giving dangerously too much additional power to the U.S. government. If Congress were given the police power, it could have done anything it wanted with the state governments, including abolish them.

3. *Create a federal system that gives most political powers and functions to the U.S. government.* The next alternative would be to divide up the powers and functions of government between the national and state levels. One way to do this would be to give the state governments a list (an *enumeration*) of a few things that they could do, such as "regulate crime, health care, property, education, and marriage." Then the U.S. government would be given all the other functions that governments do. This could be done by some sort of a catch-all phrase whereby the U.S. government would be given the power to regulate "everything else." In this option, the U.S. government would reserve the power to do most things governments that do. The term for this would be "*reserved*" powers. The state governments, then, would perform only the few remaining "*enumerated*" powers.

4. *Create a federal system that give most political powers and functions to the state governments.* This would essentially be the opposite of option three described above. The U.S. government could be given a list of a few specific functions that they would be allowed to do, such as a "create a national system of money and provide a national military,." Then the state governments would be given a catch-all provision that allows them to do "everything else." In this option, then, the state governments would continue to do most things that governments do. The U.S. government would do only a relatively few things that governments do, but it would be supreme in those areas. In technical terms, this option would give the U.S. government a few *enumerated powers*, and the states would keep all the *reserved powers* of government.

5. *Keep a confederal system.* There was another option considered briefly by the delegates. A few of the delegates suggested that Hamilton's proposal to give Congress the police power could be adopted as long as the states could defensively block Congress if the states didn't like Congress's use of its police power. Specifically, these delegates proposed giving states a power to "negative" laws passed by Congress. This essentially would give the state governments a veto over Congress. The other delegates at the convention immediately rejected this proposal as a return to confederalism. That is, if the states could "negative" anything Congress did, then the situation would be the same as existed under the Articles of Confederation. The U.S. government would not be able to tax, regulate commerce, have an army and navy, or do anything if a state blocked it from doing so. This design would simply perpetuate the problems of the Articles of Confederation, not solve them.

The Philadelphia Convention coalesced around two options for creating a federal system: options three and four in the list above. The delegates agreed the specific powers and functions of government would be divided between the U.S. and state governments, but they disagreed about which level of government should be given more functions. It's critical to understand the subtle but substantial difference between these two similar options. There are an infinite number of possible things a government might do. Governments fix potholes, collect garbage, provide health insurance for the poor, limit the size of advertising signs along the highway, and require minimum entrance exam scores to gain admission to state-run colleges. Governments also define crimes, determine child custody when divorces occur, print money, and provide military defense of the nation. There are countless other things governments might do in the unforeseeable future. For example, before the automobile and smart phones were invented, no one ever imagined that governments would someday prohibit "texting while driving." Indeed, there are literally an *infinite* number of possible things governments might regulate. Yet it's humanly impossible to list all the things a government might ever do. How, then, does one divide that list up between two governments? The solution is to list the specific powers that you want to give to one government, and then simply say the other government gets "all the rest."

As an analogy, let's say your long-lost wealthy grandmother just died, and she never accepted visitors in her mansion. When you go to her mansion to clean it out, it turns out she was a hoarder. Room after room is packed to the ceiling with boxes and objects. It would take a ridiculous amount of time cataloging every single trinket and scrap of paper just so your extended family can divide up what they want from the inheritance. Let's assume you don't want to have to deal with the family drama of dividing up the house, land, and other assets. So, you can simply say to whoever is sorting out her inheritance "Just give me any loose cash you find lying around, and you can have everything else!"

The difference between option three and option four above is which government gets a few powers, and which government gets "everything else." Both alternatives three and four propose a federal system of government, but each option distributes power between the U.S. government and the state governments in radically different ways. Option three says "the states get a small finite number *n* of powers, and the U.S. government gets a large *infinity-minus-n* number of powers." Option four, on the other hand, is precisely the opposite. It says "the U.S. government gets a small finite number *n* of powers, and the state governments gets a large *infinity-minus-n* number of powers." To return to our crude grandmother's inheritance analogy, option three says "the states get the loose cash, the U.S. government inherits everything else." Option four would say "the U.S. government gets the loose cash, and the state governments inherit everything else."

As another brief analogy, let's assume a principal at an experimental school wants to divide power between the teacher and students. If the principal tells the students "you may conduct class however you want" then the students have the police power. Now imagine instead that the principal says "only the teacher gets to assign grades or discipline anyone, but other than that the students can conduct class however they want." In this case, the teacher has enumerated powers and the students have reserved powers. If, on the other hand, the principal says "the students may design their own assignments but the teacher has say over everything else," then the students have enumerated powers and the teacher has reserved powers. There's an enormous difference between these options.

The majority of the delegates at the Philadelphia Convention voted for what we've been calling option four. That is, the Convention voted to give the U.S. government a list of a few specific functions of government, and let the states keep doing all the other things that governments do. That is, the U.S. government would have enumerated powers and the states would have reserved powers. The delegates rejected options one through three because they believed each of those options gave too much additional power to the U.S. government. Only option four gave just enough additional power to the U.S. government to create a federal system, but no more.

To implement this compromise in the Constitution, the enumerated powers of Congress were placed in Article I, Section 8 of the Constitution. These included the power to tax and spend, to have an army and navy, to regulate commerce among the states, and a couple dozen other specific powers. Also, the Necessary and Proper Clause was added at the end of Article I, Section 8. This clause allows Congress to do anything implied by the specific list. So, for example, Article I, Section 8 expressly states only that Congress may "raise" an army." But the

Necessary and Proper Clause, however allows Congress to feed, clothe, house, train, equip, and transport the army because all these things are "necessary and proper" for Congress to "raise" an army. In addition, it was initially assumed all remaining government powers that were not listed in Article I, Section 8 would be reserved to the states. Only a few years later, though, the Tenth Amendment was added to the Constitution to make that expressly clear. Federalist Paper No. 45 summarized it this way: "The powers delegated by the proposed Constitution to the federal government, are few and defined. Those which are to remain in the State governments are numerous and indefinite."

Remember that the U.S. had just fought a revolution against a strong central government. The delegates therefore believed that any strong national government is dangerous to the liberty of the people. This is important to understand because, as we shall see in the upcoming chapter focusing on federalism, the nature of U.S. federalism today is vastly differently from when the U.S. was first created.

Bicameralism

There was another major issue that the delegates at the Philadelphia Convention grappled with that threatened to break up the young United States. This question was how the states should be represented in the new national legislature. Recall once again that the former colonies, now states, were all practically their own separate independent nation-states. Most people thought of themselves primarily as citizens of their states, not as "Americans." The people living in different states even distrusted the people in other states. The people living in states with small populations especially feared that states with bigger populations would try to assert political dominance over smaller states. Ultimately, this could occur by invasion and conquest, just as larger nations often subjugate smaller nations. Because of this fear, the small states wanted each state to receive equal representation in the new Congress. Whether each state received one vote or one-hundred votes, the delegates from the states with smaller populations insisted that each state receive an equal number of votes as every other state. This way the smaller states would be politically able to band together and block any attempts by the larger states to politically oppress the smaller states. At that time, New Jersey had a smaller population relative to the other states. Accordingly, the delegates from New Jersey put forth what was called the *New Jersey Plan*, which would create a Congress where each state received an equal number of votes.

The states with large populations, on the other hand, wanted representation in the new Congress to be based on each state's population. The more population, the more votes that state should receive. The delegates from bigger states believed the New Jersey Plan was grossly unfair. Since the new U.S. government would be able to tax, the more people in a state, the more taxes that state would be paying toward the national budget. For example, if a large state has ten times as many people as a small state, then that state's citizens will pay ten times as much tax money to the U.S. government. Most of the operating budget of the U.S. government would therefore come from only a handful of states with the biggest populations. Because of this, the big states believed that the only fair solution would be to give bigger states more say in taxation and spending. At that time, Virginia had the largest state population along with New York. The delegates from Virginia put what was called the *Virginia Plan*. This would give the states votes in Congress in direct proportion to their state population, such as one Congressional representative for every 10,000 people. The exact ratio wasn't important as long as the more population a state has, the more votes that state would get in the Congress.

Both the New Jersey Plan and the Virginia Plan had other elements to their proposals, but both are most remembered for how they would have allocated power between the small states versus large states. This is because the division between big states and small states actually threatened to split up the United States. The smaller states were afraid to continue in a union with the larger states if the smaller states had no way to protect themselves from the larger states. Yet the large states believed it was unjust to give the small states an equal vote in taxing and spending given that the large states would be paying most of the taxes. Finally, the delegates from Connecticut, a state that had an average-sized population at the time, suggested a compromise. The national legislature would be called the "Congress." Yet the Congress would be *bicameral*, meaning "two chambers." In other words, Congress would have two separate legislatures that together made up the Congress. In one chamber called the *Senate*, each state would be assigned an equal number of votes. The other chamber would be called the *House of Representatives*, where votes would be in proportion to the state's population. The greater the state's population, the greater the number of votes that state would receive in the House. For any proposed policy to become U.S. law, however, *both* chambers would have to agree to that law by a majority vote. In this way, any proposal the small states objected to would be blocked by the Senate. Likewise, any proposal the large states disliked would be blocked by the House of Representatives. This meant that only those proposals that both the small states and big states were satisfied with would pass both chambers of Congress to become law. Also, because the main concern of the large states was having their fair say in taxation, the compromise had one other provision. Any proposals to raise or lower taxes would have to begin in the House of Representatives: "All Bills for raising Revenue shall originate in the House of Representatives." (Constitution Article I, Section 7).

The *Connecticut Compromise*, as it was called, was extremely popular with the delegates both from the big states and from the small states. It passed overwhelmingly at the Philadelphia Convention. Everyone was so satisfied with the compromise and the peace it brought between the small and large states that the compromise quickly became also known as the "*Great Compromise.*" The term "great" was used here in both senses of the word: important and wonderful. Still today, any proposals involving taxation must begin in the House of Representatives. And, for any proposal in any area of public policy to become law, that proposal must be passed by a majority of both the House and the Senate.

Note that under the Great Compromise, there is no legislative body called "Congress" that is other than the House and Senate together. As an analogy, there is no such thing as a "coin" that is something other than the two sides of the coin referred to as "heads" and "tails." Similarly, there is no "Congress" other than the two chambers called the House and Senate. That is, there is no third legislative chamber called "Congress." The word "Congress" is simply the combined name for the two legislative chambers of the House plus the Senate when referring to them collectively. The House plus the Senate equals the Congress.

The Constitution and Slavery

As divisive as other political issues were at the 1787 Constitutional Convention, one issue was more politically divisive than any other. The Constitutional Convention almost split up over the issue, thus almost ending the experiment of the United States as a single nation. Slavery was this most divisive issue.

Enslaved Africans had first been brought to the "New World" in the 1600's. After that, slavery had spread throughout the colonies. By the time of U.S. independence, white European enslavement of black Africans was widespread. It was almost entirely concentrated in the Southern colonies, however, where around 400,000 people were enslaved. This was due to the heavy use of slave labor in the mostly agricultural economy of the South. Large-scale planting, tending, and harvesting of crops was extremely labor-intensive. Southern white plantation owners had discovered that enslaved labor was far cheaper than paid labor. By 1787, when the Constitutional Convention met in Philadelphia, slavery had almost entirely died out in the Northern states. It was as in the process of being outlawed by the Northern states on moral grounds as well. The Northern anti-slavery delegates and the Southern pro-slavery delegates were bitterly divided over the issue of slavery.

Even the key founding Fathers were divided over the issue of slavery. Not surprisingly, those from Northern states were against slavery and did not own slaves. Benjamin Franklin was from Pennsylvania. He had once owned slaves, but had changed his views and now was in favor of abolishing slavery. John Adams was from Massachusetts, and Alexander Hamilton and John Jay were from New York. All of them vocally opposed slavery, and some of them even joined and supported abolitionist groups in their states. At the same time, however, they knew that making slavery a major national political issue would tear the country apart. To prevent this from happening, they did not actively oppose slavery in the Southern U.S. It was only more strongly anti-slavery Northerners that openly tried to block slavery being enshrined in the Constitution.

All the leading Southern Founding Fathers, on the other hand, owned slaves. George Washington, Thomas Jefferson, and James Madison all were from the Southern state of Virginia, and all owned slaves. Ironically, all of them wrote privately that they were morally opposed to slavery and hoped to eventually free their slaves. Only Washington, though, actually freed his slaves before he died. Jefferson and Madison had money problems in their later years and so chose to keep their slaves for their financial value rather than set them free. Despite these actions, both Jefferson and Madison believed not only that slavery would gradually come to an end, but that it *should* die out. It was only more radical pro-slavery Southerners who made slavery a political issue by threatening to take the Southern states out of the Union if slavery was not protected by the Constitution.

In short, most of the key Founding Fathers would have been content to avoid the issue of slavery in the Constitution. Other delegates to the Constitutional Convention, however, held stronger views about slavery. This was especially true of the Southern delegates who were themselves wealthy slave owners and insisted that the Constitution must protect slavery. There were three particular constitutional issues involving slavery that the delegates grappled with.

1. The Three-Fifths Compromise. As we just saw in the previous section, the Great Compromise had created a bicameral legislature called the Congress. This Congress would be comprised of a Senate where each state would be represented equally, and a House of Representatives where each state would be represented in proportion to their population. Once the Great Compromise had been adopted, it gave rise to another question. How would each state's slave population be counted as part of each state's total population? The clearest records we have regarding the slave population at that time is from the 1790 census. According to those data, slaves were one-third (33%) of the population of the Southern states. The largest slave populations by proportion were in Virginia and South Carolina. Slaves made up 42% of Virginia's population and 43% of South Carolina's population. The South's overall population was smaller than the North. However, since there were few slaves in the North, the free white population of the South was much smaller than the free white population in the North. Southern whites realized that unless slaves were counted as part of the Southern populations, southern slaveholding states would have far fewer representatives in the House than would Northern free states. This would mean the North could easily outvote the South on questions of slavery in the House. If so, then Congress might try to regulate, restrict, or perhaps even abolish slavery. To make all this less likely to occur, the Southern delegates to the Philadelphia convention insisted that slaves be counted fully as part of each state's population when determining state representation in the House of Representatives.

Many of the Northern delegates were outraged by this demand by the Southern delegates. To the Northern delegates, it was grossly unfair and hypocritical for Southern whites to insist that slaves are property, but then also to insist that slaves are people when it is beneficial for the free whites to treat them that way. Also, counting slaves as if they were part of the free white population would actually give Southern whites *more* than their fair share of votes in the House of Representatives. That is, it would be give Southern whites a disproportionately large share of votes in the House despite their smaller population. Mathematically, it would essentially give Southern whites almost two votes for every one Northern white vote. Yet for the Southern delegates, counting slaves as part of the South's population was necessary if the South was to have any hope of blocking anti-slavery votes in the House. The delegates on both sides angrily debated whether Southern whites should be allowed to count slaves when being assigned votes in the House of Representatives.

Historical records, including Madison's notes of the Convention, are unclear about who came up with the resulting compromise, or how the precise compromise was reached. The compromise the delegates arrived at, though, became infamously referred to as the "*Three-Fifths Compromise.*" Under this compromise, neither the North nor the South fully got its way. Instead, each slave would be counted as three-fifths of a human being when counting a state's population. Neither side was very happy with the result, but it was enough to keep the peace between the North and the South on this issue.

It's important to understand that the Three-Fifth's Compromise did *not* give *any* civil, political, or legal rights to slaves. It did *not* give each slave three-fifths of a vote, nor did it give slaves *any* representation in the House of Representatives. Instead, the number of slaves in a state were counted, that number was multiplied by 3/5, and then that number was added to the number of free whites of living in the state. In other words, the Three-Fifth's Compromises magically pretended that the free white population of the South was much larger than it really was. Then, those free whites were given votes in the House of Representatives based on that new number. In short, only Southern *whites* benefitted from the Three-Fifth's Compromise; Southern blacks still received no rights whatsoever.

Also notice that this compromise gave a perverse incentive to the South to increase the number of their slaves as much as possible. The more slaves a state had, the more votes the free whites of that state would get in the House of Representatives. This meant that if a state could bring more slaves into the state, or force all their slaves to have more children, then the free whites would benefit by having more votes in the House. The Three-Fifths Compromise actually rewarded Southern whites for enslaving more people.

The delegates from both the North and South understood the hypocrisy of claiming "all men are created equal" while at the same time enshrining slavery in the Constitution. The framers of the Constitution thus carefully avoided the use of the word "slave" or "slavery" anywhere in the Constitution. The Three-Fifth's Compromise was placed in Article I, Section 2 of the original Constitution. It states that when counting the population of a state, one should count "the whole number of free persons" along with "three-fifths of all other persons." Of course, people "other than free" are enslaved.

2. The Fugitive Slave Clause. The delegates from the slave-holding Southern states realized that there was another potential problem in remaining joined in a common nation with the Northern free states. Slaves who knew the North did not have slavery would forever be tempted to escape and flee to the North. This would cause constant headache and cost for the South in policing their slaves. It would also lead to a regular loss of valuable "property" as many slaves would no doubt eventually make their way to freedom in the North. The Southern delegates therefore insisted that something be done to prevent the Northern states from being an eternal beacon of liberty to slaves. Northern delegates agreed to put into the Constitution what became known as the *Fugitive Slave Clause*. It mandated a national policy toward escaped slaves: escaped slaves had to be returned by the North. The Fugitive Slave Clause was placed in Article IV, Section 2 of the original Constitution. The text states "No Person held to Service or Labour in one State, under the Laws thereof, escaping into another, shall, in Consequence of any Law or Regulation therein, be discharged from such Service or Labour, but shall be delivered up on Claim of the Party to whom such Service or Labour may be due."

Notice first that although the Fugitive Slave Clause used the term "escape," Southern whites referred to escaped slaves as fugitives." Calling slaves "escaped" could imply that slaves were rightfully gaining freedom from bondage. The term "fugitive," on the other hand, implied that slaves were properly enslaved under Southern law. In other words, to Southern whites, a slave who ran away was a lawbreaker and fugitive from justice, just like any other criminal who tries to avoid capture.

Also, just as the delegates had avoided putting the word "slave" in the Three-Fifths Compromise, they likewise avoided the term "slave" in the Fugitive Slave Clause. Instead, they used the term "person held to service or labour." Obviously, if one is "held" to labor, this means you are "*not* free" to leave your "service or labour." In other words, you are enslaved.

The language of the Fugitive Slave Clause also made Northern compliance mandatory, not voluntary. The clause states that slaves "*shall* be delivered up." In the law, the word "shall" is obligatory, not optional. This meant that northern states were *required* by the Constitution to return escaped slaves. It was mandatory for Northern law enforcement officials to hand over escaped slaves to whoever asserted ownership of the slave. That is, the slave had to be "delivered up" to the slave owner, because the slave owner was the person "to whom such service or labour may be due."

Also, and even more disturbingly, notice that Northern states had to turn in escaped slaves to whoever asserted a mere "claim" of ownership. No evidence, documentation, or proof was needed. Anyone could merely *claim* that a black person living in the North was an escaped ("fugitive") slave. Local law enforcement authorities were then constitutionally obligated to deliver that black person into the custody of the person "claiming" ownership. Historical records are unclear regarding the exact number of escaped slaves or free blacks that were enslaved by this clause. However, in the decades between the ratification of the Constitution and the U.S. Civil War, at least hundreds and probably thousands of blacks living in the North were enslaved through false claims of past enslavement. This included many blacks that had been born and raised free in the North their entire life. Southern plantation owners would simply hire bounty hunters to go to the North, capture and imprison any blacks they saw, and "claim" ownership. Local authorities were constitutionally obliged to cooperate. One of the most famous of these stories was that of Solomon Northup. He was born free in the North but taken into slavery due to the Fugitive Slave Clause. He suffered brutally as a slave. He was able to regain his freedom only thanks to his high-level political connections he had made while a free person in the North. He wrote about his experience in a book he titled *Twelve Years a Slave*. It was published in 1853 and became a best-seller. In 2013 it was made into an award-winning major motion picture.

3. Congressional regulation of slavery. Recall from earlier in this chapter that the Philadelphia Convention had settled on creating a federal system with a national government of enumerated powers. One of those enumerated powers that Congress was given was the power to regulate commerce among the states. Soon after this listing of specific powers was drafted, the Southern delegates saw this implicated slavery. The Southern delegates wanted clarification and assurance that Congress's power to regulate "commerce" did *not* include any power to regulate slavery. This immediately resulted in the angriest debates of the entire Convention. Northern delegates now made speeches attacking the hypocrisy and immorality of slavery. One delegate famously called slavery the "curse of Heaven," meaning God would punish the United States for the sin of slavery. (In a separate context, in response to a question about slavery, Thomas Jefferson was similarly quoted as replying "I tremble for my nation when I reflect that God is just.") For Southern delegates, though, their demand was non-negotiable. They asserted that they would never have agreed to give Congress the power to regulate commerce if they thought that "commerce" included slavery. Southern delegates threatened to leave the United States and form a separate slave-holding nation if Congress could regulate slavery as "commerce." There seemed to be no middle ground or possibility for compromise. For example, a Constitutional provision stating that Congress has "one-half" of a power to regulate slavery would be meaningless nonsense. Either slavery was "commerce" or not, and so either Congress could regulate slavery or not.

The delegates were so bitterly divided on this issue that they realized that no compromise could be reached. They also realized that if they pressed the issue, both the Constitutional Convention and the United States would likely break up. To the delegates, the worst possible outcome for their Convention would be for the United States to cease existing as a single nation. So, they made a conscious decision that for the survival of the United States, they would need to ignore this particular slavery issue, by pretending that it was not an issue. Northern delegates could go to their home states and assure their citizens that the Constitution *does* allow Congress to regulate slavery as "commerce." Southern delegates could return to their home states and promise that the word "commerce" in the Constitution does *not* include slavery. To maximize support for the Constitution, however, both sides would avoid public discussions or debates with each other about which side's claim was correct. In modern sporting terms, the delegates agreed to "punt" on the issue rather than try to reach any compromise.

The delegates did, however, reach a minor compromise of sorts on this issue. They could not agree on whether Congress had the power to regulate slavery under the power to regulate "commerce among the several states." But "commerce among the several states" is separate from commerce between the U.S. and foreign nations. In other words, regulation of *domestic* slavery is different than regulation of *international* slavery. Delegates from the Southern states made a minor concession to the Northern delegates by agreeing that Congress could ban the international slave trade in the year 1808 or afterwards if it chose to do so. Yet again, though, the delegates avoided the word "slavery." Article I, Section 9 of the Constitution simply stated "The Migration or Importation of such Persons as any of the States now existing shall think proper to admit, shall not be prohibited by the Congress prior to the Year one thousand eight hundred and eight." This would give the Southerners 20 more years to "import" as many slaves as they could. The Southern delegates believed that by 1808, the South could continue the domestic slave trade within the U.S. without bringing in new slaves from Africa or the Caribbean.

Yet nothing was said in the Constitution about whether Congress could regulate slavery *within* the United States after 1808. It simply was left an open, undecided question. Many of the delegates naively believed that by 1808, this political question could be reconsidered and solved by an entirely new generation of leaders. These future leaders would have gained the wisdom of the United States' experience with slavery so as to reach a reasonable compromise on the issue. With this hope, the Constitution was ratified (formally adopted) in 1789. As we know from history, the hope that the problem of slavery could be easily solved was misplaced. The issue of slavery was not settled until three-quarters of a century later, and only after the loss of 650,000 lives in the U.S. Civil War. The seeds of the Civil War, though, were planted in Philadelphia in 1787.

SUMMARY

The founders of the United States decided to create a democratic form of national government. The also settled on a confederal system of government where the primary political power was held by the state governments rather than the U.S. national government. These principles of government were described in the first constitution of the U.S., called the Articles of Confederation. The Articles of confederation was a horrible failure, however, due to the lack of power by the U.S. government. A second constitution was then created, called simply the Constitution. In this Constitution, as part of a major compromise, the confederal system of government was changed to a federal system of government. Although the U.S. government was given power over only a few areas of public policy, the U.S. government would be supreme over the states in those areas. As part of another major compromise, the writers of the Constitution created a bicameral (two-chamber) legislature called the Congress. In the chamber called the Senate, each state has an equal number of votes. In the chamber called the House of Representatives, each state has votes in proportion to the state's population. The most politically divisive issue, however, was slavery. The framers of the Constitution decided each slave would count as 3/5 of a person when calculating the number of votes each state would get in the House of Representatives. Also, states would be required to return escaped slaves to their owners. Yet the writers of the Constitution were deadlocked over the question whether Congress would have authority to regulate slavery. They therefore postponed resolving that particular issue to the distant future.

QUESTIONS FOR REVIEW AND SELF-ASSESSMENT

1. What are the three different basic types of government based on how many people are sharing political rule?

2. What are the three different types of government based on how power is divided between the central and regional governments within a nation?
3. What is the U.S. Articles of Confederation and why did it fail?
4. What were the nature of the political compromises in the U.S. Constitution that created a federal system and a bicameral national legislature?
5. What were the three separate compromises in the U.S. Constitution that involved slavery?

Critical Thinking Questions for Reflection and Discussion

1. Is autocracy, aristocracy, or democracy better, and why?
2. Is a federal, confederal, or unitary system better, and why?
3. Was it better on balance that the Northern states compromised on the issue of slavery, or should the Northern states have stood firm against slavery, thereby causing the U.S. to split up into two nations, one free and one slaveholding?

Suggested Reading Supplements

- Articles of Confederation
- U.S. Constitution
- James Madison, *Notes on the Debates in the Federal Convention*

For Further Advanced Reading

- Catherine Drinker Bowen, *Miracle at Philadelphia: The Story of the Constitutional Convention 1787-1986*
- David O. Stewart, *The Summer of 1787: The Men Who Invented the Constitution*

CHAPTER 4: PLURALISM

THE BIG PICTURE

There are two core but opposite problems in any democracy. On the one hand, it's often difficult to achieve any political agreement. On the other hand, a consensus by a political majority might agree to oppress political minorities. A key philosophy underlying the U.S. government is that for the sake of liberty, a lack of consensus is preferred over easily achieved agreement. A government that can't agree on anything will necessarily be unable to agree on who to oppress. An important means of making agreement difficult is by having a large, diverse population with different interests. U.S. history demonstrates, however, that having a large, diverse population is no guarantee against oppressive political majorities. Political majorities have at times achieved great things, but at times they have also done awful things to various groups within the population. Indeed, the U.S. is an ongoing experiment in the degree to which democracy and liberty can succeed over a long period time.

RELEVANT TIMELINE

- 1619 First slaves brought to the English colonies in America
- 1776 U.S. Declaration of Independence
- 1787 Philadelphia Convention writes U.S. Constitution
- 1787-88 Federalist Papers published; Anti-Federalist writings published
- 1789 U.S. Constitution ratified
- 1830 Indian Removal Act passed by Congress
- 1865 Thirteenth Amendment ratified which abolishes slavery

CHAPTER OBJECTIVES

After reading this chapter, the reader should be able to:

1. Explain the debates surrounding the ratification of the U.S. Constitution.
2. Describe the different basic types of democracy, and also the Anti-Federalist argument why a large-scale democracy would not be feasible.
3. Describe in detail James Madison's theory of factions and large-scale democracy that he put forth in Federalist #10.
4. Compare and contrast aspects of the United States that make it praiseworthy with aspects that make it blameworthy.
5. Explain how the question whether large-scale democracy can survive in the long term is still unanswered.

The Ratification Debates

As we saw in the previous chapter, the Constitution contained several major political compromises over the nature of representation, federalism, and slavery. At the end of the summer of 1787, however, the Constitution was merely a proposal to replace the failing Articles of Confederation. For the proposed Constitution to become the new social contract of the United States, it needed to be ratified. "*Ratification*" means a document has been formally approved and adopted through a defined legal process. By the proposed Constitution's own requirements, it had to be ratified by two-thirds of the states in constitutional ratifying conventions. Mathematically, this meant that nine of the thirteen states had to vote to ratify the Constitution if it was going to officially replace the Articles of Confederation.

For the next couple years, the United States was deeply involved in public debate over whether the Constitution should be ratified. Much of the debate took part in pamphlets and newspaper essays where the writers did not provide their actual names. The concept of free speech was still relatively new and untested in practice. As a result, political writers at that time typically still used what had been a long-time common custom in Europe. Political thinkers would write anonymously using only a pen-name for their own legal and social protection. This way they could present the public arguments they wanted to make, but while keeping their identity a secret.

Those who wanted a strong central government supported the Constitution. They thought the proposed Constitution would add the right amount of additional power to the national government compared to the Articles of Confederation. This group soon went by the name "*Federalists.*" This term implied they wanted a division of powers between the states and the national government, but with the national government having supreme power. The Federalists were politically well-organized. The majority of the most well-known and influential early American leaders were Federalists at this time. This included Benjamin Franklin, George Washington, John Adams, Thomas Jefferson, James Madison, John Jay, Alexander Hamilton, James Wilson and many others.

Various Federalists wrote essays published in newspapers or distributed as pamphlets in which the authors argued in favor of ratification of the proposed Constitution. The most famous and influential of all these essays were called the *Federalist Papers*. They were written by a team of three Federalists: James Madison, Alexander Hamilton, and John Jay. James Madison was a Virginia politician who had been a Virginia delegate first to the Continental Congress and then to the Philadelphia Convention. He had so much influence on the writing of the Constitution and its ratification that he became known as the "Farther of the Constitution." He later drafted the U.S. Bill of Rights, and also became President of the United States. Alexander Hamilton had first risen to fame as a military advisor to General George Washington. The state of New York had then appointed Hamilton as one of their delegates to the Philadelphia Convention. After the Constitution's ratification, Hamilton became the first Secretary of the Treasury under the first President, George Washington. John Jay was a lawyer and politician from New York who had been a New York delegate to the Continental Congress. He then became a diplomat for the United States. After the ratification of the Constitution, he became the first Chief Justice of the U.S. Supreme Court. Jay wrote only a handful of the Federalist Papers that dealt with the foreign relations power of the U.S. government. Madison and Hamilton wrote all the other Federalist Papers. (Fun Fact: Alexander Hamilton very well might have become President but he sabotaged his own political career. First he was involved in a highly publicized marital affair, and then he brutally criticized his own party's presidential candidate. He was later killed in a duel with Vice President Aaron Burr in 1804).

Dividing up writing responsibilities for the Federalist Papers, Madison, Hamilton, and Jay published anonymously under the pen name of *Publius*. Publius had been an ancient Roman who favored representative democracy and helped overthrow a tyrannical monarchy. Signing their name only as Publius, the three Federalist authors wrote a series of 85 papers published in New York newspapers in 1787 and 1788. They systematically argued that the U.S. Constitution was the best possible solution to the severe problems the U.S. was suffering as a result of the failures of the Articles of Confederation. The Federalist Papers went step-by-step through the proposed Constitution, explaining and defending each section of it.

In contrast to the Federalists, other people were against the proposed Constitution. These opponents argued that the Constitution gave *too much* additional power to the new national government compared to the Articles of Confederation. This group soon became referred to as the *"Anti-Federalists."* They themselves generally disliked this term because they also wanted a division of power between the national and state governments just like the Federalists. The Anti-Federalists disliked the Articles of Confederation and generally agreed that the U.S. government was too weak under it. When it came to the proposed Constitution, however, the Anti-Federalists thought it went too far. They believed it would give a dangerous amount of additional new power to the U.S. government. The Anti-Federalists therefore preferred going back to the negotiating table. They wanted to draft a revised proposal for a U.S. government that would have powers somewhere between the Articles of Confederation and the Constitution. The Anti-Federalists therefore typically argued that the Constitution should be rejected as it currently was written. The proposed draft of the Constitution could be revised to make it more acceptable by removing or rewriting the parts to which they objected.

The Anti-Federalists, like the Federalists, anonymously published pamphlets and newspaper essays in which they argued against ratification of the Constitution.

They published under pen-names like "Brutus," "The Federal Farmer" "Cato," "Agrippa," "Centinel," and "An Old Whig." There were many others as well. Among the best-known Anti-Federalists were Samuel Adams, Patrick Henry, and John Hancock, along with a future president, James Monroe. Yet unlike the Federalists, the Anti-Federalists were not well-organized politically. For example, unlike the Federalist Papers, there was no similarly strong and coherent set of writings on the Anti-Federalist side. Probably the best individual writer who argued against the Constitution was Robert Yates, one of New York's delegates to the Philadelphia Convention, and a judge (later Chief Justice) on the New York Supreme Court. He wrote under the name of *Brutus*, another ancient Roman who had, along with Publius, overthrown the same tyrannical monarch. Yates published a series of 16 essays in the same New York newspapers as the Federalists published in. Indeed, the essays of Publius and Brutus sometimes argued specific points back-and-forth. Because Yates offered the most thorough and systematic Anti-Federalist arguments against the Constitution in response to the Federalist Papers, we will be returning to the writings of both Publius and Brutus throughout this book.

The common general theme of the Anti-Federalists was that the national government under the Constitution would be too powerful, and therefore dangerous to liberty. There were numerous specific arguments. Standing armies would end up oppressing the people. Congressional power to set its own times of elections would let it take permanent control by cancelling elections. The President might serve for life and become like a king. The Supreme Court would have the final say over the meaning of the Constitution with no power to stop them. The "necessary and proper" clause would lead to excessive Congressional power and the corresponding elimination of state sovereignty. There were many other arguments as well.

Yet the Anti-Federalists were politically disorganized. Among the Anti-Federalists, they could not agree why the proposed Constitution was bad. Nor could they agree on any alternative to the Constitution. Sometimes various Anti-Federalists even made arguments that contradicted each other. For example, Southern pro-slavery antifederalists attacked the Constitution for leaving the door open to the possibility of restricting or abolishing slavery in the future. Northern anti-slavery Anti-Federalists, however, criticized the Constitution for condoning, protecting, and even rewarding slavery. Brutus was among this latter group of Northern Anti-Federalists.

Despite the lesser organization by the Anti-Federalists, public opinion at the time was closely divided on ratification of the Constitution. The Anti-Federalists had either majorities or large minorities in more than one state legislature. By far the biggest obstacle to ratification was that the Constitution did not include a listing of basic rights of the people. There was no freedom of speech or the press listed, no religious liberty listed, and no guarantees of fair procedures for those accused of crimes. The Anti-Federalists attacked the Constitution for not expressly protecting such basic freedoms. On this particular point, the Anti-Federalists were winning the public relations battle, and ratification was in jeopardy.

According to the proposed Constitution, nine out of the 13 states were needed to ratify the Constitution in order for it to formally take effect as a replacement for the Articles of Confederation—that is, for the Constitution to become the new social contract for the United States. The Federalists narrowly won ratification of the new Constitution. It came down to a handful of votes in a few state conventions. The sixth state to ratify, Massachusetts, voted to ratify by a vote of 187-168, but even then only because of what became known as the "Massachusetts Compromise." Leading Anti-Federalists Samuel Adams and John Hancock agreed to vote for ratification only if Federalists pledged that after the Constitution was ratified, a bill of rights would be added to the Constitution. Federalists in the state agreed. This won just enough votes from Anti-Federalists to turn what would have been a defeat into a victory for the Federalists. The next four states that ratified the Constitution also adopted the Massachusetts Compromise. That is, they similarly voted for ratification only on an understanding that the Constitution would be amended to include a bill of rights after the Constitution took effect. The nine-state threshold for ratification of the Constitution was reached in 1789, thus making it the birth-year of the Constitution. Once the Constitution officially replaced the Articles of Confederation, the remaining states voted for ratification, including the large states of New York and Virginia. Yet even then the vote was close in both those bigger states, with only a three-vote difference in New York. Many Anti-Federalists in the remaining states switched their votes at this point so that their states would not be left out of the Union.

The debates between the Federalists and the Anti-Federalists are much more important than merely being a matter of historical interest. The major issues the Federalists and Anti-Federalist debated are still the *very same* major political issues debated today about the basic nature of U.S. government. How much power should the President have? How much power should Congress have? How much power should the Supreme Court have? How much power should the U.S. government as a whole have over the state governments? In debates over public policy, presidents and members of Congress regularly refer to the ideas of the Federalists and Anti-Federalists. In deciding the meaning of the Constitution, the Supreme Court regularly quotes not just the Federalist Papers, but also other writings by both Federalists and Anti-Federalists. As we'll see in some upcoming chapters, although the Federalists won the political struggle to ratify the Constitution, U.S. history has shown that both the Federalists and the Anti-Federalists were partly correct in their predictions about the future. Moreover, many scholars and politicians throughout U.S. history, including today, have shared the Anti-Federalist's concerns about the dangers of powerful central government. In short, the arguments within the ratification debates still remain highly relevant today. Understanding modern U.S. politics is thus impossible without understanding the nature of these historical debates. Indeed, the first Federalist-Anti-Federalist dispute we'll look at was the most "big picture" issue considered in their debates: whether a large-scale democracy called the United States was even a feasible idea. If a sizeable democratic nation was not possible, then all the other issues the Federalists and Anti-Federalists debated would be pointless.

Large Scale Democracy?

The ratification of the Constitution meant that it became part of the social contract of the United States. The Declaration of Independence created the United States, and the Constitution provides its basic governmental structure. Yet the writers of the Constitution also believed it was important to re-state a basic principle that was contained in the Declaration of Independence: popular sovereignty. The Preamble to the Constitution is a preface that contains no details of structure, power, or rights, but it declares the basic purpose and source of authority of the Constitution:

> "We the People, in order to form a more perfect Union, establish justice and ensure domestic tranquility, provide for the common defense, promote the general welfare, and secure the blessings of liberty to ourselves and our posterity, do ordain and establish this Constitution for the United States of America."

Through the Preamble, the Constitution incorporates and applies Locke's social contract theory. The Preamble declares that the Constitution is a social contract entered into by the people for their mutual benefit and the protection of their natural rights ("liberty") that come from god ("blessings."). The Constitution is given power ("ordained") by the people, thus establishing that the people have created the government. Only an entity with superior authority has the power to give or "ordain" power in another entity. The people, as creators of their government, inherently have supreme power over the government, not the other way around. As we discussed in an earlier chapter when we examined Locke's social contract theory, this means democracy is the only form of legitimate government, because only democracy gives the people their rightful place in the political hierarchy.

Yet a democracy the size of the United States had never before been attempted in the history of the planet. Up until the birth of the United States, the few democracies in the planet's history had been relatively small by comparison.

According to the 1790 census, the population of the United States was almost four million, and its territory already covered an area larger than any of the nations of Europe. Everyone understood that as the U.S. expanded westward, both the population and area of the United States would likely soon surpass the entirety of Europe. To many people, maintaining a democracy on that scale seemed inconceivable. Some early Americans suggested the United States should split up into several smaller, more manageable nations. This suggestion may seem extreme today given the hindsight of history. At the time, though, this was a serious argument and was a point of contention between the Federalists and Anti-Federalists.

To understand this concern more thoroughly, we must first look at different types of democracy. There are two basic types of democracy, classified by who is making the proposed laws. In a *direct* democracy all eligible voters meet to form the laws. There are no individuals separately elected to make the laws; *everyone* directly makes the laws together. This is why direction democracy is often also called *participatory* democracy or *pure* democracy. The democracy in ancient Athens, Greece over 2,000 years ago is an example of direct democracy. Every eligible voter in Athens would come together in a large assembly and collectively make political decisions for Athens. Similarly, in the United States today, many hundreds of small towns in the New England states in the Northeast have no city council or mayor. Instead, all adult voters meet regularly in the town hall to propose, debate, and vote on public policy for their towns. Also, the state constitutions of most states allow some type of statewide ballot initiatives or referendums. There the voters can decide directly on proposed statutes or proposed amendments to the state constitution. California, for example, allows a ballot initiative mechanism where voters can gain enough signatures on petitions to have proposed state laws placed directly on statewide ballots. This method of making California law completely bypasses the state legislature. California voters are famous for enacting controversial statewide laws. Some of these have involved property taxes, affirmative action, immigrant rights, same-sex marriage, medical marijuana, and animal rights, among other issues. In 2014, Californians voted to ban single-use plastic bags in stores. Similarly, in Louisiana, voters decide directly whether to approve proposed amendments to the state constitution, but such proposals must first come from the state legislature.

Although direct democracy is convenient at the small level, it becomes difficult at the large scale. Recall Thomas Paine's famous, best-selling 1776 writing *Common Sense,* in which he argued for U.S. independence. In *Common Sense*, Paine also explained the limitations of direct democracy. When a political society is small the people can all meet together to make political decisions. "Some convenient tree will afford them a State-House, under the branches of which, the whole colony may assemble to deliberate on public matters." This becomes impossible, however, as the size of the society grows:

> "As the colony increases, the public concerns will increase likewise, and the distance at which the members may be separated, will render it too inconvenient for all of them to meet on every occasion as at first, when their number was small, their habitations near, and the public concerns few and trifling. This will point out the convenience of their consenting to leave the legislative part to be managed by a select number chosen from the whole body."

In short, as the population of a society increases, it becomes infeasible for everyone to meet in one place to decide public policy. As a result, a small group of political representatives must be chosen from among the entire population. Those representatives will then meet to propose, debate, and vote on laws. This subgroup of the population represents the will and the interests of the voters who elected them.

Because most towns and nations today are too big for direct democracy, the vast majority of democracies are examples of *representative democracy.* At the time of the founding of the United States, another word came to be commonly used as a synonym for representative democracy: a *republic.* Put differently, a republic is not the same thing as democracy, but it is a *type* of democracy. This means that all republics are democracies, but not all democracies are republics. The United States is therefore both a republic and a democracy, because the terms "republic" and "representative democracy" can be used interchangeably.

FEDERALIST #10

To return to the debate at the time of the founding of the United States, everyone understood that a direct democracy for the United States was impossible. Given the large population and size of the U.S., the only viable democratic option was a representative democracy. Yet a representative democracy of such a large scale had never even been attempted in the history of the world. Many people believed such an experiment could not succeed, so that the effort would be a waste of time. This was a serious argument against continuing a "United States."

The argument against the chance of success for a large-scale democracy was made by Brutus in his essay No. I. In it, he argued that the United States would soon grow so large, that there would simply be too many people living in it. These people would be spread out across a huge country, would live in different climates, and would have vastly different interests from each other. In such a republic, the elected representatives in the legislature would be pulled in many opposing directions by their diverse voters. The representatives would therefore be unable to agree on any common interest for the nation. The government would become paralyzed with indecision. In modern terms, we would call this political "gridlock." In short, a country with such a vast territory and population could not continue to function. Brutus explained:

> The territory of the United States is of vast extent; it now contains near three millions of souls, and is capable of containing much more than ten times that number. Is it practicable for a country, so large and so numerous as they will soon become, to elect a representation, that will speak their sentiments, without becoming so numerous as to be incapable of transacting public business? It certainly is not.
>
> In a republic, the manners, sentiments, and interests of the people should be similar. If this be not the case, there will be a constant clashing of opinions; and the representatives of one part will be continually striving against those of the other. This will retard the operations of government, and prevent such conclusions as will promote the public good. If we apply this remark to the conditions of the United States, we shall be convinced that it forbids that we should be one government. The productions of the different parts of the union are very variant, and their interests, of consequence, diverse. Their manners and habits differ as much as their climates and productions; and their sentiments are by no means coincident. The laws and customs of the several states are, in may respects, very diverse, and in some opposite; each would be in favor of its own interests and customs, and, of consequence, a legislature, formed of representatives from the respective parts, would not only be too numerous to act with any care or decision, but would be composed of such heterogeneous and discordant principles, as would constantly be contending with each other.

Another Anti-Federalist writer went by the pen name *Cato*, named after an ancient Roman leader who opposed the tyranny of Julius Caesar. The identity of Cato is not known for certain, but historians believe his most likely identity was George Clinton, then-governor of New York, and a later Vice-President of the United States. In Cato's third essay, Cato similarly writes that a large, diverse democracy will result in paralysis:

> Whoever seriously considers the immense extent of territory comprehended within the limits of the United States, with the variety of its climates, productions, and commerce, the difference of extent, and number of inhabitants in all; the dissimilitude of interest, morals, and policies, in almost

every one, will receive it as an intuitive truth, that a consolidated republican form of government therein, can never *form a perfect union, establish justice, insure domestic tranquility, promote the general welfare, and secure the blessings of liberty to you and your posterity,* for to these objects it must be directed: this unkindred legislature therefore, composed of interests opposite and dissimilar in their nature, will in its exercise, emphatically be, like a house divided against itself.

In short, the chain of the Anti-Federalist logic was as follows:

Large-scale republic→many people→many different, competing interests→ no agreement among representatives in the national legislature→ Gridlock, paralysis, do-nothing national government.

Because this argument was taken so seriously at the time, the Federalists needed to respond to it. Madison did so in Federalist Paper No. 10, which many historical and political scholars consider to be the single best summary of U.S. democracy ever written. Indeed, if one looks at any introductory textbook on U.S. government, they all will have at least three documents contained in the appendix: The Declaration of Independence, the Constitution (including its amendments), and Federalist No. 10. Whether or not it is *the* best statement on U.S. democracy, it is a highly important one. Moreover, in Federalist No. 10 Madison works step-by-step through his arguments in a way that every chain in his logic is essential to his ultimate conclusion. It's critical, then, to understand every component of his theory in logical order.

Madison replies to the Anti-Federalist arguments that a large-scale democracy cannot succeed by first introducing a term. A "faction," according to Madison, is any group whose interest is adverse to the rest of the community. In other words, a faction is any group that acts in own selfish interest, rather than what's in the common best interest for the public or society. In modern language, a faction is "just looking out for themselves." Today we call such groups "special interest groups" because they focus on a narrow public policy issues. They typically act primarily to benefit their own members, whether those members be individuals or corporations. A few of the largest, most powerful examples today are the American Association of Retired Persons (AARP), the National Rifle Association (NRA), the American Trial Lawyers Association (ATLA), the National Education Association (NEA-a teachers' union) and the U.S. Chamber of Commerce (an organization of businesses). There are many hundreds of other special interest groups. Some scholars have argued that political parties such as the Democratic and Republican parties would also be considered "factions" by Madison. However, political parties as they exist today did not exist when Madison wrote Federalist No. 10. It's unclear if Madison would consider political parties to be factions. Regardless, Madison's point is that there are many groups in society who will use the tool of government for their own selfish interest if they can.

Because factions act in their own self-interest, Madison argued they are dangerous. If a faction can control the government, it will use that political power to make public policy that favors the faction over the best interests of society. The faction will enact laws that are corrupt, and oppress or abuse the rest of the public. For example, if a faction can take over a government, it might try to confiscate its opponents' wealth, deny legal rights to those the faction dislikes, and modify political procedures to guarantee themselves continued power. The question in creating any system of government then becomes how to design the government in such as way as to minimize the danger from factions.

Madison declared there were two basic ways to control the risk of factions. He said one could either remove their *causes*, or limit their *effects*, with different ways of accomplishing each. Madison discussed each possible way in turn, beginning with how to prevent factions from arising. Madison uses the example of fire and air. If air can be withheld from fire, the fire will die. Madison does not offer any other analogy, but we can also look at how to stop weeds from sprouting. Withholding water, sunlight, and water from the seeds of a weed will prevent it from growing. Similarly, perhaps the root causes of factions could be eliminated so that factions would not exist.

There were two ways Madison suggested that removing the root causes of factions could be accomplished. One way would be to eliminate all liberty. If people aren't free to share their interests with each other, form groups of like-minded people, provided political candidates and vote for them, factions won't be able to form or elect political leaders. Madison pointed out, however, that this solution is just as bad if not worse than the problem of having factions themselves. Liberty is precious, so we don't want to do away with it. As Madison puts it, the "remedy" would be "worse than the disease." This possible solution must therefore be ruled out.

The second way to stop factions from forming would be to make everyone's interest the same. The only way to do this, however, would be to make everyone identical to everyone else. Individuals will share the same interests if they are the same in every way. If they all have the same beliefs, opinions, age, sex, race, income, wealth, occupation, religion, geographic location, and so on, they would all want the same thing. But this is an impossible fantasy world that can never exist except in maybe a bizarre science-fiction story. The reality of human nature is such that people will greatly differ in their beliefs, opinions, and interests. Humans can never be made the same. In short, making humans identical is impossible, and eliminating liberty is extremely undesirable. Madison is therefore left to conclude that we either can't prevent, or don't want to prevent, factions from existing. Since removing the causes of factions is not a viable option, the only possible solution to the problem of factions is limiting the negative *effects* of factions.

In Madison's view, there are two different situations that must be addressed. A faction might be a *minority* of the population, and a faction might be a *majority* of the population. When a faction comprises only a *minority* of the population, that faction poses no democratic threat. In either a direct democracy or in a representative democracy (a republic), the majority can simply outvote the minority faction, thereby preventing the faction from taking political power.

The bigger problem occurs when a faction is a *majority* of the population. In this case, a direct democracy offers no protection, as the majority faction would outvote the rest of the public. For Madison, the solution is not just *representative* democracy, but a *large-scale* representative democracy. That is, not just a republic, but a *large* republic in both population and size. The bigger, the better. But why is a large republic the way to minimize the effects of factions? Madison provides three arguments. He first presents two weak arguments and then a strong one. His final argument is the culmination of all his reasoning. First, in a small republic, the majority faction could coordinate more easily to elect a majority of the representatives. In a large republic, on the other hand, it would be more difficult for the majority faction to organize and win numerous elections in the many election districts across the nation. Second, presumably elected representatives are the best members of the public. A republic with a larger population allows an even greater selection of good and wise people to choose from. The leaders in a large republic should be even better than in a smaller republic, and would refuse to vote as any majority faction wishes. Yet Madison realizes these responses are weak argument. It's possible that a majority faction could sufficiently organize to elect a majority of the representatives, and those representatives would then support the faction rather than resist it. Madison therefore turns to what he says is the heart of his argument. The reason a large republic is better than a small one is because of the more diverse population contained in republic of large size.

Madison explains that in a large-scale representative democracy, the public will be spread out across a vast territory. This large population will be more diverse than in a small-scale republic, and so will have many more competing interests within the population. Representatives in such a large republic will be pulled in even more directions by their voters than would representatives in a small republic. Therefore, representatives elected from across a large, diverse nation will be less likely to form a common, shared interest than would likely happen in a small nation. The larger the republic, the less likely a majority faction will form. And, when a majority faction does form, it will be harder to coordinate its actions across the huge territory of the nation. As Madison put it:

> "Extend the sphere [of the republic], and you take in a greater variety of parties and interests; you make it less probable that a majority of the whole will have a common motive to invade the rights of other citizens; or if such a common motive exists, it will be more difficult for all who feel it to discover their own strength, and to act in unison with each other."

Notice the chain of logic in Madison's reasoning here:

Large-scale republic→many people→many different, competing interests→ no agreement among representatives in the national legislature→ Gridlock, paralysis, and do-nothing national government.

The Federalist Madison is making the *exact same* argument here as the Anti-Federalist Brutus! The brilliance of Madison's conclusion is that he turns the Anti-Federalist argument on its head. According to Madison, gridlock in government is not a *bad* thing, but rather a *good* thing! Indeed, political gridlock is such a wonderful thing, that this is the very goal in designing a large-scale representative democracy! If a government cannot agree on what to do, that means that same government will not be able to agree how to abuse power or oppress those who are not members of the majority faction. The larger the republic, the less likely that a majority faction will arise and be able to agree on who to discriminate against, steal wealth from, imprison, torture, segregate, enslave, or exterminate. The larger the republic, the more everyone's liberty is better protected. What few laws do get enacted must be laws that most people agree are good for the public as a whole.

Madison argues that a great diversity of groups with society has a positive effect on representative democracy. Another term often used to refer to Madison's theory is political *pluralism*. The word "plural" means "many." The Latin phrase "*e pluribus unum*" means "out of many, one." This phrase has been part of the Great Seal of the United States since its adoption in 1782. It was the unofficial motto of the United States until the phrase "In God We Trust" officially became the national motto in 1956. The phrase *e pluribus unum* originally meant that a single nation was created out of many states. In modern times, however, the phrase has taken on a broader meaning. A single nation exists out of many different people comprised of numerous ethnicities, religions, languages, and so on.

For many decades the term "melting pot" has been used to refer to this concept. Just as many food ingredients melt together to make a single stew, many people blend together to form the United States. More recently, though, other different foods have been used in comparison, such as "salad" or "gumbo." In these foods, different ingredients come together to create a unique dish, but the individual ingredients keep their distinct forms and flavors. These newer analogies are used to indicate that although many cultures come together to form a single United States, people still maintain some of their unique cultural identities. In this analogy, part of what makes the United States special is its unique combination of many different distinct cultures. Another term often used for this concept is *multiculturalism*.

The concept of multiculturalism, however, like all political concepts, is not without controversy. There are some who argue that a truly multicultural society is not desirable because some cultural beliefs or practices are healthier or more moral than others and so should be recognized as such and preferred. For example, should a culture that practices domination and exploitation of women, sexual abuse of children, or discrimination against religious minorities be as legally protected and socially respected as other cultures? Then there are other thinkers who believe that a multicultural society where every person is a true social equal to every other person might be a desirable ideal, but that it's an unrealistic goal. These thinkers argue that the social biases inherent in human nature will always cause humans to think in terms of "us" versus "them." If that's the situation, then public policy should acknowledge this fact and be designed according to this reality, rather than hold people to impossibly perfect standards of purely unprejudiced thoughts and behavior. Given that the U.S. and global society are both increasingly multicultural, the debate over the desirability and possibility of multiculturalism will only increase in the coming years and decades.

Pluralism's Weakness

Madison's theory of representative democracy in Federalist Paper No. 10 is just that—a *theory*. In other words, the theory of political pluralism doesn't always work in practice. Having a pluralistic society does not guarantee the prevention of a politically dominant faction. Remember that Madison argued that a large-scale republic would make it less likely for a majority faction to arise and work together. Madison did *not* say, though, that a large republic would *guarantee* that majority factions would never occur. Put differently, majority factions will inevitably exist at various points throughout the history of any democratic nation. But, according to Madison they will occur increasingly less often the larger the republic becomes.

Madison himself recognized that his theory didn't always work even at the same time he was developing his theory. He published an essay in 1787, only one month before the Philadelphia Convention began, titled "Vices of the Political System of the United States." According to the Oxford English Dictionary a "vice" is an "immoral or wicked behavior." Madison called his theory of pluralism his "republican theory." Madison wrote "Where slavery exists the republican theory becomes still more fallacious." That is, the existence of slavery in the United States shows that his "republican theory" is "fallacious" (false). This is not to say the theory never works, just that it doesn't *always* work.

Slavery is merely one example—though a substantial one—of what many historians, scholars, political activists, and political leaders since America's founding have pointed to as the inconsistency of the Founding Fathers. The very philosophical foundation of the existence of the United States is based on the ideas in Locke's social contract theory, which includes the idea that we have natural rights. The Declaration of Independence announces that "all men are created equal." It also asserts we have rights to "life, liberty, and the pursuit of happiness." Yet at the same time America's leaders were creating a nation based on such high ideals, they did not fully practice these ideals.

The American founders were human beings, and like all human beings, they were not perfect. They often had mixed motives, and they had to reach compromises given what was politically feasible at the time. Like all people then and now, they did not always apply their moral ideals consistently. On the one hand, they were a collection of political geniuses who established a nation based on the great ideals of freedom and equality. On the other hand, many of the founders did not live their lives consistent with those ideals. For example, Thomas Jefferson, who wrote the words "all men are created equal," owned many slaves and never freed them, not even in his will upon his death. Ironically, in Jefferson's draft of the Declaration of Independence, he himself had included a paragraph criticizing the King of England for the slave trade:

> "He has waged cruel war against human nature itself, violating its most sacred rights of life and liberty in the person of a distant people, who never offended him, captivating and carrying them into slavery in another hemisphere, or to incur miserable death in their transportation thither . . ."

The Continental Congress, however, deleted this paragraph from the final, released version of the Declaration of Independence. They did this not only because of its obvious hypocrisy, and also because the slaveholding states did not want slavery referred to as an evil. Indeed, a majority of the signers of the Declaration of Independence owned slaves at the time.

The weakness in the theory of pluralism can be shown throughout U.S. history. Enslaved African-Americans were not the only group subjected to oppression by a majority faction. There are plenty of instances in U.S. history where a majority faction has been able to agree on a minority group to oppress. These examples include the enslavement and segregation of African-Americans, the violent removal of Native Americans from their lands, the mass imprisonment of Japanese

Americans during WWII, the denial of voting rights to women, and discrimination against gays and lesbians. For purposes at the moment, though, we'll consider those forms of discrimination most present at the time of the founding of the United States.

Native Americans were murdered on a large scale, often enslaved, and almost all were removed by violent force from their lands. Today there is only a relatively small remaining population of Native Americans in the Eastern U.S, compared to the population and lands of Native American tribes in the U.S. West. This is because official federal public policy for many decades violently removed Native Americans East of the Mississippi to "Indian Territory," which is now the state of Oklahoma. In 1830, Congress passed the Indian Removal Act, which authorized the elimination of all Native American tribes from the Southeastern U.S. After the act was passed, the several-hundred-mile forced march to Oklahoma under military gunpoint during winter led to thousands of deaths across many tribes. The Cherokee, Muscogee, Seminole, Chickasaw, and Choctaw tribes have ever since then referred to this tragic historical episode as the "Trail of Tears." Even in the U.S. West, the U.S. government repeatedly broke treaties with Native American nations and forcibly relocated tribes onto smaller and smaller parcels of property, often the most agriculturally unproductive lands. Then, in the late 1800's, Congress decided it needed to "assimilate" Native Americans into U.S. culture. As a result, thousands of Native American children were forcibly taken from their families and placed into "Indian Boarding Schools." These schools prohibited the children's traditional language, clothing, religion, and rest of their Native American culture.

The phrase "all men are created equal" was also was literally applied only to men at first. As we'll discuss in more detail in a later chapter, women could neither vote nor hold political office, and married women had few legal rights against their husbands. This legalized discrimination continued well into the 1900's. And, as we noted in an earlier chapter, even poor white men were often denied voting rights in the first decade of the new United States. For example, in 1776 John Adams wrote a letter to a fellow land-owner James Sullivan, in which Adams declared his disdain for giving the right to vote to poor white men. Adams stated white men who do not own property are just like women and children. He argue that since the poor have no ownership stake in the community, they cannot be trusted with the power of voting.

There are many examples of such hypocrisy by the early leaders of the U.S. Some of the documents that best illustrate this inconsistency are the perspective of oppressed people themselves. These include a 1777 petition by enslaved blacks to the Massachusetts legislature, comparing their situation to that of the United States fighting for independence from England. Another famous example comes from Benjamin Banneker, a free black and one of the three lead surveyors of the city of

Washington D.C. He created and published a yearly almanac, and sent a copy along with a letter to Thomas Jefferson in which he told Jefferson blacks are as intelligent as whites and deserve equality. Jefferson wrote a brief letter of thanks, but offered no support for black civil rights. Frederick Douglass was a former slave who secretly taught himself to read and then escaped to freedom in the North. He became one of the most talented and famous public speakers ever produced by the United States. On U.S. Independence Day in 1852, he gave a speech to an abolition society titled "What to the Slave is the Fourth of July?" In the speech, Douglass eloquently pointed out the utter hypocrisy of the white Christian majority who were celebrating freedom while at the same time enslaving millions of people.

Women also spoke for themselves as well. One famous example is Abigail Adams, the wife of John Adams. She wrote letters of correspondence with John in 1776 just before the U.S. declared independence. In one of her letters, she asked her husband to "remember the ladies" in the new nation's laws by giving women more legal protection against abusive husbands. John Adams wrote back, scoffing at Abigail's request for women's rights. Several decades later, in 1848, the world's first women's rights convention was held in Seneca Falls, New York. The convention issued a statement calling for legal equality for women. The "Seneca Falls Declaration" copied both the pattern and some of the text of the U.S. Declaration of Independence. Instead of seeking U.S. independence from England, however, the declaration sought equality for women against oppression by men. The declaration included the words "We hold these truths to be self-evident; that all men *and women* are created equal . . ."

Native Americans also voiced their feelings to the leaders in the U.S. government. One famous example is Chief Joseph, leader of the Nez Perce Nation. He traveled to the capitol of Washington, spoke with several cabinet officials, and gave a speech to Congress. He pointed out to them how the U.S. government had repeatedly broken its treaty promises to the Nez Perce and other tribes. He then asked that Native Americans be treated the same as other Americans, with respect given to their legal rights. His requests, however, fell on deaf ears.

The American Experiment

Despite moral inconsistency by many of the Founding Fathers of the United States, they also all understood that they were establishing a nation based on the philosophical-moral principles of democratic liberty and equality. The Founders realized that the long-term expansion and implementation of those principles would eventually mean the increasing spread of liberty to more individuals and groups. For example, even slaveholders like Jefferson, Madison, and Washington thought that slavery violated natural rights to liberty and equality. They believed slavery would slowly but eventually become extinct due to the fact it was so morally problematic. The first citizens of the United States realized the nation was going to be a grand experiment in democracy. The question was whether the stated ideals of freedom and equality could actually be lived out and fulfilled in the long term.

In 1858, Abraham Lincoln debated Stephen Douglas as they both sought to be elected the U.S. Senator from Illinois. Lincoln believed that the fact the founders of the U.S. allowed slavery to continue under the Constitution did not detract from the great moral principles found in the Constitution:

> "It may be argued that there are certain conditions that make necessities and impose them upon us, and to the extent that a necessity is imposed upon a man he must submit to it. I think that was the condition in which we found ourselves when we established this Government. We had slaves among us, we could not get our Constitution unless we permitted them to remain in slavery, we could not secure the good we did secure if we grasped for more; and having by necessity submitted to that much, it does not destroy the principle that is the charter of our liberties. Let the charter remain as our standard." Abraham Lincoln, 7th Lincoln-Douglass Debate, Alton, Illinois, Oct. 15, 1858.

In Lincoln's Gettysburg Address in 1863, he re-emphasized that the United States of American is itself an experiment in democracy. The question is whether a people can create a government based on the *ideals* of liberty and equality, and then also actually put those ideals into *practice* and still survive in the long term:

> "Four score and seven years ago our fathers brought forth on this continent, a new nation, conceived in Liberty, and dedicated to the proposition that all men are created equal. Now we are engaged in a great civil war, testing whether that nation, or any nation so conceived and so dedicated, can long endure. . . ."

Around 650,000 men fought and died in the U.S. Civil War that ended slavery in the U.S., because the *principles* of liberty and equality eventually overcame a *practice* that was inconsistent with those principles. Throughout U.S. history, this has steadily been the case across all areas of law and society. The right to vote and full legal equality has been extended to almost all groups that formerly were denied such equality. That equality is still in the process of being expanded to other groups, such as gays and lesbians. The United States has also been at the lead of fighting injustice around the world. As merely one example, but arguably the greatest example, in World War II millions of Americans fought, and over 400,000 of them died, to stop the evil of fascism. People of all races and religions from in the U.S.

fought fascism precisely because that ideology posed a grave threat to the democratic ideals for which the United States stands. Likewise, during the Cold War with the Soviet Union and China, the communist regimes of Stalin and Mao each murdered tens of millions of their own people. They hoped to extend their totalitarian ideological control to the entire planet. They likely would have done so had the U.S. not stood up to them to hold their ambitions in check. The point is that along with hypocritical actions by the United States, the U.S. has also often fulfilled and fought for its ideals.

To put the issue in sharpest focus, the United States was the first nation in the history of the planet founded on a set of philosophical *ideas*. Throughout human history, and even today, most nations have been based on membership in an ethnic or religious group. The identity of the United States, on the other hand, is comprised of a set of political principles. These beliefs are collectively known as "the American's Creed."

So what are those ideas in a nutshell? In 1918, the House of Representatives formally adopted what is called *The American's Creed,* written by the winner of a national patriotic contest to write a brief 100-word "summary of the basic principles of American political faith." The term "creed" typically refers to a formal statement of religious belief, but here it refers to the core, essential political ideas the United States represents. To call oneself an "American," meaning here a member or supporter of the United States of America, one need not be any race or religion. Instead, one must merely profess the following ideas:

> "I believe in the United States of America as a government of the people, by the people, for the people; whose just powers are derived from the consent of the governed; a democracy in a republic; a sovereign Nation of many sovereign States; a perfect union, one and inseparable; established upon those principles of freedom, equality, justice, and humanity for which American patriots sacrificed their lives and fortunes.
>
> I therefore believe it is my duty to my country to love it, to support its Constitution, to obey its laws, to respect its flag, and to defend it against all enemies."

To become an "American," then, one need only profess allegiance to the *ideals of U.S. democracy*. Because of these ideals, despite its shortcomings the United States of America has also served as an inspiration, model, and often defender of freedom and democracy around the world. Indeed, many historians, citizens, scholars, and political leaders have called the "American Experiment" the greatest experiment ever attempted in human history. Some go so far as to call the U.S. "special" or "exceptional," meaning that the U.S. is different from all other nations. The term

"American exceptionalism" is ambiguous, though, and can be taken to imply either difference or superiority, so the concept is controversial. Regardless whether the U.S. is somehow "different" or "exceptional," the political principles of the United States, combined with its substantial economic and military and strength, give it a major role in history and in the world today.

The fact that the American Experiment is a worthwhile endeavor is exemplified in a speech Ben Franklin. He wrote a few words for the ceremony at which the final draft of the U.S. Constitution was signed. Franklin, a delegate from Pennsylvania, was elderly and not feeling well enough to give the speech. One of the other delegates from Pennsylvania, James Wilson (who later became a Supreme Court justice), read the speech for him. Franklin directed his statement to the President of the Convention, George Washington. Franklin declared in part:

> "Mr. President, I confess that there are several parts of this constitution which I do not at present approve . . . I agree to this Constitution with all its faults, if they are such; because I think a general Government necessary for us . . . I doubt too whether any other Convention we can obtain, may be able to make a better Constitution. For when you assemble a number of men to have the advantage of their joint wisdom, you inevitably assemble with those men, all their prejudices, their passions, their errors of opinion, their local interests, and their selfish views. From such an assembly can a perfect production be expected? It therefore astonishes me, Sir, to find this system approaching so near to perfection as it does; Thus I consent, Sir, to this Constitution because I expect no better, and because I am not sure, that it is not the best. The opinions I have had of its errors, I sacrifice to the public good. . . ."

Franklin realized that no constitution would be perfect, but the proposed U.S. Constitution was the best that could be reasonably hoped for under the circumstances at that time. It was "good enough." He therefore supported it despite any potential problems it contained at that moment, knowing the future would offer chances for improvement. In short, Franklin thought the experiment in democracy was worth doing, and he was willing to take part in it.

Indeed, the American experiment is still ongoing. The debate between Publius and Brutus over whether a diverse, pluralistic large-scale democracy can succeed *in the long run* has not yet been fully answered. On a globally historic scale, the U.S. is still a relatively young nation, being only around 240 years old. Compared to some other nations whose civilizations have existed for thousands of years, the U.S. is a mere "toddler" among nations. Will the United States still exist as a relatively free, democratic nation 1000 years from now? Can a multicultural nation remain united in the long term based merely on shared values of liberty and equality? Or will ethnic, regional, class, religious, ideological or other factional differences eventually break the nation apart? More importantly, even if the United States still exists 1,000 years from now, will it also still have relatively high amounts of freedom and equality? Only time will tell if "a nation conceived in liberty" can practice that principle for *many* centuries and still survive, or if factions will eventually destroy that liberty.

As we go through the rest of this course learning more U.S. national government, keep in mind that both the successes and failures of U.S. democracy are testaments to the ongoing nature of the profound American Experiment. The long-term success or failure of that experiment depends on people understanding the nature of that experiment and supporting it. Once again, then, we see the fundamental importance of civics education in maintaining a flourishing democracy.

SUMMARY

Although the Federalists supported the proposed new U.S. Constitution, the Anti-Federalists opposed its ratification. The Anti-Federalists believed the Constitution would give the new U.S. national government too much power. The Federalists narrowly won the debate, however. The Constitution was ratified and replaced the Articles of Confederation. One particular issue in the debates was whether a large-scale democracy was feasible. Anti-Federalists like Brutus argued the U.S. would be too large and diverse. This would mean the elected representatives would not agree on any common public policy, thereby paralyzing the government. Federalists, especially Madison in Federalist Paper No. 10, argued that a large-scale democracy would succeed. Because the U.S. would be so large and diverse, it would be unlikely that a single majority faction would form that would oppress any minority group. U.S. history has shown, though, that Madison's theory of pluralistic representative democracy does not always work. Majority factions have often agreed on mistreating various minority groups. Nevertheless, the ideals of democracy, equality and liberty contained in the U.S. Constitution are a grand, ongoing political experiment.

QUESTIONS FOR REVIEW AND SELF-ASSESSMENT

1. What was the nature of the debates surrounding the ratification of the U.S. Constitution?
2. What are the two different basic types of democracy, and what was the Anti-Federalist argument why a large-scale democracy would not be feasible?
3. What is James Madison's theory of factions and large-scale democracy that he put forth in Federalist Paper No. 10?

4. What are aspects of the United States that make it both praiseworthy and blameworthy?
5. Why is the question whether large-scale democracy can survive in the long term still unanswered?

Critical Thinking Questions for Reflection and Discussion

1. On balance, overall was the U.S. more praiseworthy or blameworthy at the time of its founding?
2. On balance overall, is the U.S. more praiseworthy or blameworthy today?
3. How likely is it that a large-scale democracy can survive in the long run of 1,000 years?

Suggested Supplemental Readings

- Brutus, *Essay No. 1*
- James Madison, *Federalist No. 10*
- *Chisholm v. Georgia* (1793)
- *Dred Scott v. Sanford* (1857)
- *Korematsu v. U.S.* (1944)

For Further Advanced Reading

- Robert Dahl, *A Preface to Democratic Theory*
- Roxanne Dunbar-Ortiz, *An Indigenous People's History of the United States*

Chapter 5: Constitutional Democracy

The Big Picture

An ideally designed government would make it difficult for rulers to consolidate and abuse their power. This can be achieved in many ways. First, the many functions of government can be assigned to separate units within that government. Second, each of those units can be given a way to block the actions of the other units. Third, each of the units can designed so as to represent different political interests. Fourth, the rules can limit what those units can do even when they collectively agree. The writers of the U.S. Constitution applied all these concepts extensively when they designed the U.S. government. The purpose in this design was to minimize the danger that leaders in the national government would abuse their political power.

Relevant Timeline

- 1690 John Locke publishes *Two Treatises on Government*
- 1748 Baron de Montesquieu publishes *On the Spirit of Laws*
- 1776 U.S. Declaration of Independence
- 1787 Philadelphia Convention writes U.S. Constitution
- 1789 U.S. Constitution ratified
- 1803 *Marbury v. Madison* (courts have the power of judicial review)

Chapter Objectives

After reading this chapter, the reader should be able to:

1. Explain the definition, origin and purpose of separation of powers, as well as checks and balances.
2. Describe in detail how the U.S. constitution implements a separation of powers, and checks and balances, in the design of the U.S. government.
3. Explain the definition, origin and purpose of mixed government.
4. Describe how the U.S. Constitution creates a U.S. national government comprised of mixed government.
5. Explain the concept and purpose of constitutional democracy and limited government.

Montesquieu and Human Nature

Now that we've considered the Federalist-Anti-Federalist debate over the existence of the U.S. as a whole, we can start to look more at the particular design of the U.S. government. Recall from an earlier chapter that the English philosopher John Locke invented the concept of the social contract as a way to explain and justify the existence of government. These ideas were incorporated into the U.S. Declaration of Independence. In his 1690 *Second Treatise on Government*, Locke provided a few suggestions on how to design the government he envisioned. Yet it was a later philosopher that more greatly influenced the framers of the U.S. Constitution in designing the specific details of the U.S. government. Writing a few decades after Locke, the French political philosopher Baron de Montesquieu wrote a work in 1748 titled *On the Spirit of the Laws*. In this study of government and law, Montesquieu attempted to provide what he believed would be the ideal structure of government.

Montesquieu began with the premise that human nature is selfish, untrustworthy and dangerous. Since government is simply human beings with power, this means all government is untrustworthy and dangerous. Montesquieu famously declared "Every man invested with power is apt to abuse it." The more modern expression "Power corrupts, and absolute power corrupts absolutely" is something that Montesquieu probably would have agreed with. In short, the simple logic of his reasoning is:

1. All humans are dangerous
2. Government is comprised of humans

Therefore: 3. All government is dangerous

Here lies the great irony of all government. As Locke and Montesquieu both noted, humans pose a threat to each other's rights to life and liberty. Just look through history or around the world today at places without a functioning government. In almost all instances this has resulted in lawless, violent chaos. For example, the old 1800's western U.S. was called "the Wild West" for a reason. Without adequate law enforcement, outlaws ruled, and everyone needed to fend for themselves. Yet if everyone's lives are subject to the will of the strongest, "might makes right." Hence, as Locke explained, a social contract is unfortunately needed to create a government that will make and enforce laws to protect us from each other. Yet because government is nothing other than humans with power, this means all government poses a threat to our rights as well. Humans can take away our life, liberty, and property, but so can the government. The situation might be summarized as "Government: you can't live with it, but you can't live without it." Put differently, the choice is deciding which is the lesser evil: having government, or having no government. Throughout history, most people have concluded that having government is generally the lesser of the two evils.

A key question in designing the structure of any government, then, is how to minimize the risk of danger coming from government *itself*. Is there a way to design a government such that the structure of the government itself makes it difficult for those in power to selfishly abuse their power? Montesquieu believed he had invented up a two-step solution.

Separation of Powers

The first way to limit the danger of government is to divide up and distribute the functions of government into different parts of the government. This is the opposite of condensing all the powers of government together into just one governmental entity. It doesn't matter whether one refers to the different parts of government as units, divisions, departments, or branches of government. The point is to *not* have all the various powers of government concentrated in the hands of one individual or group. This concept of assigning different governmental powers to different parts of government is called the "*separation of powers.*" Making different parts of government have to coordinate and agree doesn't guarantee that the government won't abuse its power. It simply makes abuse of power less likely to occur than if all the power of government was consolidated in just one person or unit.

An analogy is the U.S. criminal justice system. It would violate basic notions of fairness, as well as constitutional due process rights, for someone accused of a crime if the prosecutor was also the "judge, jury, and executioner." Under that system, there would be too much chance for abuse of power. The prosecutor could simply charge, convict, and punish anyone the prosecutor didn't like. Instead, the criminal justice system assigns each of the different judicial roles to different entities. First, either a prosecutors or a grand jury charges people with crimes. Then, the defendant may choose that either a different jury, or a judge, have the power to decide guilt or innocence. Finally, only judges have the power of sentencing. For the criminal justice process to be abused, the prosecutor, jury, and judge would all have to conspire together to deprive people of their rights. Of course, there's no guarantee that such a conspiracy will never happen. However, abuse of power is less likely to occur under such a system than if all the decisions were made by just one person.

Montesquieu believed that of all of the endless functions that governments have, there are only three different basic powers that governments exercise. Governments make laws, enforce those laws, and interpret those laws. Making laws is also called legislating. This task should be assigned to a legislature, also called the legislative branch of government. Once the laws are made, someone needs to enforce or "execute" those laws. Enforcing laws should be assigned to the executive branch of government. Law enforcement will lead to disagreements between the executive and the legislature, or between the executive and the people, about whether the laws are being applied correctly. Because of such disagreements, someone must interpret the meaning of the laws so as to judge whether they are being correctly enforced. The judges and courts who make these decisions comprise the judicial branch of government, also called the judiciary.

Checks and Balances

Montesquieu could have stopped there with his idea for the separation of powers. He believed this was not enough, however, so he recommended adding another layer of security and protection against abusive government. He believed each of the branches of government should be given some way to block the actions of the other branches. This would allow each branch to oppose the other branches if they started to abuse power. Montesquieu recommended giving the executive a way to "reject" laws passed by the legislature if the executive thought those laws were improper. Montesquieu also proposed that the legislature should be able to "impeach" (remove) the executive for abuse of executive power. Finally, Montesquieu also suggested having a bicameral legislature. One chamber would represent the interests of the common people, and the other chamber would represent the interests of the upper-class "nobles." In this way, the legislature would even check itself.

This concept whereby each of the different branches of government is able to interfere with actions by the other branches of government later came to be known as *"checks and balances."* Notice that for a system of checks and balances to occur, there must already be a system of separation of powers. Unless power is first divided up into different governmental units, there would be no units that could check each other. Yet although checks and balances first needs a system of separation of powers, a system of separation of powers can exist on its own. That is, a separation of powers can exist without containing the added procedural safeguard of a systems of checks and balances. In short, although the ideas of "separation of powers" and "checks and balances" are highly related, they are different concepts. It's analogous to people and their clothes: People can live without clothes, but clothes wouldn't exist without people. Similarly, separation of powers can exist without checks and balances, but checks and balances cannot exist with a separation of powers.

U.S. Separation of Powers

The framers of the U.S. Constitution agreed with both Locke's and Montesquieu's beliefs that people are generally untrustworthy and dangerous. As a result, the writers of the Constitution loved Montesquieu's ideas on how to constrain the powers of government. The delegates at the 1787 Philadelphia convention put Montesquieu's concepts of separation of powers, and checks and balances, at the core of the basic structure of the U.S. government. The details of U.S. government thus not only establish the basic framework of U.S. government, they embody Montesquieu's philosophical views on human nature.

The first thing the framers did was create a system of separation of powers. The power of the United States government is divided into three branches. Article I of the Constitution creates the legislative branch, called Congress, which is given the power to make laws. To be precise, Congress is given "legislative powers" to make certain specific kinds of laws listed in Article I, Section 8 of the Constitution. We learned about these enumerated powers in the previous chapter on the compromises that went into the Constitution. As we also learned in that chapter, in the Great Compromise the small states and big states settled on a bicameral (two-chamber) legislature collectively called the Congress. Voting in one chamber, the House of Representatives, is based on population. In the other chamber, the Senate, each state is represented equally. In the original Constitution, the people elected the Representatives, but the state legislatures elected the Senators. In this way, the selection of members of Congress followed Montesquieu's recommendation that one chamber of the legislature should represent the people, but the other chamber should represent the elite aristocracy. (Much later in 1913, the Seventeenth Amendment changed the election of Senators to direct election by the people.) Because the legislature is the branch that is described first in the Constitution, the legislative branch is sometimes referred to as the first branch of the U.S. government.

The second branch of government is the executive branch, which is created in Article II of the Constitution. According to the Constitution, the top official in the executive branch is the "President of the United States," sometimes referred to by the acronym "POTUS" by political elites. The Vice-President is second in charge. The President is given an undefined "executive power," but this has always been understood to be the power of implementing and enforcing laws. Beyond the two positions of President and Vice-President, however, the Constitution does not create any other parts of the executive branch. Instead, the Constitution leaves it to Congress to decide whether and what executive branch departments and agencies should exist.

The third branch of government is the judicial branch, also called the judiciary. It is created by Article III of the Constitution. The judicial branch is comprised of the federal courts, all of which have the power to interpret the meaning of federal laws when that interpretation is disputed. The Constitution only creates the top court in the federal court system, the "Supreme Court of the United States." Political elites sometimes refer to the Supreme Court by the acronym "SCOTUS." Beyond the Supreme Court, Article III provides that Congress shall define and create the rest of the federal court system as needed.

Table: U.S. Separation of Powers

Branch	Article	Name	Separated Power
Legislative Branch	I	Congress	Make Laws
Executive Branch	II	President	Enforce Laws
Judicial Branch	III	Supreme Court	Interpret Laws

U.S. Checks & Balances

The framers of the Constitution could have stopped at separating the powers of the U.S. government into different branches. They agreed with Montesquieu, however, that additional safeguards were needed to even further reduce the chance that government would abuse power. Each of the three branches were thus given checks against the others. These mechanisms would balance the power of the three branches against each other.

The President was given several checks. As a check against the legislature, the President has the power to veto proposed laws (bills) that Congress otherwise has passed. A veto blocks the bill from becoming law. Also, no one may be appointed as a federal judge unless that person is first nominated by the President and then that nomination is confirmed a majority of the Senate. Finally, the President may pardon people of federal crimes. This check helps prevent abuse of the criminal justice process by the courts.

The Congress was given several checks against both the President and the courts. Regarding checks against the President, Congress has a counter-check against the check of Presidential vetoes. If a separate 2/3 vote in each of the two chambers of Congress votes to override a Presidential veto, then that bill becomes law despite any objection by the President. Also, in case of abuse of power by the President or other executive officials, Congress may remove those officials from office. This is a two-step process. First, a majority of the House of Representatives would vote to "impeach" the President of some alleged wrongdoing. This is merely a charge of improper behavior. The Senate would then conduct the trial of the impeachment charges. If the Senate votes by a 2/3 majority to convict the President of those charges, then the President is removed from office. Moreover, the Senate was given several checks against the President that were not given to the House. Presidential nominees to high-level executive branch positions must be confirmed by a majority vote of the Senate. The same goes for Presidential nominees for federal judgeship positions. Also, any treaties with foreign nations that the President has negotiated must be ratified by a 2/3 majority by the Senate.

The Congress also has several checks against the judicial branch. The Congress has authority to create or abolish all federal courts other than the U.S. Supreme Court. Congress may also define the jurisdiction of the federal courts to hear and decide legal issues. A Senate majority must confirm all Presidential nominations of persons to serve as federal judges. Finally, the Congress may remove federal judges from their office by the same process used to impeach executive officials. A House majority must vote to impeach the judge, and then a 2/3 vote by the Senate would convict that judge of the charges and remove them from office.

In addition, because Congress is a bicameral legislature, each chamber acts as a check on the other. Because House representation is based on population, the House tends to represent large, more urbanized states like New York, Illinois, Texas and California. On the other hand, since every state is equal in the Senate, it tends to represent the less populated, more rural states like Vermont, North Dakota, Wyoming, and Alaska. It's also often the case that control over the two chambers is split between the Democratic and Republican parties. If the two parties each have a majority in one of two chambers of Congress, then both parties may block each other's desired legislative agenda.

Also, the House tends to represent the democratic masses more than the Senate. House terms are only two years, so representatives must constantly run for reelection. This means they answer more easily to the public's desires. The Senate, however, has a somewhat more elite, aristocratic element to it. This is because there are only two senators per state, and only 100 senators total. Senators also serve 6-year terms in office, so are somewhat immune from the rapid mood swings of the public. Also, although representatives have always been chosen by the people, in the original Constitution senators were chosen by the members of the state legislatures, not the public. This meant that political elites were choosing from among themselves as to who should be senators. This was consistent with Montesquieu's idea that one of the two legislative chambers should represent the "nobles." Although the 17th Amendment in 1913 began direct public election of Senators, the Senate today still maintains a more elite character.

The Constitution does not expressly contain any check by the judicial branch against the other two branches of government. The courts nevertheless have an important check that is directly implied by the Constitution. Under the separation of powers, it is the role of the courts to interpret law. A basic principle of law is that higher law always overrides any inconsistent lower law. Article IV of the Constitution contains the Supremacy Clause, which states that the Constitution is the "supreme law" of the land. Together these principles result in the following direct logic:

1. The Constitution is the highest law in the United States.
Therefore: 2. Anything Congress or the President says or does is lower law than the Constitution.
3. Higher law always overrides lower law.
Therefore: 4. The Constitution always overrides any inconstant action by Congress or the President.
5. It is the job of the courts to interpret law, which includes saying when higher law overrides lower law.
Therefore: 6. When the Constitution overrides Congress or the President, the courts must say so.

This power of the courts to declare actions by the other branches of government to be unconstitutional is called the power of *"judicial review."* In other words, when someone legally challenges an action by the government, the courts must decide if that action contradicts the Constitution. If Congress or the President say "x", but the Constitution says "not-x," then it is the court's constitutional responsibility to declare "x" as legally null and void. For example, if Congress prohibits "indecent" speech on the internet, the Supreme Court can declare this law void if it contradicts the Free Speech Clause of the First Amendment. We'll explore this concept of judicial review in more detail in a later chapter that focuses on the judicial branch.

Below is a table of the U.S. checks and balances.

Table: U.S. Checks and Balances

	Checks against Congress	Checks against the President	Checks against the Courts
Congressional Checks	Both the House and the Senate may block proposed laws (bills) passed by the other chamber	*Congress* overrides Presidential vetoes by a 2/3 vote in both chambers. The *House* impeaches executive officers by majority vote. The *Senate* convicts impeached executive officers by a 2/3 vote. The *Senate* ratifies treaties by a 2/3 vote. The *Senate* confirms top executive branch officers by a majority vote.	*Congress* creates lower federal courts and defines federal court jurisdiction. The *Senate* confirms federal judges by a majority vote. The *House* impeaches federal judges by majority vote. The *Senate* convicts impeached judges by a 2/3 vote.
Presidential Checks	The President vetoes proposed laws (bills) passed by Congress and calls Congress into special session	--	The President nominates federal judges and issues pardons to persons who have committed federal crimes
Judicial Checks	The courts declare laws or actions by Congress to be unconstitutional (judicial review)	The courts declare actions by the President to be unconstitutional (judicial review)	--

It's important to note that the terms "separation of powers" and "checks and balances" are not found anywhere in the language of the Constitution. Neither are some of the major constitutional principles discussed in the previous chapter, such as "representative democracy" or "enumerated powers." These are all simply shorthand terms or phrases used to more conveniently refer to the concepts contained within, and created by, the text of the Constitution.

Mixed Government

Although the phrase "separation of powers" did not come into use until the founding period of the United States, the concept of separation of powers has ancient roots. Plato was the first philosopher to describe in writing the various types of government that we learned about in an earlier chapter, such as aristocracy and democracy. The various types of government are also called *regimes.* Plato's best student, Aristotle, wrote a classic study of regimes titled *Politics.* In the *Politics,* Aristotle described the different possible types of regimes and the strengths and weaknesses of each. Autocracy allows the wisest person to rule. Yet unchecked autocracy can easily become a totalitarian dictatorship. Aristocracy is government by the best team of leaders. Yet such a small group can become an elite few who abuse the system to increase their own wealth and power. Democracy gives more people a share in making the rules that will govern them. Yet rule by the poor uneducated masses can become mob rule. In short, there is no such thing as a perfect regime since human beings are flawed. It's impossible for humans to achieve ideal government on this Earth under any particular type of regime. According to Aristotle the best regime that can be reasonably hoped for is a mixture of the different types of regimes. This would create a happy middle between the opposite extremes that can occur with any single type of regime. Aristotle thus favored the concept of "mixed government," also referred to as a "mixed constitution," or a "mixed regime."

In a mixed form of government, elements of different types of regimes are blended together on the theory that laws in a mixed regime will be the most just. The logic is somewhat akin to the saying "two heads are better than one." In other words, the combined wisdom of several people is usually greater than the wisdom of any one individual. Similarly, the benefit of each type of regime can be combined into a single regime. If only one self-interested person or group is in charge, public policy will be skewed in their favor. If two persons or groups must share political power, then the laws will probably be less biased in either opposite direction. If many different persons or groups share political power, then in theory all their various biases will tend to cancel each other out. The public policy that results will not represent any one interest only, but rather the collective interest. In short, mixed government hopefully results in a moderate, balanced approach to governance.

After Aristotle developed the concept of mixed government, other political thinkers favored this idea as well. The ancient Roman historian Polybius, for example, is known for having argued in favor of mixed government. His ideas, along with Aristotle's, are often credited as the early forerunners of Montesquieu's concept of separation of powers. Indeed, in the explanation and defense of U.S.

government found in the Federalist Papers, Madison quotes and cites both Montesquieu and Polybius.

There are many ways to implement a system of separation of powers that do not incorporate the concept of a mixed regime. That is, separating the powers of making, enforcing, and interpreting laws into different branches of government does not dictate how those branches are designed. Each branch could be an autocracy, oligarchy, or democracy. For example, there is no necessary reason why the chief executive should be one person rather than a group. The head of the judicial branch could be a single judge, a handful of judges, or a large assembly of judges. Similarly, the top lawmaker could be one, a few, or many people. The legislative, executive, and judicial branches could all be comprised of one person each, a small group each, or a large group each. For example, in theory the U.S. government could be designed the opposite way it is now. Instead of electing a Presidency of one person who enforces laws, and a Congress of several hundred people who makes laws, the public could elect one person to make the laws, and elect several hundred people to enforce the laws. Or, the public could elect one person to make the laws, one person to enforce the laws, and one person to interpret the laws. This would be autocracy within every branch of government. Similarly, all three branches could be based on oligarchy, or on democracy. The point is that the separation of powers does not need to include a mixed regime.

Yet the framers of the Constitution intentionally created a mixed regime when they designed the U.S. government. They based each of the three branches of government on a different type of regime so that competing interests will be represented by each branch. The writers of the Constitution designed a Presidency of one person, which is a type of autocracy, and is analogous to a monarchy. In the Congress, the Senate can be viewed as representing either oligarchy or aristocracy since it is a relatively small group and was originally chosen by political elites themselves. The House of Representatives, on the other hand, is the most democratic part of the U.S. government. It is the largest of the bodies in the U.S. government and is elected more frequently than the other components of the U.S. national government. It is thus closer to the interests of the people than the President, Senate, or Supreme Court. Finally, the Supreme Court, since it is a small body of unelected individuals, and is chosen presumably based on merit, is a more aristocratic institution. This means the U.S. government contains a combination of monarchical, oligarchic, aristocratic, and democratic elements. Each branch of government represents a different type of regime and interest, and is assigned a different core function of government in the separation of powers.

The purpose of both separation of powers and mixed government is to help reduce the potential for government abusing its power. Dividing the powers of government into different branches means no one institution can take on too much power. Mixed government means that no one type of societal interest will monopolize government power. Without a mixed regime, the sole interest represented by the government would use that authority to give itself more wealth and power at the expense of other groups in society. A mixed regime, combined with a separation of powers and an added layer of checks and balances, all work together to limit the power of government to maximize the protection of everyone's liberties.

Table: U.S. Mixed Government and Separation of Powers

Type of government:	Rule by:	U.S. government component:	Separated power:
Autocracy/Monarchy	One	President	Enforce laws
Aristocracy	Few –the best	Supreme Court Senate	Interpret laws Make Laws
Oligarchy	Few—the wealthy	Senate	Make laws
Democracy	Many	House of Representatives	Make laws

Recall that the Great Compromise decided that for any proposal to become U.S. law, it had to be agreed to by both the House of Representatives and the Senate, and then be signed by the President. In short:

House + Senate + President = Law

Stating these institutions in terms of mixed government, the constitutional requirements for lawmaking are:

Democracy + Oligarchy/Aristocracy + Autocracy = Law.

This design means that not only are the function of government separated into different branches of government, but those branches represent different interests in society. The power of government is therefore dispersed in two different ways at the same time. These different mechanisms worth together to make it difficult for any one individual or group in society to consolidate all political power at the national level. The claim that these structures preventing tyranny is just another way of saying they protect liberty.

Original Intent

In addition to the foregoing concepts, another way to limit the power of a central government is to divide political power between that central government and other lower levels of government within that nation. This concept, called federalism, requires such extensive discussion that it will be covered on its own in the next chapter. Regardless, the concepts in this chapter and the next are fundamentally important in understanding the thinking that originally went into the writing and ratification of the U.S. Constitution. The key point is that the framers of the Constitution *intentionally* chose to create an *in*efficient form of government. This design was purposefully selected so as to maximize the protection of liberty.

This fact can be illustrated by comparing the U.S. system to the British system. There is little separation of powers, no checks and balances, and relatively no mixed government in the current government of the United Kingdom. Instead, a one-chamber (unicameral) Parliament elected by the people makes the laws. The parliament selects the prime minister and can remove the prime minister from office at any time. The prime minister has no veto power over what the parliament decides. Also, British courts have no power to overrule laws passed by the parliament. There is still a monarchy and a "House of Lords" that both hold office by heredity and not by popular election. Yet both the monarchy and House of Lords are only figureheads at this point in history, and have no functioning authority to overrule the parliament. In short, British law is entirely decided by the parliament. The law can be can be quickly and completely changed at any time if parliament decides to do so. Diagrammed, the British government lawmaking process is simply this:

Parliament = Law.

Obviously the British system is far more efficient than the U.S. system. Yet the Founding Fathers of the United States knew they were creating an inefficient form of government that would often have political gridlock. They purposefully did this because they valued liberty over efficiency. A government that can make decisions easily can also easily decide to take away people's liberty. On the other hand, a government that has a hard time getting things done also has a hard time infringing on people's rights. The creation of a complex national system of government was a deliberate choice. The principles of the separation of powers, checks and balances, and mixed government, along with enumerated powers, federalism, and a bill of rights, all make it harder for the U.S. government to enact laws. This equally makes it more difficult for the national government to pass laws that interfere with liberty.

The speeches and writings by the Founders at the time show the drafters of the Constitution mistrusted human nature. Since the Constitution was creating in large part a democracy, this meant that the people could impose tyranny on themselves. That is, a majority can oppress a minority. The Constitutional system thus is intended to prevent not just tyranny by one individual or a relatively small group, but also tyranny by a majority of the population. Indeed, because any democracy is by definition rule by the people, preventing *tyranny by the majority* is always a critical concern. Because of this, although the founders of the United States wanted a democracy, they also necessarily feared what they called "democratic excess." This was a term used at the time to refer to lawless mob rule. The Founders of the U.S. feared that the unchecked democratic masses might act based on their sudden irrational passions. This would lead the masses to create laws that would be contrary to the good of others and the nation as a whole. Hence, the complicated structures in the U.S. constitution were collectively intended to limit the likelihood of tyranny by any one individual, by a group, or even by the masses themselves.

A Written Constitution

Collectively, all the principles of the U.S. constitution form a *constitutional democracy.* This means the government is a democracy, but one that is defined and limited by a written constitution. Collectively, the constraints on government found in the Constitution establish the principle of *limited government.* Anytime a people create a nation, if those people want their government to have absolute power, then no document is needed that says so. The people can simply tell their leaders: "do whatever you want, however you want." This would be unlimited government. The founders of the U.S., however, were students of human history. They saw overwhelming evidence that human nature is inherently selfish, untrustworthy, and even dangerous. From wars to oppression to corruption, when people are given political power, most will eventually abuse that power. Two key writers of the Constitution were James Madison and Alexander Hamilton. In defending the separation of powers in their co-authored Federalist Paper No. 51, the two stated "If men were angels, no government would be necessary." But humans are not angels. Rights and liberties are always at risk of being taken away. This could done either by the individuals put in power, or by the masses using the democratic system to impose a tyranny by the majority over the minority. The founders of the U.S. believed the best way to prevent tyranny was to put strict procedural and substantive limits on the government. Together these restrictions comprise the concept of limited government.

In the landmark U.S. Supreme Court decision *Marbury v. Madison* (1803), Chief Justice John Marshall discussed that the purpose of a written constitution is to limit the powers of government:

> This original and supreme will [of the people] organizes the government, and assigns to different departments their respective powers. It may either stop here; or establish certain limits not to be transcended by those departments.

> The government of the United States is of the latter description. The powers of the legislature are defined and limited; and that those limits may not be mistaken or forgotten, the constitution is written. To what purpose are powers limited, and to what purpose is that limitation committed to writing; if these limits may, at any time, be passed by those intended to be restrained? The distinction between a government with limited and unlimited powers is abolished, if those limits do not confine the persons on whom they are imposed, and if acts prohibited and acts allowed are of equal obligation. It is a proposition too plain to be contested, that the constitution controls any legislative act repugnant to it . . .
>
> Between these alternatives there is no middle ground. The constitution is either a superior, paramount law, unchangeable by ordinary means, or it is on a level with ordinary legislative acts, and like other acts, is alterable when the legislature shall please to alter it. If the former part of the alternative be true, then a legislative act contrary to the constitution is not law: if the latter part be true, then written constitutions are absurd attempts, on the part of the people, to limit a power in its own nature illimitable. Certainly all those who have framed written constitutions contemplate them as forming the fundamental and paramount law of the nation, and consequently the theory of every such government must be, that an act of the legislature repugnant to the constitution is void. This theory is essentially attached to a written constitution, and is consequently to be considered by this court as one of the fundamental principles of our society. . .
>
> If then the courts are to regard the constitution; and the constitution is superior to any ordinary act of the legislature; the constitution, and not such ordinary act, must govern the case to which they both apply. Those then who controvert the principle that the constitution is to be considered, in court, as a paramount law, are reduced to the necessity of maintaining that courts must close their eyes on the constitution . . .
>
> This doctrine would subvert the very foundation of all written constitutions. It would declare that an act, which, according to the principles and theory of our government, is entirely void, is yet, in practice, completely obligatory. It would declare, that if the legislature shall do what is expressly forbidden, such act, notwithstanding the express prohibition, is in reality effectual. It would be giving to the legislature a practical and real omnipotence with the same breath which professes to restrict their powers within narrow limits. It is prescribing limits, and declaring that those limits may be passed at

pleasure. . . . it thus reduces to nothing what we have deemed the greatest improvement on political institutions--a written constitution . . ."

The principles of federalism, enumerated powers, separation of powers, checks and balances, and mixed government all place constraints on how and what the U.S. government does. As we shall see in later chapters, the principles contained within the U.S. Bill of Rights put further restrictions on the U.S. government. In short, all the various structures and principles contained in the written U.S. Constitution together create a U.S. government with *limited* powers. This is the one underlying foundational principle to the entire U.S. Constitution that summarizes the basic philosophy contained by all the various features found within it. Because government is made of humans, it is inherently dangerous, and therefore must be strictly limited by a written Constitution.

If You Can Keep It

The existence of a written Constitution limiting the power of government is no guarantee against tyranny. Indeed, on the final day the U.S. Constitution was drafted, Benjamin Franklin was asked whether the framers of the Constitution had created a monarchy or a republic. That is, Franklin was asked whether the public had been given rule by a king, or self-rule (self-government) by a representative democracy. Franklin replied that the writers of the Constitution had given the people "A republic—if you can keep it." In other words, *creating* democracy is one thing, but *implementing* and *keeping* democracy is another. There is no guarantee that democracy will succeed or continue to succeed. Indeed, although the original author is unknown, by the early 1800's a common saying had arisen within the U.S.: "Eternal vigilance is the price of liberty." The founders of the U.S. well understood that for any constitutional democracy to survive, its citizens must be well-educated about their constitution and its principles. The people must also care enough to keep their government within those constitutional limits by holding leaders accountable for ignoring those constraints. Otherwise, if violations of a constitution are ignored or excused, if abuses of power are allowed, then the written constitution becomes meaningless. When a constitution becomes worthless, the people will lose their hard-earned freedoms. As the famous Irish statesman and supporter of democracy Edmund Burke once declared, "The only thing necessary for the triumph of evil is for good men to do nothing." By educating people on the specific principles, structures, and rules contained in the U.S. Constitution, books about the U.S. government are doing something. However, this job of civics education is never finished. Each new generation must learn and apply these lessons in order for democracy and liberty to continue through limited government.

Summary

The French political philosopher Montesquieu proposed a system of separation of powers as the ideal structure of government. The different functions of government would be divided into different units within that government. This way, it would be difficult for any one person or group to take over the entire government and thereby abuse political power. For the same reason, Montesquieu also argued that each division of government should be given some ability to block the actions of the other divisions of government. The writers of the U.S. Constitution liked these ideas and created an elaborate system of both separation of powers and checks and balances within the U.S. national government. The Constitution creates three different branches of government. The legislative branch makes laws. The executive branch enforces laws. The judicial branch interprets laws. The Constitution then also gives each of these three branches one or more ways to influence or interfere with the workings of the other branches. In a highly related manner, the U.S. national government also is a form of "mixed government." It contains components of several different types of governments including autocracy, aristocracy, oligarchy, and democracy. This allowing each different type of societal interest to have a say in government and block actions by the other groups. The writers of the Constitution intended all these various features of the U.S. government to limit the power of the U.S. national government. To help further ensure the principles of limited government, all these constraints were placed in a detailed written constitution. However, unless the public continues to understand and uphold the constitution, the Constitution risks becoming irrelevant.

Questions for Review and Self-Assessment

1. What is the definition, origin and purpose of a separation of powers, as well as checks and balances?
2. What are the many ways in which the U.S. constitution implements a separation of powers, and checks and balances, in the design of the U.S. government?
3. What is the definition, origin and purpose of mixed government?
4. What are the ways in which the U.S. Constitution creates a U.S. national government comprised of a mixed regime?
5. What is the definition and purpose of constitutional democracy and limited government?

Critical Thinking Questions for Reflection and Discussion

1. Should the U.S. get rid of the concept of limited government by creating a parliamentary system like England, so that the U.S. government will function more efficiently?
2. Rather than have mixed government, should the U.S. adopt representative democracy in all branches of the U.S. government, so that the Congress, President and Supreme Court will each be a large elected group of people?

SUGGESTED READING SUPPLEMENTS

- U.S. Constitution, Articles I-III
- Federalist No. 47-49, 51
- *Marbury v. Madison* (1803)
- *Bowsher v. Synar* (1986)

FOR FURTHER ADVANCED READING

- Aristotle, *Politics*

Chapter 6: Federalism

The Big Picture

The writers of the U.S. Constitution made the U.S. government supreme over the state governments. This was true only in the two-dozen-or-so policy areas where the U.S. Congress was given authority to legislate. In the last two centuries, however, the size and power of the U.S. government has steadily increased. The biggest change in this regard happened because of the Great Depression. The U.S. Supreme Court re-interpreted key parts of the Constitution to allow Congress to deal with the Great Depression. Ever since then, Congress has constitutional authority to make almost any laws it wants. Only small technical exceptions still exist, and these might eventually be eliminated as well. The appropriateness of this constitutional re-interpretation is still heavily debated today, with such issues as universal government-provided health care. In other words, the size and power of the U.S. government is a major ongoing political issue.

Relevant Timeline

- 1789 U.S. Constitution ratified
- 1819 *McCulloch v. Maryland* (Congress has broad implied powers)
- 1865 U.S. Civil War ends (U.S. government defeats the Confederacy)
- 1929 The Great Depression begins
- 1932 Franklin D. Roosevelt elected President; New Deal proposed
- 1937 Roosevelt's Court-Packing Plan proposed
- 1941 The Great Depression ends
- 1942 *Wickard v. Filburn* (Congress has broad Commerce Clause power)

Chapter Objectives

After reading this chapter, the reader should be able to:

1. Describe the originally intended nature and purpose of U.S. federalism, including the Federalist and Anti-Federalist debate over it.
2. Explain how McCulloch v. Maryland and the Civil War both increased the power of the U.S. government over the state governments.
3. Explain how the Great Depression led to the U.S. Supreme Court significantly re-interpreting the Constitution to expand the power of Congress.
4. Describe how Congress today almost has the police power due to the Supreme Court's current interpretation of the Constitution.

5. Describe the basic arguments on both sides of the debate over the proper size and scope of the U.S. national government.

Laboratories of Democracy

Recall the earlier chapter on the major compromises that went into the Constitution. Remember that the writers of the Constitution decided to create a federal system of government. The United States was given separate national and state governments, with the national government supreme over the state governments. The Supremacy Clause, found in Article VI of the Constitution, established the superiority of the national government over the state government. The national government was given only a list of specifically enumerated powers, however. These were placed in Article I, Section 8 of the Constitution. These powers include the key powers of taxing and spending, having an army and navy, declaring war, and regulating "commerce . . . among the several states." In addition to that express list, Congress has any powers implied by that list. This is according to the Necessary and Proper Clause found at the end of Article I, Section 8. All other possible functions or powers of government would remain with the state governments. That is, according to the Tenth Amendment, part of the Bill of Rights, all other powers are "reserved to" the states. All this can be portrayed by a list of powers as follows:

- Article I, Section 8: Enumerated Powers of U.S. Government. Congress may:
    - tax and spend
    - create an army and navy
    - regulate interstate commerce
    - coin money
    - define how immigrants can become citizens
    - create a federal court system below the U.S. Supreme Court
    - govern the District of Columbia
    - grant copyrights, patents, and trademarks
    - provide a post office system with roads
    - a few other less substantial powers, such as to define and punish piracy
    - do anything implied by the above list (the Necessary and Proper Clause)
- Article VI: Supremacy Clause: U.S. law is supreme over state law
- Tenth Amendment: Reserved Powers of the States: Any powers not given to the U.S. government are kept by the states

But why divide power between two different levels of government? That is, why not just have a single, unitary system of government like most nations have? Wouldn't it be simpler to have only a central government that makes a uniform set of laws that the local regions then administer? As we discussed when we looked at the compromise over federalism, the early Americans were fiercely loyal to their state governments. Also recall the principles behind constitutional democracy and limited government discussed in the previous chapter. The founders of the United States feared a strong central government. Remember they were in the midst of fighting a strong central government in the form of the British King. Dividing political power between the central government and the state governments was thus another aspect of achieving limited government. If political power is split between the capitol and the states, then any group that would want to use political power for its own self-interest would have to win control of the both national and the state governments. There's no guarantee against this occurring, but it would be more difficult to achieve than if there was only a single layer of government. In that sense, the state-versus-national division of power in the U.S. federal system is sort of like another part in the U.S. system of separation of powers, or checks and balances. Federalism system is not formally considered part of those mechanisms, but it serves the same purpose. In short, federalism is yet another additional aspect of limited government in the United States.

Besides enhancing the protection of liberty, federalism promotes better public policy than a unitary system of government. Each of the 50 states is free to make their own laws experimenting with public policy. This can involve education, crime, the environment, health care, property rights, marriage, child custody, the licensing and regulation of businesses and labor, and so on. By allowing the states to develop their own unique solutions, each state is able to quickly adopt public policy to meet the individual needs of the people within the state. Each state also is free to try different public policies to see what works and what doesn't work as practical solutions to social problems. What one state discovers does work as public policy can be adopted and modified by other states. These policy successes can in turn be modified and adopted by other states. In this way, finding good public policy can occur many times faster than if only the Congress could adopt one uniform nationwide policy at a time.

Imagine, for example, if Congress created a new uniform nationwide system of public education, in which both the content of the required knowledge and the methods of teaching it were strictly regulated. The public would have to wait a generation to see what the outcome is. Would students in the new system go on to do better in college? Would they earn higher incomes as adults? If the policy doesn't work, then switching to a new policy will take another generation to see if it works instead. Change and improvement of public policy would occur at an extremely slow rate if only a single, uniform nationwide approach could be tried at any one time. If 50 states can all try different education policies, then policy reform can be explored 50 times more efficiently. Because the U.S. federal system allows and promotes policy experimentation by the states in this way, the states have been called *laboratories of democracy*.

Arguments over Federalism

When the proposed Constitution was released to the public, Anti-Federalists argued that the proposal went too far in increasing the power of the U.S. government beyond the power it had under the Articles of Confederation. One main argument in this regard was that the Constitution would allow the U.S. government to abolish the state governments. Doing so would impose a unitary system of government on the nation. Brutus was one Anti-Federalist to make this argument. In his Essay No. I, he argued that the Necessary and Proper Clause found in Article 1, Section 8, would allow Congress to abolish the state governments if it believed doing so was "necessary and proper." And, since the Supremacy Clause in Article VI says that U.S. law is superior to state law, the state governments would be legally unable to stop their elimination.

This argument was so serious that Madison took two essays in the Federalist Papers to respond to this argument. Writing in Federalist Papers Nos. 45 and 46, Madison interestingly did not disagree with Brutus' understanding of the powers of Congress. Instead, Madison made a purely political or practical argument. Madison asserted that even if Congress had such power, it would never choose to use it. Since the people at the time were more much attached to their state governments, he argued, in any conflict between the federal and state governments, the people would support their states. As Madison phrased it, the state governments would receive the "predilection and probable support of the people." Besides, since the President and Congress are elected by citizens of the states, the people would never elect a President or Congress that would oppress or abolish their own states. Moreover, Madison asserted that even in a worst-case scenario where the federal government tries to use the national military to violently take over the states, the states can and would band together. The states could combine their state militias to easily defeat any attempted federal military takeover. Although Madison did not use this analogy, essentially he was arguing that handing someone a sharp knife doesn't mean they will ever try to stab you. This is especially true if you are their friend, and if you are much bigger and stronger than they are. In short, Madison argued that Congress would never choose to use the constitutional weapon it had been given against the states.

Early Federalism

Since the Constitution was ratified in 1789, the balance of power between the federal and state governments has increasingly tipped in favor of the federal government over the states. In 1789 an extremely small federal government had a tiny budget and did very little. It performed relatively few functions such as printing U.S. money, negotiating foreign treaties, maintaining a navy, dealing with Native American tribes, overseeing the expansion of U.S. territory and the creation of new states, and so on. The state governments, on the other hand, performed almost all the functions of government at that time. Recall from Chapter 3, which discussed the biggest political compromises put in the Constitution, that the "police power" is a broad, general power of government to make any law. Using the police power given by their state constitutions, state governments were responsible for regulating almost all areas of day-to-day human life. This included regulating property, contracts, crimes, marriage and family law, businesses, schools, roads, and so on. In other words, the federal government was in charge of only a few public policy issues, but the state governments handled all other public policy matters.

The situation regarding federalism in the last half-century, however, is quite different from the situation in the early United States. The size of the U.S. government is different than the size of the United States itself, though. For example, the Louisiana Purchase occurred in 1803, which doubled the size of the United States. Yet it did not significantly increase either the size or power of the U.S. *government.* Today, on the other hand, an extremely large U.S. government has an enormous annual budget and regulates almost every area of human life from cradle to grave. This includes education, health care, transportation and workplace safety, the environment, the economy, crime, and many other policy areas that once were regulated only by the state governments. This substantial change in public policy did not happen all at once, but rather in a series of steps throughout U.S. history. Several of these events, however, are more noteworthy than others.

Numerous U.S. Supreme Court opinions throughout U.S. history have interpreted the powers of Congress in Article I, Section 8 in a way that expanded federal power. One of the most important early cases that did so was an 1819 case, *McCulloch v. Maryland.* Congress had created a national bank, even though the power to do so is not one of the expressly enumerated powers of Congress in Article I, Section 8 of the Constitution. Congress does, however, have the express constitutional power to coin money. Congress therefore argued that the Necessary and Proper Clause gave it the power to make a national bank. Basically, Congress asserted that it was necessary and proper to have a bank to aid in the making, storing, and distributing of money. The states objected, arguing that because Article I, Section 8 did not expressly give Congress the power to create banks, the power to create banks was exclusively a state power, reserved to the states by the Tenth

Amendment. The states also argued that the word "necessary" in the Necessary and Proper Clause meant "essential." It was not necessary or essential to have a bank in order to coin money. Congress responded by arguing that the word "necessary" in the Necessary and Proper Clause should be interpreted loosely, not strictly. The U.S. Supreme Court agreed with Congress. The Court concluded that the word "necessary" in the Necessary and Proper Clause does not literally mean "necessary." Instead, it means only "appropriate." That is, merely helpful or convenient. This broad interpretation greatly expanded the implied powers of Congress under the Necessary and Proper Clause.

The Civil War

The U.S. Civil War also impacted the basic nature of U.S. federalism. Recall from an earlier chapter that Jefferson had used Locke's social contract theory in writing the 1776 U.S. Declaration of Independence. That is, legitimate government is created by the people in a social contract. This established the principle of popular sovereignty and the right of the people to revolt if the government violates the terms of the social contract. Then, in 1787, the writers of the Constitution put "We the people . . . form a more perfect union" into the preamble of the Constitution, reaffirming popular sovereignty as the foundation of U.S. government. In the years leading up to the Civil War, however, Southern whites increasingly offered an alternative theory of the U.S. government. Southern whites feared the fact that the rest of the United States was growing increasingly hostile to slavery. As a way to constitutionally protect slavery from regulation or abolition, Southerners began to explain the existence of U.S. government by an alternative to Locke's social contract theory. This competing theory was called *compact theory.* It paralleled social contract theory, but argued the states had formed the U.S. government, not the people.

Southern politicians argued that the nation of the United States was not a social contract between the people. Instead, it was an agreement—a *compact*—between the state governments to form a single, "united" union of states. Basically, compact theory argued the United States was a confederate system of government, not a federal system. If the state governments had created the United States, and since by definition the creator is greater than the creation, then the state governments were supreme over the United States. In place of popular sovereignty, compact theory held state sovereignty as the highest level of sovereignty at the national level. This also meant states could vote to override, or nullify, U.S. laws the states disagreed with. This was referred to as the *nullification doctrine.*

Also, recall that in Locke's social contract theory, the people can change or abolish the government. The people can do so if the government breaks its terms of the social contract by abusing the people's rights rather than upholding those rights.

The people can even violently rebel if need be to change the government that has now lost legitimate authority. Similarly, under compact theory, if the U.S. government breaks its terms of the agreement with the states by infringing on the states' rights rather than protecting those rights, the states may change or abolish the U.S. government. This would include the right to rebel against the U.S. government and overthrow it, or leave the union of states. For a region of a nation to leave the nation as whole is called *secession*. Thus, the alleged right of states to secede from the union was called the *secession doctrine.*

After the election of Lincoln as U.S. President in 1860, Southern whites used Northern opposition to slavery as their justification for secession and rebellion. Leaders in the Southern slave states used compact theory to argue that the states were supreme over the U.S. government. They argued that the United States was not a federal system, but a "confederacy" or "confederation" of states. Since the U.S. Congress and President was moving towards restricting or abolishing slavery, it was violating the terms of the compact. A Northern majority in Congress and the new President Lincoln vowed to stop slavery from expanding into new territories. This violated the U.S. Constitution, which was the compact between the states. Other violations to the constitutional compact were being committed as well. The Northern states were refusing to return escaped slaves as required by the Fugitive Slave Clause of the Constitution. Indeed, the situation was quite the opposite. Northern states were declaring slaves escaping into their states to be free, and Northerners were helping slaves escape through a secret network of safe-houses called the "Underground Railroad." Northern states also were allowing abolition groups to speak freely and recruit new members. The term "abolition" comes from the word "abolish" meaning "to outlaw." That is, abolition groups wanted to abolish slavery. The U.S. government was doing little if anything to stop abolitionist speeches, writings, or the Underground Railroad. Southern whites came to see Northerners as their enemies due to Northern opposition to slavery. The election of Lincoln was simply the last straw that pushed Southerners to use compact theory to justify seceding from the Union of the United States. The Southern slaveholding states then formed their own "Confederate States of America" in the spring of 1861.

The remaining states in the Union, represented by the U.S. government, won the U.S. Civil War in 1865. President Lincoln, Congress, and the Northern state governments never recognized any legitimacy to the Southern-created compact theory of the U.S. government. The U.S. government victory over the Southern states essentially put to death any serious argument in favor of compact theory. In other words, the outcome of the U.S. Civil War solidly reaffirmed that the U.S. Constitution was a social contract formed by the *people* of the United States. As the Constitution's Preamble declares, "*We the people*, in order to form a more perfect union . . . do ordain and establish this Constitution for the United States of America." The

Constitution is a social contract made by the people, not a compact made by the states. The highest national political power in the U.S. is popular sovereignty, not state sovereignty.

The Constitution's Supremacy Clause, found in Article VI, was reaffirmed as well. Remember that the Supremacy Clause declares U.S. law is supreme over the states. This makes the U.S. a federal system of government, not a confederal system. States are not supreme over the U.S. government, and may not nullify federal law. Also, individual states acting on their own are not free to leave the union. They may not secede unless the people of the United States, acting as a whole through Congress, agree that part of the U.S. should be allowed to leave the U.S. Although the Civil War put the final nail in the coffin of compact theory, ever since the civil war there have been small numbers of people who still try to justify the Southern rebellion using compact theory. These individuals are commonly referred to as *neo-confederates*, meaning "new confederates."

The Great Depression

When discussing the history of U.S. federalism, the next seven decades or so after the Civil War is commonly referred to as the era of *dual federalism*. This simply means that although the U.S. government had reaffirmed its sovereignty over the state governments, the U.S. government continued to perform relatively few functions. The state governments continued to perform their many functions, and the different areas of public policy that the state and federal governments regulated rarely overlapped. Put differently, the state governments and the federal government had dual—separate, distinct--roles in governing public policy within the nation. The federal government regulated a few things at the national and international level. The state governments regulated everything else involving the day-to-day lives of their citizens at the local and state level. Another term sometimes used for dual federalism is "layer-cake federalism." This is because the diagram of federalism during this period would look simply like a layer cake, with a thick state layer at the bottom, and a thin federal layer on top.

In 1929, the worst economic depression in U.S. history began. Over several years, the stock market crashed, thousands of banks closed, millions of people lost all their money and homes, and unemployment rose to 25% of the adult working population. People stood in long lines just for free food handed out by charities. This depression soon became known as the *Great Depression*. In this context, "great" does not mean "wonderful," but "massive." Although economic historians disagree about exactly when the Great Depression ended, the most commonly given year is 1941, the start of World War II.

The state governments were overwhelmed by trying to help the people left poor, starving, or homeless by the Great Depression. More importantly, the depression was not caused by issues in any one state or group of states, but by complex economic issues at the national and international level. States were therefore largely powerless to deal with the problem or solve the crisis. Although President Hoover and the Congress tried to do some things to address the situation, they believed the federal government did not have much authority to address the problem. The Congress had little constitutional power to regulate industries, wages, prices, or the stock market, or to provide jobs, shelter, food, money, or help through other aid programs.

By the end of Hoover's term as President, a competing Presidential candidate came along named Franklin D. Roosevelt. He was more commonly known by his initials, FDR. He won the Democratic nomination for Presidency on the promise that if elected, he would give the American people a 'New Deal." A "deal" is a bargain, agreement, or contract. In one of his more famous speeches, FDR stated that the United States needed "new terms" to "the old social contract." Roosevelt promised that if elected, for the first time in U.S. history the federal government would begin to regulate public policy areas that it had never regulated before. This would include businesses, jobs, wages, prices, and the economy as whole. Roosevelt also promised that the U.S. government would begin to provide direct help to people in need. Up until that point in U.S. history, these policy areas had been regulated only by the state governments.

Roosevelt was elected President in 1932. His party, the Democratic Party, won a large majority of the seats in Congress. Roosevelt and Congress began immediately to pass New Deal legislation. This included the regulation of banks, the stock market, and agriculture, as well as the creation of a minimum wage law that effected most industries. Many businesses challenged the legality of Congress's actions. The U.S. Supreme Court used its power of judicial review to strike down most of the New Deal legislation as unconstitutional. An understanding of precisely how the court concluded this, and then later reversed itself, is necessary to understand how the Great Depression and the New Deal changed the nature of U.S. federalism.

In many different cases over several years, the U.S. Supreme Court used three different legal arguments to strike down the New Deal legislation. First, the list of the enumerated powers of Congress in the Constitution does not expressly include the New Deal policies. Article I, Section 8 does not list "requiring minimum private wages," or "limiting agricultural prices" or "providing guaranteed retirement incomes" as powers of Congress. In response, Congress and the President argued that these policies were an exercise of Congress' power under the Commerce Clause to "regulate commerce among the several states," which is expressly listed as an enumerated power. The Supreme Court, however, said that interstate commerce involved only goods traveling across state borders, but not good, services, or economic choices purely local and internal to a state. Second, because Congress was not given the power to regulate public policy that involved matters internal to the states, the Tenth Amendment reserved such power to the states. That is, according to the Supreme Court, only the states had constitutional authority to make New Deal-style public policy. Third, the Supreme Court ruled that businesses and workers possessed an unwritten "liberty of contract" that was impliedly contained in the U.S. Constitution. This meant that businesses, their workers, and consumers could agree to contract for wages and prices of goods, services, and labor free of government regulation.

President Roosevelt was re-elected President in 1936. At the start of his second term in February 1937, the Great Depression was still dragging on. FDR, the Congress, and a majority of the American people, were frustrated with the Supreme Court blocking New Deal legislation. In response, FDR proposed that Congress add several additional justices to the Supreme Court. Under the checks and balances, Congress decides how many justices make up the Supreme Court. If FDR nominated new justices, the Senate would confirm them because the Senate was controlled by FDR's Democratic Party. At first, FDR's alleged ground for the proposal was that the elderly justices needed new, younger justices to help them with their workload. The public and media immediately saw through Roosevelt's proposal, though, and named it FDR's "Court-Packing Plan." That is, the plan simply would have allowed FDR to "pack" the court with justices who agreed with the New Deal. This was FDR's real motivation. FDR soon made a speech where he admitted his frustration with the Court and his hope that by adding more justices to the Court it would finally uphold the New Deal. Yet the public, media, and even FDR's own majority party in Congress turned against his proposal. The court-packing plan was seen as a dangerous attempt to tinker with the independence of the judicial branch within the checks and balances system of the U.S. government. The plan was therefore rejected by Congress.

Despite the political death of the court-packing plan, a remarkable event occurred that historians and legal scholars still debate. Only a few weeks after FDR's proposal was announced and defeated, one of the justices on the U.S. Supreme Court changed his views about the Constitution. This created a new five-to-four majority on the Court which began to consistently uphold the constitutionality of the New Deal policies. This required a radical re-interpretation of the meaning of Tenth Amendment, the Commerce Clause, and the concept of "liberty of contract." The Court first completely abolished the concept of "liberty of contract" in a case at the end of March, 1937. The Court said there was no such right found anywhere in the Constitution, and all earlier cases indicating so had been mistaken.

Two weeks later, the Court greatly expanded Congress's power under the Commerce Clause. The Court said the power to regulate "commerce among the states" includes not only goods traveling across state borders, but any goods or services that indirectly affect interstate commerce. This is true regardless whether the goods or services are "local" or "national." The Court thus eliminated any local-versus-national or direct-versus-indirect distinctions when it came to interstate commerce. Almost all commerce was declared to either be interstate commerce itself, or to substantially affect interstate commerce. In essence, rather than having a power to regulate only "interstate" commerce, now Congress had broad constitutional authority to regulate *all* "commerce" within the United States.

Then in 1942, in a case called *Wickard v. Filburn*, the Court expanded Congress's power under the Commerce Clause even further. The Court basically said the power to regulate commerce allowed Congress to regulate any human activity, no matter how trivial the behavior, that had commercial implications. Put simply, if what you do has the potential to affect the national economy, then Congress has the constitutional authority to regulate it. Since almost every conceivable human action has some potential ability to effect the national economy, Congress has almost absolute regulatory authority under the Commerce Clause.

That same year, 1941, the Court also declared that the Tenth Amendment is essentially meaningless. The Court declared that since the Tenth Amendment doesn't specifically list what powers are reserved to the state governments, it offers no substantive legal rights or protections to the state governments. In short, the Tenth Amendment does not prevent Congress from regulating any public policy area. Even though a policy area has always been regulated only by state and local governments, Congressional regulation of that policy area does not violate the Tenth Amendment

The U.S. Supreme Court consistently upheld *all* Congressional uses of power under the Commerce Clause for several decades after the Great Depression. In the early 2000's, by a narrow 5-to-4 majority, the Court created a couple small technical exceptions to what Congress could regulate under the Commerce Clause. Most recently, in *National Federation of Independent Businesses (NFIB) v. Sebelius* in 2012, the Court considered whether Congress could mandate that individuals buy health insurance. This requirement is part of the Patient Protection and Affordable Care Act, passed in 2010. The Act is more commonly known as the "Obamacare" health program, the centerpiece of President Obama's public policy agenda. Businesses, as well as many state governments, argued that Congress had exceeded its legislative authority under the Commerce Clause by making people purchase a good they did not want to buy. In *Sebelius*, the Court decided that *inactivity*—that is, a person *not* doing something—could not be regulated as "commerce." Therefore, Congress could not use its power under the Commerce Clause to require individuals to buy health insurance if those individuals chose not to do so. In that same case, however, by another narrow 5-to-4-majority, the Court ruled that Congress *could* use its power under the Taxing and Spending Clause to tax individuals for not doing something. This meant that Congress could "fine" people by way of a tax if they don't purchase health insurance.

Together, then, according to the Supreme Court in the *Sebelius* case, the Commerce Clause and the Taxing and Spending Clause allow Congress to regulate all possible human activity or inactivity. Anything you actively *do* can be regulated or even criminalized as "commerce," and anything you do or *don't* do can be taxed. The only limitation is if some specific part of the Constitution prohibits the regulation. For example, Congress may not restrict free speech, or prohibit the free exercise of religion, or take away any other rights protected by the Constitution. (We will discuss civil rights and civil liberties in later chapters). Barring a specific constitutional limitation, however, Congress may enact almost any law it wants. In short, currently the Supreme Court has given Congress extremely broad legislative powers under the Constitution.

Recall from the chapter discussing the key constitutional compromises that when the Constitution was written, Hamilton proposed that Congress be given the power to "make all laws whatsoever." The term for this kind of broad governmental authority is called the "police power." Also recall, however, that the framers decided instead to give Congress a couple dozen specifically enumerated powers in Article I, Section 8 of the Constitution. This was to help make sure the federal government would be a government of limited powers. Today, all of the powers listed in Article I, Section 8 are included in Congress's powers under the Commerce Clause and the Tax Clause. Moreover, in *NFIB v. Sebelius*, the four-justice minority argued that the technical distinction between activity versus inactivity should be abolished, and Congress should be given the full police power under the Commerce Clause. This means that with only tiny technical exceptions remaining, Congress is almost no longer a government of enumerated powers but instead a government of the police power. The Supreme Court is thus only one justice away from making Hamilton's vision a constitutional reality.

Cooperative Federalism

The Great Depression and its consequences radically changed the nature of the U.S. government and federalism. The U.S. Supreme Court radically re-interpreted the meaning of the Constitution as a result of the New Deal efforts to grapple with the Great Depression. As a result, the federal government became much bigger and more powerful than it was before the Great Depression. The size and power of the U.S. government have almost continually expanded since the constitutional turning point in 1937. Today, Congress directly regulates almost all areas of human activity through public policies dealing with education, health care, retirement pensions, crime, the environment, transportation safety, workplace safety, consumer safety, poverty, business, wages and prices, banking, finance, economics, and many others. As merely a few specific examples, today federal government legislation provides Medicare, Medicaid, and Social Security programs which provide guaranteed health care, retirement, and disability benefits to tens of millions of people. Together these programs make up roughly half of the entire U.S. federal budget, which is approaching four *trillion* dollars annually. Before 1937, these public policy areas were almost exclusively the responsibility of state and local governments. Since 1937, people in the United States expect their national government to address every type of social or economic problem.

Remember that the era of federalism prior to 1937 was called "*dual* federalism." For the most part, the state and federal governments oversaw entirely *different* public policy areas. Also remember that in picture form, a diagram of this would look like a layer cake, so dual federalism is also often referred to as "*layer-cake* federalism." Since 1937, on the other hand, the federal government has regulated in most of the *same* policy areas as the state and local governments do. The era of federalism since 1937 is therefore referred to as "*cooperative* federalism." This term is used because the federal and state governments cooperate to regulate policy areas together. The resulting patchwork quilt of numerous overlapping regulations has led many scholars to refer to cooperative federalism as "*marble-cake* federalism." Instead of having neatly divided layers of regulations in separate public policy areas, the federal government has combined its regulations with state and local regulations. The top layer has mixed, blended and blurred with the lower layer, creating clumps of regulations in different policy areas. Hence, a visual analogy would be a *marble* cake. The diagrams below roughly illustrate the difference between dual federalism and cooperative federalism.

Diagram: Dual Federalism

U.S. Government (federal policies): international treaties, foreign policy, U.S. money, immigration, etc.
State Governments (state and local policies): businesses, the environment, health care, retirement, disability, education, crime, property, family law, etc.

Diagram: Cooperative Federalism

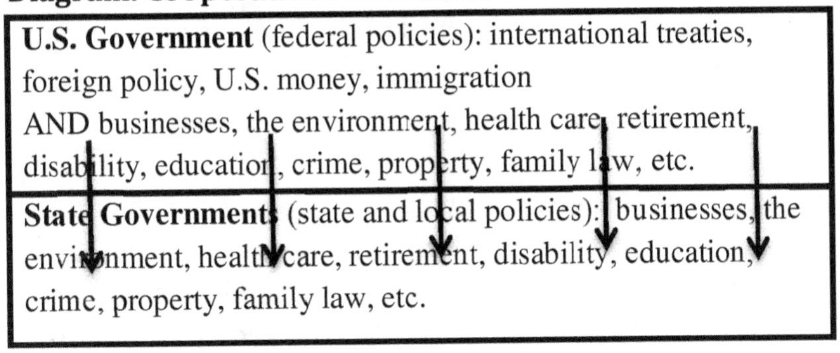

U.S. Government (federal policies): international treaties, foreign policy, U.S. money, immigration AND businesses, the environment, health care, retirement, disability, education, crime, property, family law, etc.
State Governments (state and local policies): businesses, the environment, health care, retirement, disability, education, crime, property, family law, etc.

Recall that under the Constitution's Supremacy Clause, U.S. law is supreme. This means that U.S. law overrides any contradictory state or local laws. Formally, this concept is now today as *pre-emption*. Under the pre-emption doctrine, whenever a state or local law either expressly or impliedly contradicts federal law, the federal law overrides or supersedes the state or local law. For example, several states, such as California, have legalized the medical use of marijuana. Federal law, however, outlaws all marijuana use without exception. This means that even if a state refuses to prosecute doctors who prescribe marijuana and patients who use it, the federal government can still choose to prosecute these doctors and patients under federal law. The Obama administration, for example, has decided as a matter of public health policy not to enforce federal drug laws in the case of medically prescribed marijuana. Other presidential administrations could decide differently, however, unless Congress itself decides to exempt medical marijuana in federal drug laws. Similarly, the state of Oregon currently allows doctor-assisted suicide in the case of terminally ill patients, but federal law does not allow medicine to be prescribed for such purposes. If a doctor in Oregon prescribes medication with the intent of helping a patient end their life, this still violates federal drug policy. Federal prosecutors have the option of bringing federal charges in such a case. In short, under the Supremacy Clause of the U.S. Constitution, the pre-emption doctrine allows the federal government to override state laws no matter how much the public of that state disagrees with federal policy.

Congress has still another way to obtain its public policy goals within our federal system. Through a financial program called *revenue sharing*, Congress gives the state and local governments some of the federal tax moneys it collects each year. This policy first began in relatively small amounts with the New Deal legislation to help state governments handle the problems of the Great Depression. Federal revenue sharing significantly increased in the 1960's and 1970's. Today, although the amount of revenue sharing varies from state-to-state and from year-to-year, overall roughly a quarter of state government budget revenues come from the federal government. In some states it's much higher. For example, in Louisiana in

2014, it was almost 40%. In the case of U.S. cities, the revenue sharing combined from the federal and state governments is about a third of city budgets on average. Indeed, according to one estimate, nationwide about four in ten of all state and local government bureaucrats are simply administering federal revenue sharing programs.

Although the general concept of sharing tax money between governments is called revenue sharing, any particular program that provides revenue sharing is called a *"grant-in-aid."* The shortened term "grant" is more commonly used. For example, currently the federal Medicaid Program is mostly managed by the states, and makes up a huge portion of state government budgets. In fact, Medicaid money is usually by far the largest portion of federal revenue sharing. For example, in the state of Louisiana's 2014-2015 budget, Medicaid spending made up about a third of the entire state budget.

There are two basic types of grants. *Block grants* have few or no restrictions on how the shared money is spent. *Categorical grants*, on the other hand, have many restrictions on how the money is spent. These spending conditions limit what the receiver of the money can do with the money. Medicaid, for example, is a categorical grant program because there are extensive regulations Congress places on how the states must spend Medicaid money. If a state refuses to follow the restrictions, it will not receive the money. States cannot afford to turn down a quarter or more of their annual budget, so they comply with whatever rules are imposed on them. Some members of Congress have proposed making the Medicaid program into a partial or full block grant program instead of the categorical grant program it is today. This would free up the states to experiment with health care policies that might provide better and/or more cost-effective health care. So far, however, a majority of Congress believes Medicaid should continue as a categorical grant program. This means that states will continue to follow whatever requirements Congress imposes.

There is another relatively well-known example of how Congress is able to coerce states using categorical grants with spending restrictions. Each year, every state receives millions of dollars in revenue sharing to spend on its highways. Congress places restrictions on this highway money. In the 1970's, Congress made states lower their speed limit to 55 m.p.h., although this restriction was removed a couple decades later. In 1984, Congress also mandated that states raise their drinking age to 21 or else the state would lose ten percent of its federal highway money. The state of Louisiana was the last of the fifty states to hold out against this spending condition. Louisiana finally raised its drinking age in 1996 because the state so desperately needed money that it could not afford to lose even 10% of federal highway money.

There is one final way Congress has power to coerce the state governments. As we've just seen, Congressional law overrides state law via the pre-emption doctrine. Congress can also pressure states to pass laws by placing spending conditions on categorical grants as part of federal revenue sharing with the states. With revenue sharing, Congress provides financial help to the states. Sometimes, however, Congress wants states to adopt a public policy without any financial help from Congress to accomplish the goal. When Congress simply requires a state to enact a policy without any revenue sharing, this directive is called an "*unfunded mandate.*" States hate these types of policies most of all. Not only is the state forced to follow federal policy, the state must do so at its own cost, regardless how much that might be. There are several major examples of unfunded mandates. Under the Clean Air Act, states must raise their state's air quality at their own cost in order to meet federal clean air standards. Under the Americans with Disabilities Act, states must make all their facilities and services accessible to the disabled, such as by building wheelchair ramps, installing elevators, or providing sign language interpreters. Under the law titled "No Child Left Behind," states must raise their public school performance, which might include hiring more teachers or paying teachers more. Also, under the federal Medicaid program, although states receive a large amount of federal revenue sharing, states must also provide a certain percent of matching state funds. Whenever Congress raises the amount it provides, the states must raise their matching contributions. In short, congressionally unfunded mandates require the states to enact public policy at the states' own cost, however expensive that is.

The Future of Federalism

Today, the U.S. government is still technically defined as a government of enumerated powers, but those powers are extremely broad. With a few minor technical exceptions, the Commerce Clause combined with the Taxing and Spending Clause, allow Congress to pass almost any laws. The only limitations would be specific prohibitions expressly found in the Constitution. In other words, for all practical purposes, unless there is a specific provision somewhere in the Constitution that forbids it, the U.S. Congress can do it. The Congress is therefore close to possessing the general police power. In addition, because of the Supremacy Clause found in Article VI of the Constitution, federal law overrides contrary state or local laws under the pre-emption doctrine. Congress can also coerce states do make public policy that Congress desires by placing spending conditions on revenue sharing with state governments. And, Congress can simply impose unfunded mandates on the state governments. With relatively narrow technical exceptions, the Tenth Amendment offers little if any legal protection to the states from the federal government. In short, the primary mechanism that limits the power of

Congress is merely the political process itself. That is, Congress can do whatever the people are willing to support, or at least tolerate.

Overall, this enormous increase in the size and scope of the federal government has meant that the U.S. government has moved more towards a unitary system of government. The states still exist and have independent lawmaking authority, and continue to serve as laboratories of democracy. Yet an ever-growing percent of state moneys and state workers are simply implementing federal revenue sharing programs. This means that the state governments are increasingly becoming merely administrative units of the federal government. This has been politically controversial, and has raised the question in recent decades whether the U.S should return more constitutional authority to the states. Others, though, argue the U.S. would be better off if it abolished the state governments entirely as independent lawmaking entities. Under this proposal, the state governments would officially become only administrative agencies of federal programs.

There are arguments on both sides of this issue. On the one hand, a uniform national system of public policy would be more efficient. There would be no more unnecessary duplication of programs, personnel, and costs at both the state and federal level. A single system of laws would be simpler as well. As individuals move around within the United States, they would not need to learn about a new set of laws and government programs, and get enrolled in such programs, each time they moved to a different city or state. Also, because some states have much more money than others, a unitary system would allow a more equal distribution of government goods and services. The quality of roads, public schools, public hospitals, and so on would be more even across the U.S. if resources could be shared equally at the national level. Other people have argued that the national government is needed to protect civil rights within the states. The Civil Rights Movement of the 1950's and 1960's is a classic example of this. Racial equality did not exist in the Southern states until the Federal government enforced it.

Moreover, our modern society is much more urbanized, industrialized, and complex than in 1787. Given the increasingly interconnected national and global economy, social problems typically can be addressed successfully only at the national level. Therefore, the argument goes, Congress needs broad constitutional authority to tackle modern political issues that transcend state borders. Indeed, this is one of the primary arguments behind the Patient Protection and Affordable Care Act passed in 2010, commonly known as "Obamacare," discussed earlier in this chapter. The President and a majority in Congress believed the states were not doing enough to help people afford medical insurance. Opponents, including many state governments, believed Congress overstepped its constitutional authority. This legal dispute went all the way to the U.S. Supreme Court, where a narrow margin of the Court said the law was within Congress's constitutional authority.

Finally, unlike during the founding period of the U.S., today most people feel closer to their national political leaders than to their state leaders. We see our national leaders, especially the President, in the news all the time, but our local and state leaders typically much less so. And, with other modern forms of communication, as well as modern transportation, we are much less tied to our states than people were 100 or 200 years ago. As a result, abolishing the state governments would not cause most people to feel like they were losing their identity of citizenship.

On the other hand, there are arguments in favor of keeping the state governments and their independent power. Remember the two basic reasons behind the concept of federalism. These were protecting liberty by dividing power between the state and national levels, and promoting more rapid and efficient public policy experimentation and improvement. When it comes to preventing tyranny, history has seen federalism work in both directions for the prevention of liberty. In recent decades the national government was sometimes needed to stop regional factions from imposing local tyranny. Yet at other times, the states have been at the forefront of civil rights. For example, long before the federal government became involved in the issue, many states and numerous cities prohibited discrimination on the basis of sexual orientation. At different times, then, both the national and the state levels can offer greater protection for liberty than the other can.

Also, having fifty different states allows public policy adaptability and innovation. Different regions and localities are not the same as each other when it comes to geography, demographics, economics, and so on. That is, the U.S. is not necessarily always a "one-size-fits-all" nation. People are free to move to within the U.S. to a political, cultural or physical environment of their choice. This allows for greater citizen satisfaction with the regional or local political climate of their choosing.

Moreover, local leaders often understand local problems better. This can include knowing what is needed to improve public education in the area, increase the safety of local environmental conditions, or achieve better crime prevention given the particular circumstances of the state. As a result, states regularly experiment with public policy, based on the specific needs, interests, and desires of local citizens. States further borrow and modify programs that have been successful in other states, and this cycle then repeats. State governments thus continue to serve as "laboratories of democracy," and serve as examples and models to each other. In sum, the main arguments for the existence of the states are the same today as when the U.S. was first created.

SUMMARY

The original design of the U.S. system of federalism left the states as laboratories of democracy that could experiment with public policy. Antifederalists feared the U.S. government might eliminate the state governments. Madison argued in Federalist papers #45-46, however, that this would never happen. Although the U.S. national government began as a relatively limited central government, it has evolved to be large and powerful. The Supreme Court has steadily expanded both the implied powers and the enumerated powers of Congress as found in Article I, Section 8 of the Constitution. The U.S. government's victory over the Southern states in the Civil War increased federal power over the states. However, the greatest increase in federal power happened as a result of the Great Depression and FDR's New Deal legislation. The Supreme Court re-interpreted the Commerce Clause in an extremely broad manner. Congress is now allowed to regulate any human activity that might remotely affect the national economy. This lets Congress pass almost any laws, thereby giving Congress nearly the police power today. Also, any laws passed by Congress override contrary state laws due to the Supremacy Clause. Even if Congress doesn't directly impose public policy on the states, Congress has other ways to make the states do what it wants. Congress can coerce the states to create specific policies by placing conditions on federal revenue sharing with the states, which the states cannot afford to refuse. Alternatively, Congress may simply impose unfunded mandates on the states. Taken together, these changes in the previous two centuries have greatly expanded the size and power of the U.S. national government over the states.

QUESTIONS FOR REVIEW AND SELF-ASSESSMENT

1. What was the originally intended nature and purpose of U.S. federalism? What were the Federalist and Anti-Federalist arguments regarding U.S. federalism?
2. How did McCulloch v. Maryland and the Civil War both increase the power of the U.S. government over the state governments?
3. How did the Great Depression lead to the U.S. Supreme Court significantly re-interpreting the Constitution to expand the power of Congress?
4. How does the Supreme Court's current interpretation of the Constitution allow Congress to have almost the police power?
5. What are the basic arguments on both sides of the debate over the proper size and scope of the U.S. national government?

CRITICAL THINKING QUESTIONS FOR REFLECTION AND DISCUSSION

1. On balance overall, is the U.S. government too big and powerful, too small and weak, or about the right size and power?
2. Should the states be entirely eliminated for efficiency purposes, so that the U.S. becomes a unitary system of government?

Suggested Supplemental Readings

- Brutus Essay No. V
- Federalist No. 39, 45-46
- *NLRB v. Jones and Laughlin Steel Corporation* (1937)
- *Wickard v. Filburn* (1942)
- *Garcia v. San Antonio Metropolitan District* (1985)
- *South Dakota v. Dole* (1986)
- *NFIB v. Sebelius* (2012)

For Further Advanced Reading

- David B. Walker, *The Rebirth of Federalism*

Part III: Rights and Liberties

Chapter 7: Civil Liberties

The Big Picture

A list of basic rights was not included in the text of the original U.S. Constitution. However, one was added to it immediately after its adoption. These first ten amendments to the U.S. Constitution are called the U.S. Bill of Rights. They contain basic democratic political freedoms such as the freedom of expression, religious liberty, and protections against government abuse of the criminal justice process. The Supreme Court has declared that people also have a few other rights protected by the Constitution, even though these rights are not expressly listed anywhere in the Constitution. Freedom of speech, however, is expressly listed. It is valued so highly because it is necessary for democracy to exist and is essential in the pursuit of truth in general. Together the listing of these various rights attempt to keep everyone free of government persecution. For this reason, the Bill of Rights is the foundation of what makes the United States a relatively free nation.

Relevant Timeline

- 1789 U.S. Constitution ratified
- 1791 Bill of Rights (first ten amendments) added to the Constitution
- 1868 Fourteenth Amendment added to the Constitution
- 1973 *Roe v. Wade* (right to abortion created)
- 1989 *Texas v. Johnson* (flag burning protected as free speech)
- 2015 *Obergefell v. Hodges* (right to same-sex marriage created)

Chapter Objectives

After reading this chapter, the reader should be able to:

1. Define the concept and purpose of a bill of rights, and describe the debate over whether the U.S. should have a bill of rights.
2. Describe how the U.S. Bill of Rights was written and ratified.
3. Describe the rights found in the U.S. Bill of Rights.
4. Describe the unenumerated rights protected by the Constitution.
5. Explain in detail the purpose and current protections of the Free Speech Clause of the First Amendment.

Civil Liberties

Recall from the earlier chapter on the writing of the Constitution that the main text of the Constitution lists the enumerated powers of the government in Article I, section 8 of the Constitution. Yet the Constitution did not contain a correspondingly detailed list of the rights of the people. Most constitutions in the world today have such a listing. The general term for this kind of listing is a "bill of rights." The word "bill" simply means "listing." A bill of rights is the opposite of the concept of enumerated powers. Enumerated powers are the powers specifically given to a government. A bill of rights, on the other hand, is a list of powers that the government specifically does *not* have because those powers have been taken away from the government. Put differently, a bill of rights is a list of actions people can do free from government interference, or at least with only limited regulation by government. A bill of rights, then, puts definite limits on the powers of government. Another term commonly used for such rights is the phrase *civil liberties.* In other words, a right listed in a bill of rights is also called a civil liberty.

Since a bill of rights is a list of powers the government does not have, by definition a bill of rights does not limit the power of private entities. That is, a bill of rights does not limit the actions of private individuals, businesses, schools, churches, or other private organizations. As merely one example, you may legally kick anyone out of your house for any reason you want or no reason at all. You can bar them from your home if you don't like their political views, their religion, their race, or anything else about them. If that person were to complain to you that you were violating their "constitutional rights," that person would be mistaken. Because a bill of rights places limitations only on *government,* you as a private individual are not violating anyone's rights by discriminating against them in your home. All that being said, legislatures have the authority to make laws that bar certain types of discrimination by private entities. Congress, the states, and most cities have enacted laws that bar various types of discrimination in employment, education, or housing. In short, laws *other than* a bill of rights might limit how you as a private entity may treat others.

No Bill of Rights

When the draft of the new U.S. Constitution was proposed in 1787, the lack of a bill of rights was the biggest political weakness of the proposed document. This flaw became a major political stumbling block to the ratification of the constitution. The Anti-Federalists hammered the Federalists on the fact the Constitution did not contain any express protection for basic rights such as free speech, religious liberty, fair criminal procedures, or other rights.

The Anti-Federalist Brutus, for example, made this argument in his Essay No. 2. He argued that when a social contract is formed, individuals do not give up their natural rights. In fact, the surrendering of rights is unnecessary for government to operate. Furthermore, a reservation of particular rights is needed to prevent against the tendency by rulers to abuse power for their own selfish gain by oppressing the people. Brutus argued that the Constitution needed a bill of rights or else the authority of the federal government given by the Constitution would be so broad as to be "complete" power. In particular, Brutus explained that the powers of Article I, section 8, coupled with the superiority of national laws due to the Supremacy Clause, would allow the U.S. Congress to do almost anything. Therefore, according to Brutus, specific exceptions to those powers needed to be listed in a bill of rights.

In Federalist Paper No. 84, Hamilton responded to this argument by Brutus and other Anti-Federalists. Hamilton argued against having a bill of rights. He first suggested that a bill of rights would be unnecessary. In his view, the enumerated powers of Article I, Section 8 of the Constitution did not include the Congressional power to suppress political speech, impose a national religion, torture people into false confession of crimes, or violate any other rights. Hamilton's strongest and main argument, however, was that having a bill of rights would be *dangerous* to liberty. Listing some rights, he argued, would imply a lack of other rights. Put differently, an express list of things Congress *cannot* do would imply that Congress *can* do anything not on that list. For example, if your instructor says "you have a right to use either a blue or black pen on exams" this directly implies you do not have a right to use a *red* pen. Similarly, if a bill of rights were to say *only* that you have a "freedom of speech," this would imply you do *not* have any other rights, such as a right to choose your own religion. Congress would then have the power to regulate these things. Hamilton concluded that the safest approach would be to list only what Congress *can* do, but avoid listing what it *cannot* do. Otherwise, one would need to be absolutely certain to list every possible right the people have or might ever want. Any right not listed would be forever waived, abandoned, forfeited, and relinquished. In this way, a bill of rights would severely limit the potential rights of the people.

Creating the Bill of Rights

Despite Hamilton's arguments, the Federalists were losing the public relations campaign on this issue. Several state ratifying conventions likely would not ratify the proposed Constitution without a bill of rights included. Five states ratified the Constitution only on the express written "recommendation" that a bill of rights be added. These states even proposed specific rights, such as the freedom of the press and a right of religious conscience. To win support for the ratification of the Constitution, the Federalists reached a bargain with some of the Anti-Federalists. This bargain became known as the "Massachusetts Compromise," since it gained Massachusetts voting for ratification. The Federalists promised that if the Constitution was ratified as it stood without a bill of rights, the first thing the new U.S. government would do would be to add a bill of rights. Congress would send a suggested bill of rights to the states as proposed amendments to the Constitution. Even though the final votes in some states were razor-thin margins, just enough

Anti-Federalists were persuaded by this compromise to support the Constitution. In 1789, the Constitution was ratified and therefore replaced the Articles of Confederation as the detailed social contract of the United States.

Under the process listed in the Constitution for amending it, it is a two-step procedure. First a proposal is formally made, then that proposal must be ratified (adopted). Each of these steps has two alternative methods. This means there are four possible ways to amend the U.S. Constitution.

Step One: Proposal: Formal proposal of the amendment by:

A. a two-thirds (2/3) vote of both chambers of Congress

or

B. two-thirds (2/3) of the state legislatures vote to call a national constitutional convention which will propose the amendment.

Step Two: Ratification: Approval of the proposed amendment by:

A. three-fourths (3/4) of the state legislatures vote to ratify

or

B. Three-fourths (3/4) of the states create separate, individual state constitutional conventions that vote to ratify the proposed amendment.

Throughout U.S. history, all amendments except one have been enacted by the same process. In the typical process, first there is a proposal by a 2/3 vote of both chambers of Congress, and then ratification by three-fourths of the state legislatures. The only exception was the Twenty-First Amendment, the repeal of alcohol prohibition. This amendment was enacted by a 2/3 vote of Congress followed by ratification by three-fourths of the states in state ratifying conventions.

Since the Constitution was ratified in 1789, thousands of amendments have been suggested, far fewer have been formally proposed, and only 27 amendments have made it through the final step in the ratification process. Indeed, given the first ten amendments comprising the Bill of Rights were added in 1791, there have been only 17 amendments to the U.S. Constitution in over 225 years. The infrequency of amendments shows that amending the Constitution is a politically difficult process. In recent decades, several serious proposals for constitutional amendments have failed. These include an equal rights amendment prohibiting sex discrimination in the law, as well as a school prayer amendment, a flag burning amendment, a balanced budget amendment, a campaign finance amendment, and an Electoral College amendment. The fact that amending the Constitution is so difficult illustrates the intense desire of the public to add a bill of rights, since the first ten amendments were added in a single year.

The main body of the Constitution was ratified in 1788, but by law it formally took effect in March 1789. National elections were then held according to the Constitution. The Federalists were elected to majorities in both chambers of Congress, along with their Presidential candidate, George Washington. True to their word as promised, the Federalists set out to use the constitutional amendment process to add a bill of rights to the Constitution. James Madison had been elected a representative from Virginia in the U.S. House of Representatives. Madison took upon himself the task of drafting a proposal for a bill of rights. Madison came up with a proposed list of seventeen amendments. He introduced these to Congress in June, 1789, only three months after the Constitution took formal effect. The rights Madison proposed included free speech, religious liberty, and guarantees of fair criminal process. Other rights were proposed as well. These included an amendment re-iterating the concept of popular sovereignty, which declared the people have a right to revolution because political power is derived from the people. Congress passed twelve of Madison's seventeen suggested amendments, and the state legislatures ratified ten of those twelve Congressional proposals. The two that failed were setting a fixed numerical ratio of voters to representative, and mandating that congressional pay raises enacted by Congress do not take effect until after the next Congressional election. (Fun Fact: That proposal to limit when Congressional pay raises take effect later became the 27th Amendment to the Constitution in 1992. There thus seems to be no time limit for states to consider ratifying proposed amendments).

The concept of a bill of rights is not the same as the name of particular bills of rights. The bills of rights of different governments are usually given different names to differentiate them. Some examples are the United Nations Universal Declaration of Human Rights (1948) the Canadian Charter of Rights and Freedoms (1982) and the Charter of Fundamental Rights of the European Union (2000). The bill of rights of the United States has always simply been called "The U.S. Bill of Rights." In short, when referring to the general concept of *a* bill of rights, the term is not capitalized. However, when referring to the name of the particular listing of rights in the U.S. Constitution, capitalized letters are used: *the* Bill of Rights.

The Bill of Rights

The first ten amendments to the U.S. Constitution are collectively known as the U.S. Bill of Rights. These ten amendments themselves nowhere contain the phrase "Bill of Rights." Instead, this is simply the name that has always been given to this listing of powers the U.S. government does not have. The Bill of Rights is written broadly, so that they generally apply not just to citizens, but to all individuals within U.S. territory. This makes sense as well. Recall that the theory of natural rights found in the Declaration of Independence says that *all* individuals have inalienable rights that come from god. If this is the case, then natural rights apply to all people at all times in all locations. This is true regardless whether the person is a natural-born citizen, someone who became a citizen after birth, a legal resident, or a resident in a country illegally. The theory of natural rights says such rights cannot be taken away by human government. As a practical matter, the Supreme Court follows this approach with some exceptions. For example, confessed terrorists lose some of their constitutional rights regardless if they are a U.S. citizen.

Moreover, the Bill of Rights was originally intended to place limits only on the federal government. The language of some of the Amendments indicates this expressly. For example, the First Amendment begins by saying "*Congress* shall make no law . . ." In the early 1800's, the Supreme Court initially interpreted this language to mean the Bill of Rights do not put limits on state laws. However, in the 1900's the Supreme Court changed its view and declared that most of the rights in the Bill of Rights limit what state and local governments can do as well. The court said the Fourteenth Amendment, ratified in 1868 and which expressly limits state governments, "selectively incorporates" most of the Bill of Rights. In other words, the Fourteenth Amendment applies most of the limitations of the Bill of Rights against the state governments. Today, with a few minor exceptions, the U.S. Bill of Rights protects the rights of people in all U.S. territory against interference by all levels of government. Let's briefly examine each of the amendments.

The First Amendment: "*Congress shall make no law respecting an establishment of religion, or prohibiting the free exercise thereof; or abridging the freedom of speech, or of the press; or the right of the people peaceably to assemble, and to petition the Government for a redress of grievances.*"

The First Amendment includes the most basic democratic rights, as democracy cannot exist without the freedom of speech. Without the ability to discuss public policy issues, the citizenry can't make informed decisions about such policies. Without the ability to debate the effectiveness of government leaders, citizens can't reasonably exercise their right to vote. Put simply, the people can't govern themselves if they can't discuss how they should be governed. The rights in this amendment are so important that they will receive extensive separate discussion later, both in this chapter and the next.

The Second Amendment: "*A well regulated militia, being necessary to the security of a free state, the right of the people to keep and bear arms, shall not be infringed.*"

The Second Amendment is highly debated and controversial today. The historical evidence shows that at the time, the right to bear arms was viewed to exist for three reasons: self-defense, hunting, and protection of liberty. To understand this philosophy, consider life at the time. There was no police force, 95% of the population was rural farmers, and every able-bodied adult male was in the "militia."

Because of this, guns were necessary to protect one's family against attackers, to hunt game animals for food, and to form a defense force against invasion or tyranny. For example, the "Dissent of the Pennsylvania Minority" was written by several state constitutional delegates who voted against ratification of the U.S. Constitution. Their proposal for a bill of rights included the following: "That the people have a right to bear arms for the defence of themselves and their own state, or the United States, or for the purpose of killing game." Surprisingly, the U.S. Supreme Court never ruled directly on the meaning of the Second Amendment until the case of *D.C. v. Heller* in 2008. There, the Court said the Second Amendment contains an individual right to own a firearm in one's home for self-defense purposes.

The Third Amendment: "*No soldier shall, in time of peace be quartered in any house, without the consent of the owner, nor in time of war, but in a manner to be prescribed by law.*"

The Third Amendment is often called the forgotten amendment. During the Revolutionary War, England needed lodging for its troops as they fought across the United States. England insisted the U.S. was still an English colony. English army commanders expected "English colonists" to remain "loyal" by feeding British troops and letting them stay in their homes. All this was demanded without any financial compensation being provided. The people were so angry at this practice that they restricted it in the Bill of Rights.

The Fourth Amendment: "*The right of the people to be secure in their persons, houses, papers, and effects, against unreasonable searches and seizures, shall not be violated, and no warrants shall issue, but upon probable cause, supported by oath or affirmation, and particularly describing the place to be searched, and the persons or things to be seized.*"

The Fourth, Fifth, Sixth, and Eight Amendments for the most part contain the rights of criminal defendants. These rights are also referred to as the rights of criminal suspects or the rights of the criminally accused. Collectively, they also can be referred to as *due process* rights. "Due process" simply means "fair procedure." None of these terms, however, fully captures the meaning and importance of these rights. In a tyrannical government, any person who disagrees with the government is subject to immediate arrest, fine, imprisonment, torture, or execution. The person will not be told the charges against them, they will not be told what the evidence is against them, they will not allowed to present their own side in their own defense, they will not be allowed to have a lawyer, and they will be given a biased judge who has already reached a foregone conclusion of guilt. It will often be the case that none of that person's family will ever know their loved one has been arrested, and they will never be told what happened to the individual. The person just "disappears" one day never to be seen again.

Madison, Congress, and the state legislatures that ratified the Bill of Rights wanted to prohibit government from doing any of these things that tyrannical governments do. It's critical to understand that oppressive government do these things not just to criminals, but mostly to innocent civilians. The Bill of Rights is therefore intended to protect *all* individuals living within the United State against being falsely charged and wrongly convicted. If the government begins to do any of the actions prohibited by the Bill of Rights, not only would it be unconstitutional, it would serve as a warning to the public that the government is beginning to display the marks of tyranny. Indeed, notice that collectively, the rights of criminal defendants make up the large majority of all the rights found in the Bill of Rights. Preventing and exposing tyranny was therefore an extremely important goal of the people who wrote and ratified the Bill of Rights. Government violations of these due process rights serve as "the canary in the coal mine," warning of invisible but lurking danger.

The Fourth Amendment in particular protects the privacy of your body, home, vehicle, and personal information against unreasonable government intrusion. For example, if you are walking in a public place, police generally cannot make you stop and answer questions unless the police have some "reasonable, articulable suspicion" that criminal activity is possibly occurring. Police also generally may not stop you in your automobile unless they have "probable cause" that a crime is occurring or has occurred. And, police many not enter your home without a warrant issued by a judge, and this warrant must be based on "probable cause" of criminal activity. The Supreme Court has created many specific exceptions to these rules, however. These include if you consent to the search, or if there are emergency ("exigent") circumstances where someone's life may be in immediate danger. In general, though, government may not search or seize your property without having at least some degree of suspicion that you have been engaged in wrongdoing.

In the landmark case of *Mapp v. Ohio* (1961), the Supreme Court ruled that if your Fourth Amendment or other constitutional rights are violated, then any evidence against you gained by the police through violating your rights is inadmissible in court. This is known as the "exclusionary rule," although the Court later added a few narrow exceptions. For example, one exception includes if the evidence would have been inevitably discovered anyway through other legal means.

The Fifth Amendment:" *No person shall be held to answer for a capital, or otherwise infamous crime, unless on a presentment or indictment of a grand jury, except in cases arising in the land or naval forces, or in the militia, when in actual service in time of war or public danger; nor shall any person be subject for the same offense to be twice put in jeopardy of life or limb; nor shall be compelled in any criminal case to be a witness against himself, nor be deprived of life, liberty, or* *property, without due process of law; nor shall private property be taken for public use, without just compensation.*

Among the rights listed in the Fifth Amendment are the fact that you can not be tried twice for the same crime if you were found "not guilty" the first time. A second attempt at prosecuting you would be called "double jeopardy," which is forbidden by the Fifth Amendment. You also have a right to refuse to testify against yourself in a criminal trial. This is commonly known as "pleading the Fifth."

Part of the right not to be a witness against yourself means you must be aware when the police might use whatever you say against you. In the landmark Supreme Court case of *Miranda v. Arizona* (1966), the Court announced that if you are or arrested or even under questioning based on suspicion, police must warn you of your right to not speak. The police must also let you know that if you do speak, they can use whatever you say in a court of law to convict you. Because of the case name where this ruling came from, this information came to be known as "Miranda rights" and the words the policy say came to be called the "Miranda warning."

Besides guaranteeing certain rights of criminal defendants, the last part of the Fifth Amendment guarantees that your private property, typically your home or land, cannot be taken by the government unless it is for a use that benefits the public as a whole. This power of government to take private property for a public purpose (such as for a park, road, school, etc.) is called the power of "eminent domain." If your property is confiscated by the government through the use of eminent domain, however, under the Fifth Amendment you must receive fair compensation for the value of your property.

The Sixth Amendment: *"In all criminal prosecutions, the accused shall enjoy the right to a speedy and public trial, by an impartial jury of the state and district wherein the crime shall have been committed, which district shall have been previously ascertained by law, and to be informed of the nature and cause of the accusation; to be confronted with the witnesses against him; to have compulsory process for obtaining witnesses in his favor, and to have the assistance of counsel for his defense."*

The Sixth Amendment includes several important rights, including the right to be told of the charges against you, the right to cross-examine your accusers, the right to a jury trial, and the right to an attorney. This latter right was expanded by the Supreme Court in the landmark case *Gideon v. Wainwright* (1963) to include a right to have the government provide you with a free lawyer if you can't afford one. The Supreme Court has also said your appointed lawyer must provide effective assistance of counsel for the right to assistance of counsel to be meaningful. For example, imagine you're on trial for a crime, especially where the evidence is slim, but your appointed lawyer sleeps throughout the entire trial. If you're found guilty, you would likely be able to sue for a retrial on the grounds of ineffective assistance of counsel.

The Seventh Amendment: *"In suits at common law, where the value in controversy shall exceed twenty dollars, the right of trial by jury shall be preserved, and no fact tried by a jury, shall be otherwise reexamined in any court of the United States, than according to the rules of the common law."*

Besides the protection the Bill of Rights gives to the rights of defendants in criminal cases, the Seventh Amendment guarantees certain jury trial rights in *civil* cases as well. If you sue someone in federal court, or if you are sued, you have a right to a jury trial in most cases.

The Eight Amendment: *"Excessive bail shall not be required, nor excessive fines imposed, nor cruel and unusual punishments inflicted."*

The Eight Amendment prohibits the government from inflicting torture or other humiliating or inhumane punishments. What constitutes "cruel and unusual punishment," however, is often disputed. For example, the controversial technique of "waterboarding" makes a person feel like they are drowning, but without drowning them. Parts of the U.S. military and U.S. Central Intelligence Agency (CIA) have admitted to using waterboarding on terror suspects as a means to trying to gain information from them. Whether waterboarding is a constitutionally permissible means of fighting the "war on terror" has not been yet ruled on by the U.S. Supreme Court.

The Ninth Amendment: "*The enumeration in the Constitution, of certain rights, shall not be construed to deny or disparage others retained by the people.*"

Recall Hamilton's concern in Federalist Paper No. 84 that listing the rights of the people risks losing any rights that are left off that list. When it came time to write the Bill of Rights, Madison remembered Hamilton's concern. Madison believed he could solve this problem by expressly declaring in the Bill of Rights that the people still have other rights that aren't listed. He also thought the Bill of Rights should clearly state that no court should ever interpret the Bill of Rights as implying the rights listed there are the *only* rights people have. The Ninth Amendment essentially says "The people have other rights that we haven't listed here." Since these other rights are not listed, these rights are referred to as "unenumerated rights."

The Tenth Amendment: "*The powers not delegated to the United States by the Constitution, nor prohibited by it to the States, are reserved to the States respectively, or to the people.*"

Recall our earlier discussion of the compromise over federalism in the original Constitution. A list of a few powers would be given to the federal government, and the states would keep all remaining government powers. The main body of the Constitution enumerates the powers of Congress, but left out any explanation that all other powers were still kept by the states. The Tenth Amendment adds back that sentence left out of the Constitution. It makes expressly clear that the states have reserved powers under the Constitution. Yet, as we also saw when we looked at the evolution of federalism, the Tenth Amendment has since been interpreted to be nearly meaningless today. That is, with few exceptions, the Supreme Court has declared the Tenth Amendment reserves almost no specific powers or rights to the state government.

Unenumerated Rights

Recall from the beginning of this chapter that Hamilton argued in Federalist Paper No. 84 against having a Bill of Rights. He suggested that if a list of rights is created, then any rights that are not on that list are forfeited, and government can completely interfere with those unlisted rights. Also recall that Madison believed he had solved this potential problem. The Ninth Amendment would protect any rights that were left unlisted in the Bill of Rights or the rest of the Constitution. The past two centuries have, for the most part, proven Hamilton relatively correct in his prophecy. Within only a few years after the Bill of Rights was enacted, a majority of the Supreme Court declined to interpret the Ninth Amendment as protecting any specific rights that are not already listed in the Constitution. Still to this day, no Supreme Court case has ever declared any particular right to be protected by the Ninth Amendment.

The problem is that nowhere did Madison ever list the "other" rights the Ninth Amendment refers to. The Federalist Papers do not list these other rights, nor do any writers, historians, or legal scholars of that time period. One constitutional scholar, Judge Robert Bork, famously said the situation was as if ink was spilled on the only original copy of the Ninth Amendment just after it was written. Imagine even the best modern technology is unable to determine what text is under the inkblot. The Ninth Amendment would simply say "The other rights are ___________." If this were the situation, there seems to be no principled way to determine what "other rights" the Ninth Amendment intended to list. It would simply be the whim of the justices on the Supreme Court as to how to fill in the blank. The most reasonable and fair solution, then, is to simply conclude that the Ninth Amendment is meaningless and unenforceable. This means that the only enforceable rights people have are those expressly listed in the Constitution, just as Hamilton said would happen.

Despite the Supreme Court's refusal to read any rights into the Ninth Amendment, in the late 1900's the Court began to declare a handful of rights to be protected by the Constitution even though these rights are nowhere listed in the Constitution. Rather than applying the Ninth Amendment, the Court said these unlisted, or "*unenumerated*" rights come from the Fourteenth Amendment to the Constitution, which was ratified in 1868. (We'll cover the Fourteenth Amendment in more detail in the next chapter, "Civil Rights."). There are two parts of the

Fourteenth Amendment in which the Supreme Court has protected unenumerated rights. The Privileges and Immunities Clause of the Fourteenth Amendment states "No state shall make or enforce any law which shall abridge the privileges or immunities of citizens of the United States." This clause does not specify what the particular "privileges" or "immunities" of citizens are. In the late 1900's, however, the Supreme Court declared the right to travel is a basic right that is impliedly protected by this clause.

More significantly, the Fourteenth Amendment's Due Process Clause states "nor shall any state deprive any person of life, liberty, or property, without due process of law." As we discussed earlier in this chapter, the term "due process" generally means "fair procedure." The Supreme Court has declared that the Due Process Clause requires fair procedure not just in criminal trials, but in questions such as termination of parental rights, institutionalization of mentally ill persons, denial of government benefits such as social security disability payments, and school disciplinary hearings. The Due Process Clause contains the word "liberty." In the late 1900's, the Supreme Court began to rule that there are certain rights inherent in the concept of "liberty" that cannot be taken away by the government no matter how fair the procedure. That is, the *substance* of the right will be protected regardless of *any* procedure the government might try to use to interfere with that right. As a result, this concept is known as "substantive due process."

Specifically, the Supreme Court has declared that the word "liberty" in the Due Process Clause protects a cluster of related rights. This group of rights is sometimes called the "right of privacy." A more accurate term is *familial* privacy, or privacy involving one's family. The concept of "privacy" in this context does not refer to keeping information confidential or secret. Instead, it refers to intimate private *decisions* that should be made only by one's family and not the government. In other words, "familial privacy" means you have the right to make some personal decisions involving you and your family without the government interfering with that decision or making the decision for you. This includes decisions about sex, procreation, childrearing, marriage, and the right to refuse unwanted medical treatment. Put simply, between consenting adults you can choose whether to have a romantic or sexual relationship with someone, and you can choose who to have that relationship with. You can then choose whether to get married or not. Whether you decide to get married or remain unmarried, you can choose whether to have children. If you have children, you can choose how to raise those children. You can send them to private school or teach them yourself, and you can teach them any language, or given them any religious or political views. And, if you become ill, you have a right to refuse medicine, food, and water. This is technically not a "right to die" because there is no right to accelerate death by suicide or doctor-assisted suicide. You may only refuse measures that prolong dying.

The general concept of familial privacy itself is not too controversial. After all, very few people would say, for example, that the government should be able to force people into random arranged marriages as part of a mandatory human breeding program. Yet the precise boundaries of the right of familial privacy have been controversial. The Supreme Court has declared that part of the freedom to choose whether to have children includes a right to use contraception as a means of preventing pregnancy from occurring. In 1973, in the case of *Roe v. Wade*, the Court declared that abortion was a means of contraception. That decision has resulted in decades of political battles at the state and federal level, both in legislatures and in the courts. In 2003, in *Lawrence v. Texas*, the Supreme Court expanded the right to choose a romantic or sexual partner of your choice to include same-sex relationships as well. In 2015, in *Obergefell v. Hodges*, the Supreme Court declared the general right to marriage includes a right to marry someone of the same sex. These decisions have been controversial as well. In short, it's not so much the right of privacy itself, but the *definition* of that right, that has been politically disputed. The outer boundaries of the right to familial privacy have yet to be precisely defined, and so will probably remain controversial in the future.

WHY FREE EXPRESSION?

We noted earlier that the First Amendment contains the most basic political rights. For this reason, we're going to return now to more extensively consider the two rights that make up the First Amendment. The freedom of expression will be discussed in the remainder of this chapter, and religious liberty will be covered in the next chapter. The term "freedom of speech" is sometimes misunderstood as only protecting spoken words. That is incorrect, as the First Amendment protects *all* forms of communication, not just verbal "speech." A more accurate term, then, is the "freedom of expression." The freedom of expression includes all forms of communication: writing and speaking, radio and TV broadcasts and the internet. It also includes music, art, sculpture, the tattoos you have, and perhaps the clothes or jewelry you wear. The First Amendment also expressly contains the freedom of the press and the rights of petition and assembly, all of which are included by the general term "freedom of expression." That is, you have a right to meet with other people to share ideas, to complain to the government, and say what you want in the media. But why value these rights? Why have so many people cared so much about preserving the freedom of expression?

The freedom of expression is the most important right in a democracy because it is essential for democracy to function. A government can call itself a democracy, and even have voters choose candidates in elections. Yet without a right to freedom of expression, it is not a democracy. If there is no freedom to share ideas about the candidates, then the public has no idea whether these candidates offer a genuine choice. Indeed, as often happens in nations with sham elections, the controlling political party has outlawed all opposition parties, candidates and speech. The candidates appearing on the ballot are all from the same ruling political party and have been carefully chosen by the party leaders. This may give the outer illusion of democracy, but it is not genuine democracy. With no free speech, there is no way for the voters to make informed decisions, so whatever decision they do make is not a real choice. As one example, the former dictator in Iraq, Saddam Hussein, famously announced that he received 100% of the public's vote in the country's national election. He was the only candidate allowed on the ballot.

The democratic need for free speech is analogous to the concept of "informed consent" in medicine. Imagine you agree to have your arm amputated if a doctor tells you that it's the only way to cure an infection in a cut on your finger. Only later do you find out that the doctor didn't tell you would have been equally fine had you simply washed the cut out with soap and water. Your decision to have your arm amputated was not a *genuine* choice because you weren't aware of the alternative. The doctor in such a case could be sued or perhaps even charged with a crime. Likewise, a "democracy" without free speech is a democracy in name only, but is not *genuine* democracy—it is a fraud.

Beyond the need for free speech as a means of achieving democracy, in a broader context the ability to give and receive ideas is an essential means of discovering truth. This applies to truth of all kinds, not just political truths. This can include the most mundane ideas to the most profound. If you want to know whether to bring an umbrella with you on your way to work or school, you must be free to receive information about the weather forecast, and meteorologists must be free to give you that information. Or, if you want to know whether there is a god or gods, and whether the god or gods have moral rules you're supposed to live by, then people must be free to share such ideas. There is no way you can ever hope to learn the truth about *anything* unless you are free to explore all the competing ideas about the topic you are researching. This is why the freedom of speech is often described by the metaphor of the "marketplace of ideas."

The marketplace of ideas can be compared to a physical market. In a store, brands and products compete with each other through advertising. In this way people are able to choose which product to buy. If you need toilet paper, should you buy the brand that is cheapest? Softest? Decorated with floral designs? Scented? Or made of recycled paper? Similarly, in the marketplace of ideas, people express competing ideas about politics, religion, and every other subject. All the different beliefs advertise their views and attack the flaws in each other. Only in this way can you have a realistic chance of knowing which idea is "better" or "best" or "correct," so that you can "buy" that belief. This means even the ideas you believe are false, or bad, or evil, must be allowed to equally compete head-to-head with the ideas you like. The ideas that are able to withstand vigorous criticism will come out ahead. Without such competition, you can't be certain which ideas are better, best, or correct. Again then, just as with informed medical consent or informed democratic voting, a decision to adopt idea "X" about the weather or religion is not a genuine choice unless you've been fully exposed to competing ideas. Only if you've considered ideas "Y," "Z," "QQQ" and "Not-X" can you consider whether idea "X" is worth adopting. Only then is your belief genuinely arrived at by a full and accurate comparison of the alternatives. The importance of the freedom of expression as a means of truth-finding was defended by the 1700's French philosopher Francis M. Voltaire. He famously declared "I disapprove of what you say, but I will defend to the death your right to say it."

There is another purpose for the freedom of speech that more modern thinkers have advocated. If someone were to ask you what is the most important part of your personal identity, what would you say? That is, what makes you *unique* as a human being compared to everyone else? You probably wouldn't describe your favorite color or favorite food. Instead, you would talk about personal, deeply cherished beliefs. These would include your political views, your religious beliefs about the meaning of life, and the moral principles and values that you follow. The inability to share this identity with others would deny you the ability to express your individuality. This would result in social conformity to the point where we would be little more than clones, or robots programmed by the government. Stated oppositely, the freedom to seek out, choose, and express one's beliefs are essential to personal freedom and autonomy. In short, although we have *potential* to be individuals, the freedom of expression is necessary if we hope to realize and actualize that potential. Free expression is thus essential to our very humanity.

Free Expression Rights

We've just considered the justifications most commonly given for protecting the freedom of expression. Now let's see how the U.S. Supreme Court has interpreted and applied the First Amendment's Free Speech Clause. The relevant part of the First Amendment reads "Congress shall make *no* law abridging the freedom of speech . . . " Notice that free speech would be absolutely protected if the First Amendment were read literally. Yet the First Amendment was never intended by Madison or the ratifiers of the First Amendment to be read in a literal sense. Nor has the Supreme Court ever interpreted it this way. Instead, the freedom of expression is always a matter of balancing the values of free speech versus the interest in government or society in limiting such speech. In other words, the values of truth, democracy, and individuality compete against social values like preventing violence and protecting people's reputations.

There are two ways any government might try to regulate speech. The first is regulating the method of speech. The second is regulating the content of speech. Limiting the *method* means limiting the time, place, or manner of expression. This would include things like noise ordinances that prohibit loudspeakers being used in residential neighborhoods at night. It can also include prohibiting students from yelling speeches during class time when school is in formal session. You have every right to use your own private time to tell your fellow students to worship the ghost of Elvis. On the other hand, you have no right to shout over a teacher who is presenting a math lesson during official class time. Such *time, place, and manner regulations* need to be at least "reasonable." They might be held to a higher legal standard as well if the speech is occurring in a public park, street, or sidewalk.

Besides constraining the manner of communication, the other way to limit speech is to restrict the *content*. The term "content" here means the particular topic or subject matter of the speech. The Supreme Court has generally created three different levels of First Amendment protection that apply to content-based restrictions, depending on the content.

1. *Strong protection:* Political and religious beliefs and opinions, no matter how bizarre or unpopular, are the most highly protected level of free speech under the First Amendment. These types of speech are considered to be the core of the reason for the First Amendment. The expression of political and religious beliefs therefore receive nearly absolute protection, with the exceptions noted below. As the U.S. Supreme Court once famously declared in the free speech case *Gertz v. Welch* (1972), constitutionally "there is no such thing as a false idea."

2. *Intermediate protection*: Commercial speech such as business advertising or product labeling receives a relatively high degree of constitutional protection by the First Amendment, but not quite as much as political or religious speech. For example, businesses can be required to print ingredients and nutrition information on their food products. By comparison, government can't require you to wear clothes that warn everyone about your political or religious beliefs. This is something Adolf Hitler's Nazi Germany did in requiring Jews to visibly wear a large Star of David to "warn" other Germans about their religion. Also, conduct that communicates a message is also called "symbolic" speech. Since the term "symbolic speech" might confuse people into thinking it contains verbal or written speech, however, many scholars prefer the term "communicative conduct." Such actions can be more regulated than merely spoken or written speech. The regulation of communicative conduct includes elementary and high school dress codes that regulate clothing, hair, and jewelry as a means of enforcing school discipline. Also, burning a flag as a form of political protest can be banned if the fire itself poses a danger, such as in a national forest during a drought in which a fire ban is in effect.

3. *Little or no protection*: The Supreme Court has said there are several types of expression which have little to do with the values behind the freedom of speech. That is, the speech has little to do with truth, democracy, or personal expression, and there are significant social harms caused by such speech. Therefore, society has strong reasons to prohibit such speech. Unprotected types of speech include threats, advocating immediate violence, and provoking people to react violently to you. This latter type of speech is legally called "fighting words." Also, extremely hard-core pornography is legally called "obscenity." Legally obscene materials are not protected by the First Amendment as free speech. In addition, "defamation" is falsely injuring someone's reputation. In the landmark case *New York Times v. Sullivan* (1964), the Supreme Court declared that defamation receives little protection by the First Amendment. All these types of speech have little to do with communicating ideas. Even to the degree they might, any slight value in their message is greatly outweighed by the social interests in public safety, security, or morality.

This three-tiered description is somewhat oversimplified. The various types of speech listed in the three categories often have long and complex technical legal definitions with exceptions. Also, the degree of government regulation allowed also can vary with the context. For example, more regulation of speech is allowed in prisons, government employment, public schools, and the broadcast media.

However, regardless of the content or context of speech, the Supreme Court has declared that the First Amendment never allows the government to engage in what is called *viewpoint discrimination.* Viewpoint discrimination occurs when a topic is discussed, but only one side of that topic is allowed to be presented. If, for example, a local government-owned public access cable-TV channel decided to allow political campaign advertisements, they could not accept ads only from Republican candidates but not from Democratic candidates. If that occurred, this would be impermissible viewpoint discrimination. Similarly, it would be a violation of the First Amendment if a public university held a public forum on whether the U.S. should move to a system of universal health care, but then allowed only speakers who supported the idea.

A classic example of unconstitutional viewpoint discrimination occurred in the controversial flag-burning case *Texas v. Johnson* in 1989. In Texas, as in all states, it is legal to burn the U.S. flag as a means of proper disposal of the flag. This might occur if, for example, the flag has become tattered and torn from weathering and age. Yet Texas banned burning the U.S. flag if done to show disrespect. The law was a textbook example of viewpoint discrimination, in that it allowed an activity when expressing one view, but outlawed the identical action when done to express the opposite view. Johnson was arrested for burning the U.S. flag as part of a political protest. The Supreme Court overturned his conviction, noting that both the flag-burning law and Johnson's prosecution struck at the very core of the protections of the First Amendment. That is, Johnson was expressing a political idea.

Both before and after *Texas v. Johnson*, the modern Court has generally given broad protections to speech under the First Amendment. For example, in *Snyder v. Phelps* (2011) the Westboro Baptist Church of Topeka, Kansas, led by the Reverend Fred Phelps, protested outside a Maryland military funeral of deceased Iraq War veteran Michael Snyder. The church believes that according to their interpretation of the Bible, all gay people should be killed for violation of god's laws. Because the U.S. does not execute gays and lesbians, the church believes that the U.S. government and any soldier fighting to defend it are all going to hell. The church therefore regularly protests outside U.S. military funerals in order to spread their message. They held anti-gay and anti-military signs and chanted related slogans at the funeral of Michael Snyder. These actions deeply angered Michael Snyder's father, Albert Snyder. Maryland law allows a victim of "extreme and outrageous conduct" to sue the person engaged in that conduct for "intentional infliction of emotional distress." The church, however, argued they had a First Amendment right to engage in their protest. The Supreme Court ruled on the side of the church, declaring that states many not allow this kind of civil lawsuit when the speech in question involves a public issue. Since gay rights and U.S. military policy are public issues, Albert Snyder could not sue Reverend Phelps for his offensive words, regardless how hateful the words were. The First Amendment protects political and religious ideas, no matter how "offensive" those ideas are.

As we've seen in earlier chapters, the purpose of the U.S. Constitution was to limit government, or else no Constitution would have been necessary. Similarly, and as the Court explained in *Texas v. Johnson*, and again in *Snyder v. Phelps,* the very purpose of the First Amendment was to protect unpopular ideas, or else no First Amendment would be needed. That is, a democratic majority will never outlaw speech it likes or agrees with. Instead, it will only attempt to restrict ideas it is offended by. The very point of having a First Amendment, then, is to protect the expression of offensive and unpopular views like Johnson's. Otherwise, if the First Amendment did not protect offensive speech, it would become a meaningless right. As people in the U.S. like to say, "It's a free country!" Yet it will remain so only if the people fight to keep it that way. In short, if we value the freedom of expression and want to keep it, we must do as the French philosopher Voltaire said. That is, we must defend the right to speak even by those whose views offend us.

SUMMARY

Civil liberties are our basic political freedoms. The Bill of Rights protects these freedoms by listing or enumerating our rights. A right is simply a power the government does not have. Although the U.S. Constitution did not originally contain a bill of rights, winning attacks from the Anti-Federalists on this point meant the Federalists had to agree to add a bill of rights to the Constitution. The first ten amendments to the U.S. Constitution are known as the U.S. Bill of Rights. Besides containing core political freedoms like the freedom of speech and religious liberty, there are many legal protections for persons accused of crimes. The Ninth Amendment in the Bill of Rights declares the people have other rights not listed in the Bill of Rights, but the Supreme Court has said the Ninth Amendment does not protect any unlisted rights. Instead, the Supreme Court has said the Fourteenth Amendment protects unenumerated rights even though it does not indicate that it does. These rights mostly involve a general right of familial privacy, which includes specific rights to make personal decisions involving sex, marriage, procreation, and childrearing free from government interference. The outer boundaries of these rights remain controversial because they include rights such as abortion and same-sex marriage. The First Amendment in the Bill of Rights contains the rights of free expression and religious liberty. Free speech is essential for democracy to exist, and is necessary in the search for truth. The Supreme Court has therefore said political and religious speech is almost absolutely protected by the First Amendment. Some types of speech, however, such as threats or falsely harming people's reputations, have little to do with democracy or the search for truth. Therefore, the Supreme Court has declared these other types of speech are not protected as "free" speech by the First Amendment. Regardless of the type of speech, though, the government may never allow only one side of an issue while prohibiting opposing viewpoints.

Questions for Review and Self-Assessment

1. What is the definition and purpose of a bill of rights, and what was the nature of the debate over whether the U.S. should have a bill of rights?
2. How was the U.S. Bill of Rights written and ratified?
3. What are the rights found in the U.S. Bill of Rights?
4. What are currently the unenumerated rights protected by the Constitution?
5. What is the purpose and current protections of the Free Speech Clause of the First Amendment?

Critical Thinking Questions for Reflection and Discussion

1. Should the U.S. Bill of Rights prohibit torture, even if we believe we are certain of a murderer's or terrorist's guilt?
2. Should the U.S. Bill of Rights protect burning the U.S. flag as free speech?
3. Should the U.S. Constitution protect rights not listed in the Constitution?

Suggested Reading Supplements

- Brutus, *Essay No. II,*
- *Federalist Paper No. 84*
- *New York Times v. Sullivan* (1964)
- *Roe v. Wade* (1973)
- *Texas v. Johnson* (1989)
- *Snyder v. Phelps* (2011)
- *Obergefell v. Hodges* (2015)

For Further Advanced Reading

- Akhil Reed Amar, *The Bill of Rights: Creation and Reconstruction*
- Leonard Levy, *Origins of the Bill of Rights*

CHAPTER 8: RELIGIOUS LIBERTY

THE BIG PICTURE

Most of the English Colonies in America originally had officially established religions. A diverse political coalition of different religions and different religious denominations organized to end these religious establishments. The opposition groups united around their shared religious beliefs. They then incorporated these shared beliefs into the founding documents of the United States and in early governmental practices. This importantly involved avoiding theological disputes over religious doctrines while generally promoting religiously based moral education. Collectively, these principles and practices basically require that government policy remains neutral between competing religious beliefs. And, many U.S. laws also prohibit private discrimination on the basis of religion.

RELEVANT TIMELINE

- 1776 U.S. Declaration of Independence
- 1777 Articles of Confederation
- 1785 James Madison publishes his *Memorial and Remonstrance*
- 1786 Virginia Statute for Religious Freedom
- 1789 U.S. Constitution ratified
- 1791 U.S. Bill of Rights (including the First Amendment) ratified
- 1797 Treaty of Tripoli
- 1947 *Everson v. Board of Education* (law must be religiously neutral)
- 1990 *Employment Division v. Smith* (religiously neutral laws valid)

CHAPTER OBJECTIVES

After reading this chapter, the reader should be able to:

1. Define religious establishment and describe the nature of such establishments in England's thirteen American colonies.
2. Describe the diverse political-religious coalition that argued for disestablishment around the time of U.S. independence.
3. Describe how the shared, common religious beliefs of the disestablishment coalition were reflected in the founding documents and early practices of the U.S.
4. Explain how the founders of the U.S. intended a "loose" separation of church and state, as opposed to strict separation or a "Christian nation."

5. Describe how the Supreme Court's interpretation of the First Amendment's religion clauses basically requires government neutrality between religions in various different contexts.
6. Describe some of the ways in which U.S. laws prohibits private discrimination on the basis of religion.

RELIGIOUS ESTABLISHMENTS

Besides the freedom of expression, religious liberty is another key foundation of the United States. Yet probably no other constitutional issue is as misunderstood by the public. Indeed, mistaken notions are rampant about the personal religious beliefs and original constitutional intent of the Founders of the U.S. Moreover, these incorrect ideas have caused major controversies in recent years over the role of religion and government in U.S. society. Because of the importance of this issue, combined with the exceptionally widespread misinformation about it, we will devote a full chapter to religious liberty.

To understand the thinking of the early U.S. founders on this issue, we must first look at the nature of religious liberty—or the lack thereof—in Europe and the American colonies before U.S. independence. In Europe, for well over a thousand years leading up to the time of American independence, the nations of Europe had *religious establishments.* This meant that each nation's government declared a particular denomination of Christianity to be the official religion of that nation. For example, at the time of American Independence, Lutheranism was the established religion of Germany and the Scandinavian countries. Catholicism was the established religion of France, Spain, Portugal and Italy. Calvinism, the early precursor to Presbyterianism and a couple other Protestant denominations, was established in the Netherlands in the form of the Dutch Reformed Church. And, England had the Anglican Church, part of which later became the Episcopal Church in the United States. The established religion of a nation was given preference in the law, such as financial support from the government. Also, typically members of other religions could not hold political office or receive other governmental privileges. Indeed, people who were not members of the established religion were often fined, imprisoned, beaten, tortured, or even executed.

Europe had a terrible experience with religious establishments. There were three main public policy problems caused by religious establishments. First, as was just noted, members of minority religions were severely persecuted. Members of all the disfavored religions and religious denominations were punished by law, sometimes fatally. It wasn't just official government sanction that did this, either. As a practical matter, groups belonging to the established religion were generally given partial or full immunity for committing private acts of persecution against individuals who belonged to other religions. Mobs belonging to the dominant established religion often terrorized, beat, or murdered individuals, families, and sometimes even entire communities of minority religions. As merely one atrocious example, in the 1500's thousands of Anabaptists, early forerunners of modern Baptists, were systematically hunted down and murdered in what is today Germany, Austria, and Switzerland.

Second, religious civil wars resulted from different religious denominations fighting for control of government. Each side knew that if they could take political power, they could then establish themselves as the official government religion. They could then use the law backed up by military force to persecute their religious opponents. For example, in the mid-1600's there was a war between Protestants and Catholics for control of Ireland. On the main continent of Europe, between 1618 and 1648 there was a devastating "30-Years' War" between Protestant and Catholic nations for control of the remnants of the Holy Roman Empire. Deaths from combat, disease, and starvation, were between 3 and 11 *million* people across Europe, including about a third of the population of what is now Germany and the Czech Republic.

A third main problem resulting from religious establishments was the corruption of religion. Government recognition, preference, and support of a religion typically gave the government control over the teachings and practices of that religious denomination. In other words, favoritism came with strings attached, and those in political control often pulled those strings. As merely one widespread example, the religious leaders of the established churches typically told their congregations that the political leaders were chosen by God. Therefore, the rulers had to be obeyed absolutely and without question. Basically, religious leaders indoctrinated masses with the theory of Divine Right. Most people were illiterate at the time other than the political and religious elites. As a result, the uneducated masses completely trusted and believed the interpretations of the Bible that they were given by their priests and ministers. Many political thinkers and religious reformers in the 1600's and 1700's therefore argued that religious establishments had placed the authority of man above the authority of God. Religious leaders and institutions had been corrupted by the wealth and power they were given by the political system. As a result, the sinful, corrupt teachings of humans had replaced the pure, wholesome teachings of God. These writers also often argued that true faith must be a voluntary choice of the internal human will. A false outward profession of belief forced upon one and motivated by fear of punishment would not be genuine.

In the English colonies in the Americas, only a minority of four colonies never had established churches. These colonies were Pennsylvania, Delaware, New Jersey, and Rhode Island. Most of the rest of the colonies had established the Anglican Church, also known as the Church of England. The exceptions were Connecticut,

New Hampshire, and Massachusetts, all of which were Congregationalists. They were the ancestors of the Puritans that had landed at Plymouth Rock, Massachusetts via the ship Mayflower in 1620. In sum, the majority of the colonies had established the Church of England as the established religion. This is not surprising, given that they were English colonies, and the Anglican Church was the established Church of England.

Of the three major problems that Europe had experienced as a consequence of creating religious establishments, the English colonies in America had experienced two of the three. Although the colonies had not undergone any religious civil wars, there had been heavy religious persecution of religious minorities. Some groups that experienced heavy persecution were Catholics, Baptists, and Quakers. Members of all minority religious groups, however, were denied political office and voting rights. Public speakers, newspapers, and Anglican and Congregationalist ministers regularly denounced members of other faiths as being of the devil. Anglican mobs regularly beat religious dissenters in public, occasionally burned their homes or businesses, and sometimes even murdered them. Probably the most infamous example of religious persecution in the colonies was the mass execution of alleged witches by Congregationalists. This incident is known as the Salem Witch Trials, because they occurred in Salem, Massachusetts in 1692-93.

The colonies also experienced the corruption of religious institutions. The same close, mutually-reinforcing relationship that existed in England between the government and the established Anglican Church was carried over to the colonies. Most particularly, since the Anglican Church was the established religion of most of the English colonies, it vigorously supported the authority of the English monarchy. Speech against either the King or against the colonial governors appointed by the King was outlawed in the colonies by the crime of "seditious libel." Anglican ministers not only supported such laws, these ministers condemned political criticism as sin. Criticism of the appointed rulers violated the theory of divine right of kings which was used to justify the rule of British monarchs. It was largely only ministers of the non-established religions that supported American rights, revolution and independence. Protestant (non-Catholic Christian) ministers from the non-established denominations argued that God and principles from the Christian Bible supported democracy and natural rights.

DISESTABLISHMENT

Given the widespread, systematic persecution of religious minorities in the colonies, a broad political coalition of the non-established religious groups increasingly pressed state governments to *disestablish* the state religions. These groups did not want a different established religion. Instead, they did not want *any* officially declared religion so that all people could share equal religious tolerance and liberty among themselves.

This diverse coalition included several Christian groups that were considered evangelical Protestants at the time: Presbyterians, Methodists, Lutherans, Quakers, and Baptists. Although all non-Anglicans were sometimes beaten by Anglicans, Quakers and especially Baptists suffered regular beatings at the hands of Anglicans. Today we would call these acts hate crimes. Because of this persecution, Quakers and Baptists were exceptionally vigorous in arguing for disestablishment. Since the colonial governors and local appointed officials were mostly Anglican, Anglicans who committed violence against non-Anglicans because of their faith often received little or no punishment.

Catholics also were part of the political coalition that favored disestablishment. The colony of Maryland had originally been founded by Catholics. This resulted in a significant Catholic minority in the colonies, especially in Maryland. Due to a later takeover of the colony by England, though, the Anglican Church later became the established church in Maryland. At the time, Catholics were intensely hated by Anglicans, Congregationalists, and even many evangelical Protestants. Protestants accused Catholics of being "papists" on the alleged grounds that Catholics worshipped the Pope, not God. Even after U.S. independence, for a few years the constitutions of North Carolina and South Carolina gave equal political and religious rights only to *Protestant* Christians. For these reasons, Catholics strongly favored disestablishment. Indeed, anti-Catholic bias continued well into the 20th century. For example, President John F. Kennedy was the first Catholic president. His faith was an issue during the 1960 campaign among people who questioned whether Kennedy would be more loyal to the United States or to the Pope.

Besides Protestant and Catholic Christians, there were also non-Christian minorities that actively supported the disestablishment movement. These groups included significant minorities who held religious beliefs that were much more common then than today. One significant example was an unorganized group or religious believers who rejected Christianity, but did believe in a single god who guides and helps us in this life. These individuals went by various names at the time. Historians sometimes refer to this group as Providentialists, because they believed in the providence, or wisdom and control, of God.

Another substantial minority religion at the time was *deism*. This term came from the Latin *deus*, meaning "God." Deists believed in one god, but a god who does not get involved in human affairs. It would only be in the afterlife that we would be held accountable for our Earthly actions. Deists therefore rejected concepts like prayer, miracles, or god taking human form (such as Jesus). Deism was especially popular among the educated class. Colonial leaders like Benjamin Franklin, Thomas

Paine, John Adams, and Thomas Jefferson were admitted deists. James Madison, Alexander Hamilton, and George Washington all kept their religious views extremely private in their later years. However, people close to them reported them as either being deist or as having views consistent with, or leaning towards, deism.

There were other very small religious minorities who favored disestablishment. Jews were not as socially accepted as Christians or deists, but a few thousand colonists were Jewish. Other smaller groups included, atheists, agnostics, Muslims and Hindus. These latter groups were not very politically or socially accepted at the time and so exercised relatively little influence on the founding of the U.S.

As the American colonies became increasingly democratic, evangelical Protestants, Catholics, Providentialists, Deists and Jews worked together politically. They were able to increasingly win legislative victories to disestablish Anglicanism as the established religion of several colonies. Ministers and political leaders from this loose political and religious coalition argued that disestablishment was essential to preventing the problems that had resulted in Europe and the colonies. All religions must be tolerated equally. This way believers of all religions can practice their religions free from coercion that would force them to violate their conscience. No religion should be able to co-opt the power of government. Competing religious groups must not be able to use the power of government to establish their religion over "unbelievers." Otherwise, political divisiveness could lead to bigotry, persecution between different factions, and social violence. Ultimately, sectarian differences could fragment society and lead to religious civil war. Moreover, religion must be protected from the corrupting influence of worldly money and power that results from control by, or dependency on, government.

Numerous writers argued for disestablishment. Thomas Jefferson argued for disestablishment primarily on the grounds of preventing persecution. For example, in his reflections in his *Notes on the State of Virginia*, published in 1785, Jefferson announced "The rights of conscience we never submitted, we could not submit. We are answerable for them to our God. The legitimate powers of government extend to such acts only as are injurious to others. But it does me no injury for my neighbour to say there are twenty gods, or no god. It neither picks my pocket nor breaks my leg."

Isaac Backus was a leading Baptist minister and advocate for American Independence during the Revolutionary War. He argued for disestablishment primarily on the basis of keeping religion wholesome and pure. In a widely-read sermon he published in 1773, titled *An Appeal to the Public for Religious Liberty, Against the Oppressions of the Day*, Backus stated "Now who can hear Christ declare, that his kingdom is, *not of this world*, and yet believe that this blending of church and state together can be pleasing to him?" Many other leading ministers of the time argued for disestablishment on the same grounds.

Perhaps the single most well-known document explaining the reasons for minimizing the involvement between government and religion came from James Madison. In 1784, Patrick Henry, previous Governor of Virginian but now a member of the Virginia legislature, proposed that taxpayer money be used to help pay minister salaries. A flood of petitions against the proposal poured into the state legislature. Fellow Virginian James Madison also expressed opposition to the proposal in what became a classic statement against religious establishments. In Madison's *Memorial and Remonstrance Against Religious Assessments* published in 1785, he provided all the standard arguments for disestablishment. In one of his more famous statements from his writing, he argued that official state churches tend to corrupt the purity of religious institutions, people, and teachings. Madison proclaimed "During almost fifteen centuries has the legal establishment of Christianity been on trial. What have been its fruits? More or less in all places, pride and indolence in the clergy, ignorance and servility in the laity, in both, superstition, bigotry and persecution," By the next year, 1786, Virginia had disestablished the Anglican Church as the state religion. It also had passed the Virginia Statute for Religious Freedom, written by Thomas Jefferson. The statute specifically prohibited taxpayer money from being used to support *any* religion. The statute also guaranteed everyone the right to believe and worship as they desire without any negative legal consequence.

Not everyone was in favor of disestablishment, though. Anglicans and Congregationalists typically were against disestablishment precisely because their religions were the established religions. But their antidisestablishment position was losing to the larger disestablishment movement. Antidisestablishmentarians like Anglicans and Congregationalists failed to win enough public support for their belief in antidisestablishmentarianism. The disestablishment within Virginia was part of a tide of disestablishment across the new United States. Within a decade after the U.S. declared its independence from England, most of the new states had disestablished their official state religions. By the ratification of the First Amendment in 1791, only Connecticut and Massachusetts still had established religions. (Fun Fact: the word "antidisestablishmentarianism" is the largest non-technical, non-imaginary word in the English language.)

Religious Commonalities

It's important to note that the reason Madison, Jefferson, Backus, and the other Founders were against religious establishment was *not* because they were in any way hostile towards the concept of religion. Instead, as their writings and speeches show, they wanted to avoid government involvement with religion for the *protection* of religion. The believed that prohibiting government from entangling itself with religion protected not just religious minorities, but all religious believers in general, as well as religious institutions and teachings. Put differently, keeping churches separate from the state was and is designed to *nurture* religion. Religion free from government involvement may *flourish* free of the dangers of connection with government. Religion as a whole can't thrive if one religion is allowed to use political power to favor and promote itself only, or control and persecute the rest. Understanding these philosophical premises of disestablishment allows us to see what role religion did play in the founding of the United States.

In the first couple decades of the United States' existence, there were critical but fragile political coalitions at several major steps in the birth of the new nation. First, public support had to be gained for independence. Once enough support was gained among the colonists for *declaring* independence, the revolution still had be won. That is, the same fragile political coalition had to hold together until England could be defeated and independence actually *achieved*. Then, as we saw in earlier chapters, the Articles of Confederation failed, so a new Constitution had to be both written and then ratified. Political divisions within the U.S. threatened to defeat both the writing and the ratification of the Constitution.

Even after the Constitution was ratified, the U.S. was still a young, fragile democracy. The only way any democracy can succeed is if the people in charge willingly and peacefully hand over political power of the nation to their former political enemies after lose an election. This occurred in 1800, when the losing political party (The Federalists) peacefully handed over the presidency and control of Congress to the opposing party (The Democratic-Republicans). There was no attempt by the Federalists to overthrow the election results by using the military to maintain power against the Democratic-Republicans. Once governmental power was handed over to the Democratic-Republicans, there was no violent repression of the losing Federalists. People today often fail to realize what a remarkable event the peaceful transfer of political power between opposing parties was at that time in our planet's history. Such a thing was almost unheard of. Newly elected President Thomas Jefferson, winner of the 1800 election, understood how momentous this occasion was for the success of U.S. democracy. To maintain the sense of national unity, in his inaugural address he declared "We are all Republicans, we are all Federalists."

The critical point here is that the exposure of any social divisions threatened to destroy the entire attempt at creating a United States. Religion can and often does easily divide people. If allowed to do so, religious divisions could have easily destroyed the fragile political coalitions that achieved independence or the preservation of the U.S. through the writing and ratification of the Constitution. The majority of early American leaders realized that if they were to hold together politically to achieve their dream of creating a nation, they needed to avoid social division as much as possible. They therefore focused on their *common, shared* beliefs instead. This meant avoiding divisive issues like slavery or religion to the degree possible.

Recall from the chapter on federalism that under the Constitution, states were left to decide most questions of public policy on their own. Just as the Constitution's framers left each state to decide its own policy on the question of slavery, the Constitution's framers also left each state to decide whether and how to establish or disestablish their own *state* religions. Yet the issue of religion was also unlike the question of slavery in an important way. Slavery was an all-or-nothing moral and legal issue where there was no middle ground. When it came to the issue of religion, however, the vast majority of the colonists shared a "middle ground."

The vast majority of the early Americans were religious themselves. They believed religion was the philosophical and moral foundation of any society. Recall, for example, that the English philosopher John Locke had argued that the ideas of "rights" and "democracy" are based on god's moral laws. In agreement with Locke's theory, the early Americans wanted to incorporate religious concepts into the founding of the new nation. The Founders thus needed to balance their twin goals of having a religious foundation to government while at the same time avoiding religious divisions. To do so, the political groups wanting to establish the United States tried to focus exclusively on their *shared* religious beliefs while avoiding their religious differences.

Recall the primary religious groups that banded together for disestablishment: Baptists, Presbyterians, Methodists, Quakers, Catholics, Deists, Providentialists, and Jews. Although they did not all believe in the same god, they did share some core religious beliefs in common:

1. *There is a god.* The general term for belief in one god is theism, from the Greek "*theos*" meaning "god." More specifically, this belief can be called *monotheism*, meaning "one god."
2. *Morality comes from god.* Moral goodness is defined by this one god. This morality includes such principles as honesty, peace, caring for one another, respect for elders, and so on.
3. *God's morality includes liberty and democracy.* God's morality includes every human having an equal free will to choose good over evil. This unforced choice translates politically into democratic rights, and *not* unelected monarchy or tyranny. That is, the moral ability to choose includes the ability to select one's government.

4. *God will judge us.* God will eventually judge us some day in the afterlife both for our individual moral choices, and also for our collective decisions as nations. Good actions will be rewarded, and evil (sin) will be punished.

Despite the many theological differences among the religious groups favoring disestablishment, this political coalition repeatedly focused on their shared similarities and avoided theological debates. This broad religious coalition became a political majority and won political victories for disestablishment in the 1770's, 1780's and 1790's. As a result, they changed their state constitutions and the new federal Constitution to prohibit any religion from being the established state religion.

Religion in the Founding

In early 1776, the American colonists were deeply divided on whether to declare independence from England. Although we have no exact way to measure, historical analysts estimate that roughly one-third of the colonists wanted independence, one-third did not, and one-third were somewhat undecided. Those not wanting the colonies to break free from England were called "loyalists." One reason for their loyalty was they hoped to maintain the Church of England as the established religion. This establishment would be in great jeopardy if the colonies achieved independence. To keep their special status, members of the Anglican Church tended to oppose independence. On the other hand, the same religious groups that wanted disestablishment also typically wanted the Thirteen Colonies to be independent. Independence meant that England could not impose the Anglican Church as the official state religion. Given the deep division among Americans whether to pursue independence, supporters of independence needed to maintain their unity so as to attract new supporters. Anything that might religiously divide the supporters of independence was therefore carefully avoided as much as possible. Only their shared religious beliefs were focused on. This was especially true of the belief that god is on the side of liberty and democracy, and against monarchy. Numerous writings, speeches and religious sermons at the time stated that rule by an unelected king went against god's vision of what is good. Therefore, god was on the side of American independence and democracy.

As public support for independence from England increased throughout 1776, eventually the time came to declare independence. To appeal to, and maintain support from, the various religious groups that favored independence, religious terminology in the founding documents had to remain neutral. Only general religious terms and concepts that everyone agreed to could be used. This meant that divisive sectarian terms had to be carefully avoided. They could not use the name of any one religion or religious denomination, a particular religious deity, or a particular religious text. This meant they had to avoid the use of terms like Jesus, Christ, Christian, Christianity, Bible, Biblical, Jehovah, Yahweh, Judaism, Jewish, Deism, Trinity, Protestant, Catholic, and so on. Instead, the founders used religiously neutral terms and concepts that the broad coalition of theists could all agree on and support.

The 1776 U.S. Declaration of Independence contains all of the religious beliefs the Founders had in common at the time. However, it states these beliefs using only general terms in a way they could all agree upon:

1. *There is a god.* The Declaration of Independence references "God," "Creator," "divine providence" and "Supreme Judge."
2. *Morality comes from god.* The people have "the separate and equal station to which the Laws of Nature and of Nature's God entitle them"
3. *God's morality includes liberty and democracy.* "We hold these truths to be self-evident, that all men are created equal, that they are endowed by their Creator with certain unalienable Rights, that among these are Life, Liberty and the pursuit of Happiness."
4. *God will judge us.* "Appealing to the Supreme Judge of the world for the rectitude of our intentions" and "with a firm reliance on the protection of divine Providence."

In short, the Declaration of Independence bases the moral goodness of rights, liberty, and democracy all on the existence of a supreme being who will someday judge us on how we exercise those rights. According to the Declaration of Independence, this religiously moral foundation thereby justifies the United States existing as a separate, independent nation. As we saw in an earlier chapter, though, independence requires a government, and the 1777 Articles of Confederation was the first attempt at creating a government for the United States. It continues the policy of referencing the deity in neutral, general terms. It states that god favors the U.S. having this new government: "Whereas it hath pleased the Great Governor of the World to incline the hearts of the legislatures we respectively represent in Congress, to approve of, and to authorize us to ratify the said articles of confederation and perpetual union."

At this same time, in 1776 the new Congress assigned Benjamin Franklin, John Adams, and Thomas Jefferson to design a two-sided official "Great Seal," or symbol, of the United States. Although their full design was not adopted by Congress, the religious element they suggested was the "Eye of Providence"—that is, the "all-seeing eye" of god. The final design of the Great Seal, approved by the Congress in 1782, included the Eye of Providence. Congress also added the Latin phrase "Annuit Coeptis" to the great seal. *Annuit* means "he approves" and *coeptis* means "undertakings. The phrase is therefore most commonly translated as "He approves our undertakings" or "He favors our undertakings." The Great Seal of the United States thus incorporated religious beliefs common across the various groups of Christians, Deists, Providentialists, and Jews that there is a god, and that god is on the side of liberty and democracy. The U.S. government still uses the Great Seal in various ways. The most well-known use is that both sides of the Great Seal can be seen on the back of the U.S. one-dollar bill, where it was added in 1935.

When it came time to write and ratify the Constitution in 1787, as we saw earlier this required several major compromises on politically divisive issues. Religious divisions needed to be avoided as well. There was quite a political struggle to ratify the Constitution, and it barely passed. To gain as much political support possible, the writers of the Constitution continued to apply popular disestablishment principles by not connecting the U.S. government to any particular religion. They went even further, though. Article VI of the Constitution prohibits any religious test as a qualification to serve in office in the U.S. government. Specifically, "no religious test shall ever be required as a qualification to any office or public trust under the United States." Other than those religious references, the preamble to the Constitution merely notes that the purpose of the Constitution is to "secure the blessings of liberty." In other words, liberty comes from the moral goodness of god. Consistent with the language of the Constitution, nowhere in Madison's notes of the 1787 Constitutional convention or in the Federalist Papers is there any statement that the U.S. Constitution connected the U.S. government to any particular religion. Instead, the Federalist Papers merely compare the principles of U.S. democracy to ancient Greek and Roman democracies.

The First Amendment to the Constitution, added two years later in 1791, further strengthens the principle of disestablishment. The religion clauses of the First Amendment grant the free exercise of religion to all religious groups, and they prohibit the U.S. government from making any law involving an official establishment of religion. The exact language reads "Congress shall make no law respecting an establishment of religion, or prohibiting the free exercise thereof. . ." Together these two clauses make up the Establishment Clause and the Free Exercise Clause.

Maintaining religious neutrality in the founding documents was not enough to maintain religious unity. A brand new nation, especially the first ever of its kind, is a fragile undertaking. The last thing the early Americans wanted was for religious divisions to destroy what they had worked so hard to create. To prevent religious controversy, public speeches by the early presidents, especially their official statements like their Inaugural Addresses or Thanksgiving Proclamations, continued to use neutral theistic terms. They avoided sectarian terms or references like "Jesus" or "Christ." This would allow all the various monotheistic religious groups to agree with and support these public statements. For example, President Washington referred to the supreme deity as "almighty god" and "lord and ruler of nations." President Adams used terms like "supreme being" and "author of all good." President Madison called god the "great sovereign of the universe," "beneficient parent of the human race," and "divine author of every good and perfect gift." President Jefferson was so fearful of causing religious divisions that he decided not to issue any thanksgiving proclamations during his eight years as president. He thought it was better to say nothing than to risk using any religious terms or concepts that might shatter the religious peace.

At the same time, though, the early American political leaders, wanted Americans to be religious so that the people would be morally good. Remember that one of the common religious beliefs the early Americans shared was that morality came from god. Also, we would all be judged someday by that god for our moral choices. It was commonly thought that without this belief in eventual moral accountability in an afterlife, people would abandon morality in this life. Such rejection of morality would doom any attempt at democracy to failure, because the people would forsake liberty for tyranny. President Washington, in his famous 1796 Farewell Address, expressed these ideas:

> Of all the dispositions and habits which lead to political prosperity, religion and morality are indispensable supports. . . . Where is the security for property, for reputation, for life, if the sense of religious obligation desert the oaths which are the instruments of investigation in courts of justice? And let us with caution indulge the supposition that morality can be maintained without religion . . . reason and experience both forbid us to expect that national morality can prevail in exclusion of religious principle. It is substantially true that virtue or morality is a necessary spring of popular government. The rule, indeed, extends with more or less force to every species of free government. Who that is a sincere friend to it can look with indifference upon attempts to shake the foundation of the fabric?

Washington's Farewell Address is only one example that illustrates it was both permissible and expected that public officials would promote the shared religious beliefs that morality comes from god, and that such morality is necessary for liberty and democracy.

Ever since our founding period, whenever the United States government makes an official statement referencing a god, it has continued to use neutral monotheistic terms. For example, the phrase "In God we trust" became our new national motto in 1956 (It replaced "E Pluribus Unum," the original national motto adopted in 1782). The phrase "In God We trust" had already been placed on U.S.

coins in 1865. It was added to U.S. paper currency in 1957, the year after it became the official U.S. motto. The Pledge of Allegiance had been written in 1892 and was formally adopted by Congress in 1942, but the phrase "under god" was not added until 1954. To maintain religious unity in our nation, these phrases 'In God We Trust" and "under god" carefully avoid saying *which* god. Similarly, presidential thanksgiving proclamations have continued the tradition of early Presidents in using religiously neutral names for the deity. In this way, most religious believers can hear, read, write, or say these terms with equal religious conviction. Only in the last few decades, as atheism has come to represent the belief of a significant percent of the population, have these phrases become more controversial.

The Separation of Church and State

The principle of limiting the connection between government and religion was contained in the philosophy of disestablishment. It also led to the neutral theism contained in the Declaration of Independence, the Articles of Confederation, the Constitution, the First Amendment, and in public statements by early political leaders, especially the first few presidents. This principle was that government policy, and government leaders, must carefully avoid taking any position on which monotheistic denomination or religion is the "better" or "best" or "true" denomination or religion. At the same time, however, official documents and public statements declared that religious morality was the foundation of U.S. liberty and democracy. Because of this common belief, it was generally understood at the time that public officials and public institutions should promote religious *morals*, but should avoid taking positions on religious *doctrine*. This is a critical distinction. The founders believed promoting general *moral* concepts like peace, goodness, honesty, and so on fostered religious unity and strengthened liberty and democracy. Debating *theological* concepts, on the other hand, like whether god was unitary or a trinity, or whether Jesus was divine, a prophet, or merely human, were highly *divisive* to democratic social cohesion. In short, the early Americans believed political leaders should carefully avoid taking sides in theological disputes.

As can be seen by this discussion, religion was not completely disconnected from government, nor could it be. People have moral beliefs, and those moral beliefs often come from religion. People make political choices based on their moral beliefs. Therefore, a voter or a legislator cannot help but make decisions based in part on their religious concept of morality. Our human nature is such that it is impossible for us to psychologically divorce our notions of morality from our notions of ultimate religious or spiritual meaning. Even an atheist's notion of morality, for example, is intertwined with a belief in the *absence* of any religious deity. In short, although the involvement between government and religion can be *limited*, or perhaps even *minimized*, it can never be completely *eliminated*. And, as we've just seen, most of the founders did not want it eliminated, but instead saw an important role for government for encouraging and promoting religious morality.

The common term today for limiting the involvement between religion and government is the "*separation of church and state.*" Phrases similar to this were used around the time of the founding by various writers, but it was Thomas Jefferson's wording that became the most famous particular expression of the concept. While President, he sent a letter to a Baptist congregation in 1802:

> "Believing with you that religion is a matter which lies solely between Man & his God, that he owes account to none other for his faith or his worship, that the legitimate powers of government reach actions only, & not opinions, I contemplate with sovereign reverence that act of the whole American people which declared that their legislature should "make no law respecting an establishment of religion, or prohibiting the free exercise thereof," thus building a wall of separation between Church & State."

Today there is a currently a great deal of public misunderstanding regarding the religious views of the founders of the United States government. There seem to be two opposite yet equally mistaken extremes in this regard. On the one hand today, "*strict separationists*" typically argue that the founders were mostly deists who wanted a strict separation of church and state. Under this view, the U.S. government should have no connection with any religion in any way. As we discussed earlier, though, although deists were a significant minority, many of the founders were Christians or other religions. Moreover, It is humanly impossible to complete divorce one's morality from one's spiritual views. The founders of the United States understood this, and in fact argued that these beliefs should be reliant on each other. Thus, all the religious groups in the founding coalition, including deists, generally agreed that government policy and officials should promote morality. Put differently, in most of their minds, morality was inherently religious. Protestants, Catholics, Deists, Providentialists, and Jews all therefore believed that government did have a role to play in encouraging people to follow religious morality.

On the other hand, though, many conservative Christians today argue the Founders were all devout Christians who founded the U.S. as a "Christian nation." Under this view, the Founders wanted no separation of church and state. As we have seen, though, this "Christian Nation" view is as equally mistaken as the view of strict separationists. Although Christians were probably a majority of the population at the time, this included the majority of Christians who disestablished the state religions. That same Christian majority also then supported broad *religiously neutral* declarations in the founding documents. These statements were based on the beliefs Christians shared in common with other monotheistic religions at the time. These were primarily Deism, Providentialism, and Judaism.

Ironically, at the time the Constitution was ratified, some devout Christians opposed the Constitution specifically because it did *not* connect the U.S. government in any way to Christianity. A few Christian writers labeled the Constitution as "heretical" or "blasphemous" because it was not based on principles from the Christian Bible. In their mind, the Constitution was "ungodly" because it gave equal rights and privileges to "pagans," "Jews," "Turks," "infidels," or "atheists." For example, the Rev. Samuel Wylie, minister of the Reformed Presbyterian Church in Philadelphia, wrote a book called *The Two Sons of Oil*, published in 1803. In the book, Wylie argued that Christians should not give any obedience to the new U.S. government because it was not based on Christianity. William Findley, a delegate from Pennsylvania at the 1787 Philadelphia Convention, and then a long-serving representative from Pennsylvania in the U.S. House of Representatives, wrote a response. Findley published *Observations on "The Two Sons of Oil"* in 1811. In it, Findley explained that Wylie had misunderstood that one of the very purposes of the Constitution was to *not* connect the U.S. government to any one particular religion. This avoidance was done as a matter of good public policy, for all the same reasons supporting disestablishment in general.

Indeed, the single clearest statement on this question comes from a document that both Wylie and Findley discussed in their two competing books. In 1797, the U.S. Senate ratified a treaty most commonly referred to as *The Treaty of Tripoli.* It was part of the Barbary Treaties, or Treaty of Peace and Friendship, between the U.S. and the nation of Tripoli on the West coast of Africa. The treaty was ratified unanimously by the U.S. Senate. It was then signed by Pres. John Adams, who wrote in his signing statement that he had read every word of the treaty and agreed with every word in it. The full text of the treaty was then published in major U.S. newspapers with only minimal public disagreement.

In the treaty, the U.S. agreed to do what was common practice at the time. Essentially the U.S. agreed to pay bribes to the nations on the coast of Africa to keep their pirates from attacking U.S. ships. The negotiators from the nation of Tripoli, which was predominantly Muslim, were concerned that the U.S., which was predominantly Christian, might not honor the agreement due to religious prejudice. To calm such concerns, the U.S. negotiators put into the agreement the following declaration: "The government of the United States of America is not in any sense founded on the Christian religion." Under Article VI of the U.S. Constitution, treaties are official U.S. law. This treaty was ratified only eight years after the ratification of the Constitution. It was agreed to by all U.S. Senators, the U.S. President, and apparently most the public as well. It stated literally that the U.S. government is not *in any sense* founded on the Christian religion. Reverend Wylie used this treaty as evidence to show how "godless" the U.S. Constitution and government is. Findley countered that the treaty was evidence of the proper religious neutrality of the U.S. Constitution and government.

Several decades later, during the Civil War, there was a movement by several Protestant organizations in the North to amend the Preamble to the U.S. Constitution to officially declare the U.S. to be a Christian nation. The key part of the proposal would have inserted text into the beginning of the Preamble as follows:

> "We, the People of the United States, recognizing the being and attributes of Almighty God, the Divine Authority of the Holy Scriptures, the law of God as the paramount rule, and Jesus, the Messiah, the Savior and Lord of all, in order to form a more perfect union . . ."

The proposal for the "Christian Amendment," or "Christian Nation Amendment" was submitted to Congress but Congress never voted on it. Supporters of this amendment argued that the Civil War was god's punishment on the U.S. precisely because the U.S. was *not* officially a Christian nation. In short, even Christians in the 1700's and 1800's generally recognized that the U.S. was not founded as a "Christian Nation." It's only in recent decades that the mistaken belief that the U.S. was formally founded on Christianity has arisen. However, this belief is widespread among only a few particular Christian denominations, mostly nondenominational evangelical Christians.

One point sometimes made by supporters of the "Christian Nation" argument is that the phrase "the separation of church and state" is not in the Constitution or First Amendment. This is true but irrelevant. Recall from our discussion of the U.S. Constitution so far that none of the key terms used to label the principles of U.S. national government are themselves found in the Constitution. The phrases "checks and balances," "separation of powers," "enumerated powers," "limited government," "federalism," and "representative democracy," nor even the word "democracy," are found anywhere in the U.S. Constitution. Likewise, the phrase "Bill of Rights" is nowhere found in the actual Bill of Rights. These are all simply shorthand terms and phrases used to more conveniently refer to the basic structures of the Constitution. So, too, with the phrase "separation of church and state."

The Religion Clauses

The First Amendment to the U.S. Constitution begins by stating "Congress shall make no law respecting an Establishment of Religion, or prohibiting the Free Exercise thereof." These two clauses, the Establishment Clause and the Free Exercise Clause, are really two sides of same coin. Government is prohibited from entangling itself with religion by either by requiring it or by prohibiting it. Figuring out how these clauses should be interpreted to apply in specific situations, however, has been controversial and often difficult. Indeed, in the past several decades, the Supreme Court has often gone back-and-forth in trying to determine what these clauses actually mean.

The Free Exercise Clause is the easier religious clause to analyze. Under current Supreme Court precedents, the Free Exercise Clause essentially prohibits government from making any public policy which discriminates on the basis of religion. For example, in *Church of Lukumi Babalu Aye v. City of Hialeah* (1993), the City of Hialeah, Florida outlawed "animal sacrifice" when done as part of a religious "ritual." This ordinance was passed by the city council after residents complained about the sacrifice of small animals by local members of the Santeria religion. The Supreme Court struck down the law as an unconstitutional violation of the Free Exercise Clause. The court noted that the city had banned killing animals only when done for *religious* reasons. The law allowed the identical killing of animals for *non-religious* reasons, such as euthanasia, hunting, slaughtering of animals for food, extermination of pests, or even using live rabbits to train greyhound racing dogs. The City of Hialeah could offer no compelling justification for treating the religious killings of animals different from non-religious killings. Therefore, the Court overturned the law. Had the law either allowed or banned all types of animal killing equally in the same way, rather than singling out religious activity for punishment, then the law would not have violated the Free Exercise Clause.

Indeed, as the Supreme Court had made clear earlier in *Employment Division v. Smith* (1990), people must obey generally applicable laws that are religiously neutral. In other words, people have no right to claim religious exemptions from laws merely because one's religion says otherwise. Thus, in *Smith*, the use of the natural hallucinogenic drug peyote was not protected by the Free Exercise Clause even when used as part of a religious ceremony. The Court reasoned that if exemptions to laws are allowed simply because the violation is religiously motivated, then all laws would become mere recommendations, not requirements. People would stop paying taxes, stop following traffic rules, or even commit human sacrifice, all without any ability to prosecute them if they claim a religious reason for their actions.

Although the Supreme Court's interpretation of the Free Exercise Clause is relatively straightforward, the Court has found it more difficult to create clear boundaries of the Establishment Clause. In the past several decades, the Court has applied several different theories and legal tests for determining whether a law violates the Establishment Clause. Perhaps the most famous and often-quoted statement of its meaning, though, comes from the first-ever Supreme Court case discussing the Establishment Clause in detail. In *Everson v. Board of Education* (1947), the state of New Jersey Court offered parents reimbursement for the cost of sending their children to school on public transportation. The reimbursement was equally available to parents who chose to send their children either to public schools or to private religious schools. The Court upheld the law as constitutional given its nondiscriminatory religious neutrality. The Court explained:

> The 'establishment of religion' clause of the First Amendment means at least this: Neither a state nor the Federal Government can set up a church. Neither can pass laws which aid one religion, aid all religions, or prefer one religion over another. Neither can force nor influence a person to go to or to remain away from church against his will or force him to profess a belief or disbelief in any religion. No person can be punished for entertaining or professing religious beliefs or disbeliefs, for church attendance or non-attendance. No tax in any amount, large or small, can be levied to support any religious activities or institutions, whatever they may be called, or whatever from they may adopt to teach or practice religion. Neither a state nor the Federal Government can, openly or secretly, participate in the affairs of any religious organizations or groups and vice versa. In the words of Jefferson, the clause against establishment of religion by law was intended to erect 'a wall of separation between Church and State.'

In short, the Establishment Clause requires government treat all religions and religious believers more-or-less equally by not favoring one religious group over another. This commonly applies in situations involving taxpayer subsidies for private school tuition, or when a public building provides a religious display during a religious holiday. For example, in *Zelman v. Simmons-Harris* (2002), the Court ruled that if parents may choose to use a taxpayer-provided subsidy for their child's tuition equally at either a religious or a nonreligious school, then the subsidy does not violate the Establishment Clause.

Although neutrality is the general principle, the Court has allowed relatively minor deviations from this rule. These exceptions apply if a religious practice that government is partaking in is relatively trivial and has a long history or tradition. In *Marsh v. Chambers* (1983), for example, the Court allowed a prayer by a legislative chaplain at the opening session of a state legislature because legislatures in the U.S. had a long history of doing so. In *Van Orden v. Perry* (2005), the Court upheld a small monument to the Ten Commandments on a state capitol grounds on the basis that the display merely recognized the historical role of the commandments in the nation's heritage. Yet on the same day *Van Orden v. Perry* was released, the Court also released *McCreary County v. ACLU*. In *McCreary County*, the Court declared that posting the Ten Commandments on a state courthouse wall, even though other non-religious historical documents were also posted, violated the Establishment Clause.

The inconsistency between the *Van Orden* and *McCreary County* cases shows that the Court has not yet achieved a consistent standard in applying the Establishment Clause.

Another common Establishment Clause issue, and one that much of the public misunderstands, is the issue of prayer in public schools. The Establishment Clause forbids government from sponsoring a religious activity such as prayer in a public school. Endorsing such a religious activity would favor the beliefs and practice of one religious group over others. There is a critical distinction, however, between *private* prayer and *government-sponsored* prayer. In the public school context, students and teachers may pray all they want on their own private time, even while in a public school. Individually or collectively, students may pray privately at the bus stop in the morning, on the bus, or around the flagpole before the start of school, just as students can equally engage in non-religious speech during these times. Students can then pray in hallways, during lunch in the cafeteria, or silently to themselves while class is in session all throughout the school day, just as students are equally free to discuss or meditate silently about any other topic. In study hall, students can read the Bible, Torah, Quran, Bhagavad-Gita, Dhammapada, or any other sacred texts just as the students may also read any non-religious books in this context. After school hours, student groups can use classrooms for religious meetings and prayer on an equal basis that non-religious student groups can use school facilities. Even during official school class-time, students may talk about religion if the discussion is part of a formal class discussion of history, politics, sociology, or other academic issue.

Many different types of religious activities occur every day at countless public schools throughout the U.S. All the Establishment Clause forbids is for school officials to use their authority to allow prayers to be imposed on *non-participating, non-consenting* students. This would occur if the prayer were allowed during official class time or during an official school activity, or if government resources were used to impose the prayer on others. This means that a public school teacher may not require students to say or read a prayer, nor may the teacher allow a student to say a prayer out loud to the rest of the class during official class time. Similarly, a public school principle may not allow a prayer to be broadcast over the school loudspeaker system during the official school day or at an official school event such as a football game. In any of these situations, the prayer would no longer be merely a private act, but instead the prayer would be sponsored by the government.

No Supreme Court case, and not even a single Supreme Court justice, has ever declared or even suggested that all prayer is or should be banned from public school. Indeed, the law is quite the opposite. As shown above, religious prayer may permeate the entire public school day. Such rights are protected by the free Exercise Clause, in that school officials may not treat religious speech more negatively then non-religious speech. Also, as we saw in the last chapter, the right of free expression is protected by the Free Speech Clause of the First Amendment. As a result, students are free to express their political and religious beliefs and opinions on their own private time, meaning as long as class is not officially in session. The right of free expression, however, does not include a "right" to force others to unwillingly listen to one's opinions. This means that students have no "right" to make a teacher or principal let them use official school time or use official government resources (such as a loudspeaker system), to broadcast their prayer to everyone else. In sum, the only type of prayer the Establishment Clause prohibits is *government-sponsored* prayer. In such cases neither the Free Exercise Clause nor the Free Speech Clause gives individuals a right to use the coercive power of government to impose one's views on others.

An example of this distinction between government and private speech occurred in *Santa Fe Independent School District v. Doe* (2000). There, a public high school allowed a student to use the school's loudspeaker to impose a prayer on the entire audience at an official school sporting event. The Supreme Court held that this practice violated the Establishment Clause. By using the school loudspeaker at an official school event, the speech was no longer a private prayer, but was a government-sponsored or government-endorsed prayer.

Religious Equality Today

Despite the constitutional protections for religious liberty, members of minority religions still face social prejudice. As noted earlier in this chapter there is a long history in the United States of anti-Catholic sentiment, including violence. This prejudice and violence continued in the late 1800's and early 1900's when large waves of Catholic immigrants from Europe arrived in the United States. The first and only Catholic president was not elected until John F. Kennedy in 1960. Even then, he had to overcome public concerns that he would simply obey the Pope or Catholic Church doctrine over the U.S. Constitution.

The Church of Jesus Christ of Latter-Day Saints (the Mormons) was violently persecuted during its founding period in the mid-1800's. Non-Mormons kept beating and killing Mormons, including the founder of their religion, Joseph Smith. He was murdered by a mob while imprisoned in an Illinois jail. Mormons were driven ever-farther westward until they eventually settled in what is now the state of Utah. Yet even then, Congress did not allow Utah to become a state until the Mormon Church officially gave up the practice of polygamy (marriage to multiple wives). In 2012 Republican presidential candidate and former Massachusetts Governor Mitt Romney became the first Mormon presidential candidate of a major party. Yet there has not yet been a Mormon president or vice-president.

Anti-Jewish prejudice has always been relatively common and still is today. This has included violence against Jewish people and vandalism of Jewish cemeteries and Jewish houses of worship, called synagogues. Today some conspiracy groups follow in the footsteps of Nazi propaganda by verbally attacking any Jewish people who have positions of power in politics, business, or the media. There has never been a Jewish president or vice-president. There also has never been a Jewish presidential candidate from the two major parties, but Senator Joe Lieberman was the Democratic Party vice-presidential candidate in 2000. This made him the first Jewish person to be on the presidential election ticket of a major political party.

Believers in the religion of Islam are called Muslims. Muslims have always faced prejudice in the United States, but especially after the 9/11 terror attacks on New York. Since then, and especially with the ongoing "war on terror," Muslims have been regular targets of public suspicion and distrust, and sometimes even violent attacks. This includes vandalizing of their religious houses of worship, called mosques. There has not yet been a Muslim president or vice-president, nor has a Muslim yet been on the presidential election ticket of a major political party. In 2007, however, the first Muslim was elected to Congress: Democrat Keith Ellison of Minnesota was elected to the House of Representatives.

Atheists (those who believe no religion is true) and agnostics (those who are unsure whether any religion is true) are currently the fastest-growing religious groups in the United States. Yet public opinion polls show low public regard in general for atheists and agnostics. One famous example of this contempt occurred in 1987. Then Vice-President George H.W. Bush was campaigning to be president, and was asked how he planned to win the votes of atheists. He replied "I don't know that atheists should be considered as citizens, nor should they be considered patriots." There has not yet been an openly atheistic or agnostic presidential or vice-president, nor an openly atheistic or agnostic major-party candidate on a presidential election ticket.

Despite ongoing prejudices against minority religious groups, today there are many legal protections against religious discrimination. Besides the constitutional protections against *government* discrimination that were discussed in the previous section, many U.S. laws also protect people against various types of *private* religious discrimination. A well-known and often used such law is part of the federal Civil Rights Act of 1964. The subsection of that law called "Title VII" outlaws any type of employment discrimination based on the religion of the applicant or employee. "Title II" of that same act prohibits businesses from discriminating against a customer because of the customer's religion. Also, the federal Fair Housing Act prohibits discrimination on the basis of religion in the sale or rental of housing.

There are other federal laws, and many state and local laws as well, that offer similar protections against religious discrimination.

Title VII also addresses other types of discrimination that will be discussed in an upcoming chapter on civil rights involving race and sex. Title VII treats religion differently from other types of discrimination, however, by giving religious beliefs and practices additional legal protection. Employers must provide "reasonable accommodation" for an employee's religious beliefs or practices. This means the employer has a legal duty to somewhat adjust the employee's terms or conditions of employment to allow the employee to live more consistently with the employee's religious conscience. This adjustment need only be "reasonable," however, such that it does not cause "undue hardship" on the employer. So, for example, an employer must allow an employee to take a few-minute break a couple times of day for prayer if such time is requested. On the other hand, an employer need not hold an employee's job for them while the employee goes on a year-long religious pilgrimage. Courts struggle, however, in deciding where the precise line is between what is "reasonable" versus "unreasonable" accommodation.

Many states have also tried to expand protections for religious liberty within their state through what is commonly called a "Religious Freedom Restoration Act," or "RFRA" for short. The effort to create RFRAs began after the Supreme Court's 1990 case of *Employment Division v. Smith*. Recall from the previous section of this chapter that in *Smith*, the Court ruled that there is no Free Exercise right to disobey religiously neutral laws, even if violation of the law is required by one's religious beliefs. In response, Congress and almost half the states passed variously worded RFRA statutes that offer different types of religious exemptions to otherwise neutral laws. Originally these RFRAs had broad bipartisan support among both liberals and conservatives who wanted greater protection for religious liberty. Recently, however, after the Supreme Court's ruling that a right to same-sex marriage is protected by the Constitution, a few states have considered passing newer RFRAs. These RFRAs would allow businesses to discriminate in some instances against gays and lesbians, if that discrimination was based on the religious beliefs of the business owner. For example, perhaps a restaurant owner might refuse to cater a same-sex wedding. These newer RFRA proposals have been controversial, and have generated significant political backlash. This includes from civil rights groups, and large companies that want a non-discriminatory climate for their employees in the state (such as Apple and Wal-Mart). Musical acts, organizational conventions, sporting events, and even other state governments have also threatened boycotts of any state that legalizes such discrimination.

SUMMARY

Prior to the founding of the United States, officially established religions in Europe had caused religious civil wars. Official religious establishments in both Europe and the American colonies had also led to violent persecution of religious minorities and the corruption of religious institutions. Not wanting to repeat these mistakes, a majority of the founders of the United States increasingly favored separating religion from government. By focusing on religious commonalities and avoiding religious differences, a diverse coalition of religious groups were able to maintain political unity in support of disestablishing the established Protestant denominations. This broad religious coalition held together through independence from England and through the ratification of the Constitution. To do so, the early Americans avoided taking sides regarding which particular religion was "true." Yet they still believed government leaders should acknowledge and encourage religiously-based morality. This original understanding of the separation of church and state is reflected in the language of the founding documents of the United States, as well as in speeches and writings of the founders, especially the early Presidents. Together, the Free Exercise Clause and the Establishment Clause, both found in the First Amendment, roughly require government neutrality when it comes to religion. That is, with a few minor exceptions, public policy must treat people of different religions and religious denominations equally. Many federal, state and local laws also prohibit private discrimination on the basis of religion.

QUESTIONS FOR REVIEW AND SELF-ASSESSMENT

1. What are religious establishments and what was the nature of such establishments in England's thirteen American colonies?
2. What was the diverse political-religious coalition that argued for disestablishment at the time of U.S. independence?
3. What were the shared, common religious beliefs of the disestablishment coalition, and how were these reflected in the founding documents and early practices of the U.S.?
4. How did the founders of the U.S. intend a "loose" separation of church and state, as opposed to "strict" separation or a "Christian nation"?
5. How does the Supreme Court's interpretation of the First Amendment's religion clauses basically require government neutrality between religions in different contexts?
6. What are some ways that federal laws prohibit private religious discrimination?

CRITICAL THINKING QUESTIONS FOR REFLECTION AND DISCUSSION

1. Should there be a strict separation of church and state, a "loose" separation of church and state, or no separation of church and state?
2. Should the Supreme Court reinterpret the Establishment Clause to allow government to favor one religion over others? If so, what religion should that be, and what would be the practical effect on public policy?

Suggested Reading Supplements

- James Madison, *Memorial and Remonstrance Against Religious Assessments*
- Thomas Jefferson, *Letter to the Danbury Baptist Association*
- *Everson v. Board of Education* (1947)
- *Employment Division v. Smith* (1990)
- *Church of Lukumi Babalu Aye v. City of Hialeah* (1993)
- *Santa Fe Independent School District v. Doe* (2000)
- *Van Orden v. Perry* (2005)
- *McCreary County v. ACLU* (2005)

For Further Advanced Reading

- Steven Waldman, *Founding Faith: How Our Founding Fathers Forged a Radical New Approach to Religious Liberty*
- Thomas S. Kidd, *God of Liberty: A Religious History of the American Revolution*
- Dianne Avery, Maria Ontiveros, Roberto Corrada, Michael Selmi, and Melissa Hart, *Employment Discrimination Law, 8th Edition*

Chapter 9: Slavery

The Big Picture

From before the founding of the U.S. until the defeat of the Confederate States of America in 1865, the brutal enslavement of human beings based merely on their skin color occurred in the southern states. By 1860, though, the rest of the U.S., including the newly elected President Lincoln, finally refused to allow slavery to expand any further inside the U.S. This refusal, along with other anti-slavery actions by the rest of the U.S., finally caused the southern slaveholding states to try to leave the U.S. in order to keep slavery. This resulted in the U.S. Civil War, in which hundreds of thousands of soldiers died. After several years of horrible warfare, the victorious United States kept the southern states in the U.S. and ended slavery, thereby freeing all the enslaved people.

Relevant Timeline

- 1809 Congress bans the international slave trade
- 1820 Missouri Compromise
- 1850 Compromise of 1850
- 1854 Kansas-Nebraska Act
- 1857 *Dred Scott v. Sanford* (blacks have no constitutional rights)
- 1859 John Brown's raid on Harper's Ferry
- 1860 Abraham Lincoln elected President; southern states secede
- 1861 Civil War Begins
- 1863 Emancipation Proclamation
- 1865 Civil War Ends (U.S. defeats the Confederacy); Lincoln killed

Chapter Objectives

After reading this chapter, the reader should be able to:

1. Describe the life of a slave and how the laws of the southern slaveholding states perpetuated slavery.
2. Describe the territorial expansion of slavery in the U.S. and explain how this expansion caused increasing political tension in the U.S.
3. Describe the ways in which the non-slaveholding states increasingly opposed slavery in the decade leading up to the U.S. Civil War.
4. Explain the cause of the southern slaveholding states' secession from the U.S., as explained by southern leaders themselves at the time.
5. Describe the U.S. Civil War and its most significant outcomes, especially in regards to slavery.

Domestic Slavery

The United States unfortunately has a uniquely tragic role in world history. It is known for once having the largest systematic enslavement of human beings based not on conquest in war, but based on skin color alone. Moreover, the long-term economic, social and political consequences of slavery and the Civil War still greatly affect the United States today. This means that no understanding of U.S. politics or public policy today is possible without a thorough background in, and understanding of, the role of slavery in U.S. history.

As we saw back in Chapter Three when we looked at the biggest constitutional compromises, the 1787 Constitutional Convention in Philadelphia almost broke up over the issue of slavery. However, three specific compromises involving slavery were reached. First, the 3/5 Compromise counted each slave as 3/5 of a person when calculating the representation a state receives in the U.S. House of Representatives. Second, Northern states were constitutionally required to return escaped slaves to continued enslavement in the South. Third, Congress could prohibit the international slave trade in 1808. However, the Philadelphia Convention left unresolved the major question whether Congress could regulate slavery as "commerce." Congress did eventually ban the *international* slave trade in 1808, but left domestic slavery unregulated. The North and the South were still at an impasse over whether Congress had the power to regulate slavery inside the U.S. As a result, the regulation of slavery was left entirely up to each individual state.

At the time of the ratification of the Constitution in 1789, slavery was nearly extinct in the Northern states. Slavery was formally outlawed in all the states of the North within the next few decades. In the South, on the other hand, recall that according to the 1790 census, slaves comprised about 1/3 of the population of the South. Southern whites didn't want the number of slaves to decrease, because then southern whites would have fewer votes in the House of Representatives. That is, the South wanted a high slave population to increase their representation in the House, thereby allowing them to block Northern attempts to limit slavery. Also, the Southern slave-owning class insisted on keeping the free labor they received from slaves. The agricultural economics of large-scale cotton plantations meant that slave labor was extremely profitable to plantation owners. Poor whites in the South also feared economic competition for jobs and wages if slaves were set free. Also, many poor Southern whites hoped to climb the social and economic ladder and to one day own slaves themselves. Even poor whites who believed they would never own slaves felt they were higher on the social ladder as long as there were enslaved blacks beneath them. Bogus science in the South taught that blacks were biologically inferior to whites, and southern Christianity claimed that God had created blacks to be ruled over by whites. For all these reasons, in the South slavery became enshrined as public policy and as a social institution.

Although there were urban slaves and house slaves, the majority of slaves were used for agricultural labor. The life of a field slave was brutal. It comprised long work days from sun-up to sun-down and long work weeks, with at least 6 days a week. There were no "vacations." For field slaves, work had to continue even when the temperature was over 100 degrees or below freezing. Slaves could be punished severely, such as by whipping, for failing to meet their work quotas. With rare exceptions, such as slave drivers or favored house slaves, slaves lived together in tiny, crowded one-room or two-room bare shacks. Usually these had little or no furniture, and often had dirt floors. Slaves typically had only one set of clothes. Food was usually the same simple, bare rations daily. In some cases, slaves were even responsible for finding their own food. Marriages between slaves were not recognized as legally valid. Couples and their children could therefore be sold individually at the whim of the slave owner. Enslaved women could even be raped by their master. Any children that resulted from the rape were almost always kept as slaves by the slave-owner rather than set free. Travel by slaves was not allowed except by express written permission. Even then, travel was allowed only for assigned tasks, and these written travel papers had to be carried at all times. The punishment for attempted escape was whipping, shackling, branding, maiming, or disfigurement, such as cutting off one's ear. At worst, punishment for repeated escape attempts could be death by lynching. (See Solomon Northup's autobiography, *Twelve Years a Slave,* for a particularly detailed account of slave life.)

Another part of maintaining the institution of race-based slavery was to severely suppress resistance to enslavement. Attempts by slaves to rebel against their captivity were punished by torture and often execution. The murdered person's corpse was sometimes displayed publicly as a sign to other slaves. For example, the largest slave uprising in U.S. history occurred in 1811 along the Mississippi River west of New Orleans, Louisiana. It is known as the "German Coast Uprising." At least a couple hundred slaves armed themselves mostly with hand tools. They attempted to make it to New Orleans so as to flee the U.S. by ship. They were stopped on the way by over a hundred armed whites who murdered 95 of the rebelling slaves. The heads of 18 of them were stuck on pikes (sharpened long sticks) and placed along many miles of the road along the Mississippi River. These served as a gruesome warning to other slaves not to attempt to resist their enslavement.

Public policy in the Southern states was also thoroughly designed to maintain the slave population. This included keeping slaves themselves from having the knowledge or resources to escape or rebel. To do this, most Southern states made it a crime to educate slaves or give slaves any income or property. The act of setting a slave free was legally called "manumission." Manumission was forbidden by law, even in the slave owner's will upon the slave owner's death. The law also prohibited slaves or even free blacks from owning guns. Eventually, assemblies and meetings of slaves were outlawed unless whites were present. All white persons had legal authority to stop any traveling black persons and demand to see either their written travel permission or the papers indicating they were a free black. Anyone aiding escape or rebellion by a slave was subject to death by hanging. It was illegal in the South to speak out or publish writings against slavery. In other words, there was no protection for freedom of speech. Even in the U.S. Congress, Southerners got Congress to adopt a "gag rule." For over a decade, Congress prohibited any of its members from suggesting in Congress that slavery be abolished.

All these public policies preserved slavery in the South. It was nearly impossible for any slave to plan, attempt, or succeed at escaping. Just imagine, for example, being a slave living in the Deep South, and you wish to escape to the North. As soon as it is discovered you are missing, you will be chased by men on horses who will hunt you with dogs and guns. You have no money to purchase food, no gun to defend yourself, and no horse to speed your travel. You're unable to read maps or signs, and unable to write your own forged travel papers. You must try to avoid roads and instead hide during the day. At night, you secretly walk through woods and swamps for weeks on end. This must go on through many weeks of cold and hot, rain and storms, insects and wild animals, with your sickness and injuries untreated. You have little if any food or medicine. Typically only young, able-bodied men had the physical strength to even attempt such an ordeal.

Even if you had the physical stamina to endure an escape attempt, at any moment you could be stopped by any white person. This might even be a group of whites on horseback and with guns. Regardless who it was, you would be required to show your travel papers. If caught, you will probably have your skin branded as a runaway slave, and be severely whipped or worse. You might even be "sold down the river" to a plantation owner even farther from the North. Even most fellow slaves won't help you for fear of severe punishment or execution. If you do finally make it to a "free" state, the Fugitive Slave Clause of the U.S. Constitution requires local law enforcement authorities to turn you in to anyone claiming you as their slave. Therefore, to guarantee your freedom, you must make your way all the way to Canada. Then, even if you eventually escape to freedom, you initially have no money and no education to help you start your new life. For all these reasons, most slaves never attempted to escape. Of those who tried, most failed. For one true story of successful escape, though, read Frederick Douglass' autobiography, *Narrative of the Life of Frederick Douglass*. Douglass was able to escape from slavery only by secretly teaching himself to read, and then by using a fake identity and forged travel papers. His autobiography also contains his powerful moral critique of slavery.

Although the vast majority of slavery involved whites owning blacks, in the early 1800s there was a small population of free blacks in the South. Of these, only one or two percent at most owned slaves. This was particularly true in New Orleans and other areas of Louisiana where there was a significant population of mixed racial ancestry. Most of this ownership, though, was of family members to protect them from possible ownership by whites. Recall that Southern state law prohibited setting slaves free, and taking a family member to a Northern state to set them free might mean leaving other family members behind. Yet, a few free blacks owned large plantations with many slaves purely for commercial profit. Indeed, until the U.S. outlawed the international slave trade in 1808, a majority of blacks enslaved in Africa were enslaved by competing African tribes who then sold their captives to European slave traders. Yet by the time of the Civil War, the notion that slavery was justified by white racial superiority had thoroughly ingrained itself in the dominant Southern white culture. As a result, there were extremely few black slave-owners at the start of the Civil War in 1861.

Slavery Expansion

Remember that Southern slave states needed to keep power in Congress to block possible attempts by the Northern free states at limiting slavery. Even with the fictional addition of slave numbers to the Southern white population as a result of the 3/5 Compromise, the population of the North was far greater than the population of the South. This meant that the North could easily outvote the South in the U.S. House of Representatives. The key line of defense for the South, then, was in the U.S. Senate. Slave states needed the number of slave states to always at least equal the number of free states in the Senate. Otherwise, free states could outvote slave states in the Senate, and Congress would be able to pass slavery legislation. Southern states could easily perpetuate slavery in their own states, but it was politically difficult to *expand* slavery to new U.S. territory and states. Congress always decides whether a U.S. territory becomes a state, and under what conditions it does so. For the South, the expansion of slavery into new states was critically necessary to the survival of slavery. This is why the South *absolutely insisted* that Congress allow slavery to expand into new territories and states. Southern whites and Northern whites all understood that slavery would either expand or it would die.

Throughout the first half of the 1800's, the North and South reached a series of major but difficult political compromises involving slavery. Each of these bargains attempted to maintain the delicate balance between the number of free states and slave states. In 1820, the Missouri Compromise allowed Maine to enter as a free state and Missouri to enter as a slave state. As part of the Missouri Compromise, west of Missouri a line was created dividing Northern free territory from Southern slave territory. This line cut westward across the Louisiana territory, which comprised the entire Western part of the U.S. at the time. Then, in the

Compromise of 1850, Texas was admitted as a slave state in exchange for California entering the Union as a free state. Also as part of that compromise, slavery was ended in the District of Columbia in exchange for a congressional Fugitive Slave Act that brought stricter enforcement of the Fugitive Slave Clause of the Constitution.

In 1854, Congress passed the *Kansas-Nebraska Act.* This allowed both these new states to vote for themselves whether slavery would be legal or illegal within them. Both pro-slavery and anti-slavery settlers rushed to Kansas and set up two competing state governments. In 1856 these two competing factions actually went to civil war within Kansas over the issue. This is where the term "Bleeding Kansas" comes from. After several dozen deaths in the armed conflict, federal troops had to be sent in to stop the bloodshed and the admission of Kansas as a state was postponed. Apart from this outcome, many Northerners saw the Kansas-Nebraska Act as a Southern betrayal of the Missouri Comprise. Both Kansas and Nebraska were within the territory that the Missouri Compromise guaranteed as free territory, yet the Kansas-Nebraska Act allowed for the possibility that both would become slave states.

In 1857, a landmark U.S. Supreme Court decision, *Dred Scott v. Sanford,* directly involved the issue of slavery in a major way. Although the procedure of the case is technically complex, essentially Dred Scott was slave living in Missouri, a slave state. His owner went on a business trip to the free state of Illinois, and then to part of the free area of Louisiana Territory, what would later become Minnesota. Dred Scott went along on the trip. When they returned to Missouri, Dred Scott sued for his freedom with legal help from an anti-slavery group. He argued that Illinois had abolished slavery within the state, and Congress had outlawed slavery in that part of the Louisiana Territory as a result of the Missouri Compromise. Therefore, the laws of Illinois, or the laws of Congress, or both, had made him a free man.

In what is considered by most historical scholars to be one of the worst, if not the very worst, decision in Supreme Court history, the Court ruled that Sanford was still a slave. The Court declared that no state can set a slave free. To do so would be making a non-citizen a citizen, but only the national government can make public policy on questions of U.S. citizenship. So did this mean Congress could outlaw slavery? The court said no. The majority opinion was written by Chief Justice Taney, who came from a slave state and had once owned slaves himself. He declared that slaves were not human beings but were instead property. Because of this, in outlawing slavery in the free Louisiana Territory, Congress had violated the slave owner's Constitutional right to property protected by the 5th Amendment to the Constitution, as part of the bill of rights. A document that was intended to protect the rights of the people was instead used as justification to utterly deny all rights to a people. Justice Taney went even further, though. He declared that all people of African descent, either free or slave, had never been intended by whites to be part of the social contract of the United States. Since blacks were not part of the social contract, they had no rights under the Constitution. They were not citizens, nor could they be made citizens by Congress. Since Dred Scott had no legal rights, he had no right to bring a lawsuit in federal court, and the case was dismissed.

The Dred Scott decision immediately caused a national firestorm of controversy. The Court had ruled that Congress could not restrict slavery in any U.S. territories. This meant that all the major political compromises between the North and South for the past several decades were in one fell swoop struck down as unconstitutional. And, since no state could outlaw slavery, this meant that legally, the U.S. would no longer be half-slave and half-free. Now the Constitution required that slavery be allowed *everywhere* in the United States. Slave owners could take their slaves anywhere in the U.S., and those slaves would still be enslaved. For example, there would be nothing Northern states could do to prevent a slave owner from establishing new slave-based plantations in Ohio or Pennsylvania, or building a new manufacturing plant using slave labor in Chicago or New York. Many Northern whites and free-state governments were outraged at the decision and openly refused to obey it. Southern whites and slave-state governments were in turn outraged at Northern defiance against the decision. Yet the *Dred Scott* decision had said there could be no more political compromises on the question because. That is, any attempts by Congress or the states to decide where slavery could or could not exist would be unconstitutional. Although *Dred Scott v. Sanford* did not by itself cause the U.S. Civil War, the decision probably accelerated it. After the *Dred Scott* case, the only way left to settle the issue of slavery was not through political and legal compromise, but through war.

Growing Tensions

By the late 1850's, especially after Bleeding Kansas and the Dred Scott Decision, tension was extremely high between the North and South on the question of slavery. Southern whites increasingly were outraged with the North for ignoring the *Dred Scott* decision and prohibiting the spread of slavery. Northern states also now openly defied both the Fugitive Slave Clause of the Constitution and the Fugitive Slave Act of 1850 by refusing to return escaped slaves. Northern states even passed "Personal Liberty Laws" declaring that the moment a slave set foot in their state, the slave would be become free. The few slaves that were returned from the North in the late 1850's typically required federal marshals or federal troops to enforce such returns. These incidents received both national and international press coverage. Perhaps the starkest example was in 1854. Boston was briefly put under martial law while several hundred U.S. troops made sure a single escaped slave, Anthony Burns, was returned to the South. Northerners became increasingly outraged at the enslavement of free people within their midst. At the same time,

Southerners became increasingly furious at Northern refusal to return escaped slaves.

By the late 1850's, the *abolition* movement to end slavery was still supported only by a minority of the Northern population. Yet the movement was rapidly growing in the North. Northern abolitionist groups published newspapers and helped elect officials who had anti-slavery views. Southerners, who outlawed such speeches or literature in their own states, were outraged that Northern laws continued to allow such anti-slavery "agitation." One such example was the anti-slavery novel *Uncle Tom's Cabin,* by author Harriet Beecher Stowe. It became a massive bestseller in the North, as well as in England, and was outsold only by the Bible. The book increased abolitionist feelings in the North but was banned in the South. It's impact on Northern public opinion was huge. When President Abraham Lincoln met Stowe during the Civil War, he is rumored to have said to her "So this is the little lady that started this great war."

As the abolitionist movement grew, Northerners increasingly helped slaves escape through the "Underground Railroad." The movement was led by Harriet Tubman, a former slave herself who had escaped from slavery. The Underground Railroad was neither a railroad, nor literally underground. It was many different routes out of the South. Each route was comprised of a secret series of safe houses provided by free blacks, white abolitionists, or other sympathetic persons to help shelter and hide runaway slaves. These various routes led in all directions outside the South but most went to the North. Some routes went all the way to Canada as well given the risk of capture and return within the U.S through enforcement of the Fugitive Slave Clause and the Fugitive Slave Act.

Throughout the 1850's tensions were very high between the North and South. Some Southerners already openly threatened to leave the U.S., and by military force if necessary, if the North would not leave slavery alone. One of the most famous speeches in this regard was by John C. Calhoun, a Senator from South Carolina. He was the leading proponent of the Southern "states' rights" position. He argued each state had a "right" to decide whether to enslave human beings. His 1850 farewell speech to the U.S. Senate dealt entirely with the issue of slavery. He prophesized that unless the North leaves the issue of slavery alone and ends the movement towards abolition, Northern attempts to limit slavery will lead to the break-up of the United States. Calhoun declared the South would *secede* (leave the U.S.) if need be in order to keep slavery.

Strains within the U.S. Senate over slavery came to a head in 1856. Senator Sumner from Massachusetts was brutally beaten and left permanently disabled by Senator Butler of South Carolina. Butler attacked Sumner with a cane on the floor of the Senate chamber after Sumner made an anti-slavery speech calling the expansion of slavery a "crime." This highly publicized beating polarized the nation even more.

Sumner was seen as a near-martyr in the North, whereas Butler was praised as a hero in the South.

Another, even more polarizing incident happened in 1859. A white militant abolitionist Northerner named John Brown unsuccessfully tried to inspire a slave uprising. Along with a handful of companions, he raided a military arsenal located in Harper's Ferry, Virginia. Not a single slave joined him or was freed. Brown was immediately caught by Southerners and then hung as a terrorist. Southerners fumed at the incident and believed Brown was part of a growing Northern conspiracy to end slavery by promoting slave rebellions. Fearing such revolts, the South began to better organize and arm itself with weapons to be used against possible slave uprisings. Southern states also placed even stricter regulations on slave communications, meetings, and travel. Many Northerners, however, especially abolitionists, believed Brown was a martyr for a righteous cause.

Southern Secession

During the 1850's, Northern states were able to muster enough votes in the House and Senate to get five more free states added to the Union. This now meant that on questions of slavery, both the House and Senate were controlled by majorities from Northern free states. However, the South still had one last line of defense. Remember that in the constitutional system of checks and balances, not only must the House and Senate agree on laws, but the President must sign the bill into law as well. If the President vetoes the bill, it's blocked from becoming law. A majority of presidents prior to 1860 had owned slaves themselves. Indeed, every president and presidential candidate of a major political party until 1860 had promised that they would veto any attempts by Congress to restrict or abolish slavery in South. This changed in 1860.

Abraham Lincoln was an Illinois politician who rose to fame when he ran for the U.S. Senate as a Republican. As part of the campaign, Lincoln debated Judge Stephen Douglas, a Democrat, for the seat. Their series of lengthy and highly publicized debates throughout the state of Illinois dealt entirely with a single issue: should slavery be allowed to expand any further than it already had? Douglas argued yes, the white people in each new territory and state should decide for themselves. Lincoln argued no, slavery was a moral evil and its further territorial expansion should be halted. Slavery should be contained to the territories and states only where it already existed. Lincoln narrowly lost the election to Douglas.

Lincoln's willingness to stand up against the Southern "slave power" or "slaveocracy" won him fame and admiration in the North. This propelled him to national political prominence, especially within the Republican Party, which he helped create. Lincoln made other famous speeches at the time, including his controversial "House Divided" speech in 1858. In it, he stated his belief that "'A house divided against itself cannot stand.' I believe this government cannot endure, permanently half *slave* and half *free*. I do not expect the Union to be *dissolved* -- I do not expect the house to *fall* -- but I *do* expect it will cease to be divided. It will become *all* one thing or *all* the other." Lincoln was chosen as the Republican Party's presidential nominee in 1860.

In the 1860 presidential election, there was only one major issue: the question whether slavery should be allowed to expand. As the Republican Party's candidate, Lincoln was not in favor of abolishing slavery, nor giving equal rights to blacks. Instead, his express position was slavery should be allowed to continue where it currently existed but that Congress should outlaw slavery in all other current and future U.S. territories and states. This position actually made Lincoln a moderate candidate, standing in-between those who wanted slavery to expand everywhere, and those who wanted to abolish slavery everywhere.

The Democratic Party was so divided on this issue that it split into two factions, each with its own presidential candidate. The Northern Democratic candidate Stephen Douglas argued the same position he had against Lincoln in the earlier Lincoln-Douglas debates. The white people of each new territory or state should be given the choice whether to allow slavery or outlaw it. The Southern Democrats split off from the Northern Democrats. Southern Democrats insisted slavery should be allowed in all new territories and states. They even referred to the Republican Party as the "Black Republican" party due to its stance against the spread of slavery.

Public fears over a possible breakup of the United States led to the formation of a fourth political party called the Constitutional Union Party. It took no positions on any political issues except one. Its only position was that the Union should be preserved by the North and South negotiating and compromising on the issue of slavery.

On Election Day in November 1860, Lincoln won both the popular vote and the electoral vote count. Remarkably, this occurred without him getting the vote of even a single person throughout ten southern slave states where he wasn't allowed on the ballot. In Virginia, a slave state where he was allowed on the ballot, he gained only 1% of the vote. Nevertheless, Lincoln's victory meant he was going to be the first President in U.S. history who was morally opposed to slavery, whose policy was to restrict the spread of slavery, and who was open to considering the possible abolition of slavery. Lincoln would not promise to veto Congressional attempts to restrict slavery. For the South, this meant they could no longer count on the U.S. President as being the last line of defense for slavery.

The election of Lincoln was therefore the last straw for many Southern whites. According to the 1860 census, the slave population had grown to four *million* people enslaved in the Southern states, especially in the Deep South. Slaves made up almost a third the population of each of the states of Texas, Virginia, and North Carolina. Slaves were 44% of the population of both Florida and Georgia, 45% of Alabama's population, and 47% of Louisiana's population. Slaves were even a majority of the population in Mississippi (55%) and South Carolina (57%). Also according to the 1860 census, about a third of all white families in these Deep South states owned one or more slaves. Slaves were one of the three biggest sources of wealth to Southern whites, along with land and cotton. Yet the value of both Southern land and Southern cotton depended on slave labor. Southern whites therefore believed that Lincoln posed not just a threat to slavery, but to the entire Southern economy and way of life. Most Southern whites now believed the only path left to preserve slavery would be to leave the United States.

After Lincoln's election, but before he even took office, South Carolina was the first slave state to secede. Its secession convention released an "Address of the People of South Carolina to the Slave-Holding States." In the Address, South Carolina called on the other slave states to join it, comparing their situation to when the U.S. broke away from England: "We but imitate the policy of our fathers in dissolving a union with non-slaveholding confederates, and seeking a confederation with slave-holding States." Ten other Southern slave-holding states eventually followed South Carolina's lead. Together they formed the *Confederate States of America* in early 1861. South Carolina also separately adopted a "Declaration of Secession," as did the states of Georgia, Mississippi, and Texas. All of them officially declared Northern opposition to, and interference with, slavery to be the primary cause of their secession. These declarations listed specific grievances against the North: its refusal to allow slavery to expand into new territories and states, its disobedience of the Dred Scott Decision and the Fugitive Slave Law of 1850, its allowing of abolitionist literature to be published, and its permission and help of the Underground Railroad.

The cause of preserving slave was made expressly clear in the Southern states' formal declarations. Mississippi proclaimed "Our position is thoroughly identified with the institution of slavery." Georgia announced "For the last ten years we have had numerous and serious causes of complaint against our non-slave-holding confederate States with reference to the subject of African slavery." The Commissioner from Louisiana to the Texas secession convention stated "Louisiana looks to the formation of a Southern confederacy to preserve the blessings of African slavery." The Declaration of Secession by Texas went so far as to declare:

> "We hold as undeniable truths that the governments of the various States, and of the confederacy itself, were established exclusively by the white race, for themselves and their posterity; that the African race had no agency in their establishment; that they were rightfully held and regarded as an

> inferior and dependent race, and in that condition only could their existence in this country be rendered beneficial or tolerable. That in this free government all white men are and of right ought to be entitled to equal civil and political; that the servitude of the African race, as existing in these States, is mutually beneficial to both bond and free, and is abundantly authorized and justified by the experience of mankind, and the revealed will of the Almighty Creator . . .

Arkansas' secession convention similarly passed a resolution declaring "The people of the Northern States have organized a political party, purely sectional in its character, the central and controlling idea of which is hostility to the institution of African slavery, as it exists in the Southern States; and that party has elected a President and Vice President of the United States."

Mississippi Senator Jefferson Davis became the first and only President of the Confederate States of America. Prior to doing so, he gave a farewell speech to the U.S. Senate in which he explained his state's secession. Davis declared "She [Mississippi] has heard proclaimed the theory that all men are created free and equal, and this made the basis of an attack upon her social institutions [slavery]; and the sacred Declaration of Independence has been invoked to maintain the position of the equality of the races. They have no reference to the slave. . ." Similar Senate resignation speeches were given by Louisiana Senator Judah Benjamin, who then became the Attorney General of the Confederacy, and Georgia Senator Robert Toombs, who then became Secretary of State of the Confederacy.

Then, upon ratification of the Confederate Constitution, Confederate President Davis gave a speech to the Confederate Congress. In this speech given just two weeks after the first shots of the Civil War were fired, Davis defended secession. He discussed the role of slavery in the Southern agricultural economy extensively. He declared that in the South, "brutal savages . . . were under the supervision of a superior race," and that "the labor of African slaves was and is indispensable" to the Southern economy.

The first and only Vice-President of the Confederate States of America, Alexander Stephens, had been a former U.S. Representative from Georgia. He gave a speech in Savannah, Georgia in March 1861, three weeks before the first shots of the Civil War. According to local Georgia newspaper transcripts of the speech, Stephens gave what became known as his famous "Cornerstone Speech." To a large, enthusiastic white crowd, Stephens announced:

> "The new [Confederate] constitution has put at rest, forever, all the agitating questions relating to our peculiar institution -- African slavery as it exists amongst us -- the proper status of the negro in our form of civilization. This

> was the immediate cause of the late rupture and present revolution. Jefferson in his forecast, had anticipated this, as the "rock upon which the old Union would split." He was right. . . . The prevailing ideas entertained by him and most of the leading statesmen at the time of the formation of the old [U.S.] constitution, were that the enslavement of the African was in violation of the laws of nature; that it was wrong in principle, socially, morally, and politically. . . . Those ideas, however, were fundamentally wrong. They rested upon the assumption of the equality of races. This was an error. . . . Our new government is founded upon exactly the opposite idea; its foundations are laid, its corner-stone rests upon the great truth, that the negro is not equal to the white man; that slavery -- subordination to the superior race -- is his natural and normal condition. . . . This, our new government, is the first, in the history of the world, based upon this great physical, philosophical, and moral truth."

A month later, Stephens spoke to the Virginia Secession Convention, where he re-emphasized the points in his Cornerstone Speech. He declared "The great truth, I repeat, upon which our system rests, is the inferiority of the African."

There were last-minute attempts by members of Congress, especially in the Senate, to negotiate with the South not to secede. A proposed "Crittenden Compromise" was named after its chief author, Senator John Crittenden from Kentucky. A "Peace Conference" also was held in Washington in February 1861. Negotiators both in the Senate and at the Peace Conference came up with proposals for amendments to the Constitution. The proposed Crittenden Compromise, and the Peace Conference proposals, all would have amended the U.S. Constitution to give the South the right to expand slavery and the right to have slavery in the South forever. However, these proposals failed to gain enough political support. Northerners were against any compromise that allowed slavery to expand or that preserved slavery forever. Southerners were against any compromise that did not preserve slavery and allow it to expand. There was no middle ground.

Civil War

Within a month after the peace negotiations failed, the first shots were fired by Southern troops at U.S. Fort Sumter in South Carolina in April 1861. The U.S. Civil War had begun. One way or the other, the war would finally settle the debate over slavery. Intentionally avoiding the problem of slavery during the writing of the Constitution had merely prolonged confronting the issue. Resolving the question was inevitable.

At the start of the war Lincoln's stated goal was merely to keep the Union united. However, in less than two years he decided to make the war expressly a war to end slavery. This was done for several reasons. First, he realized that even if the South was restored to the union, the issue of slavery would still be just as problematic. Slavery had been the root cause of the war, and so the issue needed to be settled once and for all. Also, the South was using its slaves during the war to help the Southern war effort. Slaves grew crops for troops, transported troops and supplies, built defenses, and so on. Every freed slave would be one less person the South would be able to force into aiding the Southern war effort. Moreover, the European powers had so far remained neutral in the war. This was because England and France depended heavily on agricultural trade with the South. For example, British textile mills needed Southern cotton to maintain clothing production. Northern naval blockades of Southern ports therefore risked war with Britain and France. Indeed, the South was trying to gain diplomatic recognition from England and France and perhaps military aid from them as well. Lincoln realized that making the war expressly a moral crusade to end slavery would make it hard for European nations to sympathize with the South or to object to blockades of the South.

In September 1862, Lincoln finally announced that unless the South surrendered by January 1, 1863, he would declare all the slaves in the rebelling states to be free. The border states of Kentucky, Missouri, Maryland, and Delaware still allowed slavery but had not joined the confederacy. To maintain political support from the border states, Lincoln decided for the time being not to address the issue of slavery in those states. When the deadline passed without any Southern States surrendering, Lincoln issued the Emancipation Proclamation on January 1, 1863. The Emancipation Proclamation made all the slaves in the Confederacy technically free, but it took Northern victory in the Civil War to actually implement it.

In November of 1863, there was a dedication of a cemetery and memorial for fallen soldiers at Gettysburg battlefield. While the war was still raging elsewhere, Lincoln appeared at the dedication and gave his famous *Gettysburg Address.* A mere 272 words, it states:

> Four score and seven years ago our fathers brought forth on this continent, a new nation, conceived in Liberty, and dedicated to the proposition that all men are created equal. Now we are engaged in a great civil war, testing whether that nation, or any nation so conceived and so dedicated, can long endure. We are met on a great battlefield of that war. We have come to dedicate a portion of that field, as a final resting place for those who here gave their lives that that nation might live. It is altogether fitting and proper that we should do this. But, in a larger sense, we cannot dedicate -- we cannot consecrate -- we cannot hallow -- this ground. The brave men, living

> and dead, who struggled here, have consecrated it, far above our poor power to add or detract. The world will little note, nor long remember what we say here, but it can never forget what they did here. It is for us the living, rather, to be dedicated here to the unfinished work which they who fought here have thus far so nobly advanced. It is rather for us to be here dedicated to the great task remaining before us -- that from these honored dead we take increased devotion to that cause for which they gave the last full measure of devotion -- that we here highly resolve that these dead shall not have died in vain -- that this nation, under God, shall have a new birth of freedom -- and that government of the people, by the people, for the people, shall not perish from the earth.

The Gettysburg Address is generally considered one of the best speeches in U.S. and world history. In the Address, Lincoln notes the United States is a great experiment with an as-yet-undetermined outcome. That experiment is whether a nation "conceived in liberty" and equality can then carry out those ideas. Can a nation consistently *practice* liberty and equality and still survive as a flourishing democracy in the long run? Can the United States not simply *declare* that all men are created equal, but can it actually *treat* all people equally, and still continue to exist as a nation?

While the North was now winning the war, Lincoln won re-election in November of 1864. He then gave his famous *Second Inaugural Address* in March 1865. By this time the Civil war had resulting in roughly 650,000 deaths. In the speech, Lincoln asserted that the Civil War was God's punishment against the entire United States, *both* the North and South, for either having or allowing slavery. He graciously hoped the North and South would reunite on friendly terms, "with malice towards none." On April 9, General Robert E. Lee, the commander of the Southern armies, surrendered. The U.S. Civil War was effectively over. Two days later, in Lincoln's final speech, for the first time he publicly expressed a desire that the right to vote be extended to blacks. A zealous confederate sympathizer and prominent American actor named John Wilkes Booth was in the crowd that heard the speech. Three days later, Booth assassinated Lincoln. Lincoln had freed four million people from enslavement, but paid the price with his own life.

Summary

Although Congress banned the international slave trade in 1808, domestic slavery continued in the South. Slavery was immoral and brutal, yet in the first half of the 1800's the Southern states perpetuated the enslavement of African-Americans through strict state laws. The South also gained several major national compromises allowing slavery to expand into additional U.S. territory and states.

During this time, the public in the Northern non-slave states increasingly opposed slavery. A series of slavery-related incidents throughout the 1850's caused increasing serious tension between the slaveholding states and the non-slaveholding states. When Lincoln was elected President in 1860, he was the first president ever to oppose the expansion of slavery. Southern whites knew that if slavery became confined to a limited geographic territory, the superior political numbers of the rest of the U.S. would eventually abolish slavery. Lincoln's election was therefore the "last straw" that led the Southern states to secede from the U.S. and form a Confederate States of America. The leaders of the Confederacy explained that they were leaving the U.S. to preserve the institution of human slavery. The Southern secession resulted in the Civil War between the Northern free states and the Southern slave states. At first U.S. President Lincoln tried to say the war was not about ending slavery, but he soon realized doing so was inevitable. In his Emancipation Proclamation, he announced the slaves would be freed. The United States of America finally defeated the Confederate States of America in 1865. As a result, slavery was abolished and four million people were set free.

Questions for Review and Self-Assessment

1. What was the life of a slave like, and how did the laws of the Southern slaveholding states perpetuate slavery?
2. How did slavery expand in the U.S., and how did this expansion cause increasing political tension in the U.S.?
3. How did the non-slaveholding states increasingly oppose slavery in the decade leading up to the U.S. Civil War?
4. How did Southern leaders defend the slaveholding states' secession from the U.S. at the time of secession?
5. What was the nature of the U.S. Civil War, and what were its most significant outcomes, especially in regards to slavery?

Critical Thinking Questions for Reflection and Discussion

1. Should the non-slaveholding states have stopped the spread of slavery sooner, even if that meant a civil war would have occurred sooner?
2. Why do modern "neoconfederates" argue that the South was not fighting to keep slavery, when southern leaders themselves said at the start of the Civil War that was why they were seceding and fighting?
3. What does the Confederate battle flag represent?

Suggested Reading Supplements

- *Dred Scott v. Sanford* (1857)

- Solomon Northup, *Twelve Years a Slave*
- Abraham Lincoln, *Second Inaugural Address*
- Ken Burns, *The Civil War* (video documentary series)

FOR FURTHER ADVANCED READING

- James MacPherson, *Battle Cry of Freedom: The Civil War Era (Oxford History of the United States).*

Chapter 10: Civil Rights

The Big Picture

A civil right protects against unjustified discrimination. One common type of irrational discrimination is treating people differently merely because of their race or skin color. After the U.S. Civil War, the U.S. tried to rebuild the southern war-torn states by educating the newly freed blacks and by giving them equal legal rights. Southern whites, however, soon used violence and the law to physically isolate blacks and to deny them equal political rights. After a century of whites-only rule in the Southern states, the U.S. government finally ended this discrimination through new laws. Since that time period, other racial minorities, religious minorities, women and sexual minorities have also received more equal treatment in the law across the U.S. Preventing any type of arbitrary discrimination requires that we understand where irrational prejudices come from.

Relevant Timeline

- 1865 Thirteenth Amendment ratified (abolition of slavery)
- 1868 Fourteenth Amendment ratified (equal protection of laws)
- 1870 Fifteenth Amendment ratified (racial equality in voting)
- 1877 Reconstruction ends
- 1896 *Plessy v. Ferguson* (racial segregation is constitutional)
- 1920 Nineteenth Amendment ratified (voting rights for women)
- 1954 *Brown v. Board of Education* (segregation unconstitutional)
- 1964 Civil Rights Act of 1964
- 1965 Voting Rights Act of 1965
- 2015 *Obergefell v. Hodges* (right to same-sex marriage)

Chapter Objectives

After reading this chapter, the reader should be able to:

1. Define civil rights and explain the historical significance of race discrimination in the U.S.
2. Describe civil rights in the South during and after reconstruction.
3. Describe how segregation and voting discrimination were finally ended by the Civil Rights Movement and several new U.S. laws.
4. Describe the history and current legal status of discrimination against women and sexual minorities.
5. Explain the several primary sources of irrational prejudices.

What are Civil Rights?

A *civil right* is the freedom from arbitrary discrimination. Notice the critical word *arbitrary,* meaning "unjust," "unfair," "irrational," or "unreasonable." Many people are confused about the concept of "discrimination." This is probably because there are two meanings of the word "discriminate." One meaning of discriminate is to "recognize differences," as in "she has a discriminating taste for fine food" or "young toddlers are often not yet able to discriminate between left and right." Another common use of the term "discriminate," however, means to treat someone unjustly because that person is different. There are endless ways people are different from each other. Yet historically, some of the most common and substantial kinds of this type of discrimination have involved race, religion, and sexual identity.

Not all "discrimination" in the first sense of the word is "discrimination" in the second sense of the word. That is, treating someone *differently* is not necessarily treating someone *unjustly.* To be clear, *not all differential treatment is unjust.* The law treats people differently all the time, yet we as a society find nothing wrong with it, or even believe it's a good thing. That is, much differential treatment is fair and reasonable. For example, only families with lower incomes qualify for government-provided student loans. Wealthy students are discriminated against. But, this public policy makes sense because there is only so much taxpayer money available. In choosing who gets such financial aid, then, it makes sense not to give government loans to millionaires. Also, people in the U.S. can't marry or legally drive cars until they turn 16, vote until they turn 18, or drink alcohol until they turn 21. These laws discriminate against the young because only at a certain age do we become mature enough to drive, vote, or handle liquor. We might debate about where the proper age cutoff should be, but we can all agree that two-year-olds are not mature enough to safely engage in any of these acts. We all want the law to treat two-year-olds different than adults.

As another example, only people with the best high school GPA's or college entrance exam scores are admitted as public university students. This means people with lower grades and standardized test scores are being discriminated against by government. Yet again, though, we have only limited resources to provide higher education. So, our society has decided that it makes sense to provide advanced education only to those who seem most likely to intellectually succeed in college. Similarly, government agencies and businesses try to hire the most qualified experts for many jobs. This means less qualified workers are being discriminated against by government and businesses. However, we accept and desire this policy. We don't want someone with an IQ of 65 to be designing, building, or operating nuclear power plants, planning military strategy, crafting economic policies, writing health care legislation, performing brain surgery, and so on.

You can probably think of other examples where the law treats people differently and it's a good thing the law does so. All these illustrations show that the concept of "civil rights" is not simply a question of being treated differently. A "civil right" is the freedom not to be treated differently *for an unfair reason.* The question in every situation is whether treating people differently is *reasonable and justified* or *arbitrary and unjustified.* Is the differential treatment in question just or unjust? For example, treating someone differently based on irrational prejudice, ungrounded fears, or false stereotypes is unjust. In short, civil rights do not provide a "freedom from discrimination" but only a "freedom from unjustified discrimination. "

Throughout U.S. history, there have been numerous public policies based on unfounded fears, irrational prejudices, and negative stereotypes. Two of the more major and common types of such arbitrary discrimination, however, have been discrimination based on race, and discrimination based on sexual identity. Sexual identity includes sex, gender, and sexual orientation. The philosopher George Santayana famously said "Those who cannot remember the past are condemned to repeat it." Knowing the past is therefore essential to learning how to avoid similar injustices today and in the future.

Race Discrimination

In the history of almost every country on the planet, the dominant ethnic groups have at some point oppressed minority ethnic groups. Ethnic groups have discriminated against, gone to war against, enslaved, or sometimes even committed genocide against, each other within and across their nations. Throughout U.S. history the dominant majority ethnic group has been people of European ancestry. Another term sometimes used for this group is "White Anglo-Saxon Protestants," or "WASP" for short. This demographic may change within the next few decades if current population trends continue. However, for the time being, this is still the case.

Practically every ethnic group in the U.S. has at some time or another suffered as a result of public policy that was prejudiced against non-whites. Indeed, some historical scholars have argued that of all the public policy issues the United States has ever been involved in, the biggest and most important public policy issue throughout U.S. history has been that of race. Regardless whether it is the most important issue, or one of the most important, race has certainly has played a huge role in the history of American politics. It continues to do so today as well.

There are many sad episodes of mistreatment of minority ethnic groups throughout U.S. history. Public policy toward Native American tribes involved consistent oppression. This included treaty-breaking, land theft, forced relocation, massacres, wars, physical isolation on "reservations," and confiscation of reservation lands through "allotment" to white settlers. From the late 1800's through well into the 1900's, Congress also authorized the systematic abduction and "re-education" of Native American children into white culture in boarding schools. This was part of a Congressional policy of "assimilation." The goal was to eliminate the separate identity of Native Americans tribes and to instead force them to become part of the dominant culture. It was only in the latter half of the 20th Century that Congress began to allow Native American tribes to re-assert their cultural identity and maintain more aspects of their tribal sovereignty.

U.S. policy towards various groups of Asian-Americans has been highly discriminatory as well. Chinese immigrant labor had worked especially on building railroads in the Western U.S. during the mid-to-late 1800s. This included the first Transcontinental Railroad. Chinese immigrants worked for a fraction of the wages for which non-Chinese laborers worked. They were forced to live in racially segregated communities that came to be known as "Chinatowns." After an economic depression in the U.S. began in 1873 and lasted many years, white workers in the west used Chinese laborers as scapegoats for the inability of whites to find jobs. White mobs attacked several dozen communities of Chinese immigrants throughout the Western U.S., killing many Chinese immigrants. At this same time, state laws in the Western U.S. outlawed most ownership of property or businesses to Chinese-Americans or other Asian-Americans, denied voting rights to Chinese-Americans or other Asian Americans, and segregated Chinese-Americans and other Asian-Americans into specific neighborhoods. State laws in the Western U.S. also banned marriage between whites and people of Asian ancestry.

Decades later, after the nation of Japan attacked Hawaii's Pearl Harbor in 1941, President Franklin D. Roosevelt and the U.S. Congress authorized the mass imprisonment of all Japanese-American men, women, and children who lived along the west coast of the U.S. This was done out of an unfounded fear that Americans with Japanese ancestry would be disloyal. They were transported and imprisoned in "internment camps" in the interior of the U.S. away from the west coast. Even though many of these same Japanese-Americans were then allowed to fight for the United States in the U.S. military, their families remained imprisoned for the duration of World War II. This imprisonment was upheld against constitutional challenge in the 1943 U.S. Supreme Court case *U.S. v. Korematsu*. The Court said the imprisonment was justified by "wartime necessity."

Latino-Americans, especially Mexican-Americans, have also suffered racial injustice. Before Texas became part of the United States, it was originally part of Mexico. At first, Texans of both Mexican and European ancestry joined together to fight for Texan independence in 1836. Texas then joined the U.S., even though

Mexico still claimed the territory as its own. Texas was firmly established as part of the U.S. after the 1858 U.S. victory in the Mexican-American War. Yet after the U.S. victory, thousands of Mexican-Americans were violently driven off their land by whites. This happened in the newly conquered territories of California, Arizona, New Mexico, and Texas, especially along the Rio Grande valley. This land theft occurred even against the numerous Mexican-Americans that had fought with white Texans on the side of the United States against Mexico. For decades afterwards, Mexican-Americans in this part of the United States faced pervasive discrimination when it came to their ability to seek jobs and their attempt to exercise the right to vote. They were also victims of regular violence by whites against them if they resisted any of these forms of discrimination to which they were being subjected.

Many other racial or ethnic groups have faced discrimination in the U.S. as well. Various European immigrants sometimes suffered harsh prejudice, especially Irish-American Catholics in the mid-1800's. They were fleeing famine in Ireland but were often victims of violent anti-immigrant hostility when they arrived in the United States. People of Jewish, Arabic, and other Middle-Eastern ancestry have similarly faced hostilities upon arrival to the United States, and they still often do.

Despite the suffering caused by racial discrimination against various ethnic groups within the United States, however, around the world the U.S. is most known for having oppressed one particular racial group: its own citizens of African ancestry. Therefore, we'll pay particular attention to this history. In the previous chapter on slavery, we saw how brutal human slavery was, and how it tore the United States apart. In this chapter, we'll examine how the struggle for equal legal rights for African-Americans evolved after the Civil War.

RECONSTRUCTION

The U.S. Civil War lasted from 1861-1865. The South had been ruined physically and economically, but more importantly the social and legal institution of slavery had been destroyed. The South needed to be rebuilt, or "reconstructed" in every way. The period of U.S. history from 1865 to 1877 is therefore known as *reconstruction*. During this time, the U.S. government put many public policies in place which attempted to reconstruct the south.

The U.S. government defeated the Confederacy in April 1865. By the end of the year, Congress and the states had amended the U.S. Constitution to abolish slavery everywhere in the U.S. The *Thirteenth Amendment* reads "Neither slavery not involuntary servitude . . . shall exist within the United States." (See the film "Lincoln" for an excellent, largely historically accurate account of the Congressional passage of the Thirteenth Amendment.).

The abolition of slavery hardly settled the matter of black rights, though. Throughout the Southern states, legislatures at both the state and local level passed what became known as *"Black Codes."* These codes did many different things restricting the rights of the newly freed blacks. For example, the Black Codes often restricted blacks from owning land, or said where they could own or rent land, or limited the types of contracts they could make. Sometimes the codes restricted the assembly and travel of blacks. The Black Codes did much more than this, though.

Basically, the Black Codes were attempting a return to something close to slavery or indentured servitude, but without calling it such. Southern white lawmakers adapted employment law and criminal law to re-impose something close to indentured servitude. The Codes often required blacks to sign employment contracts that said the employee could leave at any time, but then the employee would have to forfeit a huge sum, often up to a year's wages. Also, the Codes typically defined the crime of "vagrancy" as being either poor or unemployed. If a black person was convicted of vagrancy or any other crime, a heavy fine would be imposed. If the convicted black person couldn't pay the fine—which was common--then by court order the black person would be leased to a white person to work for them for free until the fine was paid off. This practice was called "convict leasing." Even simple crimes committed by a black person were punishable by sizeable fines as compared to if a white person committed the same crime. By defining unemployment as a crime punishable by a large fine with a sentence of mandatory labor, Southern laws effectively re-created the equivalent of slavery and indentured servitude. In one instance, the all-white local government of St. Landry Parish, Louisiana, created their Black Code merely by modifying their former slave code. Their new Black Code simply replaced the word "slave" with the word "negro," and the words "owner" or "master" with the word "employer."

The Black Codes did other things as well. They sometimes prohibited blacks from owning firearms, as had been the case under slavery. This prevented blacks from possessing the means to defend themselves against armed whites. Moreover, under the Black Codes, free blacks still were not citizens, and so typically were not allowed to vote, serve on juries, or testify against whites in court. In sum, although slavery had been abolished, the Black Codes still treated blacks as a distant second-class group of people to whites.

Lincoln's Vice-President was Andrew Johnson, a former Senator from Tennessee. He had been the only Southern Democrat that remained in the U.S. Senate after the South seceded. Lincoln therefore picked him as his vice-presidential candidate in the 1864 election to symbolize national unity. Johnson became President when Lincoln was assassinated.

Johnson did little to enforce civil rights in the South. He even vetoed Congressional attempts to pass civil rights legislation. The large Republican majority in Congress overrode most of his vetoes, though. Congress also was able to bypass Johnson through the Constitutional amendment process. In response to the

Black Codes, in 1868 Congress and the states added the Fourteenth Amendment to the Constitution. It has several parts, including a declaration that anyone born within the United States is a citizen. This provision made all slaves citizens, thereby overturning the Supreme Court's *Dred Scott v. Sanford* ruling in 1857. The effect of the Citizenship Clause today means that children born in the U.S. are citizens regardless whether their immigrant parents are here legally or in violation of U.S. immigration law.

Another key feature of the Fourteenth Amendment is the Equal Protection Clause. It declares "no state shall deny to any person the equal protection of the laws." The Equal Protection Clause is one of the most important parts of the Constitution. Along with the rest of the Fourteenth Amendment, it provides the foundation of constitutional civil rights within the United States.

Despite the passage of the Thirteenth and Fourteenth Amendments, though, blacks still were not guaranteed voting rights. The right to vote is also called "the franchise." To be "disenfranchised" means one is denied the right to vote. Voting rights are also called the right of "suffrage." This comes from the Latin *suffragium*, meaning "voting." To guarantee black suffrage, the Fifteenth Amendment was added to the Constitution in 1870. It states "the right to vote shall not be denied on account of race . . ." Although seemingly redundant with the Fourteenth Amendment, supporters basically argued that it was better to be safe than sorry. Given the previous Southern white evasion of the Thirteenth Amendment through the Black Codes, Southern whites might try to do the same with the Fourteenth Amendment. Therefore, the Fifteenth Amendment was added as extra security for voting rights for the newly freed blacks. Because the Thirteenth, Fourteenth, and Fifteenth Amendments were all enacted within a short time period as a consequence of the outcome of the Civil War, they are collectively referred to as the *Civil War Amendments.*

It was only after Republican President Ulysses Grant took office in 1869 that U.S. troops occupying the South began implementing the Civil War Amendments. Enforcement made the southern states give at least some respect to the legal rights of free blacks. According to the 1870 census, the black population comprised 34% of the South's population. Blacks were even a majority of the population in Mississippi (55%) and South Carolina (57%). With federal enforcement of voting rights, Mississippi elected two black senators, and South Carolina's congressional delegation was majority black. In Louisiana, a black lieutenant governor was elected and almost 30 blacks were elected to the state legislature. Also, the federal government's *Freedman's Bureau* provided aid and education, including the creation of schools and colleges, for newly freed blacks across the entire South.

WHITE SUPREMACY

Despite civil rights progress in the South during reconstruction, violent white defiance was widespread. This included organized resistance from white paramilitary groups like the Ku Klux Klan (KKK) which began in Tennessee, and the White League, which formed in Louisiana. At its peak, the KKK had somewhere between 250,000 and 500,000 members. It initially was led by former Confederate General Nathan Bedford Forrest. Many historical scholars refer to these white supremacist groups as the military wing of the Democratic Party in the South during this time. Federal officials overseeing reconstruction at the time estimated that at least hundreds if not thousands of blacks were murdered across the South trying to exercise their legal rights.

In the state of Louisiana alone, there was almost constant violence. This included several massacres of blacks, often including their white Republican supporters as well. Massacres occurred in New Orleans in 1866 and Coushatta in 1874, as well as a decade after Reconstruction in Thibodeaux in 1887. In Colfax, Louisiana in 1873, the worst massacre during all of Southern reconstruction occurred. Over 100 black men were murdered for attempting to exercise their voting rights. Three of the white attackers were killed during the massacre. Local whites referred to the incident as a black "riot," thereby attempting to justify the massacre to federal law enforcement officials. Not a single attacker was ever convicted. White state prosecutors would not prosecute white killings of blacks, and a federal attempt to prosecute was dismissed because this type of murder was not a federal crime. A monument erected by local whites to honor the three dead white attackers still stands in the Colfax cemetery. The monument states the three men "fell in the Colfax riot fighting for white supremacy."

After a decade of enduring continually uncooperative, obstructive, and violent Southern whites, Northerners grew exhausted. The North was tired of trying to enforce civil rights in the South by occupying it. A majority of Northerners finally lost the political will to continue to oversee that the South was respecting the civil rights of free blacks. The final death of reconstruction occurred in the contested 1876 Presidential election between Republican candidate Hayes and Democratic candidate Tilden. The electoral vote count was close, and several Southern states offered two competing vote counts. One count favored Hayes, the other count favored Tilden. The state legislatures in the disputed Southern states agreed to let Hayes have their electoral votes, but only if Hayes and the Republican Party agreed to end reconstruction. The Republican Party agreed, so Hayes became President in the spring of 1877. He and the Congress immediately ended the policy of reconstruction. U.S. troops were withdrawn, thereby ceasing the enforcement of civil rights for blacks in the South.

After the U.S. government stopped enforcement of civil rights in the South, Southern whites at first could not re-impose white supremacy through the normal political process. This was because there were now too many black voters and black elected officials who could block the passage of laws to recreate white supremacy. Southern whites therefore first needed to retake political power some other way. The only way whites could retake political power was by stopping blacks from voting. This would allow white voters to elect all white officials, who would then re-impose white supremacy. Since whites lacked the political power to do this legally, they turned to widespread, systematic terrorism. The KKK and other paramilitary white supremacist groups rose up again. They threatened, beat, stabbed, shot, lynched and otherwise murdered thousands of black leaders and political activists. Regular black citizens were similarly terrorized if they exercised, or tried to exercise, their right to vote. Homes, schools, businesses, and churches of black voters, activists, and elected officials were burned as well. Black voting dropped substantially. Whites were then able to retake political power by electing whites in all lawmaking positions at the local, state, and federal level in the South.

Economically, the end of reconstruction left the large majority of blacks in poverty. White plantation owners had been given back almost all their land by President Andrew Johnson. This occurred despite the fact that the white owners had purchased the land almost entirely from money made by slave labor. There had been ideas to give each newly freed black "forty acres and a mule" so that blacks could become financially self-sufficient. Yet there was not enough political support for any such proposal. As a result, free blacks had no farmland of their own. Since agriculture was still the primary basis of the economy, farming was the only way most people could earn a living. Free blacks therefore had to go back to work for white land owners as *sharecroppers*. This meant that blacks would be leased cropland in exchange for a large share of the crops to be given to the landowner at harvest time. Free blacks often became sharecroppers on the same plantations where they had been slaves. Their former owner was now their landlord.

Once whites took back political and economic power in the South, they manipulated legal technicalities that allowed them to bypass the Fourteenth and Fifteenth Amendments. They did this through two methods of re-establishing white supremacy: voting discrimination and segregation. These mechanisms solidified and perpetuated legal rule by white supremacy for almost a century. As we shall see shortly, it was not until the 1960's that such voting discrimination and segregation were federally outlawed. More importantly, the U.S. government finally began to actually *enforce* civil rights laws. This long delay in enforcement meant that for a century after the Civil War, the South lived in a racial class system based on the alleged supremacy of whites over blacks. A social system where one race has superior legal privileges to another race is also called a racial *caste* system. In short, the South defeated the North's efforts at reconstruction for 100 years. Man historians therefore conclude that the South lost the Civil War, but it won Reconstruction.

Voting Discrimination

When Reconstruction ended, Southern whites regained political power through widespread, systematic terrorism. Since few blacks voted because of the fear of being murdered, all-white governments were elected. The first thing the newly elected white leaders did was to pass laws to prevent blacks from voting themselves back into power. To do this, state and local governments in the South passed a series of laws that made it extremely difficult for blacks to vote. These laws carefully evaded the Fourteenth and Fifteenth Amendments, yet achieved the same result as overt racial discrimination. This was done through many mechanisms, but the following are some the most common.

Poll taxes. You had to pay a fee in order to vote. The former slaves, now free blacks, had received no education, income, or property when they were enslaved. As noted earlier in this chapter, there had been a proposal to give each former slave 40 acres and a mule to become self-sufficient farmers. The plan was politically defeated, and the large plantations were given back to their white owners. Free blacks were largely forced to be sharecroppers with little income, often renting land from the very same whites who had been their former owners. Because of this, it was difficult for many free blacks to afford the poll taxes. The white majority in the South wasn't extremely concerned about poor whites who could not afford the poll taxes. Besides, the poll taxes were often selectively enforced only against blacks. In other words, when it came time to pay the poll tax, it was strictly enforced against blacks, but either enforced leniently or not at all against whites.

Literacy tests. You had to pass a literacy test before you could vote. Remember from the previous chapter that the slave laws had made it a crime to give any education to slaves. After abolition, the federal Freedman's Bureau set up many schools for blacks. Yet Southern whites refused to teach in these schools. As a result, even after many years of reconstruction, a large percent of free blacks were still illiterate. In such a case it was difficult or impossible to pass a literacy test. As black education increased over the years, the tests were eventually rigged so that it was impossible to pass the test. For example, the author of this textbook earned both a Ph.D. and a J.D., each with a focus on studying the U.S. Constitution. One of the many different literacy tests used in Alabama asked ten questions about the U.S. Constitution. The author failed the test, scoring only four points. The test asked only obscure trivia questions about the Constitution that not even constitutional experts bother to learn. Since even whites would fail this test, when it was actually administered the passing scores were different for whites and blacks, or the test would be waived for whites.

Grandfather Clauses. In 1898, the Louisiana legislated decided that too many poor or illiterate whites were unable to vote because they could not afford the poll tax or they could not pass the literacy test. Therefore, the law was changed so that you were exempt from the poll and literacy tests if your *grandfather* could vote prior to 1867. Recall that 1867 was the year prior to the ratification of the Fifteenth Amendment, which guaranteed the right to vote regardless of race. No blacks could legally vote in the South prior to 1867, whereas whites could. This meant that the "Grandfather Clause" exempted only whites from the poll and literacy tests. Several other Southern states later copied Louisiana's use of a Grandfather Clause, but not all. In some cases, the rich, well-educated whites were content that poor, illiterate whites could not vote due to poll taxes and literacy tests.

One-Race Party Primaries: Remember Lincoln had been a Republican. The Republican Party had strongly supported the Civil War, the abolition of slavery, and Reconstruction. As a result, whites in the South hated the Republican Party and overwhelmingly voted for the Democratic Party. After Reconstruction ended and white supremacy was reestablished, not *one single* Republican candidate was elected to any local, state, or federal position in any of the states of the former Confederacy. The South was therefore called the "Solid South." The Democratic Party in the Southern states refused to let blacks take part in any party conventions, nominating process, or primary elections within the Democratic Party. This guaranteed that only white—and white supremacist---Democratic Party candidates would appear on the ballot. Since Southern whites voted so overwhelmingly Democratic during this time, whoever was the Democratic candidate would win the local election. Racial discrimination by Southern Democrats therefore guaranteed that only white supremacist politicians would be elected to local offices in the South. Political historians view Southern Democrats during this time as essentially a third political party in addition to the Republican Party and the national (non-Southern) Democratic Party.

Racial gerrymandering: "Gerrymandering" is manipulating the boundaries of a voting district. This is done to maximize the chance of winning by one political party, usually by concentrating voters of one party into the district. This particular electoral mechanism is also called "diluting" the votes of one's opposition. In short, gerrymandering is rigging a voting district boundary to make it more likely you will win and your opponent will lose. Gerrymandering can be based on many different factors, but Southern state legislatures engaged in racial gerrymandering. Black voting strength was diluted so that to the degree possible, whites comprised a majority of every voting district. This meant that even if every black voter turned out to vote for a black candidate, a white candidate would still be elected. (Fun Fact:

the term "gerrymandering" goes back to 1812. The governor of Massachusetts, Elbridge Gerry, redrew a voting district to benefit his own party. People said the bizarrely shaped district looked like a salamander. Someone combined "Gerry" with "Salamander" to make the word "gerrymander." Ever since then, the term refers to manipulation of voting district boundaries.)

All these methods of voting discrimination worked together. Besides these various laws, whites continued to use death threats, arsons, beatings, lynchings, and other violence against blacks who even tried to vote or become politically active. Also, blacks could lose their job with a white employer, and be unable to find another job with a white employer, if the employer found out a black employee tried to vote or become politically active. When all these discriminatory laws and practices were implemented, not *one single* black was elected to any public office in the entire South. The voting rate by Southern blacks in the South plummeted to .2 percent. This figure is not two percent, but *point-two*-percent, or two-tenths of one percent. Eventually but slowly, these discriminatory laws and practices were eliminated over the fierce and often violent objections by white southern voters and politicians. Chronologically this changed happened in the following order.

- 1915: The U.S. Supreme Court ruled that Grandfather Clauses violated the Fifteenth Amendment.
- 1948: The U.S. Supreme Court ruled that Southern Democrats may not exclude Blacks from primary elections because doing so violates the Fourteenth and Fifteenth Amendments.
- 1964: The Twenty-Fourth Amendment to the U.S. Constitution was ratified, which outlawed poll taxes in federal elections.
- 1965: Congress passed the Voting Rights Act of 1965, which (among other things) outlawed literacy tests. Also, for the first time since reconstruction, the U.S. government began to once again enforce voting rights in the South.
- 1966: The U.S. Supreme Court ruled that poll taxes in state and local elections violate the Fourteenth Amendment.
- 1982: Congress amended the Voting Rights Act of 1965. The addition prohibits "any practice or procedure" that results in voting discrimination, regardless of intent. This had the effect of outlawing racial gerrymandering, among other things.

Notice that the end of the Civil War was 1865, and the Voting Rights Act was 1965. The South had formal political rule by white racial supremacy for a full 100 years after the Civil War. Again, this is why most historians say the South lost the Civil War but won Reconstruction. In other words, the South lost the shooting war, but won the political battle to preserve white supremacy and prevent racial equality for a full century.

At the height of the Civil Rights Movement in the early 1960's, the U.S. government and civil rights groups helped Southern blacks register to vote. Southern whites frequently resorted to violence and terrorism to stop the efforts. As just a few examples, in the year 1963 alone there were many instances of bloodshed that received prominent media coverage around the nation and the world. Mississippi NAACP (National Association for the Advancement of Colored People) leader Medgar Evers was assassinated in Jackson, Mississippi. In another part of Mississippi, several voter registration volunteers were murdered by KKK and local police working together (see the film "Mississippi Burning"). Across the South, there were arsons and bombings of black churches, one of which killed four young girls in Birmingham. Two years later in 1965, numerous civil rights activists were beaten and several murdered in or near Selma, Alabama. Then just three years later in 1968, the foremost leader of the civil rights movement, Martin Luther King, was assassinated in Memphis, Tennessee. The former hotel where he was murdered is now the National Civil Rights Museum.

Racial Segregation

Voting discrimination was only one of the two primary ways Southern whites implemented white supremacy. Voting discrimination created white *political* supremacy. White *social* supremacy, on the other hand, was created by a widespread system of *racial segregation* in the South. By law and by custom, blacks were forced to be physically separated and isolated away from whites in every way humanly imaginable. This included neighborhoods, schools, shops, restaurants, theaters, courtrooms, trains, busses, hospitals, hotels, churches, restrooms, water fountains, parks, swimming pools, beaches, the military, jails, prisons, and even cemeteries, among other ways. As merely one other example, most Southern courtrooms had two Bibles that court witnesses could place their hands on to swear their oath of truthfulness. One Bible was for whites to touch, and one for blacks to touch. All these many forms of segregation were collectively referred to as "Jim Crow" laws. Jim Crow was a black character in an old 1800's minstrel show.

Besides Jim Crow laws, other laws and practices kept the races separate as well. Interracial dating was not legally forbidden, but was socially taboo. Persons caught doing so could be violently beaten. Interracial marriage was a crime with a long prison term. White homeowners were forbidden by law from selling their homes to a "noncaucasian," even if the owner wanted to do so. Even if this was not forbidden by law, the title deeds to white-owned property contractually prohibited the new owner from ever selling to a black person. In legal terms this is called a "restrictive covenant." The sum total of Southern racial segregation was similar to many of the things Germany did to Jews in the 1930's, prior to forcing Jews into concentration camps and systematically murdering them.

The legality of segregation was challenged in the 1896 U.S. Supreme Court case of *Plessy v. Ferguson.* Louisiana law required "equal but separate accommodations" for white versus black railroad passengers. Homer Plessy was 7/8 white and 1/8 black, but was not allowed to sit in a white car. Southern laws typically defined a person as "black" if they were as little as one-sixteenth black. That is, if any one of your great-great-grandparents was black, the law classified you as black. Plessy argued that the Fourteenth Amendment's Equal Protection Clause prohibited racial segregation. The Court, however, declared that laws which make the races "separate but equal" do not violate the Fourteenth Amendment. The Court said the Civil War Amendments were intended to create *political* equality only (such as voting rights), not *social* equality, and the Constitution can't make the races mix if they don't want to. Moreover, the court explained that social legislation must only be "reasonable" to be constitutional. In this case, Louisiana was upholding public peace and order based on longstanding social traditions and customs. The court was implying that violence would result if the races mixed. The court went further and declared that segregation is not intended to stamp blacks with a badge of inferiority, unless blacks choose it take it that way. This was an obviously false statement, however, because everyone at the time, both white and black, Northern and Southern, understood the white supremacist nature of racial segregation.

With the ruling in *Plessy v. Ferguson*, it was clear to everyone that the Supreme Court was not going to interfere with the racial caste system in the South. Although technically the case only involved segregated train cars, the effect of the case was to uphold the principle of racial segregation across the entire Southern social structure. After *Plessy v. Ferguson*, Southern whites expanded segregation in every way they could conceive. (See the film "The Help" for a mild portrayal of segregation in Jackson, Mississippi at the start of the Civil Rights era, and see the film "Something the Lord Made" for a portrayal of racial prejudice in general during the height of segregation.)

The Supreme Court case of *Plessy v. Ferguson* established the constitutional doctrine of "separate but equal." In reality, though, the "equal" part of "separate but equal" was never anywhere near equal. Blacks could sit only in the balcony in theaters and courtrooms. They could sit only in the back of busses, or had to give their seat up to a white person, or both. Facilities for blacks, such as schools, were vastly inferior compared to the same facilities whites had. These facts were ignored by the Supreme Court for several decades. Eventually, in the late 1940's and early 1950's, the Supreme Court started to more strictly enforce the "equal" part of "separate but equal." In the context of schools, for example, this meant equal funding for school buildings, teacher salaries, textbooks, course offerings, lab supplies, busses, extracurricular activities, and so on.

It's easy to compare equality of spending, but what about intangible things that are hard to numerically measure? In other words, what about equality in things such as educational, social, and career opportunities that segregation might hinder? Eventually the Supreme Court had to decide not only this question, but whether the negative stamp of segregation was itself unequal. In the landmark, unanimous 1954 Supreme Court ruling *Brown v. Board of Education of Topeka, Kansas*, the Supreme Court finally ruled that segregation was unconstitutional. The Court declared that stamping an entire race as inferior through legally enforced physical isolation is inherently *un*equal. Racial segregation thus violates both the letter and spirit of the Equal Protection Clause of the Fourteenth Amendment. *Plessy v. Ferguson* was overruled, and the "separate but equal" doctrine was no longer valid law. Although the case dealt with segregation in the context of schools, the case destroyed the justification for segregation as a whole. In the next several years, the Court made clear their ruling applied to all the various contexts of segregation. However, because the Equal Protection Clause only prohibits discrimination by government, Congress later passed the Civil Rights Act of 1964. It prohibits racial discrimination by *private* businesses and employers.

Southern whites hated *Brown v. Board of Education*, and openly and violently resisted it. Southern governors, legislatures, school boards, police departments, and judges all refused to enforce the ruling. They redrew school attendance zones, tore down and relocated schools, and in some cases even closed entire school districts rather than allow black children to go to school with white children. In one famous example, in 1957 the Governor of Arkansas used state National Guard troops armed with guns to block nine black children from going to Little Rock Central High School. U.S. President Eisenhower ordered the Governor to stop doing so. The governor simply withdrew the state National Guard, leaving the "Little Rock Nine" black schoolchildren unprotected. Mobs of angry whites threatened to attack any black children trying to enter the school. President Eisenhower then sent over 1,000 armed troops from the 101st Airborne Division to enforce integration at Little Rock Central High School. Troops and federal marshals stayed for the rest of the school year to protect the black children and their families from violence by whites. Eisenhower also federalized all 10,000 National Guard troops in Arkansas so that the Governor could not use them to block further attempts at school integration. The school board in Little Rock then closed the Little Rock public schools for a year as a final effort to prevent integration. Within a year, however, enough whites wanted their children to receive a public education that a new school board was elected. The schools were re-opened the following year on a racially integrated basis.

Yet widespread white opposition to school integration continued. White school boards and local legislatures closed existing schools near the border of segregated neighborhoods. In place of those former schools, new schools were opened deep in the middle of white neighborhoods and deep in the middle of black neighborhoods. Then, by drawing attendance zones in a certain way, white leaders could guarantee the schools would be either all-white or all-black. In response, the Supreme Court gave U.S. District Courts wide powers to order desegregation. This included the power to redraw attendance zones or even bus students between segregated schools. As a result, many whites decided to move to other cities or states rather than have their children attend racially integrated schools. This contributed to "white flight" out of urban areas. Court oversight of formerly segregated school districts has gone on for many decades due to the difficulties in desegregating them. For example, a federal court ruling in 2014 declared there would be no legal duty to further desegregate the Little Rock schools after the year 2018.

The Civil Rights Movement

As explained earlier, Southern whites imposed racial segregation in nearly every facet of life, not just education. Black political activists had been fighting voting segregation and voting discrimination throughout the Jim Crow period. These efforts finally began to achieve wider publicity across the U.S. and the world in the 1950's as television ownership became commonplace. Television coverage by national and international news organizations exposed white supremacy in the South. As a result, black activists, with increasing support from whites, began to achieve political success in the 1950's and 1960's. These efforts are collectively known as the *Civil Rights Movement.*

Historians generally consider that the modern Civil Rights Movement began with one especially famous example of black resistance to segregation. This occurred in 1954 in Montgomery, Alabama. A woman named Rosa Parks was a local leader in the NAACP. In violation of law, she refused to give up her bus seat to a white person. She peacefully submitted to arrest at the next bus stop. Rosa Parks' arrest sparked the start of the Civil Rights Movement. The Rev. Dr. Martin Luther King, Jr., went to Montgomery and helped organize a year-long boycott of the Montgomery bus system. King rose to prominence as a civil rights leader as a result of his work on the boycott. Throughout the next decade, he and countless other leaders and ordinary citizens overcame many obstacles and much hardship in their struggle to achieve legal equality for blacks. Some black leaders such as Malcolm X and his Black Panther organization argued that violence should be used if necessary to achieve racial justice. King was able to persuade the large majority of civil rights activists, however, that only peaceful, nonviolent means should be used to achieve their goals. As the premier leader of the Civil Rights Movement, King received the Nobel Peace Prize in 1964 for his efforts.

Another famous example of the struggle for civil rights began in 1961. Groups of protestors comprised of both whites and blacks rode Greyhound busses in the South in order to protest bus segregation. These "freedom riders" were frequently beaten by white mobs with the willing cooperation of local police. One freedom rider bus was even fire-bombed. Remarkably no passenger died as they were all able to escape the bus. Across the South, civil rights marchers and sit-in demonstrators were regularly beaten, fire hosed, and attacked by police dogs. Some of the most famous such images come from Birmingham, Alabama. There, the local police chief, "Bull" Connor took a militant, violent stand against the peaceful, nonviolent civil rights protesters seeking to end segregation.

Another famous and perhaps worst example happened in 1962. A federal court had ordered the University of Mississippi in Oxford, Mississippi to admit its first black student, James Meredith. The Governor of Mississippi refused to stop large crowds of whites from violently rioting. In fact, his speeches implicitly urged them to do so. President John F. Kennedy sent several hundred armed U.S. marshals to defend Meredith. On the night of September 29, hundreds of armed whites besieged the federal marshals who holed up in the main administration building on the campus. This is where whites thought the federal marshals were hiding Meredith. Although several dozen marshals were shot, remarkably none of them was killed, but two journalists died in the nightlong shootout. None of the white attackers died because President Kennedy had given the marshals strict order to *not* return fire except with tear gas and smoke canisters. President Kennedy then sent in several thousand U.S. troops who arrived by morning. They prevented further violence by whites, and the troops stayed for a year to protect Meredith. This was the final occasion where armed northerners, the federal marshals, fought against armed southerners, the white rioters, to establish racial equality in the South. For this reason, some historians have called this event "the Battle of Oxford" or "the last battle of the Civil War."

As a result of the Civil Rights Movement, racial segregation and voting discrimination were both outlawed. Toward the end of these achievements, Martin Luther King made a famous speech on March 28, 1963. A quarter million supporters of the Civil Rights Movement marched in Washington, D.C. Speaking on the steps of the Lincoln Memorial, King said the U.S. had originally given a "promissory note" to blacks that they would receive equality. However, the promissory note was a "bad check." When blacks tried to cash it, it came back marked "insufficient funds." In other words, the U.S. had promised equality, but the promise was not yet honored. King then turned to what became the theme of his speech. He repeatedly stated "I have a dream" of different manifestations of racial equality. His most remembered line is "I have a dream that my four little children will one day live in a nation where they will not be judged by the color of their skin, but by the content of their character." What became known as King's "I Have a Dream" speech is generally recognized as one of the greatest speeches in U.S. history, perhaps second only to Lincoln's Gettysburg Address.

Despite the work of King and many others, a decade after the Supreme Court's desegregation ruling in *Brown v. Board of Education*, many Southern governments still refused to comply with it. Finally the Supreme Court, Congress, and the President all became much more active in achieving desegregation through stronger court rulings, Congressional legislation, and Department of Justice enforcement of federal laws. It took late into the next decade for racial integration to be substantially implemented across the South. Even the Supreme Court didn't rule that the Equal Protection Clause protected a right to interracial marriage until the 1967 case of *Loving v. Virginia.* White supremacy therefore reigned in the South for a century after the end of the U.S. Civil war. As noted earlier, this is why historians often say the South lost the Civil War, but won Reconstruction.

The Civil War is sometimes referred to as the "Second Founding" of the United States, given that the U.S. re-emphasized the principle of equality found in the original Declaration of Independence. Correspondingly, the Civil Rights Movement is sometimes referred to as "The Second Reconstruction." Abraham Lincoln gave freedom to everyone by ending slavery, and Martin Luther King spearheaded equal justice under law for blacks. King was helped by countless other leaders who fought for civil rights, but King was and is recognized as the leader of the movement. These new principles of racial equality he led the way in establishing are different from those in the initial founding of the U.S. This makes Lincoln and King "Founding Fathers" of the U.S. today as much as the original Founders were. This is why monuments to both Lincoln and King are now located on the National Mall in Washington, D.C. near the monuments to Washington and Jefferson.

Although full social equality for people of all races has not yet been achieved in the U.S., in 2008 Barack Obama became the Democratic Party nominee for president. This made him the first black nominee of a major political party to serve on its presidential election ticket, either as a presidential or vice-presidential candidate. His election as President in 2008 and his subsequent re-election in 2012 reveals that the U.S. has made substantial progress towards racial equality.

Women's Rights

Besides the struggle for racial and religious equality under the law, women and sexual minorities have struggled for sexual equality under the law. When the Fourteenth Amendment's Equal Protection Clause was first ratified, it was intended to give legal equality only to black *men*. The Supreme Court then interpreted this principle to apply to all races. Today, any form of race discrimination in the law must be justified by a "compelling" government need. In other words, the government must show it has a reason of overriding importance for not treating people of different races equally. In the 1960's, however, the Supreme Court began to apply the Equal Protection Clause not just to questions of race discrimination, but *sex* discrimination as well. To understand the effect of this change, we must examine how the law originally treated women.

At the time the U.S. Constitution was written, women in general had fewer legal rights than men. Women couldn't vote or serve on juries. They were barred from many professions especially more socially prestigious ones such as doctor, lawyer, judge, clergy, and elected official. *Married* women, however, had fewer legal rights than unmarried women. Married women lost their separate legal identity to their husband under the old English common-law doctrine called "*coverture*." The wife's identity was "covered" by the husband's identity. But what did this mean?

In practical effect, under coverture the husband-wife relationship was roughly equivalent to how the law treats the legal relationship between parents and young children. A young child can't own property, inherit, earn income, or enter into contracts. They are deemed too immature to make such decisions on their own, so their parent has authority to make those decisions. Similarly, a married woman could not do any of these things on the theory she did not have the intellectual capability or sound judgment to do so. Therefore, the husband got to control all these decisions on behalf of his wife. Also, just as a parent is held responsible for the misbehavior of a young child, the husband was held responsible for the misdeeds of his wife. This meant he could even "discipline" or "correct" his wife's disobedience. This included using "reasonable" physical punishment, just as a parent can use corporal discipline on a young child. The husband even had a "right" to sexual relations with his wife whether she consented or not. This meant that under the legal definition of rape, a husband could not be guilty of "raping" his wife. All this loss of the married women's identity to her husband was symbolized by losing her family name. In marriage to John Smith, Jane Doe became merely "Mrs. Smith," meaning "the wife of Smith." As wedding ceremonies often say, "two become one." Under coverture, the resulting "one" was the husband. The wife essentially became the husband's property, almost to the extent of slavery. A divorce was extremely difficult to obtain, and was allowed only in extreme cases of abandonment, abuse, infidelity, or mental illness on the part of the husband. At least this was an improvement over the original English common law, where divorce could not be obtained unless the English Parliament voted to grant it.

As resistance against this and other legal oppressions against women, a group of women including Elizabeth Cady Stanton and Lucretia Mott organized the first women's rights convention in Seneca Falls, New York, in 1848. The convention was attended by some men who supported them as well, including the only African-

American attendee at the conference, Frederick Douglass. The outcome of the Seneca Falls Convention was the Seneca Falls Declaration. It directly paralleled the U.S. Declaration of Independence. Instead of listing the grievances of the Thirteen Colonies against the British Empire, however, it listed the grievances of women against men. The Seneca Falls Declaration used almost identical language as the beginning of the U.S. Declaration of Independence, but was modified slightly: "We hold these truths to be self-evident: that all men *and women* are created equal . . ."

As the movement for women's rights grew, the doctrine of coverture was modified to lessen the legal hardship it imposed on married women. Coverture was a question of state law, not federal law. Accordingly, beginning in the mid 1800's, several states began to abolish parts of coverture. It wasn't until well into the 1900's, however, that all of the various components of coverture were abolished. For example it wasn't until 1993 that the last states (Oklahoma and North Carolina) finally removed the "marital rape exception" from their rape statutes. Husbands are therefore no longer immune from being prosecuted for the rape of their wife. The only remaining vestige of coverture today is that many women still choose to take their husband's last names upon marriage. However, the law no longer legally requires this.

Besides the abolition of coverture, women received the constitutional right to vote in the Nineteenth Amendment to the U.S. Constitution, ratified in 1920. Since the right to vote is also called the right to "suffrage," the movement to gain the right to vote for women was called the Women's Suffrage Movement. Some leading "suffragettes" were Sojourner Truth, Lucretia Mott, Elizabeth Cady Stanton, Alice Paul, and Susan B. Anthony. (Fun Fact: in 1979 Susan B. Anthony became the first real woman to appear on a U.S. coin—a dollar coin-- as opposed to the fictional "Lady Liberty.") Even women themselves were not fully united within the movement, though. For example, Sojourner Truth was not treated with equal respect as other women's rights leaders because she was black. This led her to give a speech at a women's rights conference in which she famously asked "Ain't I a Woman?" Nevertheless, although the success of the Women's Suffrage Movement gave women equal political rights, women were still barred from several professions, received lower wages for the same jobs, and had limited marriage and divorce rights.

Inspired by the success of the Civil Rights Movement for blacks, the demands for women's rights grew as well. In the 1960s the Women's Rights Movement began to more forcefully argue in legal cases that the Supreme Court should apply the Equal Protection Clause to questions of sex discrimination. The Court did so, but the legal standard the Court applied was so weak that the Court mostly upheld the sex discrimination in question. As a result, women's rights groups lobbied Congress to propose an *Equal Rights Amendment* (ERA) that would be added to the

Constitution. It stated "Equality of rights under the law shall not be denied or abridged by the United States or any state on account of sex." It passed Congress in 1972 with a seven-year deadline for the states to ratify it. Congress later added a three-year extension to the deadline. The constitutionally necessary three-fourths of the state legislatures still had not ratified it by the final 1982 deadline. The ERA was ratified by only 35 states, three short of the 38 states necessary.

Despite the political defeat of the proposed ERA, the Supreme Court then began to provide stronger protection from the Fourteenth Amendment's Equal Protection Clause against sex discrimination. For example, in the 1996 case *U.S. v. Virginia*, the Court considered whether the State of Virginia could ban women from the Virginia Military Institute (VMI), a state-run all-male military college. The court declared that government may not treat men and women differently without an "exceedingly persuasive justification" for doing so. Virginia argued that women didn't want, and couldn't handle, a rigorous and strict military education. The Court explained that such negative sexual stereotypes of women could not be an important enough reason for treating men and women differently. Virginia's discriminatory admission policy was therefore unconstitutional, as Virginia could not meet the high legal standard required for such discrimination.

The standard the Court applied in *U.S. v. Virginia* is the current constitutional test that applies whenever *government* discriminates on the basis of sex. Congress, however, has passed statutes that prevent certain types of *private* discrimination on the basis of sex. For example, the Civil Rights Act of 1964 bans employers from applying different standards of hiring, promotion, pay, benefits, or working conditions to employees because of the employee's sex. There is a limited exception, however, if sex is a "bona fide occupational qualification." This means either a man or woman is genuinely required for the job due to some unique nature of the job. So, for example, a domestic violence shelter for women may hire only women and not men to serve as rape counselors.

The first woman to serve in Congress was in 1917. Since then, over 300 women have served in the House of Representatives and Senate, as well as served as heads of Cabinet departments and federal administrative agencies. Two women have been the vice-presidential candidates of major parties. Geraldine Ferraro was the Democratic Party's vice-presidential candidate in 1984, and Sarah Palin was the Republican Party's vice-presidential candidate in 2008. In 2016, the Democratic Party chose Hillary Clinton as its presidential candidate. This made Clinton the first woman nominated by a major political party as its presidential candidate.

LGBT Rights

Besides the question of sex discrimination, in the past few decades related types of discrimination involving sexuality have also been debated and litigated heavily. These related kinds of discrimination mainly involve discrimination based on sexual orientation and sexual or gender identity. The most common term currently used to encompass sexual minorities is "LGBT," which stands for "Lesbian, Gay, Bisexual, and Transgender." Although the term is intended to collectively refer to all sexual minorities, there are other groups that are not technically included in this list. For example, people who are unsure about their sexuality are *questioning* their sexuality, and *intersex* persons are born with some mixture of both male and female genitalia, or neither. Thus, some activists have proposed the term LGBTQ or LGBTQI be used instead. Other writers have suggested a simple but broad general term be used, such as GSM, for "Gender and Sexual Minorities." However, no new replacement term for LGBT has yet gained common, generally accepted usage.

For most of U.S. history until only the past few decades, there was extreme social disapproval of sexual minorities. An individual who was discovered to be LGBT would probably be fired from their job and ostracized from their friends, family, and community. Homosexual activity was even a serious crime, punishable by harsh sentences. Life could be so difficult for someone who was LGBT that most people hid their true sexual identities even from their families and closest friends. Those who were discovered sometimes committed suicide rather than face the continued humiliation. This was especially true among youth. The first openly LGBT organizations seeking to change this social climate were created after World War II. However, the modern gay rights movement began in in the late 1960's and early 1970's, inspired by the Civil Rights Movement for blacks. It was during this time that the term "gay" was first used by LGBT activists who urged LGBT individuals to "come out" to their friends and family and express "gay pride" rather than shame.

Compared to other social movements, the gay rights movement has had relatively rapid success at changing societal attitudes towards sexual minorities. Recent opinions polls show that a majority of people in the U.S., especially among the younger generations, now favor social and legal equality for LGBT people. Yet the law has been slow to catch up to these evolving social norms. There have only been a handful of Supreme Court cases involving legal discrimination against LGBT persons. The current status of federal LGBT rights can be summarized by only a few of those cases. In *Romer v. Evans* (1992), the Supreme Court declared that the Equal Protection Clause prohibits state law from expressly denying gays and lesbians all protection of the law. In *Lawrence v. Texas* (2003), the Court held that consenting adults may choose a romantic or sexual partner of their choice, including someone of the same sex, without that behavior being criminalized. Finally, in the landmark 2015 case of *Obergefell v. Hodges*, the Court declared that the Fourteenth Amendment's Due Process and Equal Protection Clauses together give same-sex couples the same right to marry as opposite-sex couples. In other words, state and local governments may not prevent couples from legally marrying simply because of the sex of one or both of the people getting married.

Although some state and local governments have resisted equal rights for LGBT persons, others have provided *more* legal protection for LGBT persons than federal law provides. For example, many states and numerous cities currently protect LGBT people from discrimination in employment, housing, education, and public accommodations. As merely one example, the State of Oregon prohibits businesses from discriminating against LGBT customers. After the Supreme Court's *Obergefell* decision, a bakery refused to provide a wedding cake to a same-sex couple. Oregon fined the bakery for violating the state anti-discrimination statute. On the other hand, Congress has yet to provide any express legal protections to sexual minorities in any federal statutes. Most recently, the question of how transgendered people should use sex-segregated bathrooms has become a public policy issue. As the United States continues to grapple with how to address sexual minorities in the law, new policies will be developed at the local, state, and federal level in coming years.

Civil Rights Today

The activities and success of the Civil Rights Movement for blacks not only inspired the modern women's rights and gay rights movements, it inspired other civil rights movements in the late 1960's and 1970's as well. For example, Mexican-Americans, led by Cesar Chavez, fought for better and more equal legal treatment of Mexican-American immigrants and migrant workers. This movement also called itself the "Chicano Movement," which in turn inspired other Latino groups, and then other non-Latino immigrant groups as well, to join in similar legal struggles. Today, many different civil rights groups fight for legal rights for racial minorities. One of the largest such organizations is the Mexican-American Legal Defense and Education Fund (MALDEF), which represents the interest of Latino-Americans in the United States.

Also, the American Indian Movement (AIM) sought to achieve better legal justice for Native Americans. This included gaining enforcement of long-ignored treaty rights, improving social and economic conditions for Native Americans living on reservations or in urban areas, and reducing anti-Indian violence. The confrontational tactics of AIM in the 1970's sometimes resulted in occupations of government facilities. This included a highly publicized siege and shootout with the FBI on the Pine Ridge Indian Reservation in South Dakota in 1975. Today, AIM continues its efforts to achieve greater economic and legal equality for Native American individuals and tribes. One current goal of AIM that is widely covered in the news is AIM's efforts to get sports teams to use Native American mascots only with permission and only in a way Native Americans believe is respectful of their cultural identity.

Despite ongoing prejudices against people because of their racial or sexual identities, today the various civil rights movements have gained many legal protections against such types of discrimination. These protections are often found in the same laws that prohibit religious discrimination, discussed in the earlier chapter on religious liberty. As discussed in this chapter, there are constitutional protections against *government* discrimination on the basis of race or sex. In addition to these constitutional protections, many U.S. laws also protect people against various types of *private* discrimination on the basis of race or sex.

One of the most widely used laws prohibiting such discrimination is part of the federal Civil Rights Act of 1964. The subsection of that law called "Title VII" outlaws employment discrimination because of the applicant or employee's "race, color, religion, sex, or national origin." of the applicant or employee. "Title II" of that same act prohibits "public accommodations" from discriminating against a customer because of the customer's race, color, religion, or national origin. Public accommodations include stores, restaurants, hotels, and entertainment facilities. Sex is excluded from Title II so as to allow, among other possible examples, private male-only or female-only clubs, or separate men's and women's dressing rooms, locker rooms, or bathrooms. "Title IX" of the same act prohibits any entity that receives federal funds from discriminating on the basis of sex. This requires, for example, that colleges that receive federal student loan money to provide equal opportunities for both men's and women's athletic participation.

Besides the Civil Rights Act of 1964, the federal Fair Housing Act prohibits discrimination in the sale or rental of housing on the basis of race, color, national origin, religion, sex, disability, or whether the family has children. Also, the Americans with Disabilities Act (ADA) prohibits discrimination in employment on the basis of disability, and requires both public buildings and private businesses to be accessible to people with disabilities. The ADA also requires that employers make "reasonable accommodation" for their employee's disabilities, as long as the accommodation does not cause "undue hardship" on the employer. So, for example, an employer would be required to raise a desk up a few inches so that a person in a wheelchair could use the desk. An employer would not be required by the ADA, however, to hire a blind person as an airplane pilot, or a person in a wheelchair as firefighter. These types of accommodations would cause "undue hardship" to the employer and so would not be "reasonable" under the ADA. Yet, just as courts struggle with where to draw the line between reasonable versus unreasonable religious accommodation, courts also have difficulty with the precise line between "reasonable" versus "unreasonable" disability accommodation.

Besides the laws just discussed, there are other federal laws, and many state and local laws throughout the U.S., that prohibit other types of discrimination. For example, no Congressional statute expressly prohibits any type of discrimination on the basis of sexual orientation. Yet almost half the states and numerous cities throughout the U.S. have outlawed employment, housing, and/or public accommodation discrimination because of sexual orientation or gender identity (such as being transgendered).

Xenophobia

Psychologically, all the various forms of arbitrary discrimination are based on an irrational fear or misunderstanding of the unfamiliar or unknown. The formal term for this is "*xenophobia.*" This is a Greek word that literally means "fear of strangers." In modern terms, xenophobia is defined as "an irrational or unreasonable fear, distrust, or hatred of strangers, foreigners, or anything perceived as foreign or different." Some fears are rational. If someone is threatening you with a weapon, your fear makes good sense. On the other hand, if you fear someone *only* because they wear a hat on their head, or speak with an accent, or eat food you've never seen before, then your fear is unreasonable. These things do not actually pose any real danger to you. With xenophobia, you simply fear or dislike someone *only* because of a harmless difference between your identity and theirs, such as the color of their skin, or who they love. Psychologists and social scientists have discovered at least three significant causes of xenophobia.

1. Low Self-Esteem. Commonly, a person with low self-esteem is able to manufacture a false sense of "self-esteem" by putting down others. In other words, the person with low self-esteem makes a comparative judgment that "I am better than that other person, so therefore I have self-worth." This is comparative or relative self-worth, rather than an absolute self-worth. A healthy self-worth says "My self-worth does not depend on the worth of others." For example, racial supremacists try to make themselves feel better about themselves by believing that other races are inferior. In fact, this was a primary argument Southern white slave owners used during the U.S. Civil War to get non-slave-owning whites to fight for slavery. Slave owners argued that the existence of slavery showed that poor whites were at least "better than" blacks. Correspondingly, the ending of slavery would mean that poor whites were "no better than" blacks.

2. Scapegoating. Often, people with problems look for "someone" or "something" to blame for those problems. This is equally true for broader social problems like unemployment. These large-scale problems can often can translate into mass blaming of some group. This is called "scapegoating." An individual or group is falsely blamed or assigned sole responsibility for some bad thing occurring. In reality, however, that person or group might be only a small part, or no part, of the cause. The classic, tragic example was Hitler's Germany. The Nazis blamed all of Germany's problems on the Jews, despite the fact that Germany's economic and social problems were complex and Jews were not one of the causes.

3. Indoctrination. Many children are raised in families, churches, communities, or even nations where false, negative stereotypes about others are taught. These children grow up to become adults who dislike or fear the "other" group. This hated group could be a different nationality, religion, race, sexuality, or any other group. These negative ideas do not need any evidence or rational argument. If all children are taught is a particular belief, most of them grow up conforming to that idea without questioning it. For example, the members of the Westboro Baptist Church in Topeka, Kansas believe that everyone in the United States except for their congregation is going to hell. They claim this is because the United States does not execute all gays and lesbians. Their young children often appear as enthusiastic participants in their public anti-gay demonstrations. The only reason these children grow up believing what they do is because it's the only thing they've ever been told by their family and church. (See the film "American History X" for a fictional illustration of all three bases of xenophobia, and their consequences. Also read the book *The Social Animal,* by Elliot Aronson, for a summary of studies on the causes of xenophobia.)

SUMMARY

A civil right is the freedom against arbitrary or irrational discrimination. One type of unjustified discrimination is treating people differently merely because of their race, ethnicity, or skin color. There are many instances of this throughout U.S. history, but a particularly infamous example is the treatment of people of African ancestry. The Civil War ended slavery. Afterwards, Reconstruction of the South at first gave the former slaves, now free blacks, equal rights under the law. This included voting rights that were enforced. Once Reconstruction ended, however, Southern whites used widespread violence to retake political power. All-white legislatures re-established white supremacy by force of law. This was done through a detailed system of voting discrimination and an elaborate system of forced physical segregation of blacks away from whites, called "segregation." It took until the 1950's and 1960's for all three branches of the national government to finally work together to end rule by white supremacy in the South. This would not have occurred, however, if not for the ceaseless struggle by blacks before and during the Civil Rights Movement to gain racial equality. The end of white supremacy was achieved only over the fierce and often violent resistance by Southern whites. Besides race discrimination, lengthy periods of legal discrimination have also occurred against women and sexual minorities. In recent decades, the U.S. has rapidly advanced to give these groups much more equal treatment in the law. All such types of unjustified discrimination are caused by prejudice based on irrational dislike or unfounded fear of difference in others.

QUESTIONS FOR REVIEW AND SELF-ASSESSMENT

1. What are civil rights, and what is the historical significance of race discrimination in the U.S.?
2. After the Civil War, how did the U.S. at first give blacks equal legal rights, but then how did the Southern states re-impose white supremacy?

3. How were segregation and voting discrimination finally ended by the Civil Rights Movement and several new U.S. laws?
4. What is the history of discrimination against women and sexual minorities, and how does current law address sexual equality?
5. What are the several primary sources of irrational prejudices?

Critical Thinking Questions for Reflection and Discussion

1. Apart from legal equality, how much social equality do all the different races have in the U.S. today?
2. Should women and men be treated completely equally under the law, such by the military draft and with unisex public restrooms?
3. How can we be certain whether our dislike or fear of someone is rational or irrational?

Suggested Supplemental Readings

- Seneca Falls Declaration
- 13th, 14th, and 15th Amendments to the Constitution
- *Plessy v. Ferguson* (1896)
- *Brown v. Board of Education* (1953)
- Martin Luther King, *I Have a Dream*
- Civil Rights Act of 1964
- Voting Rights Act of 1965
- *U.S. v. Virginia* (1996)
- *Lawrence v. Texas* (2003)
- *Obergefell v. Hodges* (2015)

For Further Advanced Reading

- Juan Williams, *Eyes on the Prize: America's Civil Rights Years, 1954-1965*
- Eleanor Flexner and Ellen Fitzpatrick, *Century of Struggle: The Woman's Rights Movement in the United States*
- Lillian Faderman, *The Gay Revolution: The Story of the Struggle*
- Elliot Aronson, *The Social Animal*
- Dianne Avery, Maria Ontiveros, Roberto Corrada, Michael Selmi, and Melissa Hart, *Employment Discrimination Law, 8th Edition*

PART IV: INSTITUTIONS

Chapter 11: Congress

The Big Picture

Although they share legislative power, the House and Senate serve as political checks on each other. Despite this tension, members of both chambers engage in several common activities, primarily investigation and lawmaking. These responsibilities require organization so Congress can function expertly and efficiently. Nevertheless, passing legislation remains complex and politically difficult. All members of Congress also share the overriding goal of getting re-elected. Because of this, politics drives the members of Congress to regularly agree to increase the size and scope of the federal government, but without adequately paying for it. Increasing public benefits without raising taxes wins votes, but has left the U.S. with an enormous, growing, and problematic national debt.

Relevant Timeline

- 1789 U.S. Constitution ratified
- 1913 Seventeenth Amendment ratified (direct election of the Senate)
- 1935 Congress creates Social Security
- 1965 Congress creates Medicare and Medicaid
- 2010 Congress passes Patient Protection and Affordable Care Act

Chapter Objectives

After reading this chapter, the reader should be able to:

1. Describe the difference in composition and roles between the House and Senate.
2. Describe the major powers and functions shared by all members of Congress.
3. Describe how, and explain why, Congress organizes itself through party leadership and the committee system.
4. Describe the major steps in the federal legislative process.
5. Explain how the politics of Congressional elections and public policy has resulted in a large national debt.

House and Senate Differences

The first article of the U.S. Constitution creates and defines the federal legislative branch, called Congress. Article I gives Congress "legislative powers," meaning the power to make laws. As we saw in an earlier chapter, when the Constitution was written, the "Great Compromise" created a bicameral national legislature comprised of two chambers. In the House of Representatives, each state has representation in proportion to its population. In the Senate, each state has equal representation, with two senators per state. Together these two chambers make up the Congress. Let's now look at some more detailed differences between the House and Senate.

The House of Representatives is based on population. If this were calculated purely on a mathematical basis, this would mean a state with an extremely small population would have their representation rounded down to zero. However, the Constitution provides that no matter how small a state's population is, the state will receive a guaranteed minimum of one representative. Because state populations change over time, the Constitution requires that a *census* be taken every ten years. A "census" is a precise count of every individual in the entire population. Then, the number of seats each state gets in the House is adjusted according to how that state's population has changed. This process is called *reapportionment,* which simply means to recalculate the allocation of representatives to each state. This also typically means the boundary lines of Congressional districts must be redrawn. This process is called *redistricting*.

Under the current formula Congress uses to apportion representatives to the population, there are 435 representatives in total across all the 50 states. However, neither the District of Columbia, nor U.S. territories like Puerto Rico, Guam, American Samoa, and the Northern Marianas Islands have voting rights in Congress. The Constitution requires that each of these representatives must be at least 25 years of age, will receive a two-year term in office, and have no limit on their possible number of terms. All members of the House come up for re-election every two years. Federalist Paper No. 52 explains that given the short two-year term of office, the representatives will constantly need to seek re-election. This will make the representatives keep a close connection to the people, reacting quickly to the people's will. In this way, the House of Representatives was designed to be a more *populist* institution than the Senate. The word "populist" comes from the root word "people." It means that the House represents and responds rapidly to the desires of the people. The House could have been made even more populist, however, since elections could have occurred every year, as many Anti-Federalists wanted.

The Constitution defines the Senate as well. Each state is assigned two senators. The current number of 50 states in the Union means there are currently 100 senators total. Adding the number of senators with the number of representatives, this means Congress has 535 members in total between its two chambers. According to the Constitution, senators must be at least 30 years of age, receive 6-year terms in office, and have no limit on their possible number of terms. Also under the Constitution, senators are elected in what are called *staggered* elections. This means that only one-third of the Senate comes up for re-election every two years. The six-year terms of office of different senators therefore only partially overlap with each other. Put differently, every two years all of the House is up for re-election, but only one-third of the Senate. After six years, or three Congressional election cycles, all the Senators will have been up for re-election. Then the six-year election cycle begins again, with the first third of Senators coming up for re-election.

According to Federalist Paper No. 62, the framers of the Constitution designed the Senate to serve as a check against the democratic masses represented by the House. In other words, the Senate was intended to be a more elite, aristocratic institution. It would be politically insulated from, and serve as a balance against, rapid and intense changes in public mood. This is indicated by the older age requirement and the longer term in office compared to the House of Representatives. The more prestigious nature of the senate is also reflected in the fact there are far fewer senators than representatives. In addition, under the original Constitution, senators were not elected by the public, but were instead elected by the state legislature in each state. In this way, it was the elites choosing the elites. The Seventeenth Amendment in 1913, however, altered the selection of senators to popular elections. This change was part of Progressive-era reforms which favored democratic participation by the public. However, even with direct elections of senators, still only one-third of the Senate is up for re-election every two years. This means that the Senate can block the wishes of the public as expressed by the House, but the public will not be able to vote all the Senate out of office for 6 years. By that time, the public's anger will probably have lessened or perhaps even have disappeared and been forgotten.

Federalist No. 62 also explains that the longer terms in the Senate compared to the House allow senators to become more experienced in various areas of public policy. After serving just three terms, for example, a Senator has spent 18 years intensively studying public policy. Becoming top policy experts should in theory allow Senators to make better, wiser laws. Moreover, the greater constancy of membership in the Senate compared to the House, caused by the staggered elections of the Senate, provides for greater stability in government. This is especially beneficial in the relationship between the United States and foreign nations. For all these reasons, the Senate is still viewed today as more aristocratic than the House. One further bit of evidence that demonstrates this is the fact that members of the House often leave the House to run for the Senate. Yet no one ever leaves the Senate to run for the House. The Senate is in turn a common stepping-stone to the Presidency, along with being a state governor or vice-president.

Besides these differences in the composition of the House and Senate, there are some differences in powers between House and Senate. As part of the Great Compromise, the writers of the Constitution also required that any bills that raise revenues (that is, taxes) must originate in the House, not the Senate. As part of the checks and balances within the Constitution, the House has authority to pass, by a majority vote, bills of impeachment of the President, other top executive officials, and federal judges. The Senate then conducts the trials of those impeachment charges. The accused is removed from office upon a 2/3 vote of the Senate finding the accused guilty of the impeachment charges brought by the House. Before the U.S. can formally join an international treaty, the Senate must ratify the treaty by a 2/3 vote. Also, before Presidential nominees for top-level executive positions or federal judgeships can be appointed to their office, the Senate must confirm those nominations by a majority vote. The table below summarizes the differences between the House and Senate.

Table: House and Senate Differences

	House of Representatives	**Senate**
Method of representation	Varies in direct proportion to population	Each state gets an equal number
Members of Congress per state	Minimum of one	Two each
Constitutional requirements	Minimum age of 25	Minimum age of 30
Length of term and number of possible terms	2 years; unlimited number of terms	6 years; unlimited number of terms
Elections	All seats up for election every two years	One-third of seats up for election every two years (staggered elections)
Democratic role	More populist	More aristocratic/elitist
Unique powers	Initiates revenue bills; Impeaches president by majority vote	Conducts impeachment trial and convicts by 2/3 vote; Ratifies treaties by 2/3 vote; Confirms high-level executive nominees by majority vote; Confirms federal judicial nominees by majority vote

Congressional Powers and Functions

As we saw in the chapter on federalism, the framers of the Constitution originally gave Congress enumerated powers in Article I, Section 8 of the Constitution. Included in these powers were the powers to tax and spend, to regulate commerce among the states, to raise and regulate the armed forces of the United States, to declare war, and to make any laws necessary and proper to execute their expressly listed powers. As we also saw in the chapter of federalism, modern Supreme Court decisions have interpreted the Commerce Clause and the Tax and Spending Clause in the Constitution to give the Congress almost the entirety of the police power, with minor technical exceptions. To briefly recap Congressional power, Congress can make any human activity a crime, and can tax any human nonactivity. This "activity-nonactivity" distinction is controversial and is only one Supreme Court justice away from being eliminated, which would give Congress the full police power. In short, except for any express limits placed on Congress by the constitution, such as the Free Speech Clause, or the Equal Protection Clause, Congress can make almost any law it wants to make.

Apart from the specifically enumerated powers given to Congress by the Constitution, there are several other powers that Congress possesses either inherently or by implication. Ironically, even though the Constitution discusses only Congress' power to make laws, the members of Congress actually spend only a small amount of their time lawmaking. The large majority of their time is spent performing other tasks. First, in order to know what laws to make, or how to improve existing laws, Congress must investigate social problems. For example, in deciding what health care legislation to write, Congress must understand the answers to many questions. What percent of the population has health insurance? What does and doesn't that health insurance cover? How much does that insurance and medical care cost? How do people without health insurance pay for health care? How can those costs be lowered? How safe and effective is the medical care that medical patients receive? How might this be improved? Congress must spend extensive amounts of time obtaining thorough, detailed answers to these questions before it can begin to formulate public policy solutions to these problems. This *investigation* of political, social, economic, legal, and other issues is the primary way members of Congress spend their time.

A subset of investigation is called Congressional *oversight.* Here, the particular issue Congress investigates is how well executive branch departments and agencies are performing their responsibilities. For example, are the Centers for Medicare and Medicaid Services, part of the Department of Health and Human Services, effectively performing their responsibilities to provide health care to people over age 65, or with low-incomes, or with disabilities? And is the Veteran's Health Administration, part of the Department of Veteran's Affairs, providing timely and effective medical treatment to sick and injured military veterans? If not, what legal reforms can Congress pass to improve these health care programs? How are the agencies implementing these programs performing? How can those agencies be held more accountable? All these types of investigations are part of Congressional oversight of the executive branch.

Another substantial part of the work of members of Congress is what is called *client service* or *casework*. This is where representatives and senators help members of the public with their problems. Most often, the problems people bring to their elected officials are problems navigating government bureaucracy. For example, maybe you applied for but were turned down for Medicaid, or social security disability. Or maybe the Veteran's Administration Hospital you normally go to said you weren't eligible for a treatment option that you've heard other veterans have received for free. If the government agency can't or won't help, often individuals turn to their elected official to get help. Members of Congress don't usually try to solve these problems themselves. Instead they usually assign their staff to do this type of work. Even if the staff isn't able to ultimately solve the individual's problem, voters feel like their elected official has at least listened to them and tried to help. This generates good will on the part of that person, who will then speak positively about their experience with their friends, family, neighbors, and coworkers. People who feel ignored by their representative will similarly spread their negative opinion about that official. Thus, elected officials cannot politically afford to ignore requests for help from voters or potential voters. Good politicians know how to achieve good public relations.

Congressional Party Leadership

As noted earlier in this chapter, Congress is comprised of 535 people. Any organization, but especially one as large and important as Congress, needs to run smoothly, efficiently, and effectively. Congress has two different major internal organizational structures that help coordinate its day-to-day activities. These two organizational mechanisms are party leadership, and the committee system.

Each chamber in Congress is managed along political party lines. The two major political parties are the Democratic Party and the Republican Party (we'll talk about them much more in an upcoming chapter). Political party organization is needed because someone needs to coordinate the functioning of the House and Senate. Almost all members of Congress belong to one of the two major political parties. As a result, the Democratic and Republican parties themselves have agreed that the party with a majority of members in a Congressional chamber will manage that chamber. For example, if the Republican Party has a majority of members in the House of Representatives, then the Republican Party leaders in the House will manage the operations of the House. They have authority to control what bills are voted on, the procedure by which those bills are voted on, how long the debate will be on those bills, which representatives are assigned to which committees, and so on. There are dozens of party leadership positions in each chamber of Congress, but the following are some of the more notable ones.

Speaker of the House. This is a position created by Constitution, and is by tradition elected by the members of the House. That is, the Speaker of the House will be elected by whichever political party has a majority in the House. This is a very politically powerful position, with a great deal of influence over the activity of the House. The Speaker has enormous influence over the details of public policy bills voted on by the House, and can often block proposed legislation the Speaker dislikes. Also, the Speaker of the House is next in line for the Presidency after the Vice-President, should anything happen to both the President and Vice-President.

House Majority Leader. The Constitution makes no mention of political parties or their leaders in Congress, so the House itself has created the party leadership positions that exist within the House. The House Majority Leader is also elected by the House members from the political party with the most seats in the House. This position is second in power within the House, after the Speaker of the House. The House Majority Leader deals more with the internal decision-making of the majority party than does the Speaker of the House, who is more formally in charge of the entire House of Representatives. Yet the House Majority Leader still has great influence over public policy coming out of the House.

House Minority Leader. This position is elected by the House members from the minority political party in the House. The House Minority Leader is therefore in charge of governing the internal workings of the minority political party in the House. The House Minority Leader will also be the top leader of the minority party who negotiates with the majority party in an effort to achieve the public policy desired by the minority party.

President of the Senate. The Constitution says the Vice-President of the United States is also President of Senate. This is largely an administrative position, meaning the Vice President is supposed to manage the parliamentary procedure of Senate meetings. However, the Constitution says the Vice-President only gets to cast a vote whenever the vote of the full Senate is tied. In other words, the Vice-President only casts tie-breaking votes. This rarely occurs, however, and the Vice-President normally has many other important duties assigned by the President. All this means the "President of the Senate" has relatively little power in the Senate.

President Pro Tempore. The Constitution says that in the Vice-President's absence as President of the Senate, the Senate itself should choose a temporary, acting President of the Senate. "*Pro tempore*" is a Latin term meaning "for the time being." The English word "temporary" comes from the same Latin origin. Since the President Pro Tempore is elected by the Senate, the position is chosen by whichever political party has a majority in the Senate. For over a hundred years, the majority party has simply chosen its most senior member of the Senate to fill this position. The President Pro Tempore usually lets other more junior senators manage parliamentary procedure in the Senate so they can gain experience with those rules. Thus, despite an impressive title, the position has relatively little power beyond that of other Senators. The most important aspect of the position is that the President Pre Tempore is next in line for the Presidency after the Vice-President and Speaker of the House.

Senate Majority Leader. Again, since the Constitution makes no mention of political parties or their Congressional leaders, the Senate itself has created the party leadership positions that exist within the Senate. Like its counterpart in the House of Representatives, the Senate Majority Leader is elected by the Senators from the political party with the most seats in the Senate. This is the most politically powerful position in the Senate, akin to the power wielded by the Speaker of the House. The Senate Majority Leader has a great deal of authority to schedule votes or block them from occurring, and to influence the substance of legislation.

Senate Minority Leader. Also like its counterpart in the House of Representatives, this position is elected by Senators from the party in the Senate minority. The Senate Minority Leader manages the internal governance of the minority party Senators, and is the lead mediator between the Senate majority and the Senate minority.

The Committee System

The Constitution makes no mention of Congressional committees. However, on the very first day of the first Congress in 1789, both the House and Senate created committees. Even before that, the Constitutional Convention in 1787 had committees working on the writing of the Constitution. Indeed, almost all legislative bodies, and most organizations have committees. The larger the organization, the greater the need for committees. In Congress, the vast majority of the work is done in committees. This includes investigation, oversight, and drafting legislation.

Committees exist for two main reasons. First, it's a simple question of division of labor. It's much more efficient to distribute the workload by delegating particular tasks to particular groups. Imagine how little Congress would accomplish, for example, if all 535 members of the House and Senate had to investigate the same subject matter at the same time before anyone moved on to a different issue. It would take months or years to deal with a single subject, while all other pressing problems would be completely ignored. Committees therefore allow Congress to investigate and write proposed legislation dealing with economic and financial problems, social issues, health care reform, educational improvement, environmental protection, terrorism prevention, and foreign policy crises, all at the same time. Also, assignment of members of Congress to committees allows representatives and senators to develop public policy expertise in the subject matter of their committees. In theory, more well-informed legislators should be able to create wiser, better laws. Indeed, after many years of serving on the same committee, members of Congress often become some of the top experts in the U.S. or even the world in that policy area.

Both the House and the Senate have a separate committee system within each chamber. In both chambers, though, each separate committee is based on a public policy topic. These policy areas include education, health care, foreign policy, energy, the environment, and so on. The committees in the two chambers of Congress largely duplicate each other. However, this is necessary because under the bicameral system, each chamber does its work independently of the other as part of the checks and balances of the U.S. federal government. The party leadership in each chamber assigns members of Congress to serve on several committees within their own chamber. That is, representatives are assigned to House committees, and senators are assigned to Senate committees.

Permanent committees are called *standing* committees. Temporary committees are variously called *select, special,* or *ad hoc* committees. There are also a few *joint* committees that include members of both chambers of Congress. The most common joint committees are called Conference Committees. These attempt to negotiation compromises when there are differences between similar bills passed by both the House and Senate. We'll talk more about the legislative process shortly.

Here are the standing committees in each chamber:

House Standing Committees:

- Agriculture
- Appropriations
- Armed Services
- Budget
- Education and the Workforce
- Energy and Commerce
- Ethics
- Financial Services
- Foreign Affair
- Homeland Security
- Intelligence
- Judiciary
- Natural Resources
- Oversight and Government Reform

- Rules
- Science, Space, and Technology
- Small Business
- Transportation and Infrastructure
- Veteran's Affairs
- Ways and Means

Senate Standing Committees:

- Agriculture, Nutrition, and Forestry
- Appropriations,
- Armed Services
- Banking, Housing, and Urban Affairs
- Budget
- Commerce, Science and Transportation
- Energy and Natural Resources
- Environment and Public Works
- Finance
- Foreign Relations
- Health, Education, Labor, and Pension (HELP)
- Homeland Security and Government Affairs
- Judiciary
- Rules and Administration
- Small Business and Entrepreneurship
- Veteran's Affairs

Each standing committee has several *subcommittees* as well. These subcommittees subdivide the public policy area over which their committee has jurisdiction. In other words, each subcommittee deals with a subtopic within the larger public policy area of their committee as a whole. Both the House and Senate each have several dozen subcommittees in total. For example, the Senate HELP Committee has three subcommittees: Subcommittee on Children and Families, Subcommittee on Employment and Workplace Safety, and Subcommittee on Primary Health and Aging. Congressional committees accordingly assign tasks to their relevant subcommittees. For example, Healthcare.gov is the official government website where individuals may sign up for government-subsidized health insurance. The website did not initially work as planned or scheduled. To find out what went wrong, the House Committee on Energy and Commerce assigned its Subcommittee on Investigation and Oversight to hold a hearing. Often, however, many subcommittees across multiple committees will work on investigation or oversight of a public policy issue simultaneously. This typically occurs with major political issues such as investigation of the 9/11 terror attacks, or development of major new social programs such as the Patient Protection and Affordable Care Act, also commonly known as "Obamacare."

The Legislative Process

A Congressional *bill* is a formal proposal in either the House or Senate for a law. The process by which a bill becomes a law is called the legislative process. The procedural rules by which laws are made in Congress is extremely detailed and complicated. Even members of Congress take years to learn all the obscure rules. There are a few basic steps, however, that explain most of what occurs. Knowledge of these basic elements of the legislative process allows for an understanding of probably about 95% of news involving proposed laws. That 95% will be described here. However, the remaining 5% contains numerous additional details and exceptions to the procedure. A diagram of the basic overview of the legislative process that we'll discuss here is located at the end of this chapter after the chapter summary and the chapter review questions.

Not all proposed laws are called bills. To be labeled a bill, a proposed law must be *sponsored* by an actual member of Congress. This means a representative or senator puts their name on the bill and formally introduces it into the lawmaking process in the chamber to which that member belongs. Only a Congressional representative can sponsor and introduce a bill into the House of Representatives, and only a Senator can sponsor and introduce a bill into the Senate. Once a bill is introduced to a chamber, the party leadership of that chamber will assign consideration of the bill to the most relevant committee or committees. Each committee chair will in turn assign the bill to the most relevant subcommittee or subcommittees.

The real work on the bill will begin in the subcommittee. The subcommittee has total authority to do anything it wants with the bill. The subcommittee can conduct an investigation, hold hearings, listen to verbal testimony, and solicit written comments from experts and concerned citizens and residents. The subcommittee can entirely rewrite the bill if it wants, including amending the bill to achieve the opposite effect of the original bill. The subcommittee can also do nothing with the bill. Once the subcommittee has finished with their handling of the bill, they will send the bill back up to their larger committee. The whole committee also then has absolute authority to do whatever it wants with the bill. It can conduct investigations, hold hearings, solicit comments and testimony, entirely rewrite the bill, or do nothing with it. Over 90% of all bills go no further than this step in the legislative process. The bill "dies in committee." Most likely this is because the committee does not like the bill, or it simply is not a top priority given other more pressing issues to deal with at the moment.

On the other hand, a majority of a committee can votes to pass on their final draft language of a bill to the parent chamber of the committee. Either the full House or the full Senate will then evaluate the bill. At this point, the full House or the full Senate will not conduct any more investigation of the bill. However, they can still vote to amend or completely rewrite the language of the bill. If the bill cannot get a majority vote on the floor of the full House or the full Senate, then the bill is dead.

If either chamber votes to pass the bill, the other chamber still needs to consider the bill. Recall that in the Great Compromise, both the House and Senate must agree on a proposed law for it to become actual law. This means that if the other chamber has not yet considered the bill, then the bill must be sent over to the other chamber for sponsorship and introduction into the legislative process in that other chamber. Thus, if the House passes a bill that was introduced only in the House, that bill is sent over to the Senate. If the Senate passes a bill that introduced only in the Senate, that bill is sent over to the House. In the other chamber, the entire process begins as usual, with sponsorship, assignment to a committee and subcommittee, and investigations and rewritings. The other chamber may do whatever it wants with the bill. This includes amending it so that it says the opposite of what the other chamber wanted, or rewriting it so that it has nothing to do with what the original topic of the bill in the other chamber. The bill might also die in committee in the other chamber. Or, the bill might be brought to the full floor of the other chamber for a vote yet fail to win a majority. Bills are regularly passed by either the House or the Senate, but then die in the other chamber.

Only if both the full House and full Senate pass the bill by separate majority votes does the bill continue in the legislative process. According to the Constitution, and as part of the Great Compromise, for a bill passed by both chambers of Congress to become law, it must be the identical bill. If there are any differences, and there often are, then the two different versions of the bill are sent to a special Joint Conference Committee. This committee is made up of an equal number of members of both the House and Senate. There, a compromise version of the bill is negotiated and then sent back to both the House and Senate. According to the internal rules of Congress, the compromise bill can no longer be investigated or amended. Both the floor of the full House and the floor of the full Senate must separately vote either up or down on the bill as it is. They must either accept it entirely, or reject it entirely. If either chamber rejects the compromise bill, it is dead. If they both pass it, now the same bill has been passed by both chambers.

Once the full House and full Senate by separate majority have voted to pass the same bill, then according to the Constitution that bill is sent to the President for consideration. The President has three options: sign the bill, veto the bill, or do nothing. If the President signs the bill within ten days, it becomes law. If the President rejects the bill, the President does so by an expressly written *veto* of the bill, part of the checks and balances in the Constitution. The bill is then sent back to Congress, where the House and the Senate have a chance to override the veto. Also under the checks and balances, if both chambers vote separately by a two-thirds margin to override the President's veto, then the bill becomes a law.

If the president decides to neither sign nor veto the bill, then what happens depends where the bill is in the timeline of the legislative process. If the President neither signs nor vetoes the bill, then the bill automatically becomes law within ten days. This is true unless the two-year Congressional term expires within that ten-day time period. In that case, the bill does not become law. Instead it must begin the entire legislative process all over again at the start of the next Congressional term, when the newly elected Representatives and Senators have taken office. The death of a bill that the President doesn't sign because of the expiration of a Congressional term is called a "pocket veto." Rather than sign the bill, the President simply "pockets it." In other words, the President does nothing to it, allowing it to die as the time limit for the bill to become law expires.

Presidential threats to veto bills are more common than actual vetoes. Often Congress will rewrite the bill to address the President's objections prior to sending the bill to the President. Vetoes tend to happen when the party in control of Congress is different than the party of the President. In this situation, sometimes Congress sends bills to the President that it knows the President will veto, simply to make a political statement. It forces the President to go on official record vetoing whatever policy Congress wants. Congressional overrides of presidential vetoes are rare, though. It's politically difficult to get even a simple majority of both chambers of Congress to agree to a bill. It's extremely difficult to get a two-thirds supermajority of both chambers to agree. Even members who originally voted for the bill often won't vote to override a veto if the President comes from the same party as that member. This is to avoid embarrassing the leader of their party and thereby stay on good terms with the President, who can offer help with the member's re-election campaign. Indeed, a 2004 study by the Congressional Research Service counted almost 1500 vetoes up to that time in U.S. History, but only just over 100 veto overrides.

The foregoing information about the legislative process is probably enough so that an observer of political news can understand roughly 90% of the news about where a bill is in the legislative process. Knowledge of one other aspect of the legislative process will bring that understanding up to around 95%. With 435 members, the House has strict time limits on debate. Each speaker might be assigned only a few minutes, or sometimes only a minute or less, to voice their support or opposition for a bill. The Senate, however, has only 100 members today. The first Senate in 1789 had even fewer members. There were only 26 Senators from the original 13 states. Ever since that first Senate, because of the small number of members in the chamber, the Senate puts no time limits on debate. Every speaker is able to talk for as long as they wish. Senators soon realized that if they opposed a bill that the majority was going to approve, it could be single-handedly blocked by never yielding their turn to talk. This ability to speak endlessly and thereby bring the Senate legislative process to a standstill is called a *filibuster*.

Senate procedure allows only one way to interrupt a filibuster, by a vote to end the filibuster. This procedure is called *cloture*. By Senate rules, if three-fifths of the Senate (60%) vote to end the filibuster, the cloture vote succeeds, and the filibuster is ended. Otherwise, if the cloture vote fails to get the needed supermajority, then the filibustering Senator may begin speaking again.

Actual filibusters are rare. More often, Senators will threaten to filibuster. The rest of the Senate then has several options. They can accommodate that Senator's wishes by changing the bill, or they can avoid bringing that bill up for a vote altogether. In the alternative, the Senate can proceed ahead and plan to vote for cloture when the Senator filibusters. Successful votes for cloture are rare. Each Senator knows that if they vote to cloture each other's filibusters, then all of them will lose the power of the filibuster. A famous example of cloture occurred during the legislative process of the Civil Rights Act of 1964 and the Voting Rights Act of 1965. Senators from the Southern states tried to collectively filibuster both those pieces of legislation. The all-white Southern senators did not want to allow racial equality in the South either by ending segregation or by ending voting discrimination. The Senators from the non-Southern states, however, joined together to cloture both filibusters. In both cases, the Senate then passed the bills, and they went on to become major laws that are still important today.

Today, Congress has become highly partisan, with Senators typically voting either for or against cloture merely along party lines. This means that to get most Senate bills passed, the party in control of the Senate effectively needs 60 votes, not 51. This has resulted in very little work getting done in the Senate in recent years. Whichever party is in the minority can easily block actions by whichever party is in the majority at that moment. For example, presidential nominees for the federal courts have in some cases been blocked for years by the opposition party. As a result of this gridlock, both major political parties have threatened at different times to end the filibuster rule. Only a majority vote is needed to change a Senate procedure. Thus, at any time the party that happens to be in the majority party could end the minority party's ability to filibuster. Because this would end so much power both major political parties have to block each other, the possibility of ending the filibuster is referred to as "the nuclear option."

Again, a diagram of the basic steps of the legislative process that were discussed here is located at the end of this chapter after the chapter summary and the chapter review questions. As can be seen from the diagram and the description of the procedure just presented, the legislative process is long, complex, and politically difficult. Besides the process summarized here, there are numerous other procedural technicalities that are part of the parliamentary procedure of Congress. Both political parties regularly take advantage of these rules to stall or block legislation which they dislike. Indeed, only a small percent of bills ever make it through the entire legislative process to become law. For example, a study of the 110th Congress, from 2006-2008, found that roughly 85% of all bills died in committee. Only four percent made it through the full legislative process to become law.

Congressional Politics and Policy

Many modern scholars have studied Congress and observed what its members do. Most of these scholars agree that the top priority of members of Congress is getting re-elected. There are many things a member of Congress might hope to achieve by being a member of Congress. This includes helping the public, having fame, achieving power and prestige, or earning lots of money. Yet none of these benefits can occur unless one is actually a member of Congress. All the advantages of being in Congress depend on *remaining* a member of Congress. Therefore, staying in Congress is the necessary top priority that supersedes all other priorities. This means that almost everything a member of Congress does has the goal of getting re-elected. Public speaking, news interviews, mailings and other advertising, client service, taking popular stands on issues, avoiding controversial positions, and other actions are calculated to win public favor. Likewise, the way any campaign money is spent is done with the explicit goal of getting re-elected.

The public policies a member of Congress creates or supports is also done with the goal of getting re-elected. This includes large, expensive "entitlement" programs. The term "entitlement" is used because if a person meets the legal qualifications to receive the financial benefits from these programs, then that person is legally entitled to receive those benefits. These programs include *Social Security*, which provides guaranteed retirement pensions and disability payments to retired workers who paid into the system. *Medicare* offers guaranteed health care for retirees who paid into the system. This includes doctors' visits, medical devices and prescription drug benefits. *Medicaid* grants guaranteed health care to individuals with lower incomes. There are numerous other smaller benefits program as well, including food, housing, and student loans for low-income individuals. Benefit programs are almost never eliminated, and rarely reduced. Think about this: when was the last time you heard a congressional or presidential candidate of any political party say "I promise if elected, I will cut *your* government benefits!" Instead, Congress almost always continues to expand the size and scope of the federal government. They either create new benefit programs or raise benefit payments in the programs that already exist. This is why the U.S. government continues to grow in size despite any efforts to constrain that growth.

Also, whenever possible, members of Congress will have Congress allocate money to their specific voting districts, rather than as part of a general spending program across the country. This is commonly done for construction projects such as new or improved roads, bridges, schools, or courthouses. All these projects are in each member of Congress' home districts. These projects are called "pork barrel projects" or "pork barrel spending," or often simply "pork" for short. These pork barrel spending projects provides jobs for the voters in a particular Congressional district. The representative or senator from that district can then claim direct credit for those jobs in their re-election campaign.

In line with this single-minded re-election goal, Congress rarely raises taxes in the amount necessary to pay for its spending. Again, when was the last time you heard a candidate of any political party say its supporters "I promise if elected, I will raise *your* taxes!" Despite increased spending, either taxes go unraised, or they are raised only slightly, and not enough to pay for the spending increase. Candidates and elected officials often promise that small new taxes will be enough to pay for new spending. Yet once the taxes come in, it's usually the case that future tax revenues were underestimated. This typically happens due to accounting assumptions that the economy will be booming and so the resulting tax revenues will be high. These overly optimistic projections were made because no politicians want to claim (a) the economy will do poorly under their plan, and (b) taxes will have to be raised a *lot* higher to pay for increased spending. In short, politicians promise lots of benefits with little or no suffering from taxes. "All gain, no pain" usually turns out to be wrong.

The National Debt

There is a substantial consequence of this consistent voting pattern by members of both parties in Congress to increase federal spending without sufficiently increasing taxes to pay for it. In the vast majority of years throughout U.S. history, Congress has spent more than it has received in revenue from taxes. This means that almost every year Congress must borrow money to pay its bills. Historically, Congress used to borrow the most money in years when the U.S. was at war. This was especially true during World War II, when the U.S. borrowed huge amounts of money temporarily. Regardless of why Congress is borrowing money, the lending comes in the way of people buying government *bonds*. A bond promises to pay back the money in the future, with interest. Entities such as individuals, businesses and even governments that want to lend the U.S. money buy U.S. bonds. Then the U.S. pays back those bondholders the principal on the bonds plus interest. This is roughly the same concept as paying back a credit card debt or bank loan such as a home mortgage. The federal government borrows money by selling bonds, and then the federal government repays those bonds with interest. The U.S. government not only pays for occasional wars with the sale of these bonds, but it also pays for its annual general operating expenses. This includes large benefit programs like the Social Security, Medicare, and Medicaid, the peacetime U.S. military, and other programs like federal highways and the national parks.

So where does this borrowed money come from? That is, who can afford to loan the U.S. money? Some of the major purchasers of U.S. bonds are wealthy foreign governments such as China, Japan, and England. Many smaller countries have bought U.S. bonds as well, hoping to have a stable source of savings while also earning a profit from the interest payments they receive. Banks, employer-provided pension funds, and even individuals who manage their own retirement accounts also all buy U.S. bonds hoping to make a profit from the interest payments. For example, most U.S. workers with retirement accounts typically make a small regular monthly purchase of a mixture of business stocks and government bonds. Then, in retirement, the retired worker gets a monthly check based on their stock and bond investments.

The U.S. government also has borrowed several trillion dollars from itself. This might sound odd at first so a brief explanation is needed. Congress created "trust funds" to pay future amounts of Social Security and Medicare as more of the population continues to age. There is supposed to be several trillion dollars stored in these "trust funds." Congress, however, realized that it could use that money to pay for benefit programs without raising taxes. As a result, Congress has spent *all* of these trust funds to pay for *current* operating expenses of the federal government. In other words, Congress has borrowed from itself, promising to pay itself back in the future as those funds come due. Without money in the trust funds, this means Congress will later have to either raise taxes by a lot, or cut spending by a lot, or both. Otherwise Congress would be unable to pay the Social Security and Medicare payments owed to seniors at the amounts promised. Some people have compared this practice to placing an "I.O.U." note into your piggy bank. In other words, when you need money now, you use up your current savings, but plan to restore your savings in the future when your financial situation improves. This assumes, of course, that you'll have the ability and discipline to restore your savings. If not, then when you need to borrow money from yourself again you'll be in trouble, since you won't have any savings.

The amount a government budget is short each year—that is, the yearly amount that spending exceeds income-- is called the annual *deficit*. The cumulative total of all current and past deficits is the combined government *debt.* The debt of the United States is called the *national debt.* In most years, the federal government has a large deficit. As a consequence, the U.S. has a large national debt. In most years, the total national debt grows significantly bigger as well. For the past decade, the annual deficit has been between a half-trillion and a trillion dollars each year. Altogether, as of 2016, the total national debt is 19 trillion dollars. This amount is expected to rise by roughly a half-trillion dollars or more per year throughout the next decade. The annual *deficit* can be decreasing (e.g. from 500 billion one year down to 400 billion the next year), yet the total *debt* can still be increasing, because the new deficit is added to the total debt already existing. Thus, politicians will sometimes misleadingly say "I reduced the deficit" while ignoring the fact that the debt still increased.

Each year, Congress pays several hundred billion dollars *only* as *interest* payments on the debt, but makes no payments on the principal of the debt. That is, each year Congress makes no payments on the debt itself, which keeps growing. Congress only pays the interest on the money borrowed. This is done just to keep from defaulting on the debt. This is analogous to how an individual with a large credit card debt must at least make a minimum payment on the credit card debt each month. This interest payment is necessary to avoid having the card canceled and the total debt sent to a collection agency.

Almost everyone who has considered this problem, including members of both major political parties, considers the growing national debt to be a serious issue. Debt itself is not necessarily a problem, but debt can become a problem when it becomes *too much* debt. Small amounts of debt can be financially sustainable as a small debt requires only small interest payments to maintain. A large and growing debt, however, becomes unsustainable because eventually there is not enough money to make even the interest payments on a debt. For example, for a person with a middle-class income, charging $100 per month on a credit card is probably sustainable, but charging $10,000 per month is not financially sustainable. The question is at what point a borrowing habit becomes unsustainable.

Congress itself has an official nonpartisan office staffed with professional experts that provides Congress with economic and financial analysis of U.S. public policies. This office is called the *Congressional Budget Office* (CBO). In a 2015 CBO report, it projected that future increases in the national debt over the next 10 years will continue to grow in an "unsustainable" manner. The report then declared:

> "Such large and growing federal debt would have serious negative consequences, including increasing federal spending for interest payments; restraining economic growth in the long term; giving policymakers less

flexibility to respond to unexpected challenges; and eventually heightening the risk of a fiscal crisis."

Notice that the CBO report warns that the national debt could lead to a "fiscal crisis." The word "fiscal" means government finances. If Congress became unable to afford payments on the debt, the federal government could simply print more money to pay off the debt. However, this would likely cause the U.S. to go into a period of high *inflation*, meaning the prices of consumer goods and services increase. Yet salaries, wages, or fixed-incomes (such as retirement pensions or government benefits like Social Security or disability payments) almost always lag behind inflation. This would be mean most ordinary workers and retirees would be stretched thin financially. This would probably cause an economic *recession*. A recession happens when the overall size of the U.S. economy, as measured by the *Gross Domestic Product* (GDP), decreases for six consecutive months or more.

If enough additional money is added to the system, *hyperinflation* can happen, whereby the prices of consumer goods and services rise rapidly on a monthly, weekly, or even daily basis. Hyperinflation can in turn cause a more severe form of a recession, called a *depression*. Economists have no agreed-upon definition of an economic depression, other than that it is worse than a recession. This might be a bigger decrease in the size of the economy, or a longer period of time for the decrease, or both. At the start of the Great Depression, for example, the overall size of the U.S. economy decreased by a third (33%) over a four-year period, from 1929 to 1933.

There are many historical examples around the world of the negative effects of hyperinflation. Two examples even come from U.S. history. The Continental Congress printed so much money to pay for the Revolutionary War, that the money became almost worthless. Similarly, the Confederate States of America printed so much money to pay for their side of the Civil War that their money became practically worthless as well. The most famous example of hyperinflation in world history, though, is Germany shortly after World War I. To pay off its huge war debts, the German government simply printed large amounts of money. At the height of the resulting hyperinflation, a loaf of bread that hypothetically cost one deutschmark at the start of 1922 cost over a billion deutschmarks by the end of that same year. Germany went through economic chaos and its Weimar government collapsed as a consequence. Indeed, many historians see Germany's severe economic problems as having a large role in giving rise to Hitler and the Nazis.

As bad as hyperinflation can be, however, there is a worst-case scenario. The federal government could simply refuse to make any further bond payments which it owes due to interest on the national debt. Basically, the U.S. government could declare bankruptcy. However, the U.S. government owes trillions of dollars in bonds to tens of millions of individuals in their retirement accounts, as well as to countless businesses and even other governments around the world. As a result, bankruptcy of the U.S. federal government would quickly cause a national and global economic depression. This outcome is therefore unlikely, as the federal government would probably print money to avoid such a disaster. As noted above, though, the solution of printing large amounts of money would bring the serious problem of hyperinflation. Hyperinflation would therefore merely be the lesser of two evils, compared to government bankruptcy. The unfortunate choice would simply be between a *possible* global depression versus a *likely* global depression.

Given the seriousness of the national debt problem, there are several possible solutions to avoid a future crisis. Congress could (1) raise taxes, (2) reduce spending, or (3) enact a combination of tax increases and spending cuts over time. Congress has repeatedly failed to address the situation in this manner, however. This failure is due to the negative political consequences that happen to politicians who raise taxes and/or cut spending. To correct this situation, in the past few decades many individuals and organizations have suggested adding an amendment to the U.S. Constitution that would require Congress to pass a balanced federal budget each year. In comparison, almost all the state governments in the United States are required by their own state constitutions to balance their yearly operating budgets. In 1995, the U.S. House of Representatives passed a proposal for a federal balanced budget amendment. However, the proposal lost in the Senate by one vote. Congress therefore has never sent a balanced budget amendment to the states for possible ratification. Regardless of any solution that is eventually applied, the problem of the national debt is not going to disappear anytime soon. Indeed, at its current rate of increase, it will only get worse. The U.S. national debt will therefore continue to be a significant political issue in national politics for the foreseeable future.

Summary

The two legislative chambers of the U.S. Congress were intended to play, and do play, different roles in U.S. democracy. The House of Representatives more strongly reflects the ever-changing, rapidly shifting swings in public opinion. The Senate, on the other hand, is more slow and deliberative in making changes to public policy. Besides making laws, the members of Congress perform other functions, such as investigating problems in government and society, and helping voters with problems. To accomplish all their functions, both chambers of the Congress have two organizational structures. These are a leadership system based along political party lines, and a committee system designed to improve expertise and efficiency in Congress. The federal law-making process itself requires a lengthy and complex procedure, such that very few proposals for laws ever become laws. Despite the several functions of Congress, however, the main goal of members of Congress is to get re-elected. This priority drives all their decisions in how they perform their various legislative responsibilities. Members of Congress therefore continually promise voters they will increase government spending, but without raising taxes to pay for that spending. This means the U.S. government does not take in enough tax revenues to pay for its spending. As a result, the federal government needs to borrow huge amounts of money every year to continue its operations. This has created an enormous cumulative national debt, which by most estimates is growing at an unsustainable rate.

Questions for Review and Self-Assessment

1. What are the differences in composition and roles between the House and Senate?
2. What major powers and functions are shared by all members of Congress?
3. How and why does Congress organize itself through party leadership and the committee system?
4. What are the major steps in the federal legislative process?
5. How have the politics of Congressional elections resulted in a large national debt?

Critical Thinking Questions for Reflection and Discussion

1. Should the Constitution be amended so that Congress is a unicameral (one-chamber) legislature based solely on population?
2. Should the Constitution be amended to require Congress to balance its budget each year?

Suggested Reading Supplements

- Alexander Hamilton and James Madison, Federalist Nos. 52-53, 62-63
- *McGrain v. Daugherty* (1927)
- House.gov
- Senate.gov

For Further Advanced Reading

- Richard Fenno, *Home Style: House Members in their Districts*
- David Mayhew, *Congress: The Electoral Connection*

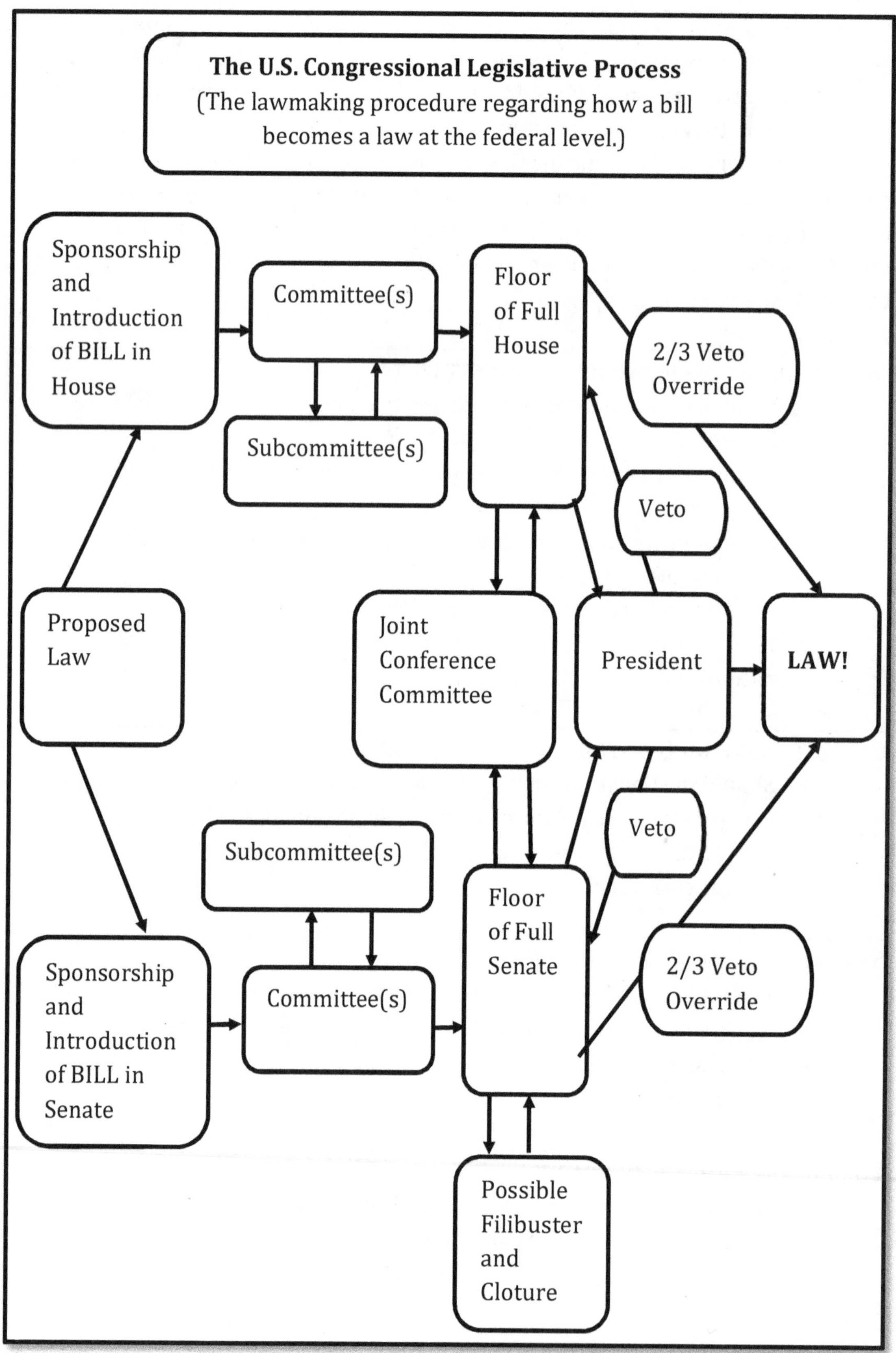
The U.S. Congressional Legislative Process
(The lawmaking procedure regarding how a bill becomes a law at the federal level.)
Sponsorship and Introduction of BILL in House
Committee(s)
Subcommittee(s)
Floor of Full House
2/3 Veto Override
Veto
Proposed Law
Joint Conference Committee
President
LAW!
Veto
Subcommittee(s)
Floor of Full Senate
2/3 Veto Override
Sponsorship and Introduction of BILL in Senate
Committee(s)
Possible Filibuster and Cloture

CHAPTER 12: THE EXECUTIVE

THE BIG PICTURE

The President, the top-most executive official in the U.S., has only a few but important powers that are listed in the U.S. Constitution. The practical effect of these powers is that the President has substantial authority over foreign policy, but relatively little authority over domestic policy. The President's primary domestic power is the ability to convince others to do what the President wants. This influence is largely determined by how popular the President is. Aside from the President, though, a large executive branch carries on most of the everyday functioning of the federal government.

RELEVANT TIMELINE

- 1789 U.S. Constitution ratified
- 1789-97 George Washington presidency
- 1861-65 Abraham Lincoln presidency; U.S. Civil War
- 1913 Federal Reserve System created
- 1933-45 Franklin D. Roosevelt presidency
- 1953 *Youngstown Sheet and Tube Co. v. Sawyer* (executive powers)
- 1973 War Powers Act

CHAPTER OBJECTIVES

After reading this chapter, the reader should be able to:

1. Describe what the Constitution declares regarding Presidential qualifications, as well as how the President is chosen and removed from office.
2. Describe the powers given the President by the Constitution, and what overall power the writers of the Constitution expected the President to have.
3. Compare and contrast Presidential power over domestic policy versus foreign policy.
4. Explain how various factors affect Presidential popularity.
5. Describe the major components and functions of the federal bureaucracy.

THE PRESIDENCY

Article II of the Constitution creates and empowers the executive branch of the U.S. government. At the head of the executive branch is the President. The President is the primary, individual elected leader of the United States. The Constitution also provides the President with a 4-year term in office. The original

Constitution did not put a limit on the number of terms the President can serve. The first president, George Washington, was extremely popular at the end of his second term and could easily have been elected to a third term. However, wishing to establish a positive democratic example, he chose not to run for a third term. Following the example set by Washington, every President after him who had a chance at a third term self-imposed this two-term limit on himself. This was true until Franklin D. Roosevelt, who was elected four times to office. FDR was elected President in 1932, 1936, 1940, and 1944. He died in office during his fourth term. This meant that the Presidency was becoming the equivalent of a life term in office. Congress and the state legislatures therefore decided to amend the Constitution to limit the President to two elected terms in office. This became the Twenty-Second Amendment in 1951.

The Constitution requires that the President be at least 35 years old, whereas Congressional Representatives or Senators must be only 25 and 30 years old, respectively. In this way, the Constitutions' framers hoped the President would be the wisest U.S. leader from having more life experience than members of Congress. Also, the writers of the Constitution feared a foreign-born President might be more loyal to their original homeland, and not the U.S. The Constitution therefore mandates that the President be a natural born citizen. This requirement has prohibited several successful high-level elected officials in the U.S. from running from president. Some of the more well-known examples are Arnold Schwarzenegger (former governor of California), Madeline Albright (Secretary of State under President Bill Clinton); and Henry Kissinger (Secretary of State under President Richard Nixon).

The President is chosen by an unusual mechanism unique to the United States. This system is called the *Electoral College.* The Constitution does not use the term "Electoral College." However, that phrase has been commonly used since the early 1800's to refer to the Constitutional plan for selecting the President. Under the Electoral College, the President is not directly elected by the people in a national vote. Instead, the President is chosen indirectly by the people through a complicated multi-step process.

First, according to Article II and the Twelfth Amendment of the Constitution, each state is assigned a number of *electoral votes.* The electoral votes each state receives is equal to the number of representatives plus the number of senators that the state has. In other words, each state's electoral vote is its number of representatives plus two. This means that the largest state, California, has over 50 electoral votes. Since each state has two senators and at least one representative, the smallest states like Alaska and Wyoming have the resulting minimum of three electoral votes.

On the day of the presidential election, voters are technically not voting for a presidential candidate. Instead, each state has a number of individual *electors* equal to the electoral votes of the state. Voters are actually voting for electors who favor one candidate or another. After the presidential election, these electors then meet together in their respective states on an assigned day and cast their electoral votes for the President.

There is another complication, though. Each state legislature decides how its electoral votes will be allocated between presidential candidates. All but two states, Maine and Nebraska, have decided that whichever Presidential candidate gets the most individual votes by the public within that state will receive *all* of that state's electoral votes. For example, Louisiana has eight electoral votes. Let's assume that in Louisiana, candidate Smith receives 40% of the vote, and candidates Jones and Doe each receive 30% of the vote. Even though Smith did not win a majority of individual votes within the state, Smith is awarded all eight of Louisiana's electoral votes. The electors who favor Smith are the ones who will represent Louisiana when the electors meet to cast their electoral votes for President. On the assigned meeting day, all eight electors will cast their electoral votes for Smith.

According to the Constitution, whichever presidential candidate receives a majority of electoral votes will become President. In other words, just winning the most electoral votes nationwide does not provide victory to a candidate unless that candidate wins more than 50% of the electoral votes overall. Currently there are 538 electoral votes possible, so a candidate needs 270 electoral votes to win. If no candidate has a majority of electoral votes, than the U.S. House of Representatives must choose the President from among the top three candidates who received the most electoral votes. The delegation from each state in the House must cast a single vote as a state. A majority vote (more than 50%) of the states is required for the winning candidate to become President. The House of Representatives has chosen the president twice: Thomas Jefferson in 1800, and John Quincy Adams in 1824.

The Electoral College is often viewed as obsolete, confusing, and undemocratic. For example, because of the mathematics of the Electoral College, a presidential candidate who won the electoral votes of the top eleven most populous states could become president without receiving even a single individual vote in any other state. Indeed, four times in U.S. history the candidate who became president due to winning the electoral college received fewer individual votes nationwide than his opponent. This occurred in 1824 (John Quincy Adams), 1876 (Rutherford B. Hayes), 1888 (Benjamin Harrison) and 2000 (George W. Bush).

There are several reasons the framers of the Constitution created such a system. Small states liked the idea because it guaranteed them a minimum of three electoral votes regardless how small their population. A direct vote by the people might give a small state even less influence in presidential elections. Slave states also liked the plan. The Three-Fifths Compromise gave Southern whites more votes in the House of Representatives, which then also gave Southern whites more influence over Presidential elections since electoral votes are based mostly on the number of representatives each state has. Also, as Hamilton discusses in Federalist Paper No. 68, the writers of the Constitution believed that a small group of electors might exercise better judgment in choosing the President than would the public at large. Although the electors would strongly consider the public's vote, they could ignore it if they believed the public had made a bad choice. As a practical matter, though, the electors have always voted as they originally pledged based on the public votes within their states.

Even if the original reasons for having the Electoral College are no longer valid, the Electoral College is unlikely to be replaced with a different system, such as direct election of the President by the public. Replacing the Electoral College is a low political priority since the Constitution is politically difficult to amend. Any political interests that believe they benefit from the current system will oppose change. Small states especially believe they have more influence with the Electoral College than they would have without it. Indeed, in 1969 the House passed a proposed constitutional amendment to abolish the Electoral College and replace it with election of the President by popular vote. However, the proposal was filibustered in the Senate by enough smaller states that cloture votes failed. The proposal was therefore abandoned and never reconsidered. As a result, the Electoral College will probably still be with us for the foreseeable future.

The Constitution also describes how the president can be removed from office prior to an election for wrongdoing. Recall that under the system of checks and balances, this is a relatively straightforward two-step process. First, the House of Representatives would by a majority vote issue charges of *impeachment* alleging some wrongdoing by the President. Second, the Senate would conduct the trial of those charges. The President will be acquitted of the charges unless 2/3 of the Senate votes to convict the President. Conviction of impeachment charges does not mean the President is convicted of a crime, but rather the President is simply removed from office.

Article II of the Constitution specifies the legal basis for impeachment of all executive officials including the President and Vice-President. The legal grounds are "treason, bribery, or other high crimes and misdemeanors." Treason is betraying one's country, and bribery is accepting money in return for a favor. Constitutional scholars generally agree the phrase "or other high crimes and misdemeanors" can be read as "or other serious wrongdoing." This could be a serious crime such as murder or rape, or abuse of power such as starting a war to gain popularity just before an election. It could also include neglect of duty, such as taking a year-long party cruise while leaving the Vice-President in charge.

No President has ever been removed from office by the impeachment process, but three were affected by the process. Presidents Andrew Johnson and Bill Clinton were each charged by the House but then acquitted by the Senate. In both cases, whether they actually broke any laws was disputed. President Richard Nixon resigned rather than be put through the impeachment process. He knew he was going to be found guilty by the Senate of ordering top law enforcement officials to cover up crimes Nixon had been involved with. Nixon therefore left office before the House could even vote on impeachment charges. Note that it's technically easier for Congress to remove a President from office (1/2 House, 2/3 Senate) than for Congress to override a presidential veto (2/3 House, 2/3 Senate). Yet because of the historical example set by the failure of Congress in 1868 to remove President Andrew Johnson from office purely on political grounds, since then members of Congress have reserved the impeachment process for only exceptional situations.

Specific Presidential Powers

Article II of the Constitution gives a broad "executive power" to the President. This includes the general power of enforcing laws under the system of separation of powers. However, the precise boundaries of this power are vague and still being determined. The most famous Supreme Court discussion of the undefined executive power came in 1952. In *Youngstown Sheet and Tube Co. V. Sawyer*, the Court indicated that Presidents have power over domestic policy if either the Constitution or Congress have expressly given the President such authority. If the Constitution and Congress are both silent on an issue, the President might have some limited leeway to act. If Congress has already established its own policies, then the President has very little freedom to oppose those policies.

Article II also lists several specific powers of the President. Although the Constitution does not specify categories of these powers, they can be grouped into executive, legislative, and judicial powers.

As the top executive officer of the United States, the President is the administrative chief of the federal government. Accordingly, as part of the checks and balances system, the Constitution gives the President authority to nominate the heads of the Cabinet departments and independent agencies, subject to Senate confirmation. Implied in this power to oversee the federal executive branch is such things as management of employees who work in the federal government, or management of federal government property, such as administrative buildings or national parks.

The Constitution also declares the President is "Commander-in-Chief" of the armed forces of the United States. As Commander-in-Chief, the President has sole and final authority to give commands regarding strategies or tactics of the U.S. military. For example, in 1945 at the end of World War II, the final decision whether and how to use the first U.S. atomic bomb on Japan rested solely with President Harry S. Truman. The assignment of the title and position of Commander-in-Chief to the President ensures that a civilian is always in charge of the military. This was because the framers of the Constitution feared a strong military might overthrow democracy and take political power for itself, and away from the people. Indeed, during the drafting of the Constitution, out of fear of a strong central military, one framer proposed that the size of the standing federal army be limited to 3,000 soldiers. George Washington, who presided over the Constitutional Convention, jokingly replied that he was fine with such a limit as long as the Constitution also limited any invading army to 3,000 soldiers. Obviously an invading foreign government would never respect such a limit, so after Washington's humorous remark the framers agreed not to put any limit on the size of the U.S. military. [Fun Fact: George Washington is the only President to have led troops in battle as Commander-in-Chief while President.]

Also, although the Constitution does not expressly list this power, as the nation's top elected leader the President is the chief ambassador of the U.S. to the rest of the world. When important international meetings occur, the President is the topmost representative that the U.S. can send. Acting in this capacity, the President may do things like negotiate treaties, plan defensive strategies with allies, and coordinate plans to improve the international economy.

To help fulfill all these executive roles, the President nominates top administrators, top civilian leaders of the U.S. military, and U.S. ambassadors to foreign nations. However, all these appointments are subject to Senate approval as stated in the Constitution. This is part of the checks and balances system.

Also to carry out the roles of chief administrator, chief diplomat, or Commander-in-Chief, the President issues "*executive orders.*" Although the Constitution does not mention the term "executive order" or describe any such power, the Supreme Court has declared the President may issue them. Executive orders can involve management of executive branch personnel and property, such as mandating affirmative action in hiring or banning snowmobiles in national parks. Executive orders can create military policy, such as by sending military advisors to a foreign nation, or ordering air strikes against a terrorist base camp. Executive orders can also establish foreign relations policies, such as recognizing a new government after overthrow of the previous one, or expelling an ambassador from a nation to protest that government's actions. Other executive orders can enforce Congressional policy within the limits of such authority given to the President by those Congressional statutes. For example, under the Patient Protection and Affordable Care Act (a.k.a. "Obamacare"), the President ordered the executive branch to delay enforcement of several provisions of the law to give businesses and state governments more time to comply with the law. Executive orders have the force of law and must be obeyed unless a court rules otherwise.

The Supreme Court has narrowly limited the President's authority to issue executive orders. Executive orders must not cross the boundary between enforcing laws and making laws. Therefore, the President may not simply raise or lower taxes, or create a new federal benefit program. Doing so would be in violation of the separation of powers, as Congress has primary authority to make domestic laws using the legislative process required by the Constitution. If the President oversteps these implied constitutional limits on executive orders, people affected by those orders may sue in federal court to block them. The precise limits of the President's authority to create and enforce policy via executive orders rather than the legislative process remains to be clearly defined by the Supreme Court.

The President is also given some legislative powers in the Constitution. As we've seen under the checks and balances, the President may veto bills passed by Congress. Also, the President may propose bills. By customary respect, the Congressional leadership will automatically assign a member of Congress to sponsor and introduce the President's proposed bills. There is no guarantee that they will ever pass, however, and most die in committee just as other bills do. In addition, the Constitution says that the President may call Congress into special session. This could occur if there was a national emergency and Congress needs to meet but is adjourned on recess at the time.

The Constitution also requires the President to inform Congress every year regarding the "state of the union." In other words, once a year the President must tell Congress what the President thinks is the current condition of the United States as a whole. From Presidents George Washington through Herbert Hoover, this report was looked at as a mere formality. However, Franklin Roosevelt realized the power of a new invention called radio. He therefore turned the State of the Union Address into a yearly public relations event. With the rise of television, all Presidents give a long state of the union speech that is always a big yearly media event. Presidents typically use the speech to propose new legislation or to tell Congress and especially the viewing public how wonderful the nation is under the President's leadership and policies. Or, the President explains how great the nation would be if only Congress would do what the President wants.

Finally, the Constitution also gives the President several judicial powers. Under the checks and balances, the President nominates all federal judges. This includes judges on the U.S. Supreme Court as well as all other levels of the federal courts. However, all nominations are subject to Senate confirmation. Some scholars argue the power to nominate federal judges is the most potent power the President possesses. This is because Supreme Court rulings can affect the basic structure and powers of government, as well as the rights of the people within the United States, for decades or even centuries. For example, as we saw when we looked at the history of federalism, in the 1930's the Court re-interpreted the meaning of the Constitution. This paved the way for a vastly larger, more powerful federal government today and likely for a long time to come.

Article II of the Constitution also states the President "shall have power to grant reprieves and pardons for offenses against the United States, except in cases of impeachment." A pardon essentially has the effect of legally pretending that the person never committed the crime. This allows a President to apply leniency whenever the President believes mercy would be a better policy than punishment. There is almost no limiting or qualifying language to this power. As long as an offense is a crime under federal law, the President has absolute power to pardon individuals for committing those offenses. This is true regardless how severe the offense. The president's power to pardon can occur anytime time after the commission of the offense, including before or after arrest, trial, conviction, or sentencing. The pardon can be granted to a single person or an entire class of persons. For example, President Washington pardoned all of the Whisky Rebellion participants, President Lincoln pardoned all Confederate soldiers, and President Carter pardoned all individuals who evaded the military draft during the Vietnam War. The only exception to the pardoning power is that a pardon may not restore someone to political office if they have been impeached.

The Constitution also requires no particular procedure to grant a pardon, mandates no necessary reasons that must be given for the decision, and provides no judicial review of the decision once it is made. In short, the President has sole discretion whether to grant a pardon or why. Indeed, in the last days of President Clinton's final term as President, he pardoned a fugitive on the FBI's top-ten most-wanted list. The fugitive also happened to be the husband of a top Democratic Party donor. Despite public outrage and Congressional threats to pass legislation limiting the President's power to pardon, no such legislation was ever enacted. Even had such a law been passed, most likely a federal court would have ruled the limitation unconstitutional. This is because the Constitution gives the President an unconditional power to pardon.

The President's power to pardon was most famously used when President Ford pardoned former President Nixon for any of his involvement in the crimes surrounding the Watergate scandal. Nixon had ordered executive branch officials and employees to secretly use their power to illegally investigate and destroy Nixon's political opponents. Some of the people involved in the illegal activities were caught when they broke into Democratic Party Headquarters in the Watergate Hotel in Washington, D.C. The investigation into the Watergate burglary eventually revealed Nixon's crimes and abuse of power. President Ford's decision to pardon Nixon was controversial and opposed by much of the public. Many political scholars believe the pardon probably played a large role in causing Ford to lose the 1976 presidential election.

Presidential Power: Original Intent

How much overall power did the framers of the Constitution generally intend or expect the President to have? This was another point of debate between the Federalists and the Anti-Federalists. Some Anti-Federalists such as Cato and Brutus argued that the public should fear the enormous powers given to the President. They suggested that the power to veto laws and the position of commander-in-chief, combined with the power to pardon people of crimes, together would allow a President to become a king. Specifically, the President could use the military to take over the country, pardon all the criminal co-conspirators who helped, and then veto any attempt by Congress to stop the takeover. These arguments sought to turn public opinion against the ratification of the Constitution.

The Federalists responded to these arguments. The most famous reply was made by Hamilton in Federalist Paper No. 70. Rather than counter-argue that the President would be weak, Hamilton argued that the nation needed a President with "vigor" and "energy." To defend his point, he compared two alternative methods by which the presidency could be designed.

During the writing of the Constitution, early drafts of the Constitution contained what is called a *plural executive.* That is, it would be a presidency of several people. This group would be a committee or council that would make decisions by majority vote. Several of the first state constitutions briefly provided plural executives in their state governments. This was done out of fear of a strong executive after the bad experience they had under rule by the British King. It was only near the end of the Constitutional Convention that the plan for a plural executive was changed to a plan for a *unitary executive.* In other words, it would be a presidency of one person. In Federalist Paper No. 70, Hamilton explains that a unitary executive is preferable to a plural executive. One person can act more quickly and decisively than can a group of people. A group could end up in disputes, delay, or gridlock when prompt action is needed. Imagine, for example, if after the terror attacks of 9/11 the U.S. had five presidents, all of which believed the U.S. government should respond in very different ways. There would be no majority vote of agreement. If they all gave conflicting orders to the U.S. military, chaos would result.

Up until the Great Depression of the 1930's, Presidents were not expected to do much. The public generally wanted presidents to just "leave them alone." Although some presidents like Lincoln wielded a great deal of power, most presidents were content to do little, and they promised little. As we saw in the chapter on federalism, though, public expectations changed with the Great

Depression. Since then, the people of the U.S. have wanted their presidents to do a lot. Scholars therefore refer to the presidents from Franklin D. Roosevelt (FDR) through today as the "modern presidency." Since FDR, the U.S. has become a more complex economy, with advanced transportation and communication technology. Also, the lack of a parliamentary system means Presidents are largely politically independent of Congress, since Presidents can only be removed by the difficult impeachment process. Presidents since FDR have thus realized they can use modern media to their advantage as a "bully pulpit" to bypass Congress and speak directly to the people.

These and other factors have psychologically caused people to look increasingly to the president as the best single leader to solve problems. Modern presidents therefore exercise more power than did presidents before them, and the public has higher expectations of presidents today compared to the past. Today, the public wants presidents to do almost everything, such as create a thriving economy with high-paying jobs for everyone, provide ample government benefit programs for anyone in need, and all while lowering taxes at the same time. In short, the public wants their presidents to be miracle workers, and presidents know this. Indeed, when was the last time you heard a presidential candidate of any political party promise that if elected, they won't do much? Because of unreasonable public demands on the power of the presidency, today presidential candidates make extravagant promises in order to get elected. These promises are impossible for any one human being to fulfill, regardless how politically powerful they are as President. In turn, the failure of presidents to live up to unrealistic expectations helps contribute to voter distrust and apathy.

Presidential Power and Foreign Policy

Regardless of the intentions of the Constitution's framers or the demands of the public, how much *actual* overall power do presidents today possess? Scholars of the presidency generally agree that the power of the President differs greatly between influence over foreign policy versus influence over domestic policy. In the area of foreign policy, presidents have a great deal of power.

In the 1800's and early 1900s, many presidents were "isolationists." The doctrine of isolationism argues that the U.S. is better off if it does not become entangled in foreign alliances or wars. Even President George Washington made this point in his Farewell Address. Much of the public throughout U.S. history has been, and still is, isolationist. For example, before the Japanese attacked Pearl Harbor, a majority of U.S. public opinion was against helping England fight against Nazi Germany. This prevented President Franklin Roosevelt from declaring war against Germany until the U.S. was itself attacked during World War II. Yet despite any isolationist tendencies, most Presidents have used the U.S. military in one way or another to achieve foreign policy goals.

As Commander-in-Chief of the U.S. military, and as chief ambassador of the United States to the World, the President can often almost single-handedly establish the official stance of the United States towards foreign nations. This is true even though the Constitution divides foreign policy between the Congress and the President. Recall that under the checks and balances, Congress has the power to declare war. Once it does so, as commander-in-Chief the President has total authority over the conduct of that war. Since World War II, however, the President has often sent armed forces into combat without Congressional authorization. During both the entire Korean War and the entire Vietnam War, for example, Congress never formally declared war. Even as the Vietnam War dragged on for many years, every year the escalation of troop levels and bombings were purely presidential decisions.

Because several presidents had acted as if they had the power to declare war, Congress became concerned that it was losing its Constitutional authority to declare war. To address this situation, after the Vietnam War Congress passed the *War Powers Act* in 1973. It is also often called the *War Powers Resolution* since Congress itself referred to the act by different names when it was passed. Yet Congress passed the law by overriding President Nixon's veto according to the required constitutional process, thus making it official U.S. law.

Regardless of the precise name of the War Powers Act, the act limits the ability of Presidents to keep troops in combat without Congressional approval. Under the War Powers Act, the President may introduce troops in combat, but then must remove them within 90 days at most unless Congress authorizes the combat to continue. The constitutionality of the War Powers Act has never been tested. Even without the War Powers Act, according to the Constitution Congress also is responsible for raising, regulating, and funding the armed forces. Thus, if Congress does not like what the President is doing militarily, it can threaten to withhold funding for the operation. This is unlikely to happen, however. If a member of Congress voted against providing financial support to armed forces, that vote would be extremely politically unpopular. Members of Congress therefore always want to claim "I support the troops!" This means that as a practical matter, Presidents can introduce armed forces into combat without Congressional approval. The primary factor hindering Presidents from doing so is lack of support from the *public* rather than Congress. Yet if the public supports the President, Congress is likely to do so as well.

Aside from war, Presidents also have a great deal of influence over peacetime foreign policy. Recall under the checks and balances that Presidents may negotiate treaties, but to become law the Senate must ratify those treaties by a 2/3 vote. This limits what domestic policies the President can commit the United States to enacting. Yet Presidents still have broad influence over foreign policy. Presidents increasingly favor using international "executive agreements" rather than treaties. Although the Constitution does not mention "executive agreements" the Supreme Court has upheld their use. The key difference is that an agreement must be passed using merely the general lawmaking process. That is, the agreement must be passed by a majority vote in both the House and Senate, then signed by the President. Presidents prefer this method because it's often easier to get the support of a majority of both chambers rather than support by 2/3 of the Senate. For example, this is why President Bill Clinton used this process to get Congress to pass the North American Free Trade Agreement (NAFTA) in 1994.

Presidents also have the power to establish or disestablish formal relations between the United States and foreign nations. Whether we are at war or at peace with other nations, Presidents can order the U.S. Department of State to either receive or refuse to receive ambassadors sent by foreign governments. By accepting an ambassador, the U.S. recognizes that person as an official representative of an official government. This means the U.S. formally recognizes that government as legitimate, which is to accept that nation's legal existence. For example, communists took over mainland China in 1949 and established the People's Republic of China (PRC). The non-communist government fled to the island of Taiwan, which established the Republic of China (ROC). For several decades, both the United Nations and the U.S. recognized only the ROC and not the PRC as the legitimate government of China. The U.N. changed its recognition from the ROC to the PRC in 1971. Finally in 1979, President Jimmy Carter granted formal U.S. diplomatic recognition to the PRC as the legitimate government of China instead of the ROC. However, the U.S. still maintains in informal relationship with the democratic ROC.

Presidents also are able to establish broad foreign policy doctrines merely by declaration. In 1823, President James Monroe declared that the U.S. would not tolerate any more interference in the Western Hemisphere by the nations of Europe or other outside countries. The *Monroe Doctrine* became a cornerstone of U.S. foreign policy for at least the next two centuries. President John F. Kennedy, for example, asserted the Monroe Doctrine as justification for a naval blockade of Cuba to keep Russian missiles out of that country. This resulted in the tense Cuban Missile Crisis in October, 1962. It was the closest the U.S. and Soviet Union ever came to nuclear war. Fortunately, the crisis ended after 10 days when Russia agreed to withdraw from Cuba.

In 1947, President Harry Truman established what became known as the *Truman Doctrine.* It said the United States would contain the attempted communist expansion of the Soviet Union to other nations beyond where communism currently existed. This policy of "containment" became the guiding principle of U.S.-Soviet relations during the Cold War.

After the 9/11 terror attacks on New York City in 2001, President George W. Bush declared that the U.S. would no longer tolerate the existence of terrorist organizations or nations that give shelter or aid to terrorist organizations. This included a right of the U.S. to pre-emptively attack such groups or governments. These foreign policy principles have often been called the *Bush Doctrine*. The doctrine was used to justify war against the Taliban government in Afghanistan for harboring the terrorist group Al-Qaeda, led by Osama bin Laden. Osama bin Laden masterminded 9/11 terror attacks. Relatedly, the 2003 invasion of Iraq was justified as a pre-emptive attack on the dictator Saddam Hussein. This was based on the grounds that he might acquire weapons of mass destruction and then give them to Al-Qaeda or other terrorist organizations.

Indeed, the title of Commander-in-Chief has been exceptionally important since World War II. Since then, the U.S. has had the most powerful military force in the world. This is partly a result of the U.S. having the largest economy and biggest national government budget of any nation on the planet. Yet it also has been a result of foreign policy decisions by Presidents and Congress to maintain high military spending levels. At first, the huge military spending was a result of fighting the "Cold War" with the Soviet Union, including in proxy wars in Korea and Vietnam. In the late 1980's and early 1990's, however, the Soviet Union collapsed and broke up into its member nations. Since the Soviet Union no longer existed, the Cold War ended. This left the U.S. as the only remaining military "superpower" on the planet.

Then, on September 11, 2001, the U.S. suffered a horrible terrorist attack in which almost 3,000 people were killed. In response, U.S. military spending increased significantly at the height of military involvement in Afghanistan and Iraq as part of the "War on Terror." Depending on how military spending is measured, the U.S. was spending almost as much or more money on its military then all the rest of the nations of the world combined were spending on their militaries. This led political observers to declare that the U.S. was now was a "hegemon." A "hegemony" exists when a nation easily dominates all other nations it has relationships with. For example, at its height, the ancient Roman Empire was a hegemon. Some political observers have even used the term "hyperpower" to describe the U.S. since the term "superpower" seemed inadequate to them. With both Russia and China increasing their military spending, however, whether or for how long the U.S. will remain a hegemon remains to be seen.

Domestic Policy and Presidential Approval

Presidential power over domestic policy is much weaker than presidential policy over foreign policy. When it comes to domestic policy, Presidents have relatively little power acting alone to accomplish what they want. Presidents can propose laws, but under the separation of powers only Congress can makes laws. This means that with the relatively small exception of executive orders, domestic policy is largely determined by Congress. Whether the President wants a major new policy in the areas of health care, education, the environment, crime, taxes, or any other area of domestic policy, that proposal will become policy only if the Congress passes it as legislation. The only power the President has to change domestic policy is to try to coax Congress to enact the President's policy wishes. The President must similarly convince political parties, interest groups, and the people in general to put pressure on Congress to pass legislation the President wants. In short, acting individually, any U.S. President has extremely little power to change domestic policy. The only thing a President can only do in this regard is try to persuade other actors in the political system to support and enact the President's desired policies.

Given that the main power any President has over domestic policy is the power of persuasion, what makes a president persuasive, especially when trying to convince Congress to pass the President's desired legislation? Many factors play a role, including the personality of the president. Yet perhaps the single factor that studies have shown to be most consistently important is presidential popularity. A President that the public likes will be more persuasive with Congress than a President that the public dislikes. Survey questions typically measure this as *presidential approval*. Although the wording might vary slightly from poll to poll, the survey question usually asks something like: "Do you approve or disapprove of the way the President is performing the job of President?" The percent of the public that replies "approve" to that question is called the president's *approval rating*. For example, a president with an approval rating of 60% or more is very popular at that moment with the public. A president with an approval rating of only 40% or less, however, is unpopular at that moment. Various businesses and organizations include the mass news media measure public opinion on a regular basis. Measures of presidential approval in particular are usually available on a weekly basis. Since survey research began in the 1940's, we now have several decades of public opinion data to draw some conclusions about several factors that strongly impact presidential approval.

The Economy. There is a strong correlation between the public's views of the condition of the economy and presidential approval. For example, if unemployment or inflation is high, presidential approval will likely be low. As we just saw when considering presidential power over domestic policy, though, it is Congress, not the President, which can pass laws affecting the economy. The President is almost completely powerless in this regard acting alone. Indeed, in the increasingly interconnected global economy, no one person, not even the President of the United States, can control or predict the economy. Even the best scientific models of the economy have dozens of variables, yet still are extremely incomplete and inaccurate. For example, every industrialized nation has teams of the best economics experts as top financial advisors to the government. Yet none of them teams foresaw the near collapse of the global financial system in 2008. After the near collapse, the best policies recommended by these same experts brought only a slow, unsteady and uncertain global recovery. Likewise, the President has neither a crystal ball nor a magic wand. The public does not understand this and so falsely assigns the President mythical powers over the national economy. Human psychology is at work here. Humans don't want to believe that life is so complex that it's sometimes beyond our ability to understand or control. In other words, people often have trouble accepting that things sometimes "just happen." So, when either good or bad things happen, people tend to want clear, simple explanations as to the cause, so they know who to either thank or blame. God is commonly given the credit for good things, and the devil is blamed for bad things. Short of thanking god or cursing the devil, what single human being has the most power to either cause things or prevent them? A significant percent of the public believes that person must be the President. People therefore give Presidents both mistaken credit and false blame for the economy.

Presidents and presidential candidates are all well aware of this false understanding on the part of the public, and take full advantage of it. When the economy is good, Presidents joyously take credit for it, even though they know the economy is largely beyond their control. When the economy is bad, opponents of the President gleefully blame the President, even though they know the President has little impact on the economy. A classic example of this occurred in the 1992 Presidential election. The economy was doing poorly at the end of President George H.W. Bush's first term in office as he ran for a second term. The governor of Arkansas, the opposition candidate, was previously unknown by the nationwide public. He hung a banner in his campaign headquarters to remind all his campaign staff: "It's the economy, stupid!" After steadily hammering Bush on the poor economy throughout the entire campaign season, Bill Clinton became the next President. Even then, Clinton won with only 43% of the popular vote because a third-party candidate, Ross Perot, won 19% of the vote by attacking Bush's record on the economy as well.

Rally-'round-the-flag effect. In times of national crisis or emergency, or national celebration, there is a temporary but noticeable spike in presidential approval. The people look to the President for leadership and inspiration. After the triggering event, presidential approval slowly returns to its previous baseline levels. The same example just used to illustrate the effect of the economy on presidential approval can also be used to illustrate the rally-'round-the-flag effect. President George H.W. Bush approval ratings were roughly 89% when the first Gulf War was won. Yet over time, as public memory of the overwhelming victory faded, so too did the rally-'round-the-flag effect. By the time of the election, the poor economy had become the dominant factor in presidential approval. Bush, Sr. therefore lost to Bill Clinton. As another example, after the 9/11 terror attacks on the World Trade Center in New York City, President George Bush Jr.'s approval ratings were the highest ever recorded for a president. Just over 90% of the public approved of the way President Bush Jr. was handling the job of President. Once again, though, as 9/11 became memory, those approval ratings returned within the range of normal levels.

The honeymoon period. Whenever a couple marries, the stereotype is that the newlyweds are blissful at the start of the marriage. They can do no wrong in each other's eyes. Over time, however, they start to get on each other's nerves, and the blissful honeymoon period ends. The same concept applies somewhat to new presidential terms. Scholars and the media consider the first 100 days of a new presidential term in office to be the rough estimate of the honeymoon period between a president and the public. The period of 100 days is only a rough estimate, though. Sometimes the period of public goodwill toward a new President will last shorter or longer than 100 days depending on the circumstances. The honeymoon period occurs because even people who voted against the President are often willing to give the new President a chance to make a fresh start of things. Much of the public gives the new President the benefit of the doubt, and takes a "wait and see" approach. However, as the President inevitably starts to make decisions some people disagree with, their initially generous attitude towards the President disappears.

The unique aspect of the honeymoon period is that is predictable. The future state of the economy is unpredictable, and future crises or emergencies are similarly unknowable. Therefore, the honeymoon period is generally the only time Presidents know in advance they will have generally high approval ratings. The level is usually around 60% or more at the start of the honeymoon period. Since a popular President is more persuasive at convincing Congress to pass legislation the President desires, the honeymoon period is a once-in-four-year opportunity. The President needs to "hit the ground running" at the start of the honeymoon period to take advantage of the public's temporary goodwill. Presidents will therefore pressure Congress during this period to move quickly in passing the President's public policy agenda. Once the honeymoon period is over, as politics returns to usual, the President will be less likely to get legislation passed that the President wishes to have enacted. Thus, every new President is advised by political advisors to have detailed legislation already written to present to Congress the moment the President takes the oath of office.

Scandals. One might presume that scandals have the opposite effect of the rally-'round-the-flag effect, and cause presidential approval to temporarily but noticeably decrease. Such is not the case, though. Scandals have an unpredictable effect on presidential approval. Some scandals destroy a presidency, such as happened with President Nixon and the Watergate scandal. Other scandals have no effect on presidential approval ratings. This was the situation with President Clinton and the sexual scandal involving himself and one of his aids, Monica Lewinsky. As another example, President Reagan had several scandals during his presidency. One, the Iran-Contra affair, included nationally-televised live coverage of Congressional hearings investigating the scandal. Despite this, President Reagan's public approval ratings were generally unharmed. For this reason, President Reagan earned the nickname the "Teflon President" because scandals would not "stick" to him. In short, there is not much political scientists can say in general about the likely effect of scandals on presidential approval.

Presidential History

A full historical account of the U.S. Presidents would require its own separate book. Here we'll summarize only in the briefest possible manner the presidency of a few of the early presidents, as well as all the modern presidents (from World War II through today). This information is found in the table below. Again, though, this section barely skims the surface of all that occurred during these presidents' terms in office.

Table of Selected Information about Selected U.S. Presidents

President	Years Served	Political Party	Select Noteworthy Items or Historical Events
George Washington	1789-1797	None	First President, ran without opposition, voluntary left Presidency after two terms
John Adams	1797-1801	Federalist	Alien and Sedition Acts criminalized opposition
Thomas Jefferson	1801-1809	Democratic-Republican	Louisiana Purchase doubled size of U.S.; Lewis and Clark Expedition explored U.S.
James Madison	1809-1817	Democratic-Republican	War of 1812 against England ended in peace treaty
***			
Andrew Jackson	1829-1837	Democratic-Republican	"Jacksonian Democracy" = democratic populism; removal of Native Americans

***			
Abraham Lincoln	1861-1865	Republican	U.S. Civil War defeated the Confederacy, ended slavery; assassinated while President
***			
Theodore Roosevelt	1901-1909	Republican	"Trust-buster" (ended big monopolies); Panama Canal
***			
Woodrow Wilson	1913-1921	Democratic	U.S. and allied victory in Europe in World War I
***			
Franklin D. Roosevelt	1933-1945	Democratic	Great Depression; New Deal; U.S. and allied victory in WWII (against Germany and Italy)
Harry S. Truman	1945-1953	Democratic	U.S. and allied victory in WWII (against Japan); start of Cold War with Soviet Union; Berlin Airlift; Korean War
Dwight D. Eisenhower	1953-1961	Republican	Began interstate highway system; truce in Korean War
John F. Kennedy	1961-1963	Democratic	Cuban Missile Crisis; pushed civil rights and space program; assassinated while President
Lyndon B. Johnson	1963-1969	Democratic	Passed civil rights laws; "Great Society" legislation; escalated war in Vietnam
Richard Nixon	1969-1974	Republican	Truce in Vietnam War; resigned presidency due to Watergate Scandal
Gerald Ford	1974-1977	Republican	Pardoned former Pres. Nixon
Jimmy Carter	1977-1981	Democratic	Iran Hostage Crisis; Energy crisis; Egypt-Israel peace
Ronald Reagan	1981-1989	Republican	Won Cold War with Soviet Union by military spending; "Reaganomics" tax cuts
George H.W. Bush	1989-1993	Republican	Won Gulf War against Iraq

Bill Clinton	1993-2001	Democratic	Best post-WWII economic expansion; Monica Lewinsky scandal and impeachment
George W. Bush	2001-2009	Republican	9/11 attacks; "War on Terror"; Afghanistan and Iraq Wars; 2008 financial crisis
Barack Obama	2009-2017	Democratic	Massive deficit spending to address post-2008 recession; "Obamacare" health insurance

The Federal Bureaucracy

The President is merely at the top of the federal executive branch. The rest of the executive branch is comprise of the federal bureaucracy. Regardless how popular or unpopular the president is, a huge administrative bureaucracy continues on with the day-to-day operations of the federal government. Immediately below the President in the executive chain of authority is the Vice-President. Together, the President and Vice-President oversee the Executive Office of the President. This office is comprised of staff who offer direct support for the day-to-day activities of the President. Next, the rest of the executive branch contains 15 Cabinet Departments and hundreds of independent agencies, altogether comprising roughly 3 million employees.

The departments and agencies of the executive branch are also known as the federal *bureaucracy*. A bureaucracy is the group of people that administer the functions of an organization. This can be either a government organization like a university, or a private organization like a large corporation. When we speak of the "federal bureaucracy," though, we are referring specifically to the bureaucracy of the United States government. Under the separation of powers in the U.S. Constitution, Congress creates and funds federal bureaucratic programs such as the U.S. military, Social Security, Medicare and Medicaid, student loan programs, and many others. Each of the numerous separate parts of the federal bureaucracy then implement and enforce the particular programs for which they are responsible.

The federal bureaucracy is composed primarily of 15 major departments known as *Cabinet departments*. The Cabinet departments are organized by policy area. Here they are listed in the order in which they were created:

- Department of State
- Department of the Treasury
- Department of Defense
- Department of Justice

- Department of the Interior
- Department of Agriculture
- Department of Commerce
- Department of Labor
- Department of Health and Human Services
- Department of Housing and Urban Development
- Department of Transportation
- Department of Energy
- Department of Education
- Department of Veterans Affairs
- Department of Homeland Security

There are also several government positions that are not considered Cabinet departments, but have been given Cabinet rank. Here are some of them:

- White House Chief of Staff
- Administrator of the Environmental Protection Agency
- Director of the Office of Management and Budget
- Ambassador to the United Nations
- U.S. Trade Representative
- Chairman of the Council of Economic Advisors
- Administrator of the Small Business Administration

Hundreds of *independent agencies* are also part of the executive branch. Congress has created them and funds them. Some agencies are led by individual heads, whereas some are led by groups called *commissions* or *boards*. Either way, they are called "independent" agencies because these heads, commissions, or boards usually receive fixed terms in office. Some receive appointment after nomination by the President and confirmation by the Senate, but some are appointed by bipartisan commissions. The theory behind having fixed terms is to offer insulation against political pressures in policy areas where Congress believes decisions should be made based on expertise and not on politics. Here's a list of some of the most frequently visible agencies that are often discussed in the news:

- Central Intelligence Agency (CIA)
- Consumer Product Safety Commission (CPSC)
- Environmental Protection Agency (EPA)
- Equal Employment Opportunity Commission (EEOC)
- Federal Aviation Administration (FAA)

- Federal Communications Commission (FCC)
- Federal Election Commission (FEC)
- Federal Trade Commission (FTC)
- National Aeronautics and Space Administration (NASA)
- National Labor Relations Board (NLRB)
- National Transportation Safety Board (NTSB)
- Occupational Safety and Health Administration (OSHA)
- Securities and Exchange Commission (SEC)
- Small Business Administration (SBA)
- Social Security Administration (SSA)
- United States Postal Service (USPS)

One extremely important and powerful agency is the Federal Reserve System, also referred to as the "Federal Reserve" or sometimes simply as "the Fed." The Federal Reserve System serves as the central bank of the United States, and is led by a Board of Governors. Federal Reserve Board members are nominated by the President and confirmed by the Senate with seven-year terms of office. The Federal Reserve Board meets regularly to manage the U.S. monetary system. For example, the Federal Reserve has legal authority to set the "prime lending rate." This figure directly affects the interest rates charged on home mortgages, car loans, student loans, and credit cards. To help stop the near-collapse of the global financial system in 2008, the Federal Reserve worked closely with Congress, the U.S. Treasury Department, major U.S. banks, and even foreign governments. Among other actions at the time, the Federal Reserve took extraordinary measures to inject over a trillion dollars into the U.S. and global economy.

Altogether, the executive branch of the federal government employs over three million people. The President is in charge of directing the operations of this entire branch, but only a thousand or so top positions are appointed by the president. These nominations need Senate confirmation under the Constitution's checks and balances. Almost all the rest of the three million employees of the federal government work in what is called the *civil service.* Employees in the civil service are not elected, nor appointed, but instead by law must be hired based mostly on qualifications. In other words, civil service employees are treated how most employees are treated at most private businesses. One exception is that civil service employees have added job protections in the law. For example, civil service employees can be fired only for being incompetent or committing some type of misbehavior. Most private businesses, on the other hand, can usually fire employees at any time and for almost any reason. As merely a few examples of the civil service, most employees of the U.S. Post Office, the National Park Service, and the Social Security Administration are civil service.

Bureaucratic Politics

Most of the work of federal administrative agencies is not controversial, as they simply implement public policy programs passed by Congress. For example, Congress, not the Internal Revenue Service (IRS), sets the tax rates individuals and corporations pay. The IRS simply collects those taxes. What is controversial is when Congress has delegated some of its lawmaking authority to agencies. For example, Congress has given the Environmental Protection Agency (EPA) limited autonomy to enact regulations controlling various types of air and water pollution. Based on this legal authority, the EPA creates environmental regulations restricting pollution from automobiles and business facilities. Similarly, the Federal Communications Commission (FCC) sets regulations governing who gets broadcast licenses for radio and television. The Federal Aviation Administration (FAA) sets rules prohibiting weapons and dangerous chemicals from being carried onto airplanes. The Occupational Health and Safety Administration governs on-the-job working conditions in industrial plants and construction sites. Congress has similarly empowered all the independent agencies with this type of independent rulemaking ability.

The U.S. Supreme Court has said this delegation of lawmaking authority is constitutional. Congress must, however, give the agency clear principles to follow regarding the narrow public policy area within the agency's jurisdiction. For example, a broad Congressional delegation to the Environmental Protection Agency (EPA) to "regulate pollution" would not be constitutional. Such a mandate does not give any guidance as to what pollution should be regulated, or how or why it should be regulated. On the other hand, a Congressional delegation to the EPA to "set limits on emissions from automobiles at levels necessary to preserve the public's respiratory health" would be constitutional. Such a precise rule gives clear guidance to the EPA as to what legal regulations it may make. An EPA regulation based on this particular delegation of authority might then regulate automobile emissions. Any specific limits on emission pollutants would then be based on current public health research as to the effect of those pollutants on adults and children.

Administrative agency authority is limited by their Congressional authorizations. Whether agencies have gone beyond those limits is a frequent issue in the courts. An entire body of law called *administrative law* deals with the legal issues arising from individuals and businesses challenging agency actions. For example, early in the Obama administration, EPA scientific experts concluded that several decades from now, global warming will probably cause some agricultural land to become unusable desert. The population will then be at risk of malnutrition or even starvation if there isn't enough food. This result clearly would injure public health. So, the EPA decided to regulate industrial emissions that lead to climate change by limiting the amount of carbon dioxide that coal-burning power plants and other factories emit. Power companies challenged these regulations in court. Were these regulations within the scope of delegated authority that Congress intended to give the EPA? In 2014, a 5-to-4 vote on the U.S. Supreme court said mostly yes. The Court upheld the EPA's authority to regulate "greenhouse gases" in some ways but not others. This was because the EPA stayed within its delegated authority on some of its regulations, but exceeded its delegated authority on some other rules it issued. In short, all independent agencies are constrained in their actions by Congress and by the courts.

Political debates over "big government" versus "small government," often mention bureaucratic rules from executive branch departments and agencies. Typically, political liberals view bureaucratic regulations as achieving positive and just results. This goes beyond clean air and safe cars. For example, wheelchair ramps need to have a minimum width and maximum angle of incline or else they are unusable. Thus, liberals see the federal bureaucracy as an entity that should be expanded so it can do more good. This is especially true in the areas of consumer and worker health and safety. Without regular inspections at food processing plants, for example, the risk of deadly foodborne illness increases, due to contamination from improper food handling and storage.

Similarly, everyone wants clean air to breathe and clean water to drink. Without government regulations restricting pollution, there is often no way to hold polluters accountable. There are hundreds or even thousands of industrial sources of air and water pollution in every city. Every gas station, for example, has surface run-off of spilled gasoline, oil, windshield wiper fluid, brake fluid, and anti-freeze. These mix together and flow downstream, affecting rivers for hundreds of miles. It would be legally impossible for a farmer who irrigates crops downstream, or a small town that relies on the river for drinking water, to prove which of the countless possible upstream polluters harmed their water supply. Government regulation at the source solves this kind of problem.

Political conservatives typically see bureaucratic regulations as costly and burdensome or even "out of control." Let's take the example of the wheelchair ramp just mentioned. Everyone agrees with the goal of equal accessibility for the disabled in the ideal. Yet if the ramp ends up merely a half-inch too narrow, or the incline is only one degree too steep, it must be redone. A small independent local business owner must spend thousands of dollars to tear it down and rebuild it until the mathematical requirements are perfectly met. Anti-pollution regulations can cumulatively cost businesses billions of dollars. These costs are then passed on to employees and consumers. This translates into fewer jobs, lower wages for employees, and higher prices for consumers.

There are also numerous horror stories of individuals ensnared in the unintended consequences of overly applied bureaucratic regulations. One example that made national news in 2013 was the story of Marty the Magician. Marty was paid to entertain at children's birthday parties. He owned a pet rabbit named Casey. In Marty's shows, he lifted Casey out of a hat or picnic basket. After zoo animals died in Hurricane Katrina, the USDA decided to increase its protection of animals that are "exhibited." Because Marty "exhibits" his rabbit, U.S. Department of Agriculture (USDA) regulations required that Marty pay for a license to display Casey. The USDA also required that Marty allow surprise inspections of his business, which was merely his home. Marty also had to notify the USDA with details of any extended travel with Casey. The regulations also required that Marty file an extensive "disaster plan" that explained how Marty will protect Casey in case of flood, fire, tornado or other natural disasters, as well as human-caused disasters such as hazardous waste spills from train derailments, nuclear accidents, terrorist attacks, and civil unrest. A disaster management expert who heard about Marty's plight volunteered to help him for free. Marty eventually filed a 34-page disaster plan for a generically named "bunny" in case he ever uses a different rabbit. Stories like this guarantee that the federal bureaucracy will continue to be the subject of political debates about big government versus small government.

SUMMARY

The President, the top elected leader of the United States, is selected by a unique constitutional system called the Electoral College. Congress may remove the President from office prior to the end of the President's term, but only for serious wrongdoing. The President has many executive powers. These include overseeing the executive branch, appointing top administrative officials, and commanding the U.S. military. The president has a key hand in lawmaking since the President proposes laws and may block Congressional proposals by vetoing them. The president also nominates all federal judges, and may issue executive orders in the performance of all these various functions. When it comes to foreign policy, Presidents are very powerful, often single-handedly being able to dictate U.S. foreign policy. Yet despite having several important powers granted by the Constitution, the President has relatively little influence over domestic policy. This is because Congress is the legislative branch of the federal government, so Presidents cannot make law. The main domestic power of the President, then, is the president's ability to persuade Congress to pass the President's policy agenda. This ability to influence Congress is based largely on the President's public popularity, which in turn is primarily influenced by the condition of the national economy. The President is merely at the top of the entire executive branch, however, which has fourteen Cabinet departments and hundreds of federal administrative agencies. With over three million employees, and a congressionally authorized ability to independently make legally enforceable regulations, the size and scope of the federal bureaucracy is at the heart of the debate over "big government versus small government."

Questions for Review and Self-Assessment

1. What does the Constitution declare are the qualifications to be President, and how is the President chosen and removed from office?
2. What powers does the Constitution give the President, and what overall power did the writers of the Constitution expect the President to have?
3. How much power does the President have over domestic policy versus foreign policy, and why?
4. How does the economy, crises, the honeymoon period and scandals affect Presidential popularity?
5. What are the major components, functions, and debates over the federal bureaucracy?

Critical Thinking Questions for Reflection and Discussion

1. Does the President have too much power, too little power, or about the right amount?
2. Does the federal bureaucracy regulate too much, too little, or about the right amount?

Suggested Reading Supplements

- Alexander Hamilton, *Federalist No. 70*
- An Old Whig, *Essay No. 5*
- *U.S. v. Curtiss-Wright Export Corp.* (1936)
- *Youngstown Sheet and Tube Co. v. Sawyer* (1952)
- *U.S. v. Nixon* (1974)
- War Powers Act (1973)

For Further Advanced Reading

- Sam Kernell, *Going Public: New Strategies of Presidential Leadership*
- Richard Neustadt, *Presidential Power and the Modern Presidents*
- James Q. Wilson, *What Government Agencies Do and Why They Do It*
- William DeGregorio, *The Complete Book of U.S. Presidents*

CHAPTER 13: THE COURTS

THE BIG PICTURE

Federal courts are responsible for interpreting federal law. Part of this authority includes the ability to legally block the other branches of government whenever they do something that violates the Constitution. The courts must be careful in using this power, however, since courts have no way of making sure that their decisions will be obeyed. Also, this controversial power makes the functioning of the courts a regular political issue. Even judges fiercely disagree amongst themselves about when they should block the actions of the other branches of government. Social science studies confirm that judges' beliefs about how to use their authority does influence their decision making.

RELEVANT TIMELINE

- 1789 U.S. Constitution ratified
- 1803 *Marbury v. Madison* (courts may enforce the Constitution)
- 1857 *Dred Scott v. Sanford* (Congress may not outlaw slavery)
- 1896 *Plessy v. Ferguson* (racial segregation is constitutional)
- 1954 *Brown v. Board of Education* (segregation unconstitutional)
- 1968 *Griswold v. Connecticut* (right to family privacy created)
- 1973 *Roe v. Wade* (right to abortion created)
- 2015 *Obergefell v. Hodges* (right to same-sex marriage created)

CHAPTER OBJECTIVES

After reading this chapter, the reader should be able to:

1. Describe the organization and authority of the federal courts.
2. Describe the source and nature of the power of judicial review.
3. Describe famous historical instances of judicial review and explain the consequences of those cases.
4. Compare and contrast judicial philosophy with political ideology, and explain how they relate.
5. Describe the main factors that social science studies reveal judges' decisions are based on.

JUDICIAL ORGANIZATION

Article III of the U.S. Constitution creates the federal judicial branch and empowers them by giving federal courts "the judicial power." Recall that under the U.S. system of separation of powers, the basic function of the courts is to interpret laws. In other words, whenever there is a disagreement about the meaning of a law, the courts have the authority to make the final determination.

The Constitution only provides a few details about the federal courts. Recall that under the checks and balances in the Constitution, all federal judges must be nominated by the President and confirmed by the Senate. Beyond that, the Constitution does not list any minimum age or other qualifications to be a federal judge. The Constitution does not even require that federal judges be attorneys. As a practical matter, though, having a legal background is an unwritten requirement. The Senate would be unlikely to confirm a nominee for a federal judicial position unless that nominee has a significant legal background.

According to the Constitution, federal judges serve in office "during good behavior." This means they receive life terms in office until they die, choose to retire, or are removed by the impeachment process for improper behavior. The behavior warranting impeachment would be similar to the standard for impeachment of the President. It would include the commission of serious crimes or other serious wrongdoing such as accepting bribes, abusing power, or neglecting duty. The impeachment process for judges is the same process as for the removal of executive officials. A majority of the House must issue articles of impeachment alleging wrongdoing, and then a two-thirds majority of the Senate must vote to find the person guilty of the wrongdoing. If the Senate convicts the federal judge, that judge is removed from office. If the Senate acquits the judge, then the judge continues to serve indefinitely.

The Constitution gives federal courts the "judicial power" over federal laws. In modern legal terminology, this is called *jurisdiction*, which means legal authority to hear and decide certain types of legal questions. The jurisdiction of the federal courts includes the U.S. Constitution, Congressional statutes, international treaties which the U.S. has joined, and rules and regulations issued by the federal bureaucracy. Federal Courts also have jurisdiction over lawsuits between different states, citizens of different states, or lawsuits involving non-U.S. citizens. Federal jurisdiction over lawsuits between businesses or citizens of different states or nations is called *diversity jurisdiction.*

Article III creates only the U.S. Supreme Court, but gives Congress the power to create the rest of the federal court system. For this reason, almost all federal courts other than the Supreme Court are called *Article III courts.* Congress currently has divided the United States into 94 geographic districts. Each state has one or more U.S. District Courts. For example, Louisiana has three federal districts: The Eastern District of Louisiana, the Middle District of Louisiana, and the Western District of Louisiana. The District Courts are the trial courts in the federal court system. If you want to file a lawsuit in federal court, or are sued in federal court, or are charged with a federal crime, your case will first be heard in the U.S. District

Court. Because U.S. District Courts conduct the first trial of your case, they are said to have *original jurisdiction*.

The U.S. is also divided into 12 geographic districts which each comprise a Federal Circuit Court of Appeals. Each Circuit Court hears appeals either from the District Courts from multiple states, or the District of Columbia. The Fifth Circuit Court of Appeals, for example, is based in New Orleans. It hears the appeals from all the U.S. District Courts in Texas, Louisiana, and Mississippi. The Circuit Courts do not conduct any trials. They only hear appeals by losing litigants in cases that have already been ruled on by the District Court. Because U.S. Circuit Courts only hear appeals, they are said to have *appellate jurisdiction*. Separate from the District Courts and Circuit Courts, Congress has also created several specialized courts, such as bankruptcy courts, tax courts, and military courts.

The U.S. Supreme Court in turn has jurisdiction to hear all appeals from the Circuit Courts of Appeals, any specialized federal courts, and all high courts within the 50 state court systems if a federal legal issue is involved. For example, in the 2000 Presidential election, Florida election law mandated how to count disputed ballots within Florida. Both presidential candidates George Bush and Al Gore, however, argued that the U.S. Constitution and federal election law were implicated by the Florida Supreme Court's application of Florida election law. Thus, because federal law was in question, the U.S. Supreme Court had appellate jurisdiction to review the decision by the Florida Supreme Court.

Let's look at another example. Assume that the Social Security Administration (SSA) office in Lafayette, Louisiana denies Jane Doe's application for disability benefits. The SSA does so on the basis that Jane did not provide enough medical evidence to prove she was disabled. If Jane still is unable to obtain benefits after going through the administrative appeals process within the SSA, she can file a lawsuit in the Western District of Louisiana, whose courthouse is located in Lafayette, Louisiana. If Jane loses her case in the federal District Court, she can file an appeal in the Fifth Circuit Court of Appeals in New Orleans. Under Congressional law, the U.S. District Court must hear any lawsuit filed, and the Court of Appeals must hear her appeal once. Both the District Court and the Court of Appeals therefore have what is called *mandatory jurisdiction*. If Jane loses her appeal, then she can ask the U.S. Supreme Court to hear her case.

The Constitution does not specify how many judges should be on the Supreme Court. Congress therefore decides this question. Under current Congressional law, there are nine judges called *justices* on the Supreme Court. Unlike the District Courts and Circuit Courts, however, most of the Supreme Court's jurisdiction is *discretionary appellate jurisdiction*. This means the Supreme Court can itself decide whether to hear the appeal in a case. By the current rule decided by the Supreme Court itself, at least four of the nine justices must agree that the case is important enough to hear. Thus, if four or more justices vote to listen to the appeal the Supreme Court will hear the case. This self-imposed requirement is therefore appropriate called the "rule of four." Each year there are typically over 7,000 cases appealed to the Supreme Court, but the justices usually agree to hear only about 150 of them at most. In deciding whether to hear a case where the Court has discretionary appellate jurisdiction, the technical legal phrase for a request that the Court hear an appeal is "a petition for a writ of certiorari." Sometimes the media will report the Court's decision either way as the Court "granted certiorari" or "denied certiorari." More simply, sometimes the shorthand phrase "granted cert." or "denied cert." will be used. Either way, these legal phrases merely indicate whether the Supreme Court agreed or declined to hear an appeal of a lower court case.

In a remaining small percent of cases before the Supreme Court, according to the Constitution the Supreme Court has *mandatory original jurisdiction.* This means the Supreme Court acts as the trial court and must hear the case for the first time, rather than on appeal. Such cases involve disputes between states, between a state and the U.S. government, or disputes between a citizen or state and a foreign government.

Once the Court agrees to hear a case, both sides in the case have a chance to file written arguments with the Court. These written arguments are called *appellate briefs* because they are a relatively short, fifty-page summary of the entire area of law and legal arguments that applies to the particular legal question in the case. Other interested parties also may file a brief on behalf of either of the litigants in the lawsuit if the interested parties have a stake in the outcome of the case. For example, if the Court is going to rule on a question of business law, then different industries, labor unions, or environmental groups might file briefs attempting to persuade the Court how to rule. These recommendations are called *amicus curiae* briefs. *Amicus curiae* is Latin for "friend of the court." The media will often shorten the phrase to just "amicus," such as "The Apple computer company filed an amicus brief in the case." Also note that the mass news media often avoid the correct legal terminology since many of their readers, listeners, or viewers might not understand the meaning. So, rather than saying "The Supreme Court today granted a petition for a writ of certiorari in a case where 50 major companies filed amicus curiae briefs," instead the media might simply report "The Supreme Court today agreed to hear an appeal of a case where 50 major companies filed briefs as friends of the court."

Once all the appellate briefs are filed with the Court, the Court will hear *oral argument* in the case. This is a chance for the lawyers on both sides to personally appear before the entire panel of judges on the Supreme Court. The lawyers then verbally explain and defend their position, as well as answer any questions the justices have, which are usually numerous.

Regardless how a case gets to the Supreme Court, after the written and oral arguments a majority vote by the Supreme Court then decides the outcome of the case. That is, whichever side can convince five or more out of the nine justices to agree with its position will win the case. It doesn't matter if the justices in the minority believe the majority opinion is outrageously wrong. However the majority rules is the court's legally binding decision. There is no higher court in the United States, so whatever the Supreme Court decides is the final determination of the legal matter in question. This is why the Supreme Court is also called a "court of last resort."

Judicial Review

Recall once again that under the separation of powers, the courts interpret laws. This function and role of the courts is not controversial. What *is* definitely controversial is the strongest power courts have in fulfilling this role: the power to declare actions by other branches of government to be unconstitutional. This power of *judicial review* essentially means that when the courts review what legislatures or executives do, courts can declare those actions illegal, and hence null and void.

The existence of the power of judicial review is for the most part not controversial, but rather how that power is used. Although neither the term "judicial review" nor its definition is found in the constitution, it can be seen as a direct implication of what *is* found in the Constitution. The writers of the Constitution were well educated. They knew that a basic principle of law is that higher law always overrides lower law. For example, state law overrides contradictory local city laws, and in turn federal law overrides contradictory state and local laws. Article VI of the Constitution expressly declares that the Constitution is the "supreme law of the land" so it must override all other laws. Under the separation of powers, the federal courts must interpret the meaning of laws. Therefore, when faced with a conflict between what the U.S. Constitution says and what the President, Congress or states are doing, the courts must say the Constitution overrides anything contradictory to it. This can be expressed logically as follows:

1. Higher law overrides contradictory lower law.
2. The Constitution is the highest law in the United States.
3. Therefore, the Constitution overrides any contradictory action by Congress, the President, or the states.
4. The courts have the power to interpret laws.
5. Therefore, when faced with a contradiction between what the federal or state executives or legislatures are doing and what the Constitution says, the courts must declare that the Constitution overrides any contradictory actions.

When the Supreme Court declares a government action to be unconstitutional, that means the action is illegal under the Constitution. Because the action is illegal, it is therefore null and void.

In 1803, the U.S. Supreme Court expressly described this logic in the landmark legal decision *Marbury v. Madison*:

> "Certainly all those who have framed written constitutions contemplate them as forming the fundamental and paramount law of the nation, and consequently the theory of every such government must be, that an act of the legislature repugnant to the constitution is void. This theory is essentially attached to a written constitution, and is consequently to be considered by this court as one of the fundamental principles of our society. . . . It is emphatically the province and duty of the judicial department to say what the law is. Those who apply the rule to particular cases, must of necessity expound and interpret that rule. If two laws conflict with each other, the courts must decide on the operation of each. So if a law be in opposition to the constitution: if both the law and the constitution apply to a particular case, so that the court must either decide that case conformably to the law, disregarding the constitution; or conformably to the constitution, disregarding the law: the court must determine which of these conflicting rules governs the case. This is of the very essence of judicial duty."

Essentially, the power of judicial review is the ability of the courts to enforce the social contract of the United States. Today, not only the U.S. Supreme Court, but all courts within the United States at both the federal and state levels possess the power of judicial review.

Again, the *existence* of this power of judicial review is for the most part not controversial. There are a few critics who believe the power of judicial review extends only over state governments, but not the other branches of the federal government. That is, some legal scholars believe Congress and the President may follow their own independent interpretation of the Constitution. However, in the regular functioning and discourse of U.S. politics, most people across the political spectrum accept the validity of judicial review over both the state and federal governments.

What is widely controversial, though, is *how* and *when* the power of judicial review should be and is used. This was, in fact, the key issue of debate between the Federalists and Anti-federalists regarding the federal courts. The Anti-federalists argued judicial review gave dangerously too much power to the federal courts. The Federalists responded to this argument, especially in Federalist Paper No. 78, written by Alexander Hamilton. There, Hamilton makes the famous statement that the judicial branch is the "least dangerous branch" of government. But why is this so? Hamilton compares the power of the courts to the powers of the other branches of government. The legislature possesses the "power of the purse." That is, the legislative branch controls money. If it wants to do something, it can raise taxes and spend money to accomplish its goals. In contrast, the executive branch possesses the "power of the sword." In other words, the executive branch, especially the President, controls the U.S. military. If the President wants something done, the President is Commander-in-Chief of the entirety of the U.S. armed forces. This is an enormous power.

Yet as Hamilton then further explains in Federalist No. 78, the courts have neither the power of the purse nor the power of the sword. Courts cannot raise taxes, nor do courts have a large budget from which they can assign money to implement their decisions. Nor do the courts command any police force or military that can go out and enforce judicial rulings. All the courts can do is issue their decisions, and then hope that the other branches of government and the public decide to voluntarily respect and obey those court decisions. If the public and other branches of government were to ignore court decisions, there would be no way for the courts to enforce their decisions. This means that the judicial branch is entirely impotent on its own, and is entirely dependent on the other branches of government to enforce court decisions. Because of this, Hamilton argued people should not worry about judicial review.

Hamilton further argued in Federalist Paper No. 81 that even if the Supreme Court abuses its power of judicial review, the impeachment process for federal judges will keep the justices in line. In other words, Hamilton argued that the fear of impeachment will keep those judges from abusing judicial review. That is, fear of losing their jobs will lead federal judges to use judicial review sparingly and carefully.

The Anti-Federalists did not agree with Hamilton's assessment, however. Perhaps most famously, the Anti-Federalist Brutus argued that judicial review was too powerful a weapon to give to the federal courts. For example, in the checks and balances in the Constitution, although the President can veto Congressional laws, Congress then has a counter-check. It can override a presidential veto by a 2/3 vote of both chambers of Congress. Yet judicial review is an unchecked check. That is, the other branches of government have no counter-check to it. The President cannot veto judicial review, and Congress cannot vote to override judicial review. Once the Supreme Court exercises judicial review, there is no way to counteract that power except to amend the U.S. Constitution, which is a very politically difficult process. Brutus went on to further argue that impeachment will not be an obstacle to judicial review. This is because using a power the courts are expressly given will not be a legal grounds for impeachment. Impeachment would be appropriate in the case of bribery, corruption, or other wrongdoing, but there is nothing wrong with using a power actually listed by the Constitution. Therefore, Brutus argued, as long as the Constitution says federal judges serve in office "during good behavior," the threat of impeachment will not deter judges from using the power of judicial review frequently or in whatever circumstances they wish.

Judicial Impact and Nominations

Once the Court has used its power of judicial review, what are the consequences of that decision? The lessons of history have shown us that both Hamilton and Brutus were each partially correct in their prophecies about the consequences of judicial review. Hamilton was correct that without support from the other branches of government, court decisions could go unenforced. In the early 1830's, the U.S. government wanted to forcibly remove members of the Cherokee Nation from their lands in Northern Georgia and Eastern South Carolina. The Supreme Court ruled in favor of the treaty rights of the Cherokee. President Andrew Jackson is recorded as having responded "Chief Justice Marshall has made his decision, now let him enforce it." President Jackson then ordered the compulsory march of the Cherokee Nation and other Eastern Native American tribes to Indian Territory (now Oklahoma) at the gunpoint of the U.S. military. Thousands of Native Americans died from starvation, freezing, and physical exhaustion. Between losing their homelands and a significant percent of their population, this forced migration became known to several tribes, especially the Cherokee, as the *Trail of Tears*.

Another example that shows the U.S. Supreme Court is powerless on its own is its 1954 ruling in *Brown v Board of Education.* The U.S. Supreme Court ruled that racially segregated public schools violated the 14th Amendment of the U.S. Constitution. Yet Southern governors, state legislatures, and local schools boards openly defied the ruling and did everything they could to obstruct integration. It was only when the both other branches of the U.S. government, Congress and the Presidency, took an active role in enforcing *Brown v. Board of Education* that public schools in the South finally became racially integrated.

Although Hamilton was correct that court rulings have no effect unless enforced by the other branches of government, Brutus was also correct that there is no counter-check to judicial review. Once the Supreme Court has ruled on an interpretation of the U.S. Constitution, there is way to reverse that ruling except for amending the Constitution. This is seldom done. As one rare example, the Supreme Court ruled in 1937 that requiring a fee to vote did not violate the Constitution. Only after the Constitution was amended in 1964 by the ratification of the Twenty-Fourth Amendment were poll taxes prohibited by the Constitution. Indeed, since the original ten amendments contained in the Bill of Rights were ratified in 1791, there have only been 17 additional amendments added to the U.S. Constitution through the present day. Many amendments have been proposed, but extremely few have been added. As a practical matter, this means the Supreme Court almost always has the final say in the meaning of the Constitution.

Brutus was further correct that impeachment is not a counter-check to the exercise of judicial review. Although investigations were begun to possibly impeach several dozen federal judges throughout U.S. history, less than a dozen federal judges have been ever impeached for wrongdoing. None of those impeachments have been for the exercise of judicial review. Moreover, no justice of the U.S. Supreme Court in particular has ever been removed from their position as judge by the impeachment process. There has never even been a serious movement to impeach the justices of the U.S. Supreme Court despite widespread public anger at the rulings. This has been true even after the most controversial Supreme Court rulings, including *Dred Scott v. Sanford* in 1856, *Brown v. Board of Education* in 1954, and *Bush v. Gore*, which decided the outcome of the 2000 Presidential election in favor of Bush over Gore. Justices on the Supreme Court know that regardless how controversial their rulings are, judges are essentially immune from impeachment on the grounds of using judicial review.

At the same time, however, strong public disagreement with controversial Supreme Court rulings can sometimes continue for decades. For example, in the landmark 1973 case *Roe v. Wade*, the Court ruled that women have a constitutional right to obtain an abortion. Public opinion on whether abortion should be legal has barely changed since then. Large minorities of the public, especially religious conservatives, still believe abortion is immoral and should be severely restricted or outlawed entirely. When conservative Republicans gain majorities in state legislatures or Congress, they regularly try to find legislative ways to minimize the right defined in *Roe v. Wade* and subsequent cases. Similarly, whenever possible, Republican Presidents attempt to appoint Supreme Court nominees that those Presidents believe will likely vote to overturn *Roe v. Wade*. Democratic Presidents do likewise in the opposite way. They typically attempt to appoint Supreme Court nominees who those Presidents believe will uphold the core of the *Roe v. Wade* decision. This example shows that by becoming involved in a controversial social issue, the Court does not necessarily settle the issue. It simply transfers the primary political battleground from the legislative arena to the judicial arena. These legal and constitutional battles over the question of abortion will continue as long as the public remains deeply divided on the issue.

Sometimes the Supreme Court's decision *not* to use judicial review can be just as controversial as when it does exercise that power. For example, in 2012, by a narrow 5-4 vote in *NFIB v. Sebelius*, the Court declined to use judicial review to overturn the Congressional mandate for individuals to buy health insurance as part of the health program commonly known as "Obamacare." By upholding the mandate to buy insurance as a valid use of the Congressional power to tax, the Court angered those who believed Congress had no constitutional authority to force people to buy a product they did not want. Was the Court abandoning its constitutional responsibility to uphold the Constitution, or was it simply acknowledging a valid constitutional power of Congress? People's perspectives on the Court's rulings depend on one's interpretation of the Constitution. One person's "right" is another person's "injustice." One person's "legislative power" is another person "constitutional violation." Hence, the Court's interpretations of the Constitution will always be politically controversial no matter how the Court rules. These controversies cause Presidential nominations to the Supreme Court to be highly politicized.

Indeed, as was noted in the previous chapter on the President, the power to nominate federal judges, especially judges to the Supreme Court, is one of the most, if not the most, important avenues a President has for long-term influence over U.S. public policy. A judge appointed at the age of 40 could spend the next half-century deciding major constitutional questions over the legal rights and powers of the President, Congress, and state governments. A single judge can tip the balance in favor of either liberal or conservative policy outcomes. Indeed, narrow 5-4 decisions are common on the court when it comes to controversial policies like abortion, the death penalty, affirmative action, gay rights, voting rights, free speech, religious liberty, and the rights of criminal defendants. *NFIB v. Sebelius,* the ruling to uphold the constitutionality of President Obama's signature health care bill, commonly known as "Obamacare," was also a split 5-4 vote. As we saw earlier in the chapter on federalism, the Court's interpretations of Congress's power under both the Commerce Clause and the Tax Clause are highly controversial. Even a single different judge could tip the scale on the Court to reverse *Sebelius* or many other previous major Supreme Court rulings.

Every President and every member of the Senate knows the huge political stakes involved in Supreme Court nominations. Thus, every President nominates people to the Court who the President believes will vote as the President wishes. Knowing this, during the Senate confirmation process the party opposite the President does everything it politically can to defeat the nomination. If the President's party is in the Senate majority, then the opposition minority party will try to filibuster the nominee. If the opposition party is in the Senate majority, they can simply avoid bringing the nominee up for a vote. This is what happened, for example, during President Obama's last year in office. Conservative Justice Scalia died, leaving the Court tied with four liberal justices and four conservative justices on the court. Whoever replaces Scalia will determine the outcome of many major constitutional issues, perhaps for many decade to come. Democratic President

Obama nominated Judge Merrick Garland to fill the empty seat on the Court. Even though Garland was considered a moderate, Senate Republicans feared he would not be as conservative as the nominee would be if a Republican won the next Presidential election. Therefore, since Republicans comprised the Senate majority, the decided not to allow Judge Garland's nomination to be voted on, in the hope that a Republican would win the fall presidential election. Regardless the outcome of this or any one particular nomination battle, every Supreme Court nomination will always likely result in a major political battle.

JUDICIAL PHILOSOPHY

All workers in any type of job have a philosophy about how they should do their job. The same is true of judges. The philosophy a judge adopts about how best to go about the job of judging is called *judicial philosophy.* There are many aspects of judicial philosophy, such as how one should treat criminal litigants. Should one be lenient and merciful towards criminal defendants, or harsh and punitive? The most publicly discussed aspect of judicial philosophy, however, is how judges should exercise the power of judicial review. In other words, what is the proper role of judges and courts in using judicial review? Although there are numerous variations, combinations, and exceptions, within judicial philosophy the main debate is between the philosophies of *judicial activism* and *judicial restraint.* These competing philosophies provide different answers regarding how freely judges should use their power of judicial review.

The philosophy of judicial activism argues that judges should not be afraid to exercise their power of judicial review. The purpose of judicial review is to uphold the main social contract of the United States, which is the U.S. Constitution. If there is any disagreement between what the Constitution says and what other branches of government are doing, the courts should not hesitate to enforce the legal limits on government placed in the Constitution. To avoid doing so would be an unethical abandonment of the Constitutional responsibility given the judicial branch. Judicial review makes sure political leaders and the public act within the limits imposed by the Constitution. Therefore, as proponents of judicial activism argue, judges should actively and without hesitation impose judicial review whenever there is a violation of the Constitution. Moreover, because judges are supposed to achieve justice, if achieving justice in a case means interpreting the Constitution in a way that changes its meaning, so be it. Judicial review will in this situation alter the Constitution's meaning in order to strike down the unjust actions by the legislative or executive branches. Judicial activists rarely call themselves by such a label, but in practice they typically believe the meaning of the Constitution should change with the times. They fear the Constitution will become obsolete and useless if it is no longer relevant to today's issues. They therefore often refer to the Constitution as a "living," or "organic" document. Judicial activists say the meaning of the Constitution should "evolve" or "grow" to accommodate new unforeseen economic, social, or technological circumstances.

On the other hand, the philosophy of judicial restraint argues that the exercise of judicial review should be rare. Legislatures and executives are democratically elected by the public. Federal court judges, though, are not elected but are instead appointed for life terms. There is no possibility of electoral accountability for their decisions. The exercise of judicial review therefore puts an undemocratic branch of government in the place of overruling decisions by the democratically elected branches of government. Any exercise of judicial review is thus not only *un*democratic, but *anti-democratic*. That is, judicial review by unelected judges blocks the wishes of the political majority acting through their democratically elected representatives. Because we wish to claim our system of government is democratic, the exercise of judicial review problematic. Judges should be therefore be restrained in their use of judicial review. As restraintists argue, the power of judicial review should only be applied in exceptional circumstances where there is a direct, blatant violation of the Constitution. Without such a clear violation, judges should uphold the law even if they disagree with it or find the law to be silly, stupid, or even unjust. Yet the only way we can have a stable meaning to the Constitution is if we look to what those who wrote and ratified it originally intended. If the meaning of the Constitution changes depending on whatever five old men and women wearing black robes happens to think at any one moment, this is governance by mere whim. Judges should therefore follow the law as it's written, and not their own personal preferences, or else the Constitution becomes meaningless and arbitrary. In short, unless the Constitution expressly forbids a government action, the action should be upheld. Yet when the Constitution is clear, it should be followed whether people like that interpretation or not. If people don't like it, the Constitution can be changed democratically through the amendment process.

To summarize this debate over constitutional interpretation, both sides believe it's important that the Constitution remain relevant to our legal and political system. The two sides disagree, however, on how that relevance should be maintained. One side believes the Constitution will remain relevant only if it has a stable meaning, but the other side believes the Constitution will remain relevant only if it has a flexible meaning. What the restraintist sees as stability the activist sees as rigidity to the point of obsolescence. What the activist sees as flexibility the restraintist sees as ungroundedness to the point of meaninglessness. Yet even this analysis oversimplifies the debate. An activist judge might, for example, strongly believe the original intent and meaning of the Constitution should be followed. So a judge's philosophy on how the Constitution should be interpreted is not necessarily the same thing as a judge's philosophy on how judicial review should be used. Either way, judicial philosophy goes to the heart of the question regarding the proper role of the Constitution and the courts in U.S. democracy.

This central debate over judicial philosophy further explains why every time there is an opening on the U.S. Supreme Court, there is a fierce political battle involving the President and the Senate. Of course, political ideology plays a huge role in Supreme Court nominations. Presidents and Senates fight over what the political ideology of a judicial nominee is and should be. Another main point of contention over candidates for the Supreme Court, however, is whether those candidates are judicial activists or judicial restraintists, and whether those judges will follow the original intent of the Constitution. Presidents typically nominate candidates who the Presidents believe will adopt the judicial philosophy preferred by the President. During Senate confirmation hearings, the Senators will then inquire and debate whether the candidate favors judicial activism or judicial restraint, as well as how the candidate believes the Constitution should be interpreted. Senators who favor one judicial philosophy will oppose judicial candidates who those Senators believe have adopted the contrary judicial philosophy. Of course, Senators also oppose judicial candidates on political grounds, but again, judicial philosophy is a key factor in the debates.

It's important to note there that the concept of judicial philosophy should not be confused with the concept of political ideology, which will be discussed in detail in the next chapter. Judicial philosophy is not the same thing as political ideology, even though there is a common misperception among the public that these concepts are the same. Political ideology is one's belief about what public policy should be. In common understanding, ideology falls on a spectrum from liberal to conservative. A judge can be politically liberal or conservative, yet still adopt either the judicial philosophy of activism or restraint. There is no necessary logical connection between political ideology and judicial philosophy. Moreover, as we shall also see in the chapter, the concept of political ideology is more complex than an either-or choice between only the two alternatives of liberal and conservative. Nevertheless, the over-simplified table below illustrates that the two concepts are not the same. This means there are many different possible combinations of political ideology and judicial philosophy on the part of judges.

Table: Combinations of Political Ideology and Judicial Philosophy

Political Ideology: / Judicial Philosophy:	Liberalism	Conservatism
Activism	Liberal activist	Conservative activist
Restraint	Liberal restraintist	Conservative restraintist

If one follows Supreme Court decisions closely, one can see examples of votes in cases that fit into all these four categories. This categorization is based on the statements the judges make in their written opinions in each decision by the Court. Even the same judges will act differently across different cases. Sometimes a liberal judge might vote for an activist outcome in one case but for a restraintist outcome in another. So, too, will a conservative judge sometimes vote for an activist outcome in one case but a restraintist outcome in a different case. For example, in the Supreme Court case of *NFIB v. Sebelius* in 2012, four liberal justices voted with Chief Justice Roberts to uphold "Obamacare" as Constitutional. In contrast to this judicial restraint, the four conservative dissenting justices would have actively used judicial review to strike down "Obamacare." However, just three years later in 2015, the situation reversed. The same four liberal justices again voted with Chief Justice Roberts, but this time they actively used judicial review to strike down state laws banning same-sex marriage in *Obergefell v. Hodges.* The same four dissenting conservative justices would have exercised judicial restraint and upheld the state law prohibitions. Thus, only Chief Justice Roberts acted consistently as a judicial restraintist across these two cases. The other eight justices alternated between judicial activism and judicial restraint. Yet at the same time, the bloc of four conservative judges also consistently argued they were merely following the original meaning of the Constitution, whereas the bloc of four liberal justices did not make such claims. This shows once again that the judicial philosophy about how to interpret the Constitution is not necessarily the same thing as the judicial philosophy regarding how judicial review should be used.

The approach a judge will use in a case can also vary depending on the type of case involves, such as whether people's lives are involved, or whether only money is at stake. In death penalty cases, for example, a judge that ordinarily uses judicial restraint might vote to give a criminal defendant the benefit of the doubt by overturning the death sentence. In short, the judicial philosophy of most judges is more complex than the simplified discussion here might indicate. And, even with the same judge, their judicial philosophy is dynamic and fluid, not static and rigid.

Judicial Voting Behavior

As we just saw, there are differing competing philosophies about how judges should use their power of judicial review. Yet what factors do judges *actually* use when deciding court cases? In other words, what influences judges to decide cases as they do? The past several decades of political science research has looked for numerical patterns of influence in federal and state court judicial decision-making. The most researched court in this regard has understandably been the U.S. Supreme Court, since it is the highest and by far most influential court in the U.S. Studies have looked at evidence whether judges vote based on influence from Congress, the President, public opinion, political interest groups, or other factors. There is unclear, inconsistent, minimal, or disputed evidence in these regards. On the other hand, current studies show clear, significant, and consistent statistical evidence that the judges vote in significant part based on their political ideology (as liberals or conservatives) and on their judicial philosophy (as activists or restraintists). In other words, and what should seem self-obvious, liberal judges vote for liberal outcomes and conservative judges vote for conservative outcomes. For example, liberal judges tend to vote to uphold the ability of women to obtain abortions, but conservative judges tend to vote to uphold community standards restricting or outlawing abortions.

Political science research studies also show, however, that these politically ideological leanings are moderated by the judges' judicial philosophies. For example, even if a liberal judge does not like a conservative law, if that judge also favors judicial restraint, then that judge will likely vote to uphold the conservative law. A conservative judge who also believes in judicial restraint will similarly tend to uphold liberal laws. For example, this phenomenon has been used to explain the vote of Chief Justice John Roberts in the 2012 Obamacare ruling in *NFIB v. Sebelius.* The Chief Justice generally votes in an ideologically conservative manner. However, in his written ruling upholding the liberal health care policy disliked by conservatives, Roberts explained that his job was not to rule based on whether he agreed with the law, but only on whether the law was consistent with the Constitution. He explained "We do not consider whether the Act embodies sound policies. That judgment is entrusted to the Nation's elected leaders. We ask only whether Congress has the power under the Constitution to enact the challenged provisions."

Another famous example of this phenomenon occurred in the 1968 Supreme Court ruling *Griswold v. Connecticut.* In that case, the state legislature of Connecticut made it a crime for doctors to prescribe contraceptives, even to married couples. The majority of the Supreme Court used judicial review to strike down the law as violating an implied "right of privacy" that was not expressly found anywhere in the U.S. Constitution. On the other hand, although dissenting Justice Stewart disagreed with the law, he could find no Constitutional reason for striking down the law. As a result, he argued for judicial restraint:

> "Since 1879 Connecticut has had on its books a law which forbids the use of contraceptives by anyone. I think this is an uncommonly silly law. As a practical matter, the law is obviously unenforceable, except in the oblique context of the present case. As a philosophical matter, I believe the use of contraceptives in the relationship of marriage should be left to personal and private choice, based upon each individual's moral, ethical, and religious beliefs. As a matter of social policy, I think professional counsel about methods of birth control should be available to all, so that each individual's choice can be meaningfully made. But we are not asked in this case to say whether we think this law is unwise, or even asinine. We are asked to hold that it violates the United States Constitution. And that I cannot do. . . . What provision of the Constitution, then, does make this state law invalid? The Court says it is the right of privacy "created by several fundamental constitutional guarantees." With all deference, I can find no such general right of privacy in the Bill of Rights, in any other part of the Constitution, or in any case ever before decided by this Court. . . . At the oral argument in this case we were told that the Connecticut law does not "conform to current community standards." But it is not the function of this Court to decide cases on the basis of community standards. We are here to decide cases "agreeably to the Constitution and laws of the United States." It is the essence of judicial duty to subordinate our own personal views, our own ideas of what legislation is wise and what is not."

In other words, even though dissenting Justice Stewart disagreed with the law on political grounds, he also believed it was not his role as a judge to vote based on his personal political preferences. His judicial philosophy of restraint therefore led him to vote to uphold the ban on contraception as constitutional. His personal political view on this issue seemed to be liberal in this case, but his philosophy of judicial restraint led him to vote for a conservative policy outcome.

Given the prominence of political ideology and judicial philosophy in how judges decide cases, the functioning of the federal courts will remain a continual political issue. This will be especially true in Presidential elections, given that the President appoints all federal judges. Indeed, the only way the public can make it likely that the Court will issue rulings the public likes is for the public to elect Presidents and Senators who will appoint judges to the Court who will rule in line with the public's wishes. However, this can sometimes take decades to achieve, given that Supreme Court justices serve for life, and vacancies on the Court occur only once every few years on average. For example, sometimes a president will serve out an entire presidential term of office without having even a single chance to nominate a judge for the Supreme Court. The public must then continue to elect President after President, and Senate after Senate, until there are enough judges on the Court who agree with the public.

The slow changeover in Supreme Court justices is why change in Supreme Court legal doctrines typically takes so long to occur. This is also why presidential nominations for the Supreme Court can result in such prolonged, heated battles in the Senate. Each judge on the Supreme Court will likely shape U.S. law for several decades during his or her time on the Court. Also, the Supreme Court's decisions can change the future meaning of the Constitution for decades or even centuries. This sometimes radically reshapes U.S. society, as occurred when the Court reinterpreted the Commerce Clause and upheld the New Deal. For better or for worse, everyone agrees we would probably live in a very different U.S. today if the Court had not ruled the way it had in the late 1930's. Unless a future Court were to reverse the New Deal rulings, which seems unlikely, the United States will continue to have a large, powerful central government for decades or centuries to come.

Summary

The U.S. Constitution creates a judicial branch comprised of a Supreme Court. The Constitution then grants Congress the power to create the rest of the federal judiciary. All federal judges must be nominated by the President and confirmed by the Senate. Federal judges then serve for life, unless they retire or are removed by the Congressional impeachment process for wrongdoing. As part of the court's responsibility to interpret laws, all courts have the power of judicial review. This is the ability to declare the actions by other branches of government to be unconstitutional. The degree to which courts should use this power is controversial and highly debated. On the one hand, it is an enormously powerful check on the other branches of government, and there is no counter-check short of amending the Constitution. On the other hand, courts are powerless to enforce their decisions without the voluntary cooperation of the other branches of government. Thus, courts risk losing political support if they exercise judicial review too frequently, or too controversially. In U.S. history, there are examples of both types of situations. Sometimes the Supreme Court has made extremely unpopular decisions the other branches of government could not overturn. In other instances, however, the other branches of government have simply ignored the Court's rulings. Even judges themselves disagree on whether judicial review should be used frequently or sparingly, and on how the Constitution should be interpreted. Indeed, scholarly studies of courts show that the top two influences in how judges make their legal decisions are probably the judges' philosophy on how to use judicial review, combined with the political ideology of the judges. This is why presidential nominations for federal judgeship positions often result in heated political debates in Senate confirmation hearings.

Questions for Review and Self-Assessment

1. What is the organization and authority of the federal courts?
2. What is the source and nature of the power of judicial review?
3. What are some famous instances of judicial review historically, and what were the outcomes of those cases?
4. What is the difference between judicial philosophy and political ideology, and how do they relate?
5. Describe the main factors that social science studies reveal judges' decisions are based on.

Critical Thinking Questions for Reflection and Discussion

1. Does the Supreme Court have too much power, not enough power, or about the right amount?
2. Should the Constitution be amended to eliminate the power of judicial review?
3. Should Supreme Court justices be judicial activists or judicial restraintists? Or does it depend on each individual case?
4. Should Supreme Court justices consider public opinion when they make their decisions?

Suggested Reading Supplements

- Brutus, *Essay Number XI, XV*
- Alexander Hamilton, *Federalist No. 78, 81*
- *Marbury v. Madison* (1803)
- *Griswold v. Connecticut* (1968)
- *Republican Party of Minnesota v. White* (2002)
- *Obergefell v. Hodges* (2015)

For Further Advanced Study

- David M. Obrien, *Storm Center: The Supreme Court in American Politics*
- Gerald Rosenberg, *The Hollow Hope: Can Courts Bring about Social Change?*
- Jeffrey Segal and Harold J. Spaeth, *The Supreme Court and the Attitudinal Model Revisited*

PART V: POLITICAL BEHAVIOR

Chapter 14: Socialization, Opinion, and Ideology

The Big Picture

People think and behave in political ways. People acquire their varied political beliefs from many different sources. These political opinions typically form around common clusters of consistent ideas. Individuals, politicians, and journalists often mistakenly think that there are only two such groups of opinion, "liberal" and "conservative." However, there are actually four basic alternative clusters of political beliefs. Each different cluster is based on a different underlying core value. Understanding these principles is key to understanding the views of U.S. political parties, and how public opinion is translated into public policy within U.S. democracy.

Chapter Objectives

After reading this chapter, the reader should be able to:

1. Define public opinion and political behavior, describe how they are measured, and explain common problems with this measurement.
2. Define political socialization, and explain the typical effect of various agents of socialization, especially the news media.
3. Define ideology and describe the common understanding of liberal and conservative based on the two dimensions of ideology.
4. Explain each ideology's core value, the ideology that results from taking that core value to its logical endpoint, and how the core values conflict with each other. Define political knowledge, interest, efficacy, trust, and tolerance, and describe their levels among the public.

Introduction to Political Behavior

Until now, this course has looked at the philosophy, structures, and institutions of the U.S. Government created by the Constitution. These basic political mechanisms include pluralism, bicameralism, enumerated powers, separation of powers, checks and balances, federalism, civil liberties, civil rights, and the three branches of government. But how do people behave within this political framework? The investigation of how individuals and groups behave within a political system is appropriately called the study of "political behavior." Stated differently, given a particular social contract, how do people act within the context of that social contract? In a democratic system, this is a four-step process. First, political *socialization* provides people with political information. Second, individuals develop political *opinions*, especially an *ideology*, based on that information. Third, those individuals then choose whether and how they will be involved in *participation* in the political system. Fourth and finally, both elected and unelected leaders provide political *representation* to the members of the public in response to public participation. This chapter will look at socialization and ideology, and the next chapter will conclude by evaluating participation and representation in the United States.

Measuring Public Opinion and Political Behavior

Political science has studied what and how people think politically for decades now. *Public opinion* is the preferences of the adult population on matters relating to government and politics. This means public opinion does not include, for example, one's views on entertainment, sports, or consumer products. It does include people's views on public policy, and political parties and candidates. Public opinion is measured using *public opinion polls*, also called public opinion *surveys*, whereby researchers ask people questions in order to measure their beliefs. Some common examples of public opinion surveys are presidential approval polls, pre-election surveys of voter preferences, and exit polls taken as people leave voting locations. Results of such surveys are often relied upon by the mass news media in their political reporting. Political leaders, candidates, parties and interest groups also use polling results to help them plan their political strategies and tactics.

The mathematics supporting the reliability and validity of such research results is well-established. Unfortunately, survey results can be, and often are, manipulated by unscrupulous political agents. With any opinion poll, there are two main things to look for to determine whether the results are trustworthy. First, the "*sample*" is the group that answered the question or questions in the survey. A sample is simply a subgroup of the larger population. To provide valid results, a survey must choose the sample randomly from the population, without bias in the selection process. Otherwise, the sample would not accurately represent the population. For example, if a national poll surveyed only women, or only people with low incomes, or only people in Northern Minnesota, or only Asian-Americans, or only people with a college degree, the results would not represent what the U.S. public as a whole thinks about the issue.

Second, the precise wording of the survey question is critical. The question must be clear, simple, and unbiased. Otherwise, the results could greatly distort or misrepresent the public's views. For example, when it comes to the issue of abortion, both pro-life and pro-choice groups claim that a large majority of the public agrees with their position. Obviously it can't be true that a majority of the public agrees with two opposite positions at the same time. This result can be explained, though, because it turns out the language the two groups use in their surveys differ vastly. A large majority of the public agrees with a statement like "Women should have the freedom to control their own bodies." At the same time, a large majority of the public also agrees with statements such as "The murder of unborn babies should be prevented." Both questions are phrased in a way to so as to produce particular answers. The results are therefore highly skewed in favor of one position or the other. When this issue is examined in a relatively unbiased way, the truth turns out to be somewhere in-between the two extremes. A majority of the public thinks abortion is morally wrong in some circumstances but not in others. In other words, that same majority believes abortion should be legal in some circumstances but not in others. As another simple example, let's assume Congress is considering changes to how doctors get paid in the federal Medicare program. The following survey questions will get very different results: "Should Congress change the health care system?" "Should Congress improve the health care system?" "Should Congress solve the health care crisis?" "Should Congress interfere with the health care system?" "Should Congress damage the health care system?"

Yet even the most scientifically conducted opinion surveys can still be mistaken when predicting what a population believes based merely on a sample of that population. Perhaps there was some unknown bias in how the sample was chosen. Or, perhaps the sample just happened to be skewed toward a particular opinion more than the general population is. Indeed, even using advanced mathematical principles to evaluate their data, social scientists can generally claim only that their opinion polls have a 95% likelihood of accuracy. That likelihood itself falls within a certain "margin of error," which is a possible range of the actual population's opinions. For example, imagine an opinion survey company asks 800 randomly chosen members of the U.S. public "Do you approve of the way the President is handling the job of President?" The news media reports the results as "55% yes, 45% no, with a plus-or-minus 3% margin of error." This means that the survey researchers are 95% confident that a range of between 52% and 58% of the general U.S. population approves of President's handling of the presidency. Note, then, that there is still a 5% chance that the actual population's opinion lies outside of the 52-58% range. Put differently, one out every 20 opinion surveys will guess wrongly about what the actual population believes. Thus, one can never be 100% certain of the results of opinion polls. Even with the most scientific opinion polls, the results are only 95% certain at best.

Public *opinion* is measured by asking people what they *think*. Political *behavior*, on the other hand, is measured by what people *do*. Actions can be measured in a variety of ways, including survey research, direct observation, evaluation of government statistics, and experimental methods. In considering scientific findings regarding either public opinion or political behavior, it's important to keep in mind there are no "laws" of human behavior. In the case of physical laws such as gravity, the behavior of objects is perfectly predictable. However, in the case of human minds, what people decide to do is not perfectly predictable. The best social scientists can do is find *trends* or *tendencies* or *likelihoods* or *probabilities* of *most* humans to behave in certain ways. In other words, all that psychological, sociological, and political studies show are what a *majority* of people *tend* to think or do in certain contexts. It may only be the case that 51% of the population believes X whereas 49% believes Y. Yet mathematically, a social scientist can accurately claim that "A majority of people tend to believe X." By using qualifying language like "tend to" or "are more likely to," it's understood that these are simply generalizations based on statistical evidence.

Actual human behavior is much more complex than simple explanations can provide, and there are always many exceptions. Nevertheless, there are some statistical trends that social science evidence reveals. For example, the claim that "basketball players are usually taller than people who don't play basketball" doesn't mean that all basketball players are tall, or that all tall people play basketball. It simply means that if one measures the height of all basketball players and of all non-basketball players, basketball players are taller *on average*. Some basketball players will be shorter than the average non-basketball-player, and some non-basketball players will be taller than the average basketball player. However, *most* basketball players are taller than *most* non-basketball-players. Let's look then, at what social science studies have found regarding how *a majority* of people think and behave politically *a majority* of the time.

Political Socialization

Socialization is the learning process by which people acquire information and beliefs. All of one's senses provide information about the world. Thus, throughout one's entire life, in every waking moment learning is occurring, which is socialization. People are socialized regarding religious and cultural ideas, or even regarding which professional sports teams to like. Here, though, we will discuss *political* socialization, which is the acquisition of information and beliefs about politics.

Each source of information is called an *agent of socialization*. There are numerous agents of socialization throughout one's life. Several majors ones are family, friends and other peers, religion, education, the mass news media, and the life cycle that people typically go through as one ages. There are a few things social scientists can say about the typical influence of several common agents of socialization. On the other hand, these agents of socialization often occur simultaneously, so that they either work together, or in opposing directions. In addition, even though social science is many decades old, it is still in its relative infancy. There are many things about human nature that science still does not understand, especially about what makes people acquire certain beliefs rather than others. Therefore, social science findings about political socialization are still limited in their answers. Moreover, keep in mind that each person's individual socialization is much more complex than any of the generalizations here would indicate.

Regarding one's parents, you'll more likely than not lean politically the way you were raised. Not surprisingly, liberal parents raise children to be liberal, and conservative parents raise children to be conservative. If your parents politically differ, you'll more likely acquire the political beliefs of your mother, since most children tend to spend more time overall with their mothers. When it comes to your friends and other peers, though, it's a "chicken-and-egg" type of question: do you like people who agree with you, or do you decide to agree with the people you like? That is, do you make friends with people because you already agree with them on things, or do you end up agreeing with your friends because they are your friends? Social science data have not yet been able to definitely show which is the case. It's probably a little of both. You seek out like-minded individuals to be friends with, and then those friends reinforce your pre-existing beliefs.

When it comes to religion, your family and the location where you're born largely determine your religion. For example, if you're born in Thailand, you and your family will most likely be Buddhist. If you're born in China, you'll most likely grow up mixed Buddhist-Taoist-Confucianist, but in Japan you'll be mixed Buddhist-Shintoist. If you're born in Central Africa, you and your family will most likely be animist. If you're born in North Africa or the Middle East your family will most likely be a Sunni Muslim, unless you're born in Iran, where you'll most likely be a Shiite Muslim, or unless you're born in Israel, where you'll most likely be a Jew. If you're born in India, you'll most likely be a Hindu, unless you're born in the Punjab province, in which case you'll most likely be a Sikh. If you're born in Europe or North or South America, you'll most likely be an orthodox (traditional) Christian, unless you're born in Utah, in which case you'll most likely be a member of the Church of Jesus Christ of Latter-Day Saints (the Mormon Church). In short, your religion depends largely on the belief your parents taught you, which in turn can largely be predicted based on the dominant religion of the culture in which you're raised.

Religions typically tell their believers about the views and behaviors people "should" have. Religious beliefs therefore translate into political beliefs that are consistent with those religious beliefs. If your church teaches you that god wants you to give lots of money to the poor, then you'll most likely end up a liberal Democrat. If your church teaches you that god thinks abortion is morally wrong, then you'll most likely end up a conservative Republican. If your church teaches that ownership of private property is a sin, you'll most likely end up supporting communism. There is strong social science evidence that most children simply adopt whatever religious beliefs they are given. Despite this evidence, most adults have a hard time accepting that their religious beliefs are largely a result of the random circumstances regarding where and to whom they were born. Even when faced with such evidence, most adults will still insist that *their* religious beliefs just happen to be correct, but the billions of people who have different beliefs were all simply indoctrinated as children.

Regardless of one's religious beliefs, most people tend to go through a typical cycle of events and stages throughout life. A typical person finishes their childhood education, starts a career, gets married, maybe buys a house, has kids, tries to save for retirement, and eventually retires. On average, as one grows older, these events tend to make one lean in a more conservative direction on the issue of taxes and law enforcement. This makes sense as well. Every penny paid in taxes out of one's hard-earned money is one less penny to provide for one's family. And, criminal lawbreakers threaten the safety and security of one's home and family. For these reasons, it's understandable that as most adults grow older, they tend to favor lower taxes and tougher law enforcement in order to preserve and protect their family and community.

Education also significantly impacts people politically. Under the age of about 14, elementary and junior high schools typically instill political values of patriotism and obedience to authority. In short, "Love your country and do what you're told." Indeed, in the United States, many people's earliest political memory is reciting the Pledge of Allegiance to the U.S. flag. Also recall how many times you were told as a child to listen and do whatever your parents, teachers, ministers, and police tell you.

Over the age of 14 studies show the more years of education a person has, especially the more years of college, the more the person tends to become politically liberal, especially on questions of equality. Scholars themselves disagree as to why this is the case, as any causes are hard to conclusively demonstrate. Nevertheless, there are two competing theories. Scholars who are themselves politically liberal claim college enlightens college students to be more liberal. Such scholars point out, for example, that the more information students learn about the benefits of political, religious, racial and sexual tolerance, the more students will favor equality and oppose discrimination of all kinds. Scholars who are themselves politically conservative claim college students are politically indoctrinated to be liberal by liberal college professors. Social scientists have taken opinion surveys of college faculty in the United States, especially faculty in the liberal arts and humanities where students are exposed to political ideas. These studies show that such faculty overwhelmingly self-identify themselves as very-to-extremely liberal. More than 80% vote Democratic, and they identify themselves as "extremely liberal" at a rate several times higher than the general population. Thus, the argument goes, after many years of hearing mostly liberal opinions and one-sided evidence from their political science, sociology, psychology, history, English, art, and philosophy professors (among others), college students tend to adopt liberal viewpoints. There is no clear evidence regarding which theory, enlightenment or indoctrination, is more accurate. As with most things in life, the truth is probably somewhere in-between.

News Media Bias

Throughout one's adult life, by far the biggest agent of political socialization for most people is the mass news media. In nations that are not democracies, there typically is no such thing as freedom of the press. Instead, the media simply serve as a tool of propaganda by the state: "All hail our glorious Leader!" In democracies, on the other hand, there is a philosophical debate about what the proper role of the media is. There are primarily two competing theories.

One view argues that the "mirror" role of the media should be to pass on bare facts without imposing any subjective interpretation of those facts. An actual mirror doesn't tell you, for example, whether you're having a good hair day or bad hair day. It just shows you what you look like, and lets you judge your own appearance. Similarly, the argument goes, the media should report only "just the facts" without any commentary, opinions, analysis, or editorializing.

Other political thinkers, however, argue for the "watchdog role" of the media. A watchdog guards its owner, barking to warn of any approaching danger. Similarly, the argument goes, since democracy is rule by the people, in a democracy the media should protect the public against misbehavior in government. The media should provide not just facts, but warnings that government is committing abuse, fraud, waste, corruption, or other scandals. By carefully scrutinizing the actions of government, political commentators and investigative journalists keep an eye on politicians and government, thereby acting as a safeguard of public liberty. In this way, the mass news media is basically an additional "check" in the system of checks and balances.

There is no "right" answer as to the "correct" role of the media in a democracy, and even journalists disagree. As a historical matter, though, the founders of the United States believed the purpose of the Free Press Clause of the First Amendment was to protect the watchdog role of the media. As a legal matter, the U.S. Supreme Court has agreed with this original intent through its interpretations of the Free Speech and Free Press Clauses. Also, as a statistical matter, the large majority of all news organizations and journalists subscribe to the watchdog role of the media. Even if they say they don't, the coverage and content of their stories says otherwise.

The problem often is that what one person thinks is the media fulfilling its watchdog role seems to another person to be blatant political bias on the part of the media. Given that journalists are imperfect human beings just like anyone else, they cannot help but have their moral, religious, and political beliefs and opinions affect how they cover the news. Some journalists are better at minimizing that influence than others, but it's psychologically impossible to forget all one's beliefs. Moreover, since media organizations are simply groups of human journalists, this means that all media organizations have their own collective political biases as well.

Political bias affects not only *how* individual journalists and news organizations cover the news, but *what* news they cover. On any given day, there are hundreds or even thousands of possible news stories to cover, and dozens, hundreds, or even thousands of facts within each story. Only a few stories can be covered, and then only a few facts within each of those stories. These choices necessarily reflect the values of the journalist or news organization reporting the stories. For example, if you watch different cable TV news channels, or read different news websites on the internet, you'll often see vastly different stories covered. One news organization will have a story as its main headline, whereas another news organization won't even mention that story at all. When both organizations cover the same story, there will be differences in how those stories are covered. This could be differences in facts or differences in perspectives on those facts, such as quotes from commentators. Therefore, regardless where you get your news, if you get your news from only a single media outlet, you're getting a politically biased and highly incomplete portrait of the news.

The only way to get a less biased, more accurate, and more complete version of the news is to get your news from a wide variety of multiple sources. Make sure your news sources approach the news from different opposing political angles and come from both inside and outside the U.S. Widely-respected English-language news organizations include the Canadian Broadcasting Corporation (CBC) and the British Broadcasting Corporation (BBC). News organizations outside the U.S. often provide coverage of stories, facts, or perspectives regarding the United States that news organizations within the U.S. do not provide.

At the same time, though, research has shown people often mistakenly perceive bias even where there is none. For example, liberals believe the mass news media has an overall conservative bias, but conservatives believe the media has an overall liberal bias. Both beliefs can't be equally true. This perception can be explained, though, by the fact that people are more likely to remember, and will react more strongly to, things they disagree with than things they agree with. This is called the *negativity bias* that humans have in general. For example, you might hear a speech by a politician and agree with 95% of it, yet the 5% that angers you will be what you most remember. So, even a news story that is carefully crafted to be even-handed and politically balanced will be perceived as biased by those who disagree with even a small portion of the story.

Aside from the question of political bias, though, the news media have several nonpolitical biases. Radio and television have a *production bias*. This means there is a bias inherent in the way broadcast news is produced. With a newspaper, magazine, or website, a news story can simply add another page if needed. The broadcast media, however, deal with finite time that cannot be expanded. With a fixed time, stories must be told briefly. This means simple stories get chosen over complex stories, and news is told only in "sound bite" quotes of only a few seconds each.

All commercial media also have a *ratings bias*. News is a business which needs advertising revenue to survive. Advertising rates are determined by the size of the audience. News stories therefore tend to be framed dramatically to get high rates. For example, rather than cover the issues in election campaigns, the news typically provides only "horse-race" coverage comparing which candidate is "in the lead" or "gaining ground" based on polling. Also, stories are oversimplified to make them more understandable to a mass audience. Dramatic stories are favored over undramatic ones. Stories are purposely framed as "good" versus "evil" to heighten their drama even if this does injustice to the participants involved.

The news media also contains what is called an *information bias.* Roughly 80-90% of all news comes from government sources. This has two results. First, journalists tend to give government officials favorable coverage, or at least not overly harsh coverage, for fear of losing access to the information they provide. Second, since there is no other source of information to verify government claims, the public does not know what to believe. For example, toward the end of the Vietnam War, it was revealed that several presidential administrations and the military had repeatedly lied to the public about how the U.S. was doing in the war. This and other examples of government dishonesty have caused public distrust and cynicism towards government and toward the media that relay government information.

Media Effects

Apart from biases that come from the media, what effect does the news media have on the audience? The media will influence its audience even in the absence of any of the biases listed above. Social scientists originally believed that the media had minimal effects on the audience. For example, people don't watch a news story and then suddenly have a revelation that all their political views are entirely wrong. Recent studies have shown, however, that media produces more subtle effects on the audience.

First, the media causes the transfer of information to the audience. The audience might not change their opinions, but they discover, or even change their mind about, the *facts*. For example, the audience will learn who is running for

President, the qualifications those candidates have, and the controversial statements each of them has made.

Second, the media induces cynicism by the public. We just discussed the various biases inherent in the news media. Politicians and their campaign advisors are well aware of these biases and take advantage of them. Politicians intentionally speak in only sound-bite slogans, and they heavily use negative advertising knowing that sensationalism attracts views. Yet people are aware of these tactics and dislike the lack of positive substance in campaigns. The public comes to distrust not just politicians, but the media as well for being an accomplice to these types of manipulation.

Third, the media sets the agenda for public discussion. The audience tends to think that what they hear on the news must be the most important news at that moment. We might not know about a famine or civil war that has been going on for years in a foreign country, until the media starts to cover it. One famous example of this phenomenon is news coverage of shark attacks. For decades, the rate of shark attacks has been roughly constant from year to year. Yet when the media suddenly starts reporting them, the audience starts talking about it and thinks something strange is happening. Nothing out of the ordinary is actually occurring. It's just that the news media have suddenly begun to report what was already happening for a long time.

Finally, the news does persuade some people to adopt political opinions, but only those who view news intermittently. At one end of the spectrum are people who have no political knowledge. The news has no opportunity to influence such people because they never pay attention to the news. At the other end of the spectrum, news addicts are so knowledgeable about politics that they are immune to having their opinions influenced. These political junkies already know the counter-argument to every argument. People in the middle of the news-watching spectrum, though, have incomplete political knowledge and opinions. At the same time, they are also occasionally exposed to new facts and opinions. These are the people, then, who are most vulnerable to influence from the news. It's like having half the pieces of a puzzle, and then you're given a few new pieces. It will change your perception of the overall picture.

Ideology: The Common Understanding

A person's political *ideology* is the total sum of all one's political beliefs and opinions. These do not necessarily have to have consistent underlying principles, but they often do. Typically when the term ideology is used it refers to a more-or-less coherently organized belief system about the proper role of government in human life. There is a common, traditional view of ideology which is mistaken and incomplete, and a more accurate and complete view of ideology. Because the mistaken view is so widespread, we need to consider it first.

Commonly, ideology is viewed as a "left-right" one-dimensional spectrum. It runs along a line with liberalism on the left and conservatism on the right. A simple diagram would look like the following.

Very Liberal—Liberal—Moderate—Conservative—Very Conservative

The terms "left" or "left-wing" are often used for liberalism, and "right" or "right-wing" are often used for conservatism. This conventional terminology goes all the way back to the French legislature in the late 1700's. The party seated in the left wing of the chamber supported revolutionary change, and the party seated in the right wing of the chamber supported keeping traditional political institutions. The slang terms "left" and "right" stuck. Today in the United States, the Democratic Party is the dominant liberal, or left-wing, political party, and the Republican Party is the dominant conservative, or right-wing, political party.

Although ideology is typically diagrammed as a line, in actuality ideology is comprised of two dimensions. Each dimension reflects a persons' belief regarding the proper role of government in different areas of life. One dimension is economic liberty. That is, what is the proper role of government in regulating economic decisions? The other dimension is social liberty. That is, what is the proper role of government in regulating our personal moral decisions? Liberals and conservatives disagree on the proper role of government in regulating these two areas of human decision-making. Any diagram of ideology must therefore have at least these two dimensions of the graph: support for individual liberty on one axis, and support for economic liberty on the other axis. The simplified graph below places support for economic liberty on the x-axis, and support for individual liberty on the y-axis. This is arbitrary, however, and the axes of the different dimensions of liberty could be switched. The graph is used merely to illustrate the point that political ideology must be graphed on two dimensions, not one.

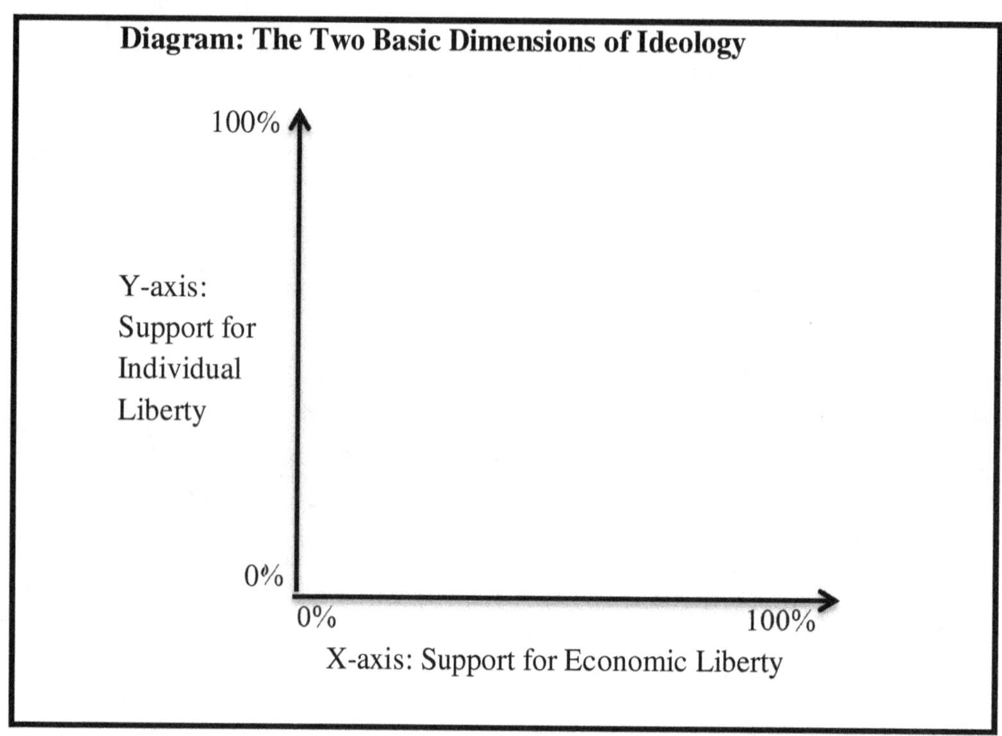

We'll come back to fill out this graph in more detail shortly. For now, though, what do the labels "liberal" and "conservative" generally mean in common usage? These ideologies are complex and have many variations and exceptions. Nevertheless, generally when citizens, journalists, politicians, or political commentators use these terms, they mean something by them. Even if their understanding is a grossly oversimplified stereotype of what a "liberal" or "conservative" believes, there is a core of overlap in the common use of these terms.

So what do most people correctly or incorrectly usually mean when they use the terms liberal or conservative? Generally, liberals favor social liberty more than conservatives, but conservatives favor economic liberal more than liberals. This is *not* to say that conservatives don't want any social liberty, or that liberals don't want any economic liberty. It's merely the case that liberals favor a higher degree of social liberty than conservatives favor, and conservatives want a higher degree of economic liberty than liberals do. State oppositely, liberals generally do *not* want government to regulate or prohibit social choices of personal morality such as abortion, marijuana use, or same-sex marriage. They *do,* however, want government involvement in economic issues such as by raising the minimum wage, taxing wealthy individuals and corporations, and redistributing that wealth to the poor through social welfare programs. Conservatives are the opposite of liberals. They generally *do* want the government to regulate or prohibit some personal and social moral choices such as abortion, marijuana use, or same-sex marriage. However, they do *not* want heavy government regulation of economic issues: they favor lower taxes overall, and a "free-market" economy with fewer regulations and less redistribution of income and wealth.

Even with these oversimplified stereotypes, there are issues that do not fit neatly into this framework. For example, liberals typically want heavy regulation of individual gun ownership, and conservatives do not. Rather than being an economic issue, this question seems more of a personal moral decision about how best to defend oneself and family. If so, then the positions of both liberals and conservatives on this issue are inconsistent with their general positions on the degree to which government should regulate social issues. Nevertheless, despite problems in these general descriptions of "liberal" and "conservative," these definitions are what most people generally mean when they use the terms. Again, most individuals do not fit perfectly into these molds, but most people have these stereotypes in mind when they use the terms to describe themselves or others. In the table below are many of the more common standard policy positions of liberals and conservatives.

Table: Standard "Liberal" versus "Conservative" Policy Positions

Political Issue	Standard "liberal" preferred policy position (usually Democratic Party positions)	Standard "conservative" preferred policy position (usually Republican Party positions)
Social and Moral Issues		
Abortion rights	Women's right to choose	Right to life of unborn fetus
Same-sex marriage	marriage equality	traditional marriage
Marijuana use	legalization	criminalization
Flag-burning	Free speech right	Not part of free speech
School prayer	Violates religious conscience of minority	Part of religious freedom of majority
Crime	lenient enforcement and sentencing	strict enforcement and sentencing
Immigration	Lenient enforcement	Strict enforcement
Guns	Restrict or eliminate	Right of self-defense
Foreign policy	Eliminate nuclear weapons	Keep nuclear deterrent
Economic Issues		
Economy	More regulation	Free-market
Taxes	Increase to fund programs	Decrease to reward success
Social welfare programs	Increase and expand the social safety net	Less income redistribution; more personal responsibility
Health care	Universal government-provided healthcare	Private individual choice via insurance
Environment	More regulation	Less regulation
Education	Uniform federal standards	Individual state standards
Minimum wage	Increase	Decrease or eliminate
Affirmative action	In favor	against
National debt	Not a problem	Reduce size of government
Campaign spending	Regulate to equalize	Unregulated free speech

Ideology: The Accurate Understanding

Despite the widespread usage of the one-dimensional either-or "liberal-conservative" framework, this is a highly incomplete and inaccurate understanding of ideology. For example, let's say Bob agrees with the conservative Republican Party position against abortion, but he also wants high taxes on the wealthy to provide free universal health care, which agrees more with the liberal Democratic

Party position. Since he half agrees with each of the two major parties, Bob would likely tell opinion pollsters that he is a "moderate" or an "independent." Susan, however, believes exactly the opposite of Bob: she favors abortion rights but wants low taxes because she believes people should be responsible for paying for their own health care. Since she half agrees with the two major parties, she too would likely tell pollsters she is a "moderate" or "independent." Yet Bob wants more government regulation than either of the two major parties want, whereas Susan wants less government regulation then either of the two parties want. Polling organizations and the news media would treat Bob and Susan as politically similar, even though they are as opposite from one another as liberals are from conservatives. The reason for this misunderstanding is the failure to see that political ideology has two dimensions, not one.

As we just described, ideology has two dimensions: social liberty and economic liberty. Mathematically, it's impossible to accurately draw two dimensions in one dimension. For example, every photo has two dimensions: height and width. If you try to draw a photo in one dimension, it will be a meaningless line. Every photo would look identical in one dimension. Separate photos of a house, a person, and a dog would all look like identical lines in one dimension! Yet clearly a house is entirely different from a person or a dog. Similarly, the two dimensions of ideology cannot be graphed accurately on a one-dimensional line. All that will be portrayed is meaningless nonsense by falsely claiming that people with opposing views are the same. Instead, the only way to diagram ideology accurately is to use a two-dimensional graph or table. Just as all two-dimensional representations need both height and width, an accurate two-dimensional drawing of ideology needs both an x-axis and a y-axis. Both axes have scales starting at zero percent and ending at one-hundred percent. That is, neither social liberty nor economic liberty is an all-or-nothing proposition. One can favor varying degrees of social liberty and economic liberty.

The introductory ideology table shown below is oversimplified because it uses only "low" or "high" degrees of liberty favored along the two dimensions. This oversimplification is purely for the sake of demonstrating that there are four ideologies, not two as is commonly believed. These four ideologies are arrived at through four possible combinations of views on social and economic liberty. There are basically two possible views towards social liberty, either supporting/favoring social liberty or opposing/disfavoring it. There are likewise two possible views towards economic liberty, either supporting/favoring it or opposing/disfavoring it. Combining these options together, two possible views of social liberty times two possible views of economic liberty results in four possible ideologies. Again, though, these are not actually rigid categories, but continuous spectrums. Ideologically a person can be anywhere in the two-dimensional plane shown. A person can also lie along the far edges, in the middle of one of the ideologies, or on the border between two ideologies. Someone can even be at the middle intersection of all the ideologies. Adding the ideologies to the simplified two-dimensional graph we provided moments ago, we get the graph below. Now, instead of two ideological points on a one-dimensional line, there are four ideological "spaces" or "areas" or "zones" on a two-dimensional graph or plane.

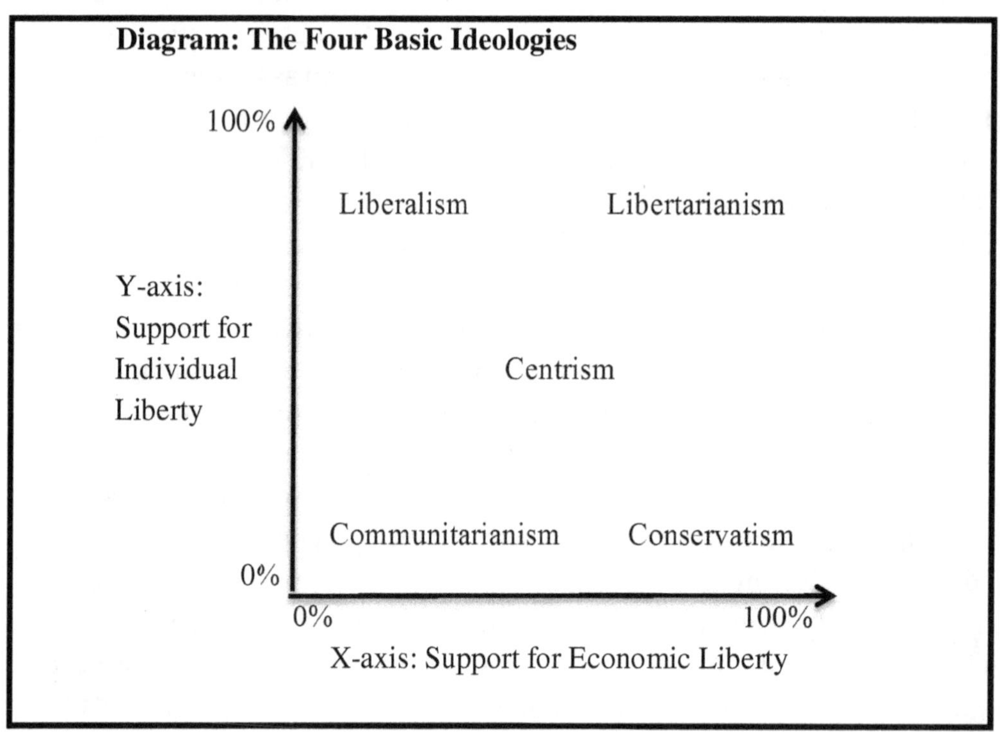

As the first chapter of this book explained, politics exists because humans disagree over resources and values. Differences in values are at the root of the competing ideologies. There are many different political values that most people recognize as worthy of support. These mainly include liberty, equality, order, morality, and pragmatism. Each different ideology is driven by a belief that these values have a *particular* ranking, with one of the values being the highest. Thus, the essential difference between the different ideologies is disagreement over which political value is the *most important* value. When there is a conflict between values, the more important value will takes precedence over the others. Moreover, other than pragmatism, which we shall see is by definition is a middle approach, political values can be taken to their extreme logical endpoints. This would mean the value is not just the *highest* political value, but the *only* political value. When this occurs, other political values are rejected. Now we can see a much more detailed two-dimensional graph of ideology, with detailed explanation immediately following the graph. Also, the ideologies are described in no particular order; for simplicity sake we will merely start in the upper-left quadrant (liberalism), and then proceed clockwise around each remaining quadrant of the graph to describe libertarianism, conservatism, and communitarianism.

Ideology Table: ***Common labels for ideologies based on their overall positions on the proper role of government in regulating social and economic liberty. Each ideology favors or disfavors social and economic liberty differently.***

100% | High social liberty | 51%	**Liberalism** (also often called **Progressivism**) --Progressives support social liberty but oppose economic liberty --Primary political value: *equality* --[extreme form: *socialism/communism/Marxism*]	**Libertarianism** (also sometimes referred to as **Individualism**) --Libertarians support both social liberty and economic liberty --Primary political value: *freedom* --[extreme form: *anarchism*]
49% | Low social liberty | 0%	**Communitarianism** (also variously called majoritarianism, populism, collectivism, authoritarianism, or statism) --Communitarians oppose both social liberty and economic liberty --Primary political value: *order* --[extreme forms: *nationalism*; *fascism/nazism*]	**Conservatism** --Conservatives favor high economic liberty but do not favor social liberty --Primary political value: *morality* --[extreme forms: *laissez faire* economics; *theocracy*]
Y-axis ↑ x-axis→	0% - Low economic liberty - 49%	51% -High economic liberty-100%

Liberalism. The word "liberal" comes from the Latin word *liber* meaning "free." Liberals increasingly prefer the term "progressive" to describe themselves. The term "progressive" comes from the root word "progress." Liberals or progressives want wants government regulation of economic decisions. This includes increasing redistribution of wealth, and the elimination of all forms of social and economic discrimination. This will achieve what progressives call "social and economic justice." In other words, to progressives, greater social and economic equality is societal progress. The political value of *equality* is therefore the underlying value of progressivism. The notion of this total type of equality is also called *egalitarianism*. However, progressives want little government regulation of personal morality. In the United States, the Democratic Party is the dominant mainstream liberal or progressive political party. The Green Party, a minor political party in the U.S. is ideologically left of the Democratic Party. That is, they are even more liberal or progressive than the Democratic Party.

The extreme form of liberalism or progressivism is variously called *socialism* or *communism*. It's also called *Marxism*, named after the founder of the extreme version of this ideology, Karl Marx. Taken to its logical extreme, everyone would have the same income and wealth. To achieve this perfect equality of economic outcome, socialism believes there should be absolute regulation of the economy. This would mean that there is no such thing as "private property." Private ownership of land, homes, or businesses is outlawed. Instead, everything would be owned in common by "the people." Since "the people" only make collective decisions through government, then as a practical matter this means the government owns everything. This means government would make all decisions on who gets what sort of housing when and where. Government would also own and run all businesses, and set all wages, prices, the type and number of goods produced, who gets them, and so on. It would a *centrally planned economy*, also often just called a "planned economy" for short. In the United States, the Socialist Worker's Party represents a socialist ideology.

Libertarianism. The word libertarian comes from the root word "liberty," meaning freedom. This also comes from the same Latin word "liber" that the term "liberalism" comes from, but the two are different ideologies. *Freedom* is the therefore the underlying value of libertarianism. Libertarians want little government regulation of either social or economic choices. They like to say the government should stay out of both their wallet and their bedroom. A staunch libertarian wants no more laws than are necessary to prevent crimes of violence against people and property. This means the only services government would provide would be a police force and military. Taxes would be just enough to pay for that these government functions and no more. All schools would be private schools, and even roads would be privately built and operated toll roads. Another term sometimes used for libertarianism is *individualism*. It's the view that an individual's choice should almost always outweigh what society, acting through government, wants the individual to do or not do. In the U.S., the libertarian ideology is represented by the appropriately named Libertarian Party.

The extreme form of libertarianism is *anarchism*. The term "anarchy" comes from the Greek *an*, meaning "no", plus *archia*, meaning "rulers." Anarchism takes the principle of small government to its logical conclusion of there being no government. Put differently, taking freedom to its logical extreme would mean no laws. To anarchists the term "legitimate government" is an oxymoron, a contradiction in terms. If one person controls another person's life, it's called slavery. Yet if two or more people control the life of a third person, it's called democracy. If a man with a gun demands you give him your money, it's called robbery. If government demands you give it your money, it's called taxation. Being ruled by any government is really just another form of slavery, and even democracy is merely enslavement of the individual by the majority. Because anarchists do not believe in willing participation in any form of government, there are no political parties that represent the anarchist ideology. Forming a political party to work within a political system would be implicitly recognizing the legitimacy of that political system.

Conservatism. The word "conservative" comes from the root word "conserve," meaning "preserve" or "safeguard." The word "conservation" has the same root meaning. Conservatives want government to preserve traditional moral order by maintaining laws that prohibit "bad" moral choices and reward "good" moral choices. The underlying value of conservatism is therefore *morality*. Morality includes rewarding hard work and success in the traditional manner by allowing people to keep the economic fruits of their own labor. This includes their wages, objects they have made, and businesses or property they have built or acquired. This means having low taxes and little government regulation of the economy. Economically this is also known as *capitalism* or *free market* economics. The Republican Party is the dominant mainstream conservative political party in the United States. The Constitution Party, a minor party in the U.S., is to the ideological right of the Republican Party. That is, they are even more conservative than the Republican Party.

There is more than one type of extreme form of right-conservatism, depending on which dimension of conservatism, moral or economic, is emphasized. One extreme form is *theocracy*, rule by religious leaders. Recall from a much earlier chapter that under theocracy, there is no such thing as "rights" when it comes to personal morality. God's moral commands may not be disobeyed, period. Theocracy therefore takes the regulation of morality to its logical extreme by eliminating all rights to make personal moral decisions. Another extreme type of conservatism is *laissez faire* economics. This theory takes reducing economic regulation to the logical extreme of having absolutely no government regulation of economic choices. Individuals should be completely free to make, sell, buy, earn or pay whatever they want without any government interference. One can support theocracy without laissez faire economics, and one can favor laissez faire economics without having a theocracy. Indeed, it is extremely rare that both ideas are combined into a single political philosophy. In the U.S., there is no political party that represents either version of the extreme form of conservatism.

Communitarianism. The word communitarian is based on the root word "community." This term indicates the interests of the group outweigh competing interests of the individual. That is, the collective rights of the community as a whole, whoever makes up a majority of people, override the rights of individuals in both economic and moral questions. An individual's selfish choices should not be allowed to disrupt or harm the good of the community. The underlying value of communitarianism is therefore order. Communitarianism is the opposite of the libertarian ideology. Libertarianism favors the individual over the group, but communitarians favor the group over the individual. Communitarianism goes by a variety of other names because no generally-agreed upon term has yet been adopted. Probably the most common term used by its supporters is communitarianism, but opponents often refer to it by other names. These include populism, majoritarianism, collectivism, authoritarianism, and statism. Currently there is no U.S. political party that represents the communitarian ideology.

A stronger version of communitarianism is *nationalism*. This is the view that the good of the nation overrules individual rights. Nationalism typically includes a blind, quasi-religious faith in the leaders of the nation. Thus, criticism of national leaders or policies is seen as akin to religious heresy and is therefore attacked or outlawed as unpatriotic or treasonous. The extreme form of nationalism is called *fascism*. The term comes from the Latin word *fasces*. This was an ancient Roman symbol of authority made of a tied bundle of sticks usually with a blade sticking out of it. Taking the value of group-imposed order to a logical extreme, fascism believes the majority should be able to impose any social and economic order it believes is best for the group. This can include discriminating against, segregating, enslaving, or even exterminating individuals or minority groups. Fascism is also commonly known as *Nazism*, although technically Nazism is a form of fascism. "Nazi" is a shorthand term for the political party of Adolf Hitler before and during World War II. Under German Nazism, millions of Jews, along with thousands of homosexuals, Gypsies (Roma), the mentally and physically disabled, Jehovah's witnesses, and political dissenters were murdered so as to "cleanse" Germany of "inferior" beings. In the United States, the American Nazi Party represents the ideology of fascism.

Centrism. Centrism comes from the root word "center" meaning "middle." It exists in-between the other ideologies. It is not an ideology in itself, but rather a blend of the four main ideologies and their core political values. In other words, centrism supports a moderate amount of reasonable government regulation of both moral and economic choices. This view is also called "moderate" because it avoids extremes, so a centrist can also be called a "moderate." The underlying value of centrism is therefore *pragmatism*, or practicality. That is, centrism takes a flexible "do whatever works" approach to policy issues, rather than adopting rigid ideological stands on what public policy always "must" or "must not" do. By way of analogy, an unhealthy diet might eat either too much or too little overall, or too few vitamins and minerals, or too much fat, sugar, or salt. A physically healthy diet is properly balanced. Similarly, governments can regulate either too little or too much, or focus excessively on one political value to the neglect of others. Politically healthy public policy therefore is a balanced approach to governance that incorporates all the political values. In contrast, the all-or-nothing, black-or-white approach taken by ideologies often result in bad policy. For example, as we saw in the chapter on Congress, progressive Congressional Democrats refuse to cut spending, while conservative Congressional Republicans refuse to raise taxes. Because neither side is willing to compromise, the U.S. now has a huge and increasingly problematic national debt. Because centrism is by definition a "middle-of-the-road" position, there is no extreme form of it. There is no such thing, therefore, as "radical centrism" or "radical moderation." Currently there is no active political party in the United States that represents a centrist political position, although individual candidates can be centrist or centrist-leaning. Also, although many centrists are "independents," a centrist is not necessarily the same as an independent. An independent voter merely lacks loyalty to any one political party, but might still have strong ideological beliefs.

Apart from the four ideologies and the middle position of centrism, *patriotism* is often mistaken as an ideology. The word "patriot" comes from the Greek *patris*, meaning "fatherland," and *patriotes*, meaning "fellow countryman." It is not an ideology itself, but simply means love of one's country. It can and does exist across and throughout all the ideologies and centrism. One can support any ideology and still greatly love one's homeland. Indeed, patriotism is like the love of parents for a child. Both parents can love their child equally strongly yet have completely opposing views about what's best for the child. For example, one parent might think it's best to be lenient with the child so as to teach the child mercy and forgiveness, whereas the other parent might believe it's best to be strict with the child so as to teach the child discipline and responsibility. Similarly, people of all ideologies, including the extreme versions, typically love their country. They simply disagree about what that means regarding public policy.

Patriotism is often confused with nationalism, but only by nationalists themselves. Recall nationalists believe criticism of government policy or leaders is by definition unpatriotic. Thus, if you hear an individual accuse someone of being unpatriotic for disagreeing with the government, that individual is expressing a nationalistic viewpoint.

Also, note that the question "*who* should rule?" is related to the concepts of ideology and patriotism, but is not the same thing. One can be equally patriotic while favoring autocracy, oligarchy, or democracy. Also, whether political power is in the hands of one, a few, or the many, the public policies enacted will depend on the ideology of the one, few, or many in charge.

Other Political Attitudes

There are several other aspects of our political views apart from ideology. These other political attitudes have been extensively measure by opinion surveys as well. To begin, ideological beliefs lead people to support policies consistent with those ideologies. Should income taxes be raised, lowered, or kept the same? Should marijuana be legalized? Should we go to war against the country of Freedonia? Should government provide free universal college tuition and health care? There are countless other public policy issues as well. Scholars, the media, and polling organizations regularly conduct opinion polls to determine where public opinion currently stands on policy issues. Public opinion often changes over time, sometimes rapidly. For example, in just a 20-year period between 1995 and 2015, overall public support for same-sex marriage increased from about 25% to around 60%, and is even higher among the younger generation.

On the other hand, sometimes public opinion on an issue remains consistent over a long period of time. For example, in the 40-year period between 1975 and 2015, roughly half the public has consistently believed abortion should be illegal in all circumstances, and roughly half has consistently believed abortion should be legal in some or all circumstances. When public opinion does substantially change on an issue, public policy will usually change in response. Legislators are elected from among the public, so tend to hold views consistent with public opinion. Even if the legislators don't agree with public opinion, they need to keep the public happy in order to win their votes. Thus, as public opinion changes, legislators correspondingly add laws, modify laws, or repeal laws. These changes reflect the shifting political attitudes among the public and among the legislators themselves.

Regardless whether public opinion is stable or unstable, different human societies disagree about the "correct" public policy answers. These societies often reach contradictory answers even within their own societies. This is true for the U.S. as well. The people of the United States have collectively decided that 18-year-olds are mature enough to vote, marry, have children, serve on juries that sentence criminal defendants to death, and die for one's country while serving in the military. Yet, at the same time, the people of the U.S. have decided that adults are not mature enough to sip even 3.2% beer until the age of 21. These public policies are inconsistent.

Regardless of the nature of public opinion, however, these opinions act on the information we have about the world. The degree to which we are aware of political information is called political *knowledge*. Generally, people in the U.S. have low levels of political knowledge. For example, in surveys of political knowledge, usually less than half of survey respondents can name the Vice-President of the United States, and less than 10% can name the Chief Justice of the U.S. Supreme Court. Similarly, public *interest* in politics is generally low within the U.S. Only a minority of survey respondents typically state they are interested in regularly following news about government or politics.

Public opinion surveys also measure the degree to which people feel they can influence public policy. This concept is called political *efficacy*. This is simply another term for effectiveness. That is, do people believe they can "make a difference" in politics if they try to do so? Within the U.S., only a minority of survey respondents say they believe their actions can or do make any impact on government policy.

Political scientists also measure the degree to which the public has political *trust* in government. During the Cold War between the U.S. and the Soviet Union in the 1950's and early 1960's, a majority of the public had faith the U.S. government was "doing the right thing" or "looking out for them." In the years from 1963 to 1974, however, a series of political events shattered the U.S. public's trust in government. President John F. Kennedy, prominent black activist Malcolm X, foremost civil rights leader Martin Luther King, and then popular presidential candidate Senator Robert Kennedy were all assassinated. The public then learned that the Pentagon and several presidential administrations had systematically lied to the public to cover up how badly the U.S. was doing in the war in Vietnam. Then in 1974, President Nixon resigned due to the far-reaching Watergate scandal that involved major illegal abuse of power by the federal government. Public confidence in political institutions was shattered, and it has never recovered. Since the early 1970's, only a minority of the public has expressed a high level of trust in the federal government.

Finally, the concept of political *tolerance* measures whether individuals are willing to grant equal basic civil liberties to people whose views they dislike or even hate. The precise measure of tolerance varies greatly depending on the specific wording of the survey question. If you ask people "Do you believe in in free speech for all, no matter their view," then 80-to-90 percent of the public responds "yes." On the other hand, if you ask people if someone whose views they hate should be allowed to engage in a particular activity, then tolerance plummets. Only around a third (33%) of the public is willing to allow someone whose views they hate make a public speech, work as a teacher, or have their book available at the local library. Nor do large majorities support actions like burning the U.S. flag, or refusing to stand and say the Pledge of Allegiance. In short, political tolerance is high in the abstract, but low in practice.

SUMMARY

What people collectively think politically is called public opinion. Social scientists measure public opinion through asking people their political beliefs in opinion polls or surveys. Everyone's beliefs are formed through acquiring information. This process of learning and forming opinions is called socialization. Different mechanisms of socialization, from education to the media to growing older, all have different impacts on our political beliefs. The sum total of our political beliefs is our ideology. Different ideologies commonly have competing underlying philosophies about the proper role of government in our lives. How much liberty should we have? What behavior should laws regulate, and what actions should we be free to do without legal interference? The common but mistaken conception of ideology is that there are only two choices, liberal or conservative. In actuality, each ideology believes differently regarding the proper role of government in regulating both our social choices and our economic choices. One can favor or disfavor regulation in either of the two public policy areas, resulting in four possible combinations of views. Therefore there are four basic ideologies: libertarian, communitarian, progressive, and conservative. Each ideology holds a different political value as the highest value. Libertarians favor liberty, communitarians favor order, progressives favor equality, and conservatives favor morality. Each competing value can be taken to its logical extreme, resulting in extreme ideologies. The moderate middle between all four ideologies is not itself an ideology, but is merely centrism with pragmatism as its core value. Besides ideology, there are many other political concepts which opinion polls measure. These concepts include political knowledge, political interest, political efficacy, political trust, political tolerance, and support for current or potential public policies.

QUESTIONS FOR REVIEW AND SELF-ASSESSMENT

1. What are public opinion and political behavior, how they are measured, and what are some common problems with this measurement?
2. What is political socialization, and what are the effects of one's parents, religion, education, the life cycle, and the mass news media as agents of political socialization?
3. What is ideology, what is the common understanding of liberal and conservative, and what are the two dimensions of ideology?
4. What are libertarianism, liberalism, conservatism, communitarianism, and centrism, including the core values of each ideology and their logical extremes?

5. What are political knowledge, interest, efficacy, trust, and tolerance, and what are their levels among the public?

Critical Thinking Questions for Reflection and Discussion

1. Are college students enlightened or indoctrinated by their college instructors?
2. Overall, is the mass news media biased towards any one ideology?
3. Which ideology is the "best" or "wisest" ideology?

Suggested Reading Supplements

- American National Election Studies (ANES) Guide to Public Opinion and Electoral Behavior, online
- *New York Times v. Sullivan* (1964)
- Spiro T. Agnew, Speech to the Midwest Republican Conference (1969)

For Further Advanced Reading

- V.O. Key, *The Responsible Electorate*
- Jonathan Haidt, *The Righteous Mind: Why Good People are Divided by Politics and Religion*

Chapter 15: Participation, Elections, and Representation

The Big Picture

Political beliefs lead to political actions. People act in many different ways politically. This includes watching and discussing the news, obeying laws, joining political parties and interest groups, and voting. Most people support either the Democratic Party or the Republican Party, but the economy often determines who wins the presidency. Overall political participation is generally declining, though, partly because of interpersonal disconnection caused by technology. Regardless, Congress imperfectly represent the public's wishes. The nature of political behavior by the all the various political actors in the U.S. reveals the essence of political power in the United States. Different facts support several competing evaluations.

Chapter Objectives

After reading this chapter, the reader should be able to:

1. Define conventional and unconventional participation, providing examples of each.
2. Define and describe voting turnout and voting determinants, explain the voting determinants in presidential elections, and explain how technology has arguably decreased overall participation.
3. Compare and contrast political parties and interest groups, explain the two-party system in the U.S., and list the most powerful interest groups.
4. Explain several of the main reasons why Congressional policy imperfectly reflects public opinion.
5. Describe the competing views of overall political power in the U.S., providing evidence in support of each view.

Conventional versus Unconventional Participation

After acquiring beliefs and opinions, people act based on those beliefs and opinions. Political scientists divide all political activities into one of two types. Political activity that lawfully uses the existing democratic system is called *conventional* participation. Such conventional political activity could include joining or supporting a political party, joining or supporting an interest group. It could also include voting, writing a letter to the editor of a newspaper, contacting an elected official, or working on a political campaign or running for office. It could even be something as simple as following political news and discussing it. *Unconventional* political behavior, on the other hand, works outside the legally accepted means of using the political system. In other words, unconventional political activity seeks to challenge and defy the existing political institutions, systems, structures, or processes by breaking the law. But why? People who engage in unconventional participation tend to believe it's their last resort. They feel alienated from politics and society. That is, they have no sense of being able to get their voice heard in the current political system using the lawful means to do so. So, those individuals go outside the law as a means of making a political statement or attempting to achieve a political goal. Illegally blocking traffic to stage a protest, occupying a government building, or vandalizing the posters or offices of one's political opponent would all be examples of unconventional participation.

Unconventional participation is itself divided into two types. *Civil disobedience* is intentional law breaking that uses only peaceful, nonviolent means to do so. Civil disobedience thus avoids hurting people or property. This nonviolence includes not physically resisting arrest, conviction, sentencing, or imprisonment. A famous example of civil disobedience is the U.S. civil rights movement led by Dr. Martin Luther King, Jr. During the 1950's and 1960's, the civil rights movement sought to achieve racial equality in the law through peacefully violating laws that enforced racial segregation or denied voting rights based on race. King's "Letter from Birmingham Jail," written as he sat in jail in 1963, is a classic defense of civil disobedience. The major start of the modern civil rights movement also began with a single famous act of civil disobedience. In 1955, Rosa Parks refused to yield her bus seat to a white person as the law required in Montgomery, Alabama. She peacefully allowed herself to be arrested so as to raise public awareness of the injustice of the laws imposing racial segregation. Outside of the United States, Mohandas Gandhi strictly adhered to a philosophy of civil disobedience as he led the nation of India to independence from Great Britain in the 1930's and 1940's. The multiple Academy Award-winning film "Gandhi" portrays these events. Indeed, Martin Luther King credited Gandhi with inspiring his use of civil disobedience as a strategy for achieving racial justice through political change. King said "Jesus gave me the message, but Gandhi gave me the method." Gandhi in turn was inspired in part by American writer and thinker Henry David Thoreau, who in 1849 was imprisoned for refusing to pay his taxes. Thoreau opposed the use of his tax money to pay for slavery and the war against Mexico. In defense of his actions, Thoreau wrote a classic essay titled "Civil Disobedience."

Whereas civil disobedience breaks the law peacefully, *unconventional* political behavior uses violence to achieve its goals. Such violent actions are commonly referred to as *terrorism*. This is the philosophy that instilling fear and terror in one's political opposition or the public at large is a valid means of achieving political goals. Civilians are therefore often the targets of terrorists. The Oklahoma City Bombing in the 1990s and the attacks against New York City and the Pentagon on September 11, 2001 are examples of terrorism within the United States.

Terrorism continues to be widely used around the world by individuals and groups who are willing to use any violent means they believe will help them achieve their political goals.

VOTING

Let's look more closely at several of the most common types of conventional political participation. Other than following political news and discussing it, the most common way most people participate politically is by voting. In the late 1700's, generally only white land-owning males could vote in the U.S. Thus, it was a democracy in name, but a plutocracy, or rule by the wealthy few, in practice. In earlier chapters we looked at how the right to vote was expanded first to non-property-owning white males, then to black males by the Fourteenth and Fifteenth Amendments in 1868 and 1870, then to women by the Nineteenth Amendment in 1920.

In addition to these expansions of voting rights, the Twenty-Sixth Amendment was added to the Constitution in 1971. It guarantees the right to vote for all individuals who are 18 years of age or older. Prior to that, only four states had a voting age lower than 21. However, during the Vietnam War in the late 1960's, over a half a million adult males were drafted to fight in Vietnam. As tens of thousands of them died, this revealed the inconsistency in U.S. law that adults were old enough to fight and die for their country, but not old enough to vote. After the Supreme Court struck down Congressional attempt to change the nationwide voting age, Congress and the states ratified the 26th Amendment. Notice that this means most 18-year-old adults today could not legally vote when the Constitution was first adopted, nor until only a few decades ago.

Voting behavior is the most commonly studied type of political behavior. This is both because voting itself is so common, and because it's relatively easy to measure. The study of voting behavior includes the study of both *whether* people vote and *how* they vote. When someone votes, they "turn out" to vote. The measure of whether people vote is therefore called voting *turnout*. Voting turnout in the U.S. is relatively low compared to most other industrialized democracies. The highest voting turnout in the U.S. occurs in Presidential elections. Roughly three-fourths of all citizens register to vote, and roughly two-thirds of those vote. This means that only between 50 and 60 percent of eligible voters turn out to vote for President. Voting turnout is generally much less in other elections. Turnout in congressional midterm elections is usually around 40%, in primary elections around 30%, and in state and local elections between 20% and 30%. Some local elections such as school board elections or local judicial elections might have only around 10% voting turnout.

This low voter turnout is troubling to people who want the U.S. to continue to be able to call itself a democracy. Of eligible adult voters, if only half vote in a Presidential election, and only half of those vote for the winning candidate, then at most only one-fourth of the adult population is choosing the President. An even smaller fraction of the adult population is choosing other elected officials at the federal, state, and local level. Recall from a much earlier chapter that if only a relative minority of the population is making all the political decisions, that system of government is by definition an oligarchy. In short, although most people in the U.S. refer to it as a democracy and would like to keep doing so, the voting turnout data suggest otherwise. This is why low voter turnout is such a political concern.

So why is voting turnout in the U.S. so low? This is especially puzzling give that education is positively correlated with turnout. That is, the more education a person has, the more likely that person is to vote. Education levels in the U.S. have slowly but steadily increased throughout the past century. Yet at the same time, voting turnout has slowly declined over the past several decades. This decline in turnout has also occurred despite the right to vote being expanded to essentially all of the adult population.

Low voter turnout in the U.S. can be partially explained by comparing the U.S. to other democracies where turnout is generally higher. There are obstacles to voting in the U.S. that do not occur in other nations. For example, in some other democracies, voting is a legally required civic duty, like jury service in the U.S. Also, to make voting convenient, election days in other countries are often national holidays. No one has to go to work or take their children to school, so the only thing they have to do that day is vote. In the U.S. on the other hand, federal elections and many state elections occur on Tuesday, a mid-week workday. In addition, citizens in most other nations simply need simply show up at the polls with their regular identification cards to vote. In almost all states of the U.S., voters must separately register in advance in order to vote. If they forget to register, or decide not to vote but later change their minds after the registration deadline, they are prohibited from voting.

Moreover, most democracies are multi-party democracies with proportional representation. Under this system, voters have more choices, and every individual vote helps increase the representation of that party in the national legislature, even if the party wins only a small minority of the vote. Voters therefore have a good reason to go vote. In the U.S., however, there are realistically only two choices of which party to vote for, and only the winning party in an election district receives any representation in the government. Supporters of minor parties, or even the major second party, often do not bother to vote if they know there is no chance of their favored party winning that district. All these various differences illustrate that there are more hindrances and disincentives to voting in the U.S. compared to most other democracies.

Once people decide to vote, *how* do they decide who to vote for? The study of factors that influence individuals to choose one candidate or party over another is called the study of *voting determinants*. The party affiliation of voters is the biggest determining factor. That is, the party generally favored by a voter is the single biggest factor in determining which candidate that voter chooses to support. Although the numbers fluctuate from year-to-year, generally both the Democratic and Republican parties each receive roughly around 40% of the vote. In other words, around 80% of voters in total vote more-or-less automatically for the party with which those voters usually affiliate themselves. This leaves around 20% of voters remaining. People in this middle group are called "independents" or *swing voters* because they can swing either way to vote either Democratic or Republican in any particular election. Swing voters thus tend to be moderate, centrist voters.

Since the two major parties are roughly tied when it comes to the percent of the public that loyally supports them, swing voters typically decide the outcomes of elections. During election campaigns, the candidates of the two opposing parties often "race to the middle" with their policies. This means they adopt moderate, centrist polices in the hope of winning over a majority of swing voters, and thereby the general election. Studies show that some swing voters are politically sophisticated and vote based on carefully evaluating the many policy positions of the candidates. These same studies also show, however, that a majority of swing voters, especially in Presidential elections but also other elections, simply vote based on how the voter perceives the condition of the economy. If the economy is good, swing voters will likely vote for the President and/or candidates from the President's party. If the economy is bad, swing voters will likely vote for the candidates from the party opposing the President. Yet as we discussed in the previous chapter on the Presidency, no one person on the planet, not even the President of the United States, can possibly control the massive, complex and unpredictable economy. This means that elections are often decided based on false beliefs by the public.

Political Parties

Besides voting, another way people commonly participate politically is by formally joining political parties, or otherwise supporting them such as by donating money to them or campaigning for their candidates. Political parties sponsor candidates for political office, and both the parties and their candidates take stands on many different political issues. A person's ideology often leads to them joining a particular political party. As we saw in the last chapter, in the United States the Democratic Party generally represents the liberal or progressive ideology, and the

Republican Party generally represents the conservative ideology. Often, though, simply advertising the ideology of a party is not enough to win a political majority. Because there's a political need for any party to get support from a majority of the voters, the parties also make appeals to groups. Each party tells various groups it will support policies that group wants, if the group supports and votes for that party in return.

Populations tend to consistently split into different certain kinds of factional groups. Historically, in all countries over time, there have been four key demographic divisions within societies that lead people to political division. These four distinctions are ethnicity, religion, geography, and socio-economic class. People across these different groups frequently struggle and compete against either other. At best, this competition results in healthy political dialogue. At worst, these conflicts have sometimes resulted in ethnic genocide, such as 1940's Germany and 1990's Rwanda. There have been religious civil wars, such as have been ongoing in Iraq and Afghanistan since the early 2000s. Brutal suppression of regional autonomy has occurred, such as Chinese rule over Tibet. Also, there has been class warfare where the rich have subjugated or enslaved the poor, such as the early 1800's Southern U.S. The opposite has also occurred, where the poor have risen up to subjugate, enslave, or slaughter the rich, such as France in the 1790s or Vietnam during the 1970's Pol Pot regime.

In democracies, all these types of demographic divisions lead the public to support different particular political parties. These social-demographic divisions are a major basis of political party differences all around the world today, and in the United States as well. Both the Democratic and Republican party regularly rely on and encourage certain different social groups to support them. These groups are displayed in the table below. The table reveals where the stereotypes of Democrats and Republicans come from. Yet these are just stereotypes, as a minority of each of the groups supports the opposite party, or is politically independent. For example, there are poor, urban, New England blacks that vote Republican, and there are rich, southern, white evangelical Protestants that vote Democratic. There are also local variations in this group support. Nevertheless, the political parties openly make appeals to these different groups, knowing that nationwide, majorities of these groups typically support them. The formal policy positions of a political party are called the *party platform.* Thus, the party platforms are designed to appeal to various groups.

Table: U.S. party demographic divisions

Demographic Category	Democratic core bases of support (nationwide average)	Republican core bases of support (nationwide average)
Ethnicity/Race	Minorities (Blacks, Latinos)	Whites
Religion	Catholics, Jews	Evangelical Protestants
Geography	Urban Centers; States in New England, Midwest, Pacific Coast	Suburbs, Rural Areas, States in South and West
Socio-Economic Class	Working Class, Unions	Upper Class, Business Owners and Executives

Yet all this begs the question why the United States has only two major political parties. Almost all other democracies on the planet today are multi-party systems. This means three or more major political parties exist and regularly get elected to public office. Even the official policy of the U.S. government for decades has been to help other countries become multi-party democracies. After the defeat of the Axis powers in World War II, after the fall and breakup of the Soviet Union, and after the U.S. ousting of regimes in Iraq and Afghanistan, the U.S. government helped conquered or newly independent nations set up multi-party democracies.

The reason the U.S. has only two major political parties is because the U.S. election system differs from most other democracies. The U.S. system is a "winner-take-all" election system, more technically known as a "single-member district with plurality winner." This means that no matter how small the percentage of the vote the winning candidate receives, that candidate becomes the sole winner as long as that candidate received more votes than any other candidate.

For example, imagine an election district with five candidates from five different political parties. In a winner-take all system with parties A, B, C, D, and E, then the candidate from party A can win a voting district with only 20.1% of the popular vote if the other candidates each receive only 19.9% of the vote. Hypothetically, if there are 100 such election districts, and the percentage of votes for the different parties is the same across all the districts, then party A can win all 100 seats in the legislature while receiving only 20% of the vote nationwide. This means 80% of the national public does not receive any representation from the parties they prefer.

Under such a system, voters realize that unless their favorite candidate or favorite party has a reasonable chance of getting the most votes, their vote for a candidate from a party in 3rd or 4th or 5th place is practically a wasted vote. Most voters' only chance to get any representation of their views is to choose one of the top two parties. This is because those are the only parties with any reasonable likelihood of winning. Much of the voting public therefore "holds their noses" and votes for the "lesser of two evils" between the top two parties. As a result, public votes for third parties are almost always *much* lower than the number of votes for the top two parties. Only on rare occasion can an exceptionally strong candidate from a third party gain a significant percentage of the vote.

In the U.S., the winner-take-all system has entrenched the Democratic and Republican parties as the dominant political parties. Votes for third parties, such as the Constitution Party or Libertarian Party, are therefore usually only a fraction of a percent or less of the popular vote. On the rare occasion when an independent candidate or third party begins to receive a sizeable following, the two major parties adjust their policies to move closer to that third candidate or party. For example, in 1992 billionaire Ross Perot ran as an independent presidential candidate. Among other stands he took, he wanted to solve the national debt and impose congressional term limits. After he won 19% of the popular vote in the national election, the Republican Party pledged to try to balance the federal budget and add a constitutional amendment imposing term limits on Congress. Perot later created the Reform Party and ran again as its presidential candidate in 1996, but gained only 8% of the vote. The Reform Party never achieved significant popular support again, and almost totally disappeared from the national political scene within a decade.

In contrast to the two-party system in the U.S., most other democratic election systems around the world use some variant of what is called *proportional representation* ("PR"). The more technical term for PR is "multi-member district with at-large representatives." Under PR, legislative representation is based at least in part on the percent of vote each party receives from the public. Let's use our example above of an election with five political parties, A, B, C, D, and E. Party A receives 20.1% of the vote and all the other parties each receive 19.9% of the vote. In a nation with 100 election districts that uses a pure PR system, the seats in the legislature are assigned based on the percent of votes each party receives nationwide rather than by individual districts. Since each party received approximately an equal 20% of the overall nationwide vote, each party receives 20% of the seats in the national legislature. In other words, all the parties A, B, C, D, and E each receive 20 seats in the legislature. Essentially all of the citizens of that nation have someone representing their views in the legislature. PR is therefore much more democratically representative of the entire population than is a two-party, winner-take-all system. This is why around the world, multi-party systems are strongly preferred to two-party systems. This is even official U.S. government policy when it helps other nations create democracies.

Nevertheless, there are several third parties in the United States that regularly provide candidates for political office, such as the Libertarian Party, the Constitution Party, the Green Party, and others. Supporters of these parties, as well as other proponents of democratic choice, have argued that the U.S. should convert to a system of PR. However, any attempts at reforming the U.S. election system to allow for a multi-party democracy would require either a federal election law passed by Congress, or perhaps even a Constitutional amendment. Either way, it would have to be supported by majorities of Democratic and Republican legislators at the federal and/or state level. This would mean willingly giving up their own two-party duopoly on power, which they are unlikely to do.

Indeed, the two major parties regularly work together to block attempts by third parties to gain access to the political process. For example, all the state legislatures have made it difficult for third parties to be listed on election ballots. In most states, these ballot restrictions require that third parties must gather the signatures of between one and five percent of the state's eligible voters to re-qualify for the next statewide ballot. In a large state like California, this can mean hundreds of thousands of signatures are needed *every* election. To get their party's presidential nominee listed as a presidential candidate in all fifty state therefore requires a huge amount of effort every four years. The Democratic and Republican parties, on the other hand, are automatically relisted on the ballots in all fifty states every election. Also, there is a private Presidential Debate Commission comprised of only Democrats and Republicans. This Commission decides which party's candidates are allowed in televised Presidential debates. Third party candidates are rarely allowed. Independent candidate Ross Perot was allowed in the 1992 debates, but the Commission then made their entrance rules stricter to keep him out of the 1996 debates.

As we've seen, there are ideologies other than liberal and conservative, and across those ideologies there are many political parties other than the Democratic and Republican parties. However, winner-take-all elections, combined with active resistance from the two major parties, makes it extremely difficult for third parties to be listed on ballots, gain public exposure, or win elections. For tens of millions of U.S. citizens who would prefer a third party, every election therefore confronts those voters with three options: Don't vote, waste a vote on a third party as a symbolic "protest" vote, or hold one's nose and vote for the "lesser of two evils."

Interest Groups and Campaign Finance

Political parties are different from what are called *special interest groups.* Special interest groups, also often simply called "interest groups," attempt to influence public policy by supporting parties or candidates, but interest groups do not provide the candidates for political office themselves as parties do. Also, whereas political parties adopt and fight for public policies across a broad range of issues, special interest groups focus their efforts usually only on one narrow policy area. Hence, the term "special" interest group means "narrow" interest as opposed to "broad" interest, or "single" interest as opposed to "multiple" interests. Political parties represent many broad interests of the public as a whole, but special interest groups represent only a narrow interest of a subgroup of the population. Here are a few of the biggest and most politically powerful special interest groups, along with their membership:

1. American Association for Retired Persons (AARP); (protecting Medicare and Social Security for the elderly)~40 million members.
2. National Rifle Association (NRA); (protecting gun ownership rights)~4 million members.
3. National Education Association (NEA) (teachers' union); ~3 million members;
4. U.S. Chamber of Commerce (businesses) ~3 million businesses in local and state Chambers of Commerce.
5. American Federation of State, County, and Municipal Employees (AFSCME) (state and local government workers); ~1.4 million members.

When an interest group has a large membership, it can raise a great deal of money through membership dues and other donations. Special interest groups formally create *political action committees (PACs)* as well as *Super PACSs*. Under congressional campaign finance laws and Supreme Court rulings interpreting those laws, PACs and Super PACS have slightly different legal rules that apply to them. The rules differ regarding how money can be donated to PACs and Super PACs and how that money can then be spent. PACs have limits on the financial contributions given them, and how much they can directly donate to political parties and candidates. Super PACs, on the other hand, may accept unlimited donations, but then may not donate to political parties or their candidates. Both PACs and Super PACs, however, may also spend their money independently of political parties and their candidates. Indeed, that's the only way that Super PACs may spend their money. Currently there are several thousand PACs and several hundred Super PACs registered with the Federal Election Commission (FEC). The FEC oversees PAC and Super PAC compliance with federal election laws. The maze of varied campaign finance rules for individuals, PACS, and Super PACS is confusing even to political candidates themselves.

PACs and Super PACs create media advertisements favoring candidates, parties, or public policy positions. They also create negative campaign ads *against* political candidates, parties, or public policy positions. These negative ads are also called "attack" ads. Collectively, in each federal election cycle, PACs and Super PACs spend hundreds of millions of dollars on negative attack ads. This is why large and powerful interest groups are feared by candidates from both major political parties. Democratic and Republican office holders and candidates usually do what they can to keep in the good graces of such interest groups as the AARP or the NRA, for fear of political retaliation otherwise.

This huge amount of spending from interest groups is also a major reason why campaign spending is such a controversial topic. Very wealthy individuals and interest groups can afford to pay for television ads or other advertising to influence elections. The vast majority of ordinary individual voters, on the other hand, cannot afford to compete with such campaign spending. This means that the messages in campaign elections are highly skewed towards the views of these wealthy interest groups, and not necessarily what most ordinary voters believe or want.

Congressional attempts at legally regulating campaign finance, however, must comply with the First Amendment's Free Speech Clause. The Supreme Court has created a complex set of rules whereby some types of legal limits on campaign contributions and spending are constitutional whereas other types of legal limits are not. In 2010, the Supreme Court in *Citizens United v. FEC* declared there are constitutional limitations on how Congress may regulate campaign finance. The *Citizens United* ruling gave rise to the existence of Super PACs. As noted earlier, the full set of campaign finance laws is complex and confusing. Basically though, as a result of the *Citizens United* ruling, wealthy and powerful interest groups are able to spend unlimited amounts of money supporting or opposing candidates. Ordinary voters as well as candidates who are not wealthy have no way to oppose such spending. Their messages are therefore drowned out by the messages coming from PACs and Super PACs.

The confusing and controversial legal framework of campaign finance has been heavily criticized on both sides of this issue as being unnecessarily complex and riddled with loopholes. For example, currently individuals and interest groups can only contribute small amounts of money to a candidate, but individuals and interest groups can spend unlimited amounts of money on their own. This means poor presidential candidates must rely on tens of thousands or even hundreds of thousands of small donations, whereas billionaires can simply spend endless amounts of their own money. Indeed, so many political candidates across all political parties are wealthy because they have a much easier time running for political office than people without such wealth. This is true for candidates for the House, but especially for the Senate and the presidency since those campaigns are the most expensive. In recent decades alone, super-wealthy presidential candidates like Ross Perot, Steve Forbes, and Donald Trump were all able to spend millions of dollars of their own money on their campaigns. Trump won the Republican Party presidential nomination in 2016, and Perot even created his own Reform Party. In 2014, for the first time in U.S. history a majority of the members of Congress were millionaires.

The two opposing sides of this political issue disagree on the solution to this skewed system. Conservatives tend to argue the Free Speech Clause of the First Amendment should forbid all Congressional campaign finance laws. If spending money on political candidates, parties, or advertising is free speech, then Congressional regulations themselves are the problem. For example, if contribution limits were repealed or overturned, this would allow wealthy individuals, PACs and Super PACs to donate endless amounts of money to poor candidates. This would equalize the ability of both poor candidates to compete with independently wealthy candidates. However, this would require either that Congress repeal all contribution limits, or that the Supreme Court declares contribution limits violate the Free Speech Clause.

Progressives, on the other hand, tend to generally argue that much more regulation is to needed to close the loopholes. They argue that money is not equivalent to speech. Since it isn't then the Supreme Court was mistaken in *Citizens United* to overturn congressionally imposed spending limits on wealthy individuals, PAC's and Super PACs. Progressives therefore argue that the *Citizens United* case should itself be overturned, thereby allowing campaign finance laws to limit how much wealthy individuals or interest groups may spend in political campaigns. This would then provide a more level playing field between rich and poor candidates. Otherwise, politics increasingly becomes the exclusive playground of the richest "one-percent" of the population.

In short, both sides see the current system as flawed. Either contribution limits need to be removed by Congress or overturned by the Supreme Court, or more spending limits need to be added by Congress and upheld by the Supreme Court. Regardless of the particular solution, unless something is changed, the current campaign finance system will continue to strongly favor that only the very wealthy can afford to run as political candidates for federal elected offices. Given the enormous and ever-increasing role money plays in U.S. elections, this issue is not going away. It will surely be reconsidered by Congress, will eventually come up again before the U.S. Supreme Court, and will remain an ongoing issue in Congressional and Presidential debates and campaigns.

Participation and Technology

We've just seen that voting, and joining or supporting political parties and interest groups are all types of conventional political participation. Yet as we also saw earlier in this chapter, in most elections within the U.S. less than half of all adult citizens vote, sometimes fewer. A far smaller percent of the public joins political parties or interest groups, write letters to the editor of the newspaper, runs for political office, contacts their elected officials, or engages in other types of political participation. Moreover, these participation rates have been slowly but steadily declining over the past 100 years or so. This is true not just for political participation but for all types of social memberships and activities. For example, fewer people join civic and fraternal organizations such as the Kiwanis, Lions Club, American Legion, or Rotary Club. Fewer people attend church. Membership in labor unions, volunteer associations, bowling leagues, and bridge clubs have been declining. All this has occurred despite the fact that education and income levels in the U.S. have increased, giving people more resources to participate. Also, voting rights have greatly expanded in the last century, yet voting and other political participation has gone down. So what accounts for this? Several thinkers have suggested that modern technology has played a significant role in this decline.

The author, political scientist, and social thinker Robert Putnam wrote a book in 2000 called "Bowling Alone." In it, he discusses the concept of *social capital.* "Capital" is wealth. Economic capital is financial wealth. Correspondingly, social capital is the amount of interpersonal social connection and involvement a person has with other people. For example, an introvert who grew up as an only child in a remote rural area might not have much social capital. On the other hand, an extrovert who grew up in a large family in a crowded urban neighborhood might have a lot of social capital. As adults, individuals who are loners have little social capital. On the other hand, people who have a large circle of friends, and are actively involved in community organizations, have a high amount of social capital. Such a person is more likely to know their neighbors. In turn, someone who knows many people living around them is more likely to care about what happen to their community and nation. This person will therefore be more likely to vote and politically participate in other ways than would a person who neither knows nor cares about many people. In short, people with high social capital will be more involved politically than people with low social capital.

Putnam argues that general levels of social capital in the population have declined over the last century for several reasons all having to do with our modern society. One important such reason is the rise of technology, especially leisure technology. Most leisure activities of today, as well as other aspects of society, are less inter-personal today than they were 100 years ago. Many activities today involve much less face-to-face human interaction, less direct in-person contact, then these activities used to require.

Here are a few of the many examples of how technology has changed how we interact in our modern lives compared to the past:

Old Form of interaction	New Equivalent
Neighborhood park	drive to state park
Neighborhood bar	drive to bar/nightclub
Town square news	TV, radio, internet
Meet to chat	phone, e-mail and internet chat
Neighborhood restaurant	fast-food, drive-thru, home delivery
Go to local concert	buy, listen to CD or radio
Go to play/theatre	watch movies or TV
Watch/play sports	watch on TV
Outdoor exercise	home exercise machines
Interactive games	computer/video games
Walk to corner store	drive to distant mall, shop on internet
Sit on front porch	stay inside with air-conditioning
Drive in open buggy	sealed in air-conditioned car.
Go to local bank	drive-through ATM machine
Live in same town	relocate often
Work in same town	commute to work in other town
Work in office	Work from home via computer
Walk to town well	use indoor plumbing
Grow gardens together	Shop at supermarket
Build homes together	Buy homes pre-made from power tools

There are many other ways technology has changed daily living. This pervasive way in which our everyday interpersonal interactions have changed has enormous implications. Studies on human communication show that the *meaning* in most human communication occurs not in the words themselves, but in things like tone of voice, facial expressions, and body language. This requires being able to see and hear the other person, regulate body space between the two people, and even touch the other person. This direct, face-to-face involvement with others creates a much greater sense of connection than does merely reading a person's words in e-mail or even hearing their voice on the phone. Putnam points out that technology has therefore reduced our social capital, thereby causing significantly less social and political involvement overall. Neal Postman, in his book "Amusing Ourselves to Death" argues that television has similarly affected our lives in a negative way. Families use to watch television together, but now they sit in different rooms. Each person watches their individual televisions, computer screens, tablets, or smartphones alone. We become lost by immersing ourselves in the technology, oblivious to the existence of other fellow humans in our immediate vicinity.

Note that in each of the examples listed above, technology has brought significant benefits, but also at an enormous and usually hidden cost as well. One hundred years ago most of us would have large extended families and also know everyone in the neighborhood, probably well. Ironically, although technology has made it easy to communicate with people far away and travel to visit them, technology has resulted in *less* human connection. In each case, technology has caused less direct, face-to-face personal interaction to occur with those around us. We can instantly send a mass e-mail to a hundred people, yet speak face-to-face with none of them. This type of communication contains much less meaning, and provides far less connection to others. The domino effect is that we care less about others, and therefore become less involved, either socially or politically.

If social bonds continue to slowly disintegrate in this way due to technological advancement, the concern is that the connections that hold democratic society together will eventually dissolve as well. Why vote, or why be willing to fight and die defending the rights of one's neighbors, if one has no sense of "community" or "nation?" This question has led some political thinkers such as Putnam to wonder whether the United States or any democracy can survive the endless growth of technology. Do the costs of technology ultimately outweigh the benefits?

Most people are not even aware of this trade-off between technology and human closeness, yet some people are. The Amish have maintained close-knit religious communities where they have substantially limited the role of technology in their lives. They are aware of the seriousness of the choice to adopt new technologies, and have consciously chosen to preserve deep, extensive human relationships rather than embrace many modern technologies. At the very least, every time a new technology is created, each Amish community goes through a careful thought process. They consider whether the technology will hurt their community rather than help it.

There is no easy answer, however, to declining political participation in the broader industrialized U.S. society. Would the U.S. and other democracies be better off returning to pre-industrial, pre-electronic technology for their own long-term health? This is unlikely to happen, at least not for the foreseeable future. It would require a radical change in everyday life that most people would probably reject. Nevertheless, the problem of low social capital and the resulting problem of low political participation is not going away. As noted earlier, such low participation risks the U.S. becoming an oligarchy rather than a democracy. Moreover, as the first chapter in this book discussed, an uninformed and passive public can give rise to demagogues who take power and abuse it in terrible ways. At the very least, then, it's worth examining how technology negatively affects democratic political society, in order to determine what can be done about it.

Representation

In a democracy, political participation by the public, especially through democratic elections, results in political representation provided by elected officials. Indeed, the theoretical function of elections is to elect leaders to enact voter-preferred policies. This in turn confers legitimacy on the government. As John Locke described in his social contract theory, and as the U.S. Declaration of Independence agreed, only governments that receive the consent of the people can claim legitimate political authority. Of course, no one is going to vote for someone who the voter thinks is going to do the opposite of what the voter wants. Yet studies comparing public opinion to Congressional laws show that Congressional policy outcomes matches the policy preferences of the public roughly only about 2/3 of the time. In other words, about 1/3 of the time Congress does the opposite of what a majority of the public wants. There are many factors that help allow this to occur.

Role of a representative. Elected officials themselves disagree about what their proper role is as representatives of the people. This debate goes back at least as far as the English Parliament in the late 1700's. A *delegate* believes their job is to vote exactly as the voters want, regardless whether doing so is in the best interests of the voters or not. That is, delegates believe it would be arrogant for a representative to presume to know better than the public. A *trustee*, on the other hand, believes the role of a representative is to act in the best interest of the voters, regardless what the voters prefer. Trustees believe that often what voters want is mistaken, dangerous, or even morally wrong. In such cases, it would irresponsible for a representative to follow the public's wishes. Despite the claims of elected officials to be either delegates or trustees, in practical reality, most if not all politicians act sometimes as a delegate, and sometimes as a trustee. Remember from the chapter on Congress that the primary, overriding goal of members of Congress is to get re-elected. Therefore, their role at any particular moment depends on what the elected official believes is the most politically beneficial approach at that moment. The term *politico* applies to this hybrid delegate-trustee role.

Party primary elections. In party *primary elections*, the Democratic and Republican parties first pick their parties' own candidates. Those primary election winners then go on to compete against each other in the final *general election*. Primary voters tend to be die-hard party members who are more extreme ideologues than the general public. That is, Democratic primary voters tend to choose very liberal candidates, and Republican primary voters tend to choose very conservative candidates. In the general election, it's therefore usually the case that a very liberal Democrat candidate competes against a very conservative Republican candidate. Recall from our earlier discussion on voting and elections that ideological candidates who win the primary elections will then suddenly "race to the middle" to take more moderate policy positions to win over centrist-leaning swing voters. Once elected, however, they are largely free to return to their true ideological leaning. They also have an incentive to do so given that the next election they will face will once again be their party's primary election. In short, in most Congressional districts, and with the Presidency as well, whoever gets elected is not ideologically in the moderate middle. Rather than being mainstream centrists, most elected federal officials tend to support policies their party members support, even if a majority of the public opposes those policies.

Members of both parties do this equally, but a classic example occurred in the early 2000s. In 1990 a woman named Terry Schiavo living in Florida was diagnosed to be in a permanently vegetative state. After years of failed medical attempts at recovery or rehabilitation, along with medical complications, in 1998 Terri's husband finally decided she would not have wanted to go on living like that. He decided to let her die by withdrawing her feeding tube. Terri's parents, however, opposed withdrawing the feeding tube on religious grounds. Religious conservatives, a core base of support within the Republican Party, pressured state and federal Republican officials to try to stop it. In 2003 the Republican controlled state legislature passed a law signed by Republican Governor Jeb Bush to block the withdrawal of the tube. Courts overturned the law as interfering with Terri and her husband's constitutional rights to refuse unwanted medical treatment. In 2005 the Republican Congress and Republican President Bush then passed an emergency law to stop the withdrawal of the feeding tube, but federal courts blocked that law as well. After seven years of litigation in court, Terri's husband finally remove the feeding tube and Terri passed away in March of 2005. Throughout the situation, many public opinions polls consistently showed that a large majority of the general public opposed political and legal efforts to stop withdrawal of the feeding tube. Despite opposition from the general public, Congress and the President tried to block remove of the tube anyway. In this case, they were simply doing what their party's *primary* voters wanted, not what general election voters wanted. This example illustrates that Congress can and does sometimes go against the wishes of the larger public out of fear of losing support from party primary voters.

Interest groups. As we discussed earlier in this chapter, most political campaign money comes not from ordinary citizen-voters, but from big donors and spenders like large and wealthy interest groups, such as industry groups or labor unions. Representatives will often vote in favor of these groups precisely because these are the groups who have the money to either support or oppose those representatives. Interest groups will be favored by members of Congress even if the public opposes such policies. Indeed, a famous survey by a political scientist named John Kingdon asked members of Congress "How did you go about making up your mind on the ___ bill?" Legislators could provide more than one answer on who was influential in their decision. Here's the ranking of the top five factors members of Congress mentioned as influential:

1. Colleagues in Congress	40%
2. Voting Constituency (public)	37%
3. Interest Groups	31%
4. Presidential Administration	25%
5. Party Leaders in Congress	10%

Notice that interest groups had almost as much influence as the public, and only 37% of Congress, just barely over a third, even said the general public had any influence on their vote.

Divided Party Government. Recall that in our federal system of separation of powers and checks and balances, for any bill to become law, it must pass both the House and Senate and be signed by the President. If all three political institutions--the House, Senate, and Presidency--are controlled by the same political party, then the public knows who to either thank or blame for policies that become federal law. For example, in the first two years of President Obama's administration, the House, and Senate, and Presidency were all held by the Democratic Party. Often, however, rather than there being unified party control, different parties will be control of these three different institutions. For example, in the last six years of Democrat Obama's presidency, the Republican Party controlled one or more chambers in Congress. This is called *divided party government* or *divided government.* Indeed, assume each of the two major political parties has an equal 50-50 chance of controlling each of the three institutions. Statistically the odds are only one out of eight that all three institutions will be in the hands of the same political party in a federal election cycle. Stated differently, we can expect that on average, divided government will occur seven out of every eight years.

Divided government raises an interesting problem about accountability. If the President and one or both chambers of Congress creates policy the public doesn't like, which party does the public blame? In such a situation, both political parties can simply point to the other as being at fault, and the voters don't know who hold accountable. Both parties realize this confusion exists, so it allows both political parties to play the blame game and avoid accountability. Democrats can say it's the Republicans' fault, and vice versa. The House can blame the Senate, and vice versa. The Congress can blame the President, and vice versa. If everyone is to blame, then the practical result is that no one is to blame. For example, since 2008, public opinion polls consistently show that over 70% of the public disapproves of how Congress is doing its job. Yet members of Congress are overwhelmingly re-elected to office. Voters hate Congress, but they love their individual representatives. This is because divided government allows each member of Congress to merely "blame the other guy," thereby escaping the voter's wrath.

Merely one example is the enormous national debt the United States has, discussed in the earlier chapter on Congress. Majorities of the public consistently want Congress to avoid new debt and repay the current debt, or at least avoid making the debt dangerously large. Yet both parties keep voting for more spending programs, more tax cuts, or both. This simply worsens the debt problem by causing the U.S. to have to borrow hundreds of billions of dollars more each year to pay for these policies. After several decades now of ballooning debt, each party continually blames the other. Congressional Democrats say its Congressional Republican's refusal to raise taxes. Congressional Republicans say it's Congressional Democrats' refusal to cut or slow spending. Yet under the checks and balances, every House, every Senate, and every President of both parties have needed to all three agree on federal budgets for them to get passed. They have all had an equal hand in causing the problem and refusing to make the difficult choices to address it. The public wants to "throw the bums out," but due to divided government the public can't tell *which* bums to throw out. The consequence is that both parties in Congress continue to add to the national debt every year, knowing they will get likely get reelected by simply blaming each other.

The incumbent advantage. An *incumbent* is a person has already been elected and served a term in office, and who is now running for re-election to stay in that same office. For example, a president who is close to finishing a four-year term and is running for re-election to a second term in office is called the incumbent candidate. The term incumbent applies to elected officials running for re-election at all levels of government, be it federal, state, or local. Regardless of the position an incumbent is running for, incumbents generally have a significant electoral advantage today. Social scientists have calculated that before the 1960's, there was almost no electoral advantage to being a Congressional incumbent. Yet today, incumbency alone appears to provide an advantage to the incumbent of somewhere between seven and ten percent of the vote. There are many reasons for this. In an age of greater federal spending, incumbents are able to do more favors for voters. Also, with the rise of the mass electronic media, incumbents receive more media coverage, and therefore have better name recognition among voters. (See the 1992 comedy film *The Distinguished Gentleman*, where Eddie Murphy's character wins a Congressional election simply because his name is the same as the previous representative from that district).

By far the biggest factor in the incumbent advantage, however, is money. For example, according to Federal Election Commission (FEC) campaign contribution data from the 2004 Congressional campaign, incumbents received a combined 1.1 billion dollars in donations, whereas all their challengers only received a combined

160 million dollars in donations. This is a seven times spending advantage for the incumbents. As we've already discussed in this chapter, the large majority of this money comes from interest groups. But why such a disparity of campaign donations? Basically, the incumbent is already a proven winner, and can already directly influence public policy on behalf of the financial donor. The challenger might lose, in which case the money would be wasted. Even if the challenger wins they won't be able to help the financial donor until the challenger actually takes office. To hedge their bets, what many interest groups do is donate to both the incumbent and the challenger, but usually much less to the challenger. This way, no matter which candidate wins, the interest group can claim that the representative owes them something.

Most political scientists who have done studies on the financing of campaigns have concluded that money is the number one influence in winning an election. Whichever candidate has more money, usually wins. This makes sense as well. A candidate who has seven times more money than an opponent can afford to take out seven times more TV ads, radio ads, newspaper ads, and internet ads. They can pay for seven times as many posters, leaflets, yard signs, and bumper stickers. They can hire seven times as many campaign workers to make phone calls or go door-to-door to speak with potential voters. The message of the candidate with more money simply drowns out the message of the candidate with less money. An analogy often made is how the amplified loudspeakers at a rock concert will drown out someone trying to yell in the crowd. The point is that if you have the money to win, you can ignore what the voters want, because all you have to do to win is outspend your opponent. Thus, winning elections is all about money. There are still other factors as well that give Congressional incumbents an advantage, such as free mailing perks, as well as printing and travel expenses paid for at taxpayer expense. Nevertheless, by far the main explanation or incumbent success is the higher campaign spending by incumbents and the interest groups supporting them.

The end result of the incumbent advantage is that members of Congress know that as long as they don't do anything too controversial, they are practically guaranteed to win re-election. They can therefore largely ignore what a majority of the public wants on a day-to-day basis. One possible solution to the incumbent advantage that has often been suggested and even tried is *term limits*. Either state law, federal law, or both, could impose a limit on the number of terms members of Congress could serve in office. For example, perhaps members of the House of Representatives could be limited to four two-year terms maximum, and members of the Senate to two six-year terms maximum.

Both groups in favor of and against term limits want the same goal, which is to prevent corruption and abuse of power by legislators. The two sides differ, however, whether term limits would be the solution to poor representation, or would cause even worse representation. Supporters of term limits argue that term limits would regularly force legislators out of office, so that the public could elect new officials who more closely represent the wishes of the current public. Opponents of term limits argue that new, inexperienced legislators are even more open to influence by interest groups than more experienced, long-term legislators.

At the moment, though, this debate is largely moot. In 1995, in the Supreme Court case of *U.S. Term Limits v. Thornton*, the Court by a narrow 5-4 margin declared term limits on Congress contradicted the Constitution, since the Constitution does not impose such limits. This means that for either state legislatures to impose term limits on Congress, or for the Congress to impose term limits on itself, the U.S. Constitution would have to be amended. However, as we've discussed in earlier chapters, this is a politically difficult process, so is unlikely to occur. As a practical matter, this means that that the advantage of Congressional incumbents is probably here to stay, unless a future Supreme Court reverses its *Term Limits* ruling.

Power in the United States

We just briefly examined the representation provided by the primary representative political body in the United States, the Congress. We saw that although Congress does implement the public's wishes about two-thirds of the time, Congress is also able to ignore or go against the public's wishes about one-third of the time, for various reasons. So considering what Congress does and does not do, what is the basic overall nature of politics in the United States? Recall from the first unit of this course that politics is power. Therefore, this question is really asking what the essence is of power in the United States. There are several competing views, but essentially two basic ones, with two variants in one of them. This results in three competing analyses of power in the United States.

One view of power in the United States is called *democratic pluralism*. This view is very similar to what James Madison predicted in Federalist No. 10. Policy is made by numerous different competing political groups, or factions, that balance each other's' power such that no one group dominates. This view typically argues that democratic pluralism is part of "The American's Creed," which we saw in the earlier chapter on factions. To recall, the elements of the American's Creed include democratic self-government based on popular sovereignty and majority rule, but with several constraints on that rule. These include limited government due to enumerated powers, separation of powers, checks and balances, and federalism. Rights and liberties are included as well, such as speech, press, religion, and the rights of the criminally accused. Equality is included, as reiterated by the Equal Protection Clause of the Fourteenth Amendment. And, a pluralistic society of diverse groups based on ethnicity, religion, economic class, region, and so on will block each other's' power. This latter concept was the particular focus of Madison in Federalist No. 10.

Madison's prediction in Federalist No. 10 seems to have held mostly true in the United States so far. That is, no one group, no single faction, has ever yet seized all political power for itself. For example, despite how powerful they are, oil companies do not absolutely rule the nation, nor have teachers' unions overthrown the government. Yet as we've also seen, even with such pluralism, over a long enough period of time, the political system cannot block a sustained desire by a majority. In other words, any determined majority usually gets its way eventually. For example, for decades the majority allowed slavery. Eventually a different majority ended slavery despite violent rebellion against ending slavery. Also, for over a century the majority wanted a small federal government. Eventually a different majority greatly increased the size and power of the federal government despite intense political and legal efforts to prevent that expansion. Regardless, the point is that the theory of democratic pluralism argues that for the most part, political power in the U.S. is generally dispersed across numerous competing groups.

A competing view of power in the United States is that policy is made by a relatively small percent of the population. This minority possesses exceptional wealth, power, interest, motivation, education, or a combination thereof. This theory of *elitism* therefore argues that although on paper the United States is a democracy, in reality it's an oligarchy, or rule by an elite few. Indeed, within the study of political science there is a theory that all politically complex organizations eventually become oligarchies. This is because the few most talented and ambitious individuals gradually rise to the top leadership where they then naturally acquire most of the power within that organization. This theory is called the "iron law of oligarchy" on the claim that it is a rule of human behavior as unbreakable as iron. Indeed, political scientists have had trouble finding many exceptions to this rule. Nevertheless, regardless whether the iron law of oligarchy is always accurate, there are two competing versions or interpretations of elitism.

One common version of this argument is that the United States is in fact a particular form of oligarchy, a plutocracy. Recall that plutocracy means rule by the wealthy. In other words, this version of elitism argues that political rule in the United States is primarily in the hands of big businesses and corporations, wealthy individuals, political party leaders and elected officials, and large and powerful interest groups. Money from elites causes the election of elites. Elites than make policy either that either neglects or oppresses the masses by enacting policies that favor elites. This might be through lowering taxes on the rich, providing taxpayer subsidies for corporations, keeping low minimum wages for workers, and so on. Since elite-made public policy favors the wealthy, the rich then have more money to spend in political campaigns getting elites elected. The result in a self-perpetuating cycle of elitism. There are some statistics that support the claim of this version of elitism. In 2012, the House was 83% male and 83% white; the Senate was 83% male and 96% white. Also, as we noted earlier, in 2014 a majority of all members of Congress were millionaires. At least demographically, Congress does not match the general public.

A different interpretation of elitism agrees political power is in the hands of a relative few. However, those few who are making most of the political decisions are the people who are most fit to govern. In other words, this is an aristocracy, or "rule by the best. There are some statistics that support this claim. Political participants tend to be older, more educated, and more professionally successful. The voting turnout of people ages 65-74 is twice that of people ages 24-35. Those with an advanced or professional degree vote at three times the rate of those with only a high school diploma. Political elites are not just more educated, but are more politically aware, interested, involved, tolerant, and confident they can make a difference. Therefore, the argument goes, these elites can rule our nation better than can the masses of common, ordinary citizens who are politically unaware, uninterested, uninvolved, intolerant, and uneducated. The masses apparently are either incapable of governing themselves or unwilling to do so. Therefore, the elites must do it for them.

Another way to state this argument is that aristocratic elites are caretakers of the United States. In other words, they act as trustees who safeguard the nation's best interests. Indeed, notice that even democratic elections are themselves an aristocratic institution. Voting for a leader presumes some people would be better rulers than others. No one votes for who they think will do the worst job. Instead the public wants democratic elections so it can vote for who it thinks is "the best" candidate to govern. Otherwise, democratic rulers would be chosen by lottery from among the entire population, just like individual citizens are chosen for jury service. This view that elitism is good is controversial, and relatively few people adopt this view, or at least not openly. It has a long history, however. As we saw earlier in the course, the founding fathers of the U.S. distrusted "democratic excess." As a result, they put checks on the whims of the masses. This included a Senate originally chosen by state legislatures rather than the people, and a President chosen by the Electoral College rather than by direct popular vote.

In short, there is some evidence in support of both the main theories of power in the United States, democratic pluralism and elitism. Within elitism, there is some evidence that supports the two alternative versions of elitism, plutocracy and aristocracy. As we've also suggested several times throughout this course, the truth is often somewhere in the middle. Therefore, although the United States is in theory labeled a democracy, overall the evidence suggests that in practice the U.S. might be a democratic-oligarchic-plutocratic-aristocratic hybrid.

Indeed, we can go one step farther and add autocracy (rule by one) into this mix. In the earlier chapter on the presidency, we saw how modern presidents have a great deal of autocratic power over foreign policy. Also, as we saw in the earlier chapter on the separation of powers, the framers of the Constitution intentionally created a "mixed government," also called a "mixed regime." The President represented autocracy, the Senate represented either oligarchy or aristocracy, the House of Representatives represented democracy, and the Supreme Court represented aristocracy. Even these labels oversimplify things given that we've just shown how all democratic elections have an aristocratic component where voters select "the best" candidates. Combining the mixed regime *theory* of the U.S. government with the evidence of how that government has worked in *practice*, the United States seems to be a democratic-oligarchic-plutocratic-aristocratic-autocratic hybrid. In short, the United States is in reality a mixture of many different types of political rule. Indeed, no system of government is ever 100 percent "pure." Every government and each political system is unique and changes over time. The mixed-government hybrid known as the United States of America will continue to evolve in the future as well.

Summary

People's political beliefs and opinions lead them to participate in politics. This can be done either through conventional, lawful activities, or unconventional, illegal actions. The most commonly measured form of political participation is voting. Voting turnout is lower in the U.S. than most other democracies due to several unique obstacles to voting in the U.S. Other common means of political participation are joining or otherwise supporting political parties or interest groups. There is a two-party system in the U.S., which is perpetuated by the winner-take-all form of elections. Special interest groups have enormous influence over political campaigns due to their ability to raise and spend money. All forms of participation have steadily decreased over the last century, however. This has been caused in significant part by the increasing technologically-induced isolation of people from each other. The sum total of the public's political participation leads to the political representation the public receives from elected officials. Members of Congress follow the public's wishes about two-thirds of the time, but go against it the other one-third of the time. There are many reasons why Congress has the leeway to sometimes ignore the public. These include party primaries, divided government, and the incumbent advantage due to imbalance in campaign spending. When we look at overall political power in the United States, there is some evidence to support each of the several main theories regarding the essence of power in the

United States. It appears, then, that in actual practice the United States is probably some type of mixed democratic-oligarchic-plutocratic-aristocratic-autocratic hybrid.

Questions for Review and Self-Assessment

1. What is conventional participation versus unconventional participation, and what are some examples of each?
2. What is voting turnout, what is the level of voting turnout in the U.S., and why is it so low? What are voting determinants, and what are the main voting determinants in presidential elections?
3. How do political parties differ from interest groups, and why are there only two major political parties in the U.S.? What are some of the most powerful interest groups, and how do campaign finance laws affect the power of interest groups? How has technology arguably influenced overall political participation of all types?
4. How well does Congress reflect public opinion, and what are several of the main reasons why Congressional policy imperfectly reflects public opinion?
5. What are the several competing views of overall political power in the U.S., and what is some evidence in support of each view?

Critical Thinking Questions for Reflection and Discussion

1. Should voting be legally required?
2. Should the Constitution be amended so that Congress is chosen based on proportional representation rather than winner-take-all elections?
3. Is technology on balance more beneficial or more harmful to society?
4. Should the Constitution be amended to impose term limits on members of Congress?
5. Which view of the nature of overall political power in the U.S. is most correct?

Suggested Reading Supplements

- American National Election Studies (ANES), *Guide to Public Opinion and Electoral Behavior*, online
- Martin Luther King, *Letter from Birmingham Jail*
- Edmund Burke, *Speech to the Electors of Bristol* (1774)
- *Citizens United v. Federal Election Commission* (2010)

For Further Advanced Reading

- Robert Aldrich, *Why Parties: The Origin and Transformation of Political Parties in America*

- Robert Putnam, *Bowling Alone: The Collapse and Revival of American Community*
- Mancur Olson, *The Logic of Collective Action: Public Goods and the Theory of Groups*
- C. Wright Mills, *The Power Elite*

APPENDIX

Appendix A: The U.S. Declaration of Independence

IN CONGRESS, July 4, 1776: The unanimous Declaration of the thirteen united States of America.

When in the Course of human events, it becomes necessary for one people to dissolve the political bands which have connected them with another, and to assume among the powers of the earth, the separate and equal station to which the Laws of Nature and of Nature's God entitle them, a decent respect to the opinions of mankind requires that they should declare the causes which impel them to the separation.

We hold these truths to be self-evident, that all men are created equal, that they are endowed by their Creator with certain unalienable Rights, that among these are Life, Liberty and the pursuit of Happiness.--That to secure these rights, Governments are instituted among Men, deriving their just powers from the consent of the governed, --That whenever any Form of Government becomes destructive of these ends, it is the Right of the People to alter or to abolish it, and to institute new Government, laying its foundation on such principles and organizing its powers in such form, as to them shall seem most likely to effect their Safety and Happiness. Prudence, indeed, will dictate that Governments long established should not be changed for light and transient causes; and accordingly all experience hath shewn, that mankind are more disposed to suffer, while evils are sufferable, than to right themselves by abolishing the forms to which they are accustomed. But when a long train of abuses and usurpations, pursuing invariably the same Object evinces a design to reduce them under absolute Despotism, it is their right, it is their duty, to throw off such Government, and to provide new Guards for their future security.--Such has been the patient sufferance of these Colonies; and such is now the necessity which constrains them to alter their former Systems of Government. The history of the present King of Great Britain is a history of repeated injuries and usurpations, all having in direct object the establishment of an absolute Tyranny over these States. To prove this, let Facts be submitted to a candid world.

He has refused his Assent to Laws, the most wholesome and necessary for the public good.

He has forbidden his Governors to pass Laws of immediate and pressing importance, unless suspended in their operation till his Assent should be obtained; and when so suspended, he has utterly neglected to attend to them.

He has refused to pass other Laws for the accommodation of large districts of people, unless those people would relinquish the right of Representation in the Legislature, a right inestimable to them and formidable to tyrants only.

He has called together legislative bodies at places unusual, uncomfortable, and distant from the depository of their public Records, for the sole purpose of fatiguing them into compliance with his measures.

He has dissolved Representative Houses repeatedly, for opposing with manly firmness his invasions on the rights of the people.

He has refused for a long time, after such dissolutions, to cause others to be elected; whereby the Legislative powers, incapable of Annihilation, have returned to the People at large for their exercise; the State remaining in the mean time exposed to all the dangers of invasion from without, and convulsions within.

He has endeavoured to prevent the population of these States; for that purpose obstructing the Laws for Naturalization of Foreigners; refusing to pass others to encourage their migrations hither, and raising the conditions of new Appropriations of Lands.

He has obstructed the Administration of Justice, by refusing his Assent to Laws for establishing Judiciary powers.

He has made Judges dependent on his Will alone, for the tenure of their offices, and the amount and payment of their salaries.

He has erected a multitude of New Offices, and sent hither swarms of Officers to harrass our people, and eat out their substance.

He has kept among us, in times of peace, Standing Armies without the Consent of our legislatures.

He has affected to render the Military independent of and superior to the Civil power.

He has combined with others to subject us to a jurisdiction foreign to our constitution, and unacknowledged by our laws; giving his Assent to their Acts of pretended Legislation:

For Quartering large bodies of armed troops among us:

For protecting them, by a mock Trial, from punishment for any Murders which they should commit on the Inhabitants of these States:

For cutting off our Trade with all parts of the world:

For imposing Taxes on us without our Consent:

For depriving us in many cases, of the benefits of Trial by Jury:

For transporting us beyond Seas to be tried for pretended offences

For abolishing the free System of English Laws in a neighbouring Province, establishing therein an Arbitrary government, and enlarging its Boundaries so as to render it at once an example and fit instrument for introducing the same absolute rule into these Colonies:

For taking away our Charters, abolishing our most valuable Laws, and altering fundamentally the Forms of our Governments:

For suspending our own Legislatures, and declaring themselves invested with power to legislate for us in all cases whatsoever.

He has abdicated Government here, by declaring us out of his Protection and waging War against us.

He has plundered our seas, ravaged our Coasts, burnt our towns, and destroyed the lives of our people.

He is at this time transporting large Armies of foreign Mercenaries to compleat the works of death, desolation and tyranny, already begun with circumstances of Cruelty & perfidy scarcely paralleled in the most barbarous ages, and totally unworthy the Head of a civilized nation.

He has constrained our fellow Citizens taken Captive on the high Seas to bear Arms against their Country, to become the executioners of their friends and Brethren, or to fall themselves by their Hands.

He has excited domestic insurrections amongst us, and has endeavoured to bring on the inhabitants of our frontiers, the merciless Indian Savages, whose known rule of warfare, is an undistinguished destruction of all ages, sexes and conditions.

In every stage of these Oppressions We have Petitioned for Redress in the most humble terms: Our repeated Petitions have been answered only by repeated injury. A Prince whose character is thus marked by every act which may define a Tyrant, is unfit to be the ruler of a free people.

Nor have We been wanting in attentions to our Brittish brethren. We have warned them from time to time of attempts by their legislature to extend an unwarrantable jurisdiction over us. We have reminded them of the circumstances of our emigration and settlement here. We have appealed to their native justice and magnanimity, and we have conjured them by the ties of our common kindred to disavow these usurpations, which, would inevitably interrupt our connections and correspondence. They too have been deaf to the voice of justice and of consanguinity. We must, therefore, acquiesce in the necessity, which denounces our Separation, and hold them, as we hold the rest of mankind, Enemies in War, in Peace Friends.

We, therefore, the Representatives of the united States of America, in General Congress, Assembled, appealing to the Supreme Judge of the world for the rectitude of our intentions, do, in the Name, and by Authority of the good People of these Colonies, solemnly publish and declare, That these United Colonies are, and of Right ought to be Free and Independent States; that they are Absolved from all Allegiance to the British Crown, and that all political connection between them and the State of Great Britain, is and ought to be totally dissolved; and that as Free and Independent States, they have full Power to levy War, conclude Peace, contract Alliances, establish Commerce, and to do all other Acts and Things which Independent States may of right do. And for the support of this Declaration, with a firm reliance on the protection of divine Providence, we mutually pledge to each other our Lives, our Fortunes and our sacred Honor.

Appendix B: The Constitution of the United States of America

Note: Below is the Constitution as originally written. Text in [Brackets] is added as labels for clarification. Text in [*bracketed italics*] has been amended.

Preamble

We the People of the United States, in Order to form a more perfect Union, establish Justice, insure domestic Tranquility, provide for the common defense, promote the general Welfare, and secure the Blessings of Liberty to ourselves and our Posterity, do ordain and establish this Constitution for the United States of America.

Article. I. [The Legislature]

Section. 1.

All legislative Powers herein granted shall be vested in a Congress of the United States, which shall consist of a Senate and House of Representatives.

Section. 2.

The House of Representatives shall be composed of Members chosen every second Year by the People of the several States, and the Electors in each State shall have the Qualifications requisite for Electors of the most numerous Branch of the State Legislature.

No Person shall be a Representative who shall not have attained to the Age of twenty five Years, and been seven Years a Citizen of the United States, and who shall not, when elected, be an Inhabitant of that State in which he shall be chosen. [*Representatives and direct Taxes shall be apportioned among the several States which may be included within this Union, according to their respective Numbers, which shall be determined by adding to the whole Number of free Persons, including those bound to Service for a Term of Years, and excluding Indians not taxed, three fifths of all other Persons.*] The actual Enumeration shall be made within three Years after the first Meeting of the Congress of the United States, and within every subsequent Term of ten Years, in such Manner as they shall by Law direct. The Number of Representatives shall not exceed one for every thirty Thousand, but each State shall have at Least one Representative; and until such enumeration shall be made, the State of New Hampshire shall be entitled to chuse three, Massachusetts eight, Rhode-Island and Providence Plantations one, Connecticut five, New-York six, New Jersey four, Pennsylvania eight, Delaware one, Maryland six, Virginia ten, North Carolina five, South Carolina five, and Georgia three.

When vacancies happen in the Representation from any State, the Executive Authority thereof shall issue Writs of Election to fill such Vacancies.

The House of Representatives shall chuse their Speaker and other Officers; and shall have the sole Power of Impeachment.

Section. 3.

The Senate of the United States shall be composed of two Senators from each State, [*chosen by the Legislature thereof*] for six Years; and each Senator shall have one Vote.

Immediately after they shall be assembled in Consequence of the first Election, they shall be divided as equally as may be into three Classes. The Seats of the Senators of the first Class shall be vacated at the Expiration of the second Year, of the second Class at the Expiration of the fourth Year, and of the third Class at the Expiration of the sixth Year, so that one third may be chosen every second Year; [*and if Vacancies happen by Resignation, or otherwise, during the Recess of the Legislature of any State, the Executive thereof may make temporary Appointments until the next Meeting of the Legislature, which shall then fill such Vacancies.*]

No Person shall be a Senator who shall not have attained to the Age of thirty Years, and been nine Years a Citizen of the United States, and who shall not, when elected, be an Inhabitant of that State for which he shall be chosen.

The Vice President of the United States shall be President of the Senate, but shall have no Vote, unless they be equally divided.

The Senate shall chuse their other Officers, and also a President pro tempore, in the Absence of the Vice President, or when he shall exercise the Office of President of the United States.

The Senate shall have the sole Power to try all Impeachments. When sitting for that Purpose, they shall be on Oath or Affirmation. When the President of the United States is tried, the Chief Justice shall preside: And no Person shall be convicted without the Concurrence of two thirds of the Members present.

Judgment in Cases of Impeachment shall not extend further than to removal from Office, and disqualification to hold and enjoy any Office of honor, Trust or Profit under the United States: but the Party convicted shall nevertheless be liable and subject to Indictment, Trial, Judgment and Punishment, according to Law.

Section. 4.

The Times, Places and Manner of holding Elections for Senators and Representatives, shall be prescribed in each State by the Legislature thereof; but the Congress may at any time by Law make or alter such Regulations, except as to the Places of chusing Senators.

The Congress shall assemble at least once in every Year, and such Meeting shall [*be on the first Monday in December,*] unless they shall by Law appoint a different Day.

Section. 5.

Each House shall be the Judge of the Elections, Returns and Qualifications of its own Members, and a Majority of each shall constitute a Quorum to do Business; but a smaller Number may adjourn from day to day, and may be authorized to compel the Attendance of absent Members, in such Manner, and under such Penalties as each House may provide.

Each House may determine the Rules of its Proceedings, punish its Members for disorderly Behaviour, and, with the Concurrence of two thirds, expel a Member. Each House shall keep a Journal of its Proceedings, and from time to time publish the same, excepting such Parts as may in their Judgment require Secrecy; and the Yeas and Nays of the Members of either House on any question shall, at the Desire of one fifth of those Present, be entered on the Journal.

Neither House, during the Session of Congress, shall, without the Consent of the other, adjourn for more than three days, nor to any other Place than that in which the two Houses shall be sitting.

Section. 6.

The Senators and Representatives shall receive a Compensation for their Services, to be ascertained by Law, and paid out of the Treasury of the United States. They shall in all Cases, except Treason, Felony and Breach of the Peace, be privileged from Arrest during their Attendance at the Session of their respective Houses, and in going to and returning from the same; and for any Speech or Debate in either House, they shall not be questioned in any other Place.

No Senator or Representative shall, during the Time for which he was elected, be appointed to any civil Office under the Authority of the United States, which shall have been created, or the Emoluments whereof shall have been encreased during such time; and no Person holding any Office under the United States, shall be a Member of either House during his Continuance in Office.

Section. 7.

All Bills for raising Revenue shall originate in the House of Representatives; but the Senate may propose or concur with Amendments as on other Bills.
Every Bill which shall have passed the House of Representatives and the Senate, shall, before it become a Law, be presented to the President of the United States: If he approve he shall sign it, but if not he shall return it, with his Objections to that House in which it shall have originated, who shall enter the Objections at large on their Journal, and proceed to reconsider it. If after such Reconsideration two thirds of that House shall agree to pass the Bill, it shall be sent, together with the Objections, to the other House, by which it shall likewise be reconsidered, and if approved by two thirds of that House, it shall become a Law. But in all such Cases the Votes of both Houses shall be determined by yeas and Nays, and the Names of the Persons voting for and against the Bill shall be entered on the Journal of each House respectively. If any Bill shall not be returned by the President within ten Days (Sundays excepted) after it shall have been presented to him, the Same shall be a

Law, in like Manner as if he had signed it, unless the Congress by their Adjournment prevent its Return, in which Case it shall not be a Law.

Every Order, Resolution, or Vote to which the Concurrence of the Senate and House of Representatives may be necessary (except on a question of Adjournment) shall be presented to the President of the United States; and before the Same shall take Effect, shall be approved by him, or being disapproved by him, shall be repassed by two thirds of the Senate and House of Representatives, according to the Rules and Limitations prescribed in the Case of a Bill.

Section. 8.

The Congress shall have Power To lay and collect Taxes, Duties, Imposts and Excises, to pay the Debts and provide for the common Defence and general Welfare of the United States; but all Duties, Imposts and Excises shall be uniform throughout the United States;

To borrow Money on the credit of the United States;

To regulate Commerce with foreign Nations, and among the several States, and with the Indian Tribes;

To establish an uniform Rule of Naturalization, and uniform Laws on the subject of Bankruptcies throughout the United States;

To coin Money, regulate the Value thereof, and of foreign Coin, and fix the Standard of Weights and Measures;

To provide for the Punishment of counterfeiting the Securities and current Coin of the United States;

To establish Post Offices and post Roads;

To promote the Progress of Science and useful Arts, by securing for limited Times to Authors and Inventors the exclusive Right to their respective Writings and Discoveries;

To constitute Tribunals inferior to the supreme Court;

To define and punish Piracies and Felonies committed on the high Seas, and Offences against the Law of Nations;

To declare War, grant Letters of Marque and Reprisal, and make Rules concerning Captures on Land and Water;

To raise and support Armies, but no Appropriation of Money to that Use shall be for a longer Term than two Years;

To provide and maintain a Navy;

To make Rules for the Government and Regulation of the land and naval Forces;

To provide for calling forth the Militia to execute the Laws of the Union, suppress Insurrections and repel Invasions;

To provide for organizing, arming, and disciplining, the Militia, and for governing such Part of them as may be employed in the Service of the United States, reserving to the States respectively, the Appointment of the Officers, and the Authority of training the Militia according to the discipline prescribed by Congress; To exercise exclusive Legislation in all Cases whatsoever, over such District (not exceeding ten Miles square) as may, by Cession of particular States, and the Acceptance of Congress, become the Seat of the Government of the United States, and to exercise like Authority over all Places purchased by the Consent of the Legislature of the State in which the Same shall be, for the Erection of Forts, Magazines, Arsenals, dock-Yards, and other needful Buildings;--And

To make all Laws which shall be necessary and proper for carrying into Execution the foregoing Powers, and all other Powers vested by this Constitution in the Government of the United States, or in any Department or Officer thereof.

Section. 9.

The Migration or Importation of such Persons as any of the States now existing shall think proper to admit, shall not be prohibited by the Congress prior to the Year one thousand eight hundred and eight, but a Tax or duty may be imposed on such Importation, not exceeding ten dollars for each Person.

The Privilege of the Writ of Habeas Corpus shall not be suspended, unless when in Cases of Rebellion or Invasion the public Safety may require it.

No Bill of Attainder or ex post facto Law shall be passed.

No Capitation, or other direct, Tax shall be laid, [*unless in Proportion to the Census or enumeration herein before directed to be taken.*]

No Tax or Duty shall be laid on Articles exported from any State.

No Preference shall be given by any Regulation of Commerce or Revenue to the Ports of one State over those of another; nor shall Vessels bound to, or from, one State, be obliged to enter, clear, or pay Duties in another.

No Money shall be drawn from the Treasury, but in Consequence of Appropriations made by Law; and a regular Statement and Account of the Receipts and Expenditures of all public Money shall be published from time to time.

No Title of Nobility shall be granted by the United States: And no Person holding any Office of Profit or Trust under them, shall, without the Consent of the Congress, accept of any present, Emolument, Office, or Title, of any kind whatever, from any King, Prince, or foreign State.

Section. 10.

No State shall enter into any Treaty, Alliance, or Confederation; grant Letters of Marque and Reprisal; coin Money; emit Bills of Credit; make any Thing but gold and silver Coin a Tender in Payment of Debts; pass any Bill of Attainder, ex post facto Law, or Law impairing the Obligation of Contracts, or grant any Title of Nobility.

No State shall, without the Consent of the Congress, lay any Imposts or Duties on Imports or Exports, except what may be absolutely necessary for executing it's inspection Laws: and the net Produce of all Duties and Imposts, laid by any State on Imports or Exports, shall be for the Use of the Treasury of the United States; and all such Laws shall be subject to the Revision and Controul of the Congress.

No State shall, without the Consent of Congress, lay any Duty of Tonnage, keep Troops, or Ships of War in time of Peace, enter into any Agreement or Compact with another State, or with a foreign Power, or engage in War, unless actually invaded, or in such imminent Danger as will not admit of delay.

Article. II. [The Executive]

Section. 1.

The executive Power shall be vested in a President of the United States of America. He shall hold his Office during the Term of four Years, and, together with the Vice President, chosen for the same Term, be elected, as follows:
Each State shall appoint, in such Manner as the Legislature thereof may direct, a Number of Electors, equal to the whole Number of Senators and Representatives to which the State may be entitled in the Congress: but no Senator or Representative, or Person holding an Office of Trust or Profit under the United States, shall be appointed an Elector.

[*The Electors shall meet in their respective States, and vote by Ballot for two Persons, of whom one at least shall not be an Inhabitant of the same State with themselves. And they shall make a List of all the Persons voted for, and of the Number of Votes for each; which List they shall sign and certify, and transmit sealed to the Seat of the Government of the United States, directed to the President of the Senate. The President of the Senate shall, in the Presence of the Senate and House of Representatives, open all the Certificates, and the Votes shall then be counted. The Person having the greatest Number of Votes shall be the President, if such Number be a Majority of the whole Number of Electors appointed; and if there be more than one who have such Majority, and have an equal Number of Votes, then the House of Representatives shall immediately chuse by Ballot one of them for President; and if no Person have a Majority, then from the five highest on the List the said House shall in like Manner chuse the President. But in chusing the President, the Votes shall be taken by States, the Representation from each State having one Vote; A quorum for this purpose shall consist of a Member or Members from two thirds of the States, and a Majority of all the States shall be necessary to a Choice. In every Case, after the Choice of the President, the Person having the greatest Number of Votes of the Electors shall be the Vice President. But if there should remain two or more who have equal Votes, the Senate shall chuse from them by Ballot the Vice President.*]

The Congress may determine the Time of chusing the Electors, and the Day on which they shall give their Votes; which Day shall be the same throughout the United States.

No Person except a natural born Citizen, or a Citizen of the United States, at the time of the Adoption of this Constitution, shall be eligible to the Office of President; neither shall any Person be eligible to that Office who shall not have attained to the Age of thirty five Years, and been fourteen Years a Resident within the United States.

[*In Case of the Removal of the President from Office, or of his Death, Resignation, or Inability to discharge the Powers and Duties of the said Office, the Same shall devolve on the Vice President, and the Congress may by Law provide for the Case of Removal, Death, Resignation or Inability, both of the President and Vice President, declaring what Officer shall then act as President, and such Officer shall act accordingly, until the Disability be removed, or a President shall be elected.*]
The President shall, at stated Times, receive for his Services, a Compensation, which shall neither be increased nor diminished during the Period for which he shall have been elected, and he shall not receive within that Period any other Emolument from the United States, or any of them.

Before he enter on the Execution of his Office, he shall take the following Oath or Affirmation:--"I do solemnly swear (or affirm) that I will faithfully execute the Office of President of the United States, and will to the best of my Ability, preserve, protect and defend the Constitution of the United States."

Section. 2.

The President shall be Commander in Chief of the Army and Navy of the United States, and of the Militia of the several States, when called into the actual Service of the United States; he may require the Opinion, in writing, of the principal Officer in each of the executive Departments, upon any Subject relating to the Duties of their respective Offices, and he shall have Power to grant Reprieves and Pardons for Offences against the United States, except in Cases of Impeachment.

He shall have Power, by and with the Advice and Consent of the Senate, to make Treaties, provided two thirds of the Senators present concur; and he shall nominate, and by and with the Advice and Consent of the Senate, shall appoint Ambassadors, other public Ministers and Consuls, Judges of the supreme Court, and all other Officers of the United States, whose Appointments are not herein otherwise provided for, and which shall be established by Law: but the Congress may by Law vest the Appointment of such inferior Officers, as they think proper, in the President alone, in the Courts of Law, or in the Heads of Departments.

The President shall have Power to fill up all Vacancies that may happen during the Recess of the Senate, by granting Commissions which shall expire at the End of their next Session.

Section. 3.

He shall from time to time give to the Congress Information of the State of the Union, and recommend to their Consideration such Measures as he shall judge necessary and expedient; he may, on extraordinary Occasions, convene both Houses, or either of them, and in Case of Disagreement between them, with Respect to the Time of Adjournment, he may adjourn them to such Time as he shall think proper; he shall receive Ambassadors and other public Ministers; he shall take Care that the Laws be faithfully executed, and shall Commission all the Officers of the United States.

Section. 4.

The President, Vice President and all civil Officers of the United States, shall be removed from Office on Impeachment for, and Conviction of, Treason, Bribery, or other high Crimes and Misdemeanors.

Article III. [The Judiciary]

Section. 1.

The judicial Power of the United States shall be vested in one supreme Court, and in such inferior Courts as the Congress may from time to time ordain and establish. The Judges, both of the supreme and inferior Courts, shall hold their Offices during good Behaviour, and shall, at stated Times, receive for their Services a Compensation, which shall not be diminished during their Continuance in Office.

Section. 2.

The judicial Power shall extend to all Cases, in Law and Equity, arising under this Constitution, the Laws of the United States, and Treaties made, or which shall be made, under their Authority;--to all Cases affecting Ambassadors, other public Ministers and Consuls;--to all Cases of admiralty and maritime Jurisdiction;--to Controversies to which the United States shall be a Party;--to Controversies between two or more States;-- [*between a State and Citizens of another State;*]--between Citizens of different States;--between Citizens of the same State claiming Lands under Grants of different States, and between a State, or the Citizens thereof, and foreign States, Citizens or Subjects.

In all Cases affecting Ambassadors, other public Ministers and Consuls, and those in which a State shall be Party, the supreme Court shall have original Jurisdiction. In all the other Cases before mentioned, the supreme Court shall have appellate Jurisdiction, both as to Law and Fact, with such Exceptions, and under such Regulations as the Congress shall make.

The Trial of all Crimes, except in Cases of Impeachment, shall be by Jury; and such Trial shall be held in the State where the said Crimes shall have been committed; but when not committed within any State, the Trial shall be at such Place or Places as the Congress may by Law have directed.

Section. 3.

Treason against the United States, shall consist only in levying War against them, or in adhering to their Enemies, giving them Aid and Comfort. No Person shall be convicted of Treason unless on the Testimony of two Witnesses to the same overt Act, or on Confession in open Court.

The Congress shall have Power to declare the Punishment of Treason, but no Attainder of Treason shall work Corruption of Blood, or Forfeiture except during the Life of the Person attainted.

ARTICLE. IV. [THE STATES]

Section. 1.

Full Faith and Credit shall be given in each State to the public Acts, Records, and judicial Proceedings of every other State. And the Congress may by general Laws prescribe the Manner in which such Acts, Records and Proceedings shall be proved, and the Effect thereof.

Section. 2.

The Citizens of each State shall be entitled to all Privileges and Immunities of Citizens in the several States.

A Person charged in any State with Treason, Felony, or other Crime, who shall flee from Justice, and be found in another State, shall on Demand of the executive Authority of the State from which he fled, be delivered up, to be removed to the State having Jurisdiction of the Crime.

[No Person held to Service or Labour in one State, under the Laws thereof, escaping into another, shall, in Consequence of any Law or Regulation therein, be discharged from such Service or Labour, but shall be delivered up on Claim of the Party to whom such Service or Labour may be due.]

Section. 3.

New States may be admitted by the Congress into this Union; but no new State shall be formed or erected within the Jurisdiction of any other State; nor any State be formed by the Junction of two or more States, or Parts of States, without the Consent of the Legislatures of the States concerned as well as of the Congress.

The Congress shall have Power to dispose of and make all needful Rules and Regulations respecting the Territory or other Property belonging to the United States; and nothing in this Constitution shall be so construed as to Prejudice any Claims of the United States, or of any particular State.

Section. 4.

The United States shall guarantee to every State in this Union a Republican Form of Government, and shall protect each of them against Invasion; and on Application of the Legislature, or of the Executive (when the Legislature cannot be convened), against domestic Violence.

ARTICLE. V. [AMENDMENTS]

The Congress, whenever two thirds of both Houses shall deem it necessary, shall propose Amendments to this Constitution, or, on the Application of the

Legislatures of two thirds of the several States, shall call a Convention for proposing Amendments, which, in either Case, shall be valid to all Intents and Purposes, as Part of this Constitution, when ratified by the Legislatures of three fourths of the several States, or by Conventions in three fourths thereof, as the one or the other Mode of Ratification may be proposed by the Congress; Provided that no Amendment which may be made prior to the Year One thousand eight hundred and eight shall in any Manner affect the first and fourth Clauses in the Ninth Section of the first Article; and that no State, without its Consent, shall be deprived of its equal Suffrage in the Senate.

ARTICLE. VI. [LEGAL EFFECT OF CONSTITUTION]

All Debts contracted and Engagements entered into, before the Adoption of this Constitution, shall be as valid against the United States under this Constitution, as under the Confederation.

This Constitution, and the Laws of the United States which shall be made in Pursuance thereof; and all Treaties made, or which shall be made, under the Authority of the United States, shall be the supreme Law of the Land; and the Judges in every State shall be bound thereby, any Thing in the Constitution or Laws of any State to the Contrary notwithstanding.

The Senators and Representatives before mentioned, and the Members of the several State Legislatures, and all executive and judicial Officers, both of the United States and of the several States, shall be bound by Oath or Affirmation, to support this Constitution; but no religious Test shall ever be required as a Qualification to any Office or public Trust under the United States.

ARTICLE. VII. [RATIFICATION]

The Ratification of the Conventions of nine States, shall be sufficient for the Establishment of this Constitution between the States so ratifying the Same.
Done in Convention by the Unanimous Consent of the States present the Seventeenth Day of September in the Year of our Lord one thousand seven hundred and Eighty seven and of the Independence of the United States of America the Twelfth In witness whereof We have hereunto subscribed our Names

AMENDMENTS I-X [THE BILL OF RIGHTS]

Amendment I

Congress shall make no law respecting an establishment of religion, or prohibiting the free exercise thereof; or abridging the freedom of speech, or of the press; or the right of the people peaceably to assemble, and to petition the Government for a redress of grievances.

Amendment II

A well regulated Militia, being necessary to the security of a free State, the right of the people to keep and bear Arms, shall not be infringed.

Amendment III

No Soldier shall, in time of peace be quartered in any house, without the consent of the Owner, nor in time of war, but in a manner to be prescribed by law.

Amendment IV

The right of the people to be secure in their persons, houses, papers, and effects, against unreasonable searches and seizures, shall not be violated, and no Warrants shall issue, but upon probable cause, supported by Oath or affirmation, and particularly describing the place to be searched, and the persons or things to be seized.

Amendment V

No person shall be held to answer for a capital, or otherwise infamous crime, unless on a presentment or indictment of a Grand Jury, except in cases arising in the land or naval forces, or in the Militia, when in actual service in time of War or public danger; nor shall any person be subject for the same offence to be twice put in jeopardy of life or limb; nor shall be compelled in any criminal case to be a witness against himself, nor be deprived of life, liberty, or property, without due process of law; nor shall private property be taken for public use, without just compensation.

Amendment VI

In all criminal prosecutions, the accused shall enjoy the right to a speedy and public trial, by an impartial jury of the State and district wherein the crime shall have been committed, which district shall have been previously ascertained by law, and to be informed of the nature and cause of the accusation; to be confronted with the witnesses against him; to have compulsory process for obtaining witnesses in his favor, and to have the Assistance of Counsel for his defence.

Amendment VII

In suits at common law, where the value in controversy shall exceed twenty dollars, the right of trial by jury shall be preserved, and no fact tried by a jury, shall be otherwise reexamined in any Court of the United States, than according to the rules of the common law.

Amendment VIII

Excessive bail shall not be required, nor excessive fines imposed, nor cruel and unusual punishments inflicted.

Amendment IX

The enumeration in the Constitution, of certain rights, shall not be construed to deny or disparage others retained by the people.

Amendment X

The powers not delegated to the United States by the Constitution, nor prohibited by it to the States, are reserved to the States respectively, or to the people.

Amendments XI-XXVII

Amendment XI

The Judicial power of the United States shall not be construed to extend to any suit in law or equity, commenced or prosecuted against one of the United States by Citizens of another State, or by Citizens or Subjects of any Foreign State.

Amendment XII

The Electors shall meet in their respective states and vote by ballot for President and Vice-President, one of whom, at least, shall not be an inhabitant of the same state with themselves; they shall name in their ballots the person voted for as President, and in distinct ballots the person voted for as Vice-President, and they shall make distinct lists of all persons voted for as President, and of all persons voted for as Vice-President, and of the number of votes for each, which lists they shall sign and certify, and transmit sealed to the seat of the government of the United States, directed to the President of the Senate; -- the President of the Senate shall, in the presence of the Senate and House of Representatives, open all the certificates and the votes shall then be counted; -- The person having the greatest number of votes for President, shall be the President, if such number be a majority of the whole number of Electors appointed; and if no person have such majority, then from the persons having the highest numbers not exceeding three on the list of those voted for as President, the House of Representatives shall choose immediately, by ballot, the President. But in choosing the President, the votes shall be taken by states, the representation from each state having one vote; a quorum for this purpose shall consist of a member or members from two-thirds of the states, and a majority of all the states shall be necessary to a choice. [*And if the House of Representatives shall not choose a President whenever the right of choice shall devolve upon them, before the fourth day of March next following, then the Vice-President shall act as President, as in case of the death or other constitutional disability of the President.]* The person having the greatest number of votes as Vice-President, shall be the Vice-President, if such number be a majority of the whole number of Electors appointed, and if no person have a majority, then from the two highest numbers on the list, the Senate shall choose the Vice-President; a quorum for the purpose shall consist of two-thirds of the whole number of Senators, and a majority of the whole number shall be necessary to a choice. But no person constitutionally ineligible to the office of President shall be eligible to that of Vice-President of the United States.

Amendment XIII

Section 1.

Neither slavery nor involuntary servitude, except as a punishment for crime whereof the party shall have been duly convicted, shall exist within the United States, or any place subject to their jurisdiction.

Section 2.

Congress shall have power to enforce this article by appropriate legislation.

Amendment XIV

Section 1.

All persons born or naturalized in the United States, and subject to the jurisdiction thereof, are citizens of the United States and of the State wherein they reside. No State shall make or enforce any law which shall abridge the privileges or immunities of citizens of the United States; nor shall any State deprive any person of life, liberty, or property, without due process of law; nor deny to any person within its jurisdiction the equal protection of the laws.

Section 2.

Representatives shall be apportioned among the several States according to their respective numbers, counting the whole number of persons in each State, excluding Indians not taxed. But when the right to vote at any election for the choice of electors for President and Vice-President of the United States, Representatives in Congress, the Executive and Judicial officers of a State, or the members of the Legislature thereof, is denied to any of the male inhabitants of such State, [*being twenty-one years of age*], and citizens of the United States, or in any way abridged, except for participation in rebellion, or other crime, the basis of representation therein shall be reduced in the proportion which the number of such male citizens shall bear to the whole number of male citizens twenty-one years of age in such State.

Section 3.

No person shall be a Senator or Representative in Congress, or elector of President and Vice-President, or hold any office, civil or military, under the United

States, or under any State, who, having previously taken an oath, as a member of Congress, or as an officer of the United States, or as a member of any State legislature, or as an executive or judicial officer of any State, to support the Constitution of the United States, shall have engaged in insurrection or rebellion against the same, or given aid or comfort to the enemies thereof. But Congress may by a vote of two-thirds of each House, remove such disability.

Section 4.

The validity of the public debt of the United States, authorized by law, including debts incurred for payment of pensions and bounties for services in suppressing insurrection or rebellion, shall not be questioned. But neither the United States nor any State shall assume or pay any debt or obligation incurred in aid of insurrection or rebellion against the United States, or any claim for the loss or emancipation of any slave; but all such debts, obligations and claims shall be held illegal and void.

Section 5.

The Congress shall have the power to enforce, by appropriate legislation, the provisions of this article.

Amendment XV

Section 1.

The right of citizens of the United States to vote shall not be denied or abridged by the United States or by any State on account of race, color, or previous condition of servitude--

Section 2.

The Congress shall have the power to enforce this article by appropriate legislation.

Amendment XVI

The Congress shall have power to lay and collect taxes on incomes, from whatever source derived, without apportionment among the several States, and without regard to any census or enumeration.

Amendment XVII

The Senate of the United States shall be composed of two Senators from each State, elected by the people thereof, for six years; and each Senator shall have one vote. The electors in each State shall have the qualifications requisite for electors of the most numerous branch of the State legislatures.

When vacancies happen in the representation of any State in the Senate, the executive authority of such State shall issue writs of election to fill such vacancies: *Provided*, That the legislature of any State may empower the executive thereof to make temporary appointments until the people fill the vacancies by election as the legislature may direct.

This amendment shall not be so construed as to affect the election or term of any Senator chosen before it becomes valid as part of the Constitution.

Amendment XVIII

[Section 1.

After one year from the ratification of this article the manufacture, sale, or transportation of intoxicating liquors within, the importation thereof into, or the exportation thereof from the United States and all territory subject to the jurisdiction thereof for beverage purposes is hereby prohibited.

Section 2.

The Congress and the several States shall have concurrent power to enforce this article by appropriate legislation.

Section 3.

This article shall be inoperative unless it shall have been ratified as an amendment to the Constitution by the legislatures of the several States, as provided in the Constitution, within seven years from the date of the submission hereof to the States by the Congress.]

Amendment XIX

The right of citizens of the United States to vote shall not be denied or abridged by the United States or by any State on account of sex.

Congress shall have power to enforce this article by appropriate legislation.

Amendment XX

Section 1.

The terms of the President and the Vice President shall end at noon on the 20th day of January, and the terms of Senators and Representatives at noon on the 3d day of January, of the years in which such terms would have ended if this article had not been ratified; and the terms of their successors shall then begin.

Section 2.

The Congress shall assemble at least once in every year, and such meeting shall begin at noon on the 3d day of January, unless they shall by law appoint a different day.

Section 3.

If, at the time fixed for the beginning of the term of the President, the President elect shall have died, the Vice President elect shall become President. If a President shall not have been chosen before the time fixed for the beginning of his term, or if the President elect shall have failed to qualify, then the Vice President elect shall act as President until a President shall have qualified; and the Congress may by law provide for the case wherein neither a President elect nor a Vice President elect shall have qualified, declaring who shall then act as President, or the manner in which one who is to act shall be selected, and such person shall act accordingly until a President or Vice President shall have qualified.

Section 4.

The Congress may by law provide for the case of the death of any of the persons from whom the House of Representatives may choose a President whenever the right of choice shall have devolved upon them, and for the case of the death of any of the persons from whom the Senate may choose a Vice President whenever the right of choice shall have devolved upon them.

Section 5.

Sections 1 and 2 shall take effect on the 15th day of October following the ratification of this article.

Section 6.

This article shall be inoperative unless it shall have been ratified as an amendment to the Constitution by the legislatures of three-fourths of the several States within seven years from the date of its submission.

Amendment XXI

Section 1.

The eighteenth article of amendment to the Constitution of the United States is hereby repealed.

Section 2.

The transportation or importation into any State, Territory, or possession of the United States for delivery or use therein of intoxicating liquors, in violation of the laws thereof, is hereby prohibited.

Section 3.

This article shall be inoperative unless it shall have been ratified as an amendment to the Constitution by conventions in the several States, as provided in the Constitution, within seven years from the date of the submission hereof to the States by the Congress.

Amendment XXII

Section 1.

No person shall be elected to the office of the President more than twice, and no person who has held the office of President, or acted as President, for more than two years of a term to which some other person was elected President shall be elected to the office of the President more than once. But this Article shall not apply to any person holding the office of President when this Article was proposed by the

Congress, and shall not prevent any person who may be holding the office of President, or acting as President, during the term within which this Article becomes operative from holding the office of President or acting as President during the remainder of such term.

Section 2.

This article shall be inoperative unless it shall have been ratified as an amendment to the Constitution by the legislatures of three-fourths of the several States within seven years from the date of its submission to the States by the Congress.

Amendment XXIII

Section 1.

The District constituting the seat of Government of the United States shall appoint in such manner as the Congress may direct:

A number of electors of President and Vice President equal to the whole number of Senators and Representatives in Congress to which the District would be entitled if it were a State, but in no event more than the least populous State; they shall be in addition to those appointed by the States, but they shall be considered, for the purposes of the election of President and Vice President, to be electors appointed by a State; and they shall meet in the District and perform such duties as provided by the twelfth article of amendment.

Section 2.

The Congress shall have power to enforce this article by appropriate legislation.

Amendment XXIV

Section 1.

The right of citizens of the United States to vote in any primary or other election for President or Vice President, for electors for President or Vice President, or for Senator or Representative in Congress, shall not be denied or abridged by the United States or any State by reason of failure to pay any poll tax or other tax.

Section 2.

The Congress shall have power to enforce this article by appropriate legislation.

Amendment XXV

Section 1.

In case of the removal of the President from office or of his death or resignation, the Vice President shall become President.

Section 2.

Whenever there is a vacancy in the office of the Vice President, the President shall nominate a Vice President who shall take office upon confirmation by a majority vote of both Houses of Congress.

Section 3.

Whenever the President transmits to the President pro tempore of the Senate and the Speaker of the House of Representatives his written declaration that he is unable to discharge the powers and duties of his office, and until he transmits to them a written declaration to the contrary, such powers and duties shall be discharged by the Vice President as Acting President.

Section 4.

Whenever the Vice President and a majority of either the principal officers of the executive departments or of such other body as Congress may by law provide, transmit to the President pro tempore of the Senate and the Speaker of the House of Representatives their written declaration that the President is unable to discharge the powers and duties of his office, the Vice President shall immediately assume the powers and duties of the office as Acting President.

Thereafter, when the President transmits to the President pro tempore of the Senate and the Speaker of the House of Representatives his written declaration that no inability exists, he shall resume the powers and duties of his office unless the Vice President and a majority of either the principal officers of the executive department or of such other body as Congress may by law provide, transmit within four days to the President pro tempore of the Senate and the Speaker of the House of Representatives their written declaration that the President is unable to discharge the powers and duties of his office. Thereupon Congress shall decide the issue, assembling within forty-eight hours for that purpose if not in session. If the Congress, within twenty-one days after receipt of the latter written declaration, or, if Congress is not in session, within twenty-one days after Congress is required to assemble, determines by two-thirds vote of both Houses that the President is unable to discharge the powers and duties of his office, the Vice President shall continue to discharge the same as Acting President; otherwise, the President shall resume the powers and duties of his office.

Amendment XXVI

Section 1.

The right of citizens of the United States, who are eighteen years of age or older, to vote shall not be denied or abridged by the United States or by any State on account of age.

Section 2.

The Congress shall have power to enforce this article by appropriate legislation.

Amendment XXVII

No law, varying the compensation for the services of the Senators and Representatives, shall take effect, until an election of Representatives shall have intervened.

Appendix C: James Madison, Federalist No. 10

The Union as a Safeguard Against Domestic Faction and Insurrection

To the People of the State of New York:

Among the numerous advantages promised by a well constructed Union, none deserves to be more accurately developed than its tendency to break and control the violence of faction. The friend of popular governments never finds himself so much alarmed for their character and fate, as when he contemplates their propensity to this dangerous vice. He will not fail, therefore, to set a due value on any plan which, without violating the principles to which he is attached, provides a proper cure for it. The instability, injustice, and confusion introduced into the public councils, have, in truth, been the mortal diseases under which popular governments have everywhere perished; as they continue to be the favorite and fruitful topics from which the adversaries to liberty derive their most specious declamations. The valuable improvements made by the American constitutions on the popular models, both ancient and modern, cannot certainly be too much admired; but it would be an unwarrantable partiality, to contend that they have as effectually obviated the danger on this side, as was wished and expected. Complaints are everywhere heard from our most considerate and virtuous citizens, equally the friends of public and private faith, and of public and personal liberty, that our governments are too unstable, that the public good is disregarded in the conflicts of rival parties, and that measures are too often decided, not according to the rules of justice and the rights of the minor party, but by the superior force of an interested and overbearing majority. However anxiously we may wish that these complaints had no foundation, the evidence, of known facts will not permit us to deny that they are in some degree true. It will be found, indeed, on a candid review of our situation, that some of the distresses under which we labor have been erroneously charged on the operation of our governments; but it will be found, at the same time, that other causes will not alone account for many of our heaviest misfortunes; and, particularly, for that prevailing and increasing distrust of public engagements, and alarm for private rights, which are echoed from one end of the continent to the other. These must be chiefly, if not wholly, effects of the unsteadiness and injustice with which a factious spirit has tainted our public administrations.

By a faction, I understand a number of citizens, whether amounting to a majority or a minority of the whole, who are united and actuated by some common impulse of passion, or of interest, adverse to the rights of other citizens, or to the permanent and aggregate interests of the community.

There are two methods of curing the mischiefs of faction: the one, by removing its causes; the other, by controlling its effects.

There are again two methods of removing the causes of faction: the one, by destroying the liberty which is essential to its existence; the other, by giving to every citizen the same opinions, the same passions, and the same interests.

It could never be more truly said than of the first remedy, that it was worse than the disease. Liberty is to faction what air is to fire, an aliment without which it instantly expires. But it could not be less folly to abolish liberty, which is essential to political life, because it nourishes faction, than it would be to wish the annihilation of air, which is essential to animal life, because it imparts to fire its destructive agency.

The second expedient is as impracticable as the first would be unwise. As long as the reason of man continues fallible, and he is at liberty to exercise it, different opinions will be formed. As long as the connection subsists between his reason and his self-love, his opinions and his passions will have a reciprocal influence on each other; and the former will be objects to which the latter will attach themselves. The diversity in the faculties of men, from which the rights of property originate, is not less an insuperable obstacle to a uniformity of interests. The protection of these faculties is the first object of government. From the protection of different and unequal faculties of acquiring property, the possession of different degrees and kinds of property immediately results; and from the influence of these on the sentiments and views of the respective proprietors, ensues a division of the society into different interests and parties.

The latent causes of faction are thus sown in the nature of man; and we see them everywhere brought into different degrees of activity, according to the different circumstances of civil society. A zeal for different opinions concerning religion, concerning government, and many other points, as well of speculation as of practice; an attachment to different leaders ambitiously contending for pre-eminence and power; or to persons of other descriptions whose fortunes have been interesting to the human passions, have, in turn, divided mankind into parties, inflamed them with mutual animosity, and rendered them much more disposed to vex and oppress each other than to co-operate for their common good. So strong is this propensity of mankind to fall into mutual animosities, that where no substantial occasion presents itself, the most frivolous and fanciful distinctions have been sufficient to kindle their unfriendly passions and excite their most violent conflicts. But the most common and durable source of factions has been the various and unequal distribution of property. Those who hold and those who are without property have ever formed distinct interests in society. Those who are creditors, and those who are debtors, fall under a like discrimination. A landed interest, a manufacturing interest, a mercantile interest, a moneyed interest, with many lesser interests, grow up of necessity in civilized nations, and divide them into different classes, actuated by different sentiments and views. The regulation of these various and interfering interests forms the principal task of modern legislation, and involves the spirit of party and faction in the necessary and ordinary operations of the government.

No man is allowed to be a judge in his own cause, because his interest would certainly bias his judgment, and, not improbably, corrupt his integrity. With equal, nay with greater reason, a body of men are unfit to be both judges and parties at the same time; yet what are many of the most important acts of legislation, but so many judicial determinations, not indeed concerning the rights of single persons, but concerning the rights of large bodies of citizens? And what are the different classes of legislators but advocates and parties to the causes which they determine? Is a law proposed concerning private debts? It is a question to which the creditors are parties on one side and the debtors on the other. Justice ought to hold the balance between them. Yet the parties are, and must be, themselves the judges; and the most numerous party, or, in other words, the most powerful faction must be expected to prevail. Shall domestic manufactures be encouraged, and in what degree, by restrictions on foreign manufactures? are questions which would be differently decided by the landed and the manufacturing classes, and probably by neither with a sole regard to justice and the public good. The apportionment of taxes on the various descriptions of property is an act which seems to require the most exact impartiality; yet there is, perhaps, no legislative act in which greater opportunity and temptation are given to a predominant party to trample on the rules of justice. Every shilling with which they overburden the inferior number, is a shilling saved to their own pockets.

It is in vain to say that enlightened statesmen will be able to adjust these clashing interests, and render them all subservient to the public good. Enlightened statesmen will not always be at the helm. Nor, in many cases, can such an adjustment be made at all without taking into view indirect and remote considerations, which will rarely prevail over the immediate interest which one party may find in disregarding the rights of another or the good of the whole.
The inference to which we are brought is, that the CAUSES of faction cannot be removed, and that relief is only to be sought in the means of controlling its EFFECTS.

If a faction consists of less than a majority, relief is supplied by the republican principle, which enables the majority to defeat its sinister views by regular vote. It may clog the administration, it may convulse the society; but it will be unable to execute and mask its violence under the forms of the Constitution. When a majority is included in a faction, the form of popular government, on the other hand, enables it to sacrifice to its ruling passion or interest both the public good and the rights of other citizens. To secure the public good and private rights against the danger of such a faction, and at the same time to preserve the spirit and the form of popular government, is then the great object to which our inquiries are directed. Let me add that it is the great desideratum by which this form of government can be rescued from the opprobrium under which it has so long labored, and be recommended to the esteem and adoption of mankind.

By what means is this object attainable? Evidently by one of two only. Either the existence of the same passion or interest in a majority at the same time must be prevented, or the majority, having such coexistent passion or interest, must be rendered, by their number and local situation, unable to concert and carry into effect schemes of oppression. If the impulse and the opportunity be suffered to coincide, we well know that neither moral nor religious motives can be relied on as an adequate control. They are not found to be such on the injustice and violence of individuals, and lose their efficacy in proportion to the number combined together, that is, in proportion as their efficacy becomes needful.

From this view of the subject it may be concluded that a pure democracy, by which I mean a society consisting of a small number of citizens, who assemble and administer the government in person, can admit of no cure for the mischiefs of faction. A common passion or interest will, in almost every case, be felt by a majority of the whole; a communication and concert result from the form of government itself; and there is nothing to check the inducements to sacrifice the weaker party or an obnoxious individual. Hence it is that such democracies have ever been spectacles of turbulence and contention; have ever been found incompatible with personal security or the rights of property; and have in general been as short in their lives as they have been violent in their deaths. Theoretic politicians, who have patronized this species of government, have erroneously supposed that by reducing mankind to a perfect equality in their political rights, they would, at the same time, be perfectly equalized and assimilated in their possessions, their opinions, and their passions.

A republic, by which I mean a government in which the scheme of representation takes place, opens a different prospect, and promises the cure for which we are seeking. Let us examine the points in which it varies from pure democracy, and we shall comprehend both the nature of the cure and the efficacy which it must derive from the Union.

The two great points of difference between a democracy and a republic are: first, the delegation of the government, in the latter, to a small number of citizens elected by the rest; secondly, the greater number of citizens, and greater sphere of country, over which the latter may be extended.

The effect of the first difference is, on the one hand, to refine and enlarge the public views, by passing them through the medium of a chosen body of citizens, whose wisdom may best discern the true interest of their country, and whose patriotism and love of justice will be least likely to sacrifice it to temporary or partial considerations. Under such a regulation, it may well happen that the public voice, pronounced by the representatives of the people, will be more consonant to the public good than if pronounced by the people themselves, convened for the purpose. On the other hand, the effect may be inverted. Men of factious tempers, of local prejudices, or of sinister designs, may, by intrigue, by corruption, or by other means, first obtain the suffrages, and then betray the interests, of the people. The question resulting is, whether small or extensive republics are more favorable to the election of proper guardians of the public weal; and it is clearly decided in favor of the latter by two obvious considerations:

In the first place, it is to be remarked that, however small the republic may be, the representatives must be raised to a certain number, in order to guard against the cabals of a few; and that, however large it may be, they must be limited to a certain number, in order to guard against the confusion of a multitude. Hence, the number of representatives in the two cases not being in proportion to that of the two constituents, and being proportionally greater in the small republic, it follows that, if the proportion of fit characters be not less in the large than in the small republic, the former will present a greater option, and consequently a greater probability of a fit choice.

In the next place, as each representative will be chosen by a greater number of citizens in the large than in the small republic, it will be more difficult for unworthy candidates to practice with success the vicious arts by which elections are too often carried; and the suffrages of the people being more free, will be more likely to centre in men who possess the most attractive merit and the most diffusive and established characters.

It must be confessed that in this, as in most other cases, there is a mean, on both sides of which inconveniences will be found to lie. By enlarging too much the number of electors, you render the representatives too little acquainted with all their local circumstances and lesser interests; as by reducing it too much, you render him unduly attached to these, and too little fit to comprehend and pursue great and national objects. The federal Constitution forms a happy combination in this respect; the great and aggregate interests being referred to the national, the local and particular to the State legislatures.

The other point of difference is, the greater number of citizens and extent of territory which may be brought within the compass of republican than of democratic government; and it is this circumstance principally which renders factious combinations less to be dreaded in the former than in the latter. The smaller the society, the fewer probably will be the distinct parties and interests composing it; the fewer the distinct parties and interests, the more frequently will a majority be found of the same party; and the smaller the number of individuals composing a majority, and the smaller the compass within which they are placed, the more easily will they concert and execute their plans of oppression. Extend the sphere, and you take in a greater variety of parties and interests; you make it less probable that a majority of the whole will have a common motive to invade the rights of other citizens; or if such a common motive exists, it will be more difficult for all who feel it to discover their own strength, and to act in unison with each other. Besides other impediments, it may be remarked that, where there is a consciousness of unjust or dishonorable purposes, communication is always checked by distrust in proportion to the number whose concurrence is necessary.

Hence, it clearly appears, that the same advantage which a republic has over a democracy, in controlling the effects of faction, is enjoyed by a large over a small republic,--is enjoyed by the Union over the States composing it. Does the advantage consist in the substitution of representatives whose enlightened views and virtuous sentiments render them superior to local prejudices and schemes of injustice? It will not be denied that the representation of the Union will be most likely to possess these requisite endowments. Does it consist in the greater security afforded by a greater variety of parties, against the event of any one party being able to outnumber and oppress the rest? In an equal degree does the increased variety of parties comprised within the Union, increase this security. Does it, in fine, consist in the greater obstacles opposed to the concert and accomplishment of the secret wishes of an unjust and interested majority? Here, again, the extent of the Union gives it the most palpable advantage.

The influence of factious leaders may kindle a flame within their particular States, but will be unable to spread a general conflagration through the other States. A religious sect may degenerate into a political faction in a part of the Confederacy; but the variety of sects dispersed over the entire face of it must secure the national councils against any danger from that source. A rage for paper money, for an abolition of debts, for an equal division of property, or for any other improper or wicked project, will be less apt to pervade the whole body of the Union than a particular member of it; in the same proportion as such a malady is more likely to taint a particular county or district, than an entire State.

In the extent and proper structure of the Union, therefore, we behold a republican remedy for the diseases most incident to republican government. And according to the degree of pleasure and pride we feel in being republicans, ought to be our zeal in cherishing the spirit and supporting the character of Federalists.

PUBLIUS.

INDEX

A

B

C

D

E

F

G

H

I

J

K

L

M

N

O

P

R

S

T

U

V

W

X

Y

Z

CPSIA information can be obtained
at www.ICGtesting.com
Printed in the USA
FSHW011655240120
66225FS

9 781935 754909